Jean Franco, born in 1924 in Dukinfield, Cheshire, was educated at Hyde Grammar School and at Manchester and London Universities. She lived for four years in Guatemala and Mexico, from 1953 to 1957, and in 1960 took up an appointment as Lecturer in Spanish at Queen Mary College, London University. In 1964 she was appointed Reader in Latin American Literature at King's College, London University, and in 1968 became Professor of Latin American Literature at the University of Essex. She is a founder-member of the Society for Latin American Studies of Great Britain and has served as Chairman since 1967. She has published many articles and translations in British periodicals and has contributed to Latin American periodicals. She is the editor of *Short Stories in Spanish* (Penguin, 1966), the author of *An Introduction to Spanish American Literature* (1969), and a contributor to the Latin American section in the *Penguin Companion to Literature*, Volume 3.

JEAN FRANCO

The Modern Culture of Latin America

SOCIETY AND THE ARTIST
Revised Edition

PENGUIN BOOKS

Penguin Books Ltd, Harmondsworth,
Middlesex, England
Penguin Books Inc., 7110 Ambassador Road,
Baltimore, Md 21207, U.S.A.
Penguin Books Australia Ltd, Ringwood,
Victoria, Australia

First published by Pall Mall Press 1967
Revised edition published in Pelican Books 1970
Copyright © Jean Franco, 1967, 1970

Made and printed in Great Britain by
Richard Clay (The Chaucer Press) Ltd
Bungay, Suffolk
Set in Monotype Plantin

CONTENTS

LIST OF ILLUSTRATIONS

List of Illustrations

ACKNOWLEDGEMENTS

I am grateful to the following for the loan of books otherwise un-obtainable: Mr J. M. Cohen, Mr Robert Roland, Mr William Rowe, Dr Fernando Debesa, Cultural Attaché at the Chilean Embassy in London, and Dr Lourenço da Silva of the Casa do Brasil, London.

I should also like to express my thanks to Señora Blanco Fombona de Hood, Cultural Attaché at the Venezuelan Embassy in London, who advised me on recent developments in Venezuelan art and architec-ture, and to the Departamento de Prensa de la Dirección de Cultura de la UCV, Caracas, for permission to reproduce the photographs in Plates 13, 14, 29, 30, 31 and 32. Plates, 4, 5, 6, 7, 8, 10, 15, 16 and 28 are published by arrangement with Illustration Research Service, London, 7, 15 and 16 being reproduced with the permission of J. Allan Cash, FIIP, FRPS, 4, 5, 6, 8 and 28 with the permission of Camera Press Ltd, London, and 10 with the permission of the Mexican Tourist Board.

The following plates are reproduced by permission of the Museum of Modern Art, New York: 1, 2 (gift of the Hon. Mrs Robert Woods Bliss), 3, 11, 12 and 17 (Inter-American Fund), 9 (Abby Aldrich Rockefeller Fund), 18 (gift of Charles E. Merrill), 19 (gift of Larry Aldrich), 20 (gift of Mr and Mrs Warren D. Benedek).

The following plates are reproduced by permission of the Departa-mento de Publicaciones del Comité Organizador de los Juegos de la XIX Olimpiada: 21, 22, 25 and 27 (photographs Manuel Garay), 23 and 26 (photographs Francisco Uribe), and 24 (photograph Leonard Soned).

J. F.

Introduction:
The Artist and Social Conscience

An intense social concern has been the characteristic of Latin-American * art for the last hundred and fifty years. Literature – and even painting and music – have played a social role, with the artist acting as guide, teacher and conscience of his country. The Latin American has generally viewed art as an expression of the artist's whole self: a self which is living in a society and which therefore has a collective as well as an individual concern. Conversely, the idea of the moral neutrality or the purity of art has had relatively little impact.

In countries like those of Latin America, where national identity is still in the process of definition and where social and political problems are both huge and inescapable, the artist's sense of responsibility towards society needs no justification. Thus any evaluation of Latin-American movements must also be concerned with the social and political preoccupations out of which they sprang. Indeed, whereas in Europe it is legitimate to study art as a self-propagating tradition in which new movements may arise as a solution to technical problems, this approach is impossible in Latin America where even the names of literary movements are different from those of Europe. 'Modernism', 'New Worldism', 'Indianism' define social attitudes, unlike 'Cubism', 'Impressionism', 'Symbolism', which refer to technique. This difference is extremely important. It has meant that, generally, movements in the arts have not grown out of a previous movement but have arisen in response to factors external to art. A new social situation defines the position of the artist, who then improvises or borrows a technique to suit his

*The term Latin America is used where a statement refers to all the countries of Central and South America, both Spanish-speaking and Portuguese-speaking; the term Spanish America is used for Spanish-speaking countries only – i.e., excluding Brazil.

purpose. Hence the history of the arts in Latin America is not a continuous development but a series of fresh starts.

It is the purpose of this book to consider some of these 'fresh starts' and to explore the artist's attitude to society and the way that he expresses this in his work. The bulk of the evidence comes from literature, although obviously such a study must take into consideration painting and architecture. The book covers both Spanish America and Portuguese-speaking Brazil. The starting date of 1888 is not an arbitrary one. That year saw the publication of *Azul* by the Nicaraguan poet, Rubén Darío: a book which heralded the emergence of Latin America's first true artistic movement, Modernism. Before this date, it is hardly possible to talk about movements, but only about the attitudes of individuals. This book is not intended as a comprehensive coverage of literature, art and music, being concerned with general trends rather than individual contributions to the arts.

THE NINETEENTH CENTURY

Nothing could be greater than the disparity between the turbulent excitement of political life in nineteenth-century Latin America and the dullness of much of its literature and painting. An extraordinary procession of eccentric despots, mad tyrants and half-civilized 'men on horseback' sweeps across the historical scene without ever being captured in the pages of the insipid historical and romantic novels of the time. Latin-American reality was too bold and strange to be grasped by writers accustomed to the narrow refinements of Paris or London. They themselves were aware of their inadequacy. With Independence, Spanish-American and Brazilian intellectuals expected a marvellous flowering of original literature, not a shadow-boxing between European fashion and American reality. But, from the first, the pursuit of art proved difficult. Brazil, under an independent monarchy, was stable enough but was flooded by imported books which made it difficult for writers to do more than follow European fashions. In Spanish America, the situation was disastrous. By 1830, nearly every part of the sub-continent presented a spectacle of civil war, violence or dictatorship; the few writers and intellectuals were either tossed to one side or forced into battle. Complaints that the pursuit of art was impossible abound in the early nineteenth century. The Argentinian poet, Esteban Echeverría (1805–51), for instance, declared:

... because of the revolutionary state of affairs, because they are absorbed in action or in the material needs of a precarious existence, men of talent cannot dedicate themselves to the thought and contemplation which is necessary for literary creation and frequently they cannot find the means of publishing their works.[1]

José Joaquín de Olmedo (Ecuador, 1780–1847) excused his scanty poetic output on the grounds that the environment was an unfavourable one:

I need a comfortable spot where I can see the countryside, the rivers, the mountains. I need friends who will criticize, judges who will applaud and even fanatics who will discuss every word, every phrase, every thought.[2]

Here we see defined the two factors which were most instrumental in preventing the development of a continuous artistic tradition: the political factor, and the lack of an appreciative and critical public.

Of these, the first was so serious in the nineteenth century as to prevent any artistic life at all for long periods. In Argentina, for instance, during the dictatorship of Juan Manuel Rosas (1829–32, 1835–52) nearly all writers were forced to go into exile. During the Civil War in Mexico between 1858 and 1860, the printing of books and newspapers was stopped or seriously curtailed for months at a time. In Venezuela, countless revolutions, interspersed with periods of dictatorship, meant the virtual eclipse of artistic life. This state of affairs has unfortunately continued to prevail in many countries, even in the twentieth century. Guatemala, Honduras, Nicaragua, the Dominican Republic, Cuba, Venezuela, Paraguay and Peru have had long periods of dictatorship, and in some of these countries – notably Paraguay, the Dominican Republic and Nicaragua – intellectual life has seemed on the verge of extinction. Even countries like

Argentina and Brazil have in recent times been controlled by men who waged a vendetta against the intellectual.*

The second factor – the lack of a critical and appreciative audience – arose as a corollary of the political and social situation. The gulf between the educated elite and the masses, which is at the root of the problem, has its origin in a social pattern formed at the time of the Conquest. In Spanish America, even more than in Brazil, the rural masses who formed the greater part of the population remained outside the main stream of colonial life. Only through religion were they united to any universal tradition, and it is only in the religious art, architecture and sculpture of the colonial period that there is any significant fusing of indigenous characteristics and more universal themes. Independence brought no narrowing of the gap between the illiterate masses and the educated and largely urban elite. The numbers of illiterates – over eighty per cent in many countries in the nineteenth century – are a significant indication of the social situation and account for the fact that many writers preferred voluntary exile in Europe to virtual isolation in their own hemisphere. They also account for the fact that there were two cultures in Latin America: an orally transmitted rural culture, tenacious of the past and untouched by recent European trends, and an urban minority culture which took its cues from Europe.

The habit of regarding European culture as the supreme standard had been deeply impressed on the Latin-American intellectual from colonial times. In those days, the source of light was Europe, whence came new books, new intellectual fashions. The fact that the Spanish colonial service required its senior officials in the colonies to be of Spanish birth undoubtedly helped to create a feeling of exaggerated regard for everything that came from Europe. After Independence, the attitude changed, but only superficially. Certainly, there was a decisive reaction in Spanish America against all things Spanish – and a rejection, too, of Spanish culture.[3] But this rejection came about,

---

* In Argentina under Perón, in Brazil under Getúlio Vargas, especially after 1936. More recently military coups in Argentina and Brazil have brought about sporadic reintroductions of censorship.

not because Spanish culture did not fit American reality, but because it was traditional, old-fashioned and not in tune with the modern world with which the new generation of Spanish-American intellectuals identified themselves. Much the same was true of Brazil which, despite its Portuguese-born monarch, also wished to identify itself with the modern world. As a Brazilian critic has observed:

> Strongly marked by its 'Europeanization', the Brazilian mind turned toward the different European markets which supplied it. It was felt that within the tomes of European wisdom must be concealed some ideal and miraculous formula. The surrounding reality was completely forgotten by the majority of the intellectuals of the early nineteenth century, to whom it seemed that the literary, artistic and philosophic moulds of Europe fitted Brazil perfectly.[4]

This exalted opinion of the up-to-date European (and especially the French) fashion was not favourable to the native artist. The upper classes of the new republics and of Brazil tended to prefer the skilled architects, painters, musicians and writers from abroad to their own native novices. Booksellers stocked mainly foreign imported books, and, in the theatre, plays by native authors never attained the success of foreign plays. So that, while the artist was fully aware of the latest European trends and identified himself with the modern, his own work was an imitation which even the people he wrote for tended to reject.

The artist was thus in a difficult position between the pull of Europe and the needs of his native culture. It was precisely this, however, which often drove him to write social criticism. He could either set up his own standard of civilized values, as Andrés Bello (Venezuela, 1781–1865) did, or he could use his knowledge of civilized and European standards to launch an attack on the backwardness of his own country. Adoption of the latter course led to satirical or polemical writing in which the writer passed judgement from a 'European' position. The satirical poems of Felipe Pardo y Aliaga (1806–68), for instance, set up England as the standard by which his country, Peru, was to be judged. Hence, we find Pardo making fun both of the 'Sovereign People – the three-coloured Tsar' who, despite their ignorance, help to decide the fate of the nation, and also of the

Creole aristocracy which he finds lazy and egotistical. Thus, although Pardo writes from a conservative viewpoint, his concern is not that Peru is following European political patterns but that it is following the *wrong* European pattern. Similarly, José Joaquín Fernández de Lizardi (1778–1827) wrote the first Mexican novel, *El Periquillo Sarniento* (The Itching Parrot,* 1816), as an attack on the backwardness of Mexic at the close of the colonial period. He exposed the weakness of the education system, the evils of a clergy without vocation, of doctors and surgeons without proper training, and of bad hospitals. His chief target is antiquated thought and attitudes, and his weapon is the European Enlightenment with which he himself feels identified.

In Argentina, the identification of the intellectual with the most advanced European ideas took on a special significance under the dictatorship of Rosas, whose championship of rural interests led him to despise European imported fashions, manners and political ideas. The attitude of the cultured man was crystallized by one of Rosas's bitterest opponents, Domingo Sarmiento (1811–88), in a polemical essay, *Civilización y barbarie: Vida de Juan Facundo Quiroga* (Civilization and Barbarism: The Life of Juan Facundo Quiroga, 1845) – generally known as *Facundo* – which specifically identified the city with civilized and European values:

> The city man dresses in European clothes, lives a civilized life . . . [in the city] are the laws, the ideas of progress, the means of instruction, municipal organization, regular government, etc. When one leaves the city area, everything changes; the countryman wears different clothes which I will call American since they are common to all countries; his way of life is different; his needs are limited and are of a special kind. They seem to be two different societies, two nations foreign to one another.[5]

Sarmiento, in common with most of his fellow intellectuals, saw himself as the upholder of the modern against the traditional, of the cultured and literate man against the illiterate barbarian, of a European idea of civilization against the centrifugal localism of

*The title refers to the hero's nickname.

rural Argentinians. And the most artistically successful novel of protest written during the nineteenth century, Esteban Echeverría's *El matadero* (The Slaughterhouse, published posthumously but probably written about 1840), dramatizes these same antinomies. This work, which is more of a short story than a novel, made an uncompromising attack on the Rosas regime. It relates an incident at the abattoir in Buenos Aires where, during the slaughtering of the animals, a bull escapes, killing a boy as he does so. The bull is recaptured and the butchers, excited by the thrill of the pursuit and capture, make a bloodthirsty ritual of the killing. As they finish off the animal, a refined-looking young man passes on horseback. They turn against him, drag him from his horse and torment him. The youth struggles valiantly against the attackers but has a haemorrhage and is left for dead. The reason for the attack on him is that he is a 'unitarian' (that is, in opposition to Rosas and his federalist party). The butchers know this because their victim carries no outward sign of support for the Rosas regime and also because he rides with a foreign saddle. He is thus identified with an 'un-American' way of life. Echeverría's own sympathies are not left in doubt. He is unmistakably on the side of refinement and civilization, against the native 'butchers'.

It is legitimate to conclude, therefore, that the social awareness of Echeverría and other writers of the early part of the nineteenth century arose out of a disparity between their refined culture and their brutal environment. But this very disparity made it difficult for them to write great works of art. They felt themselves part of Western culture and wished to work within its tradition; hence they often wrote the sort of novel or poem that Europeans were writing at the time: historical novels, Balzacian social novels, Chateaubriand-type novels of Indian life. Whereas the European writer, working from within the tradition, was able to extend his vision by the gradual acquiring of new technical terrain, no such possibility was open to the Latin American, who tended to borrow whatever instrument seemed most suited to his purpose and then abandon this when some new situation arose. But, most frequently, Latin-American experience simply could not be fitted into European moulds. In this case, the writer had to

17

abandon Europe and strike out boldly on his own: a difficult task and one which frequently made him ill at ease. The writer for whom the recording of a unique American experience was so urgent as to require him to abandon European forms was almost invariably under the necessity of justifying himself for paying more attention to the content than the form. Juan María Gutiérrez's prologue, for instance, to Echeverría's *El matadero* comes back again and again to the same point – that the author was not in a tranquil enough state when he wrote to produce a refined and finished work. Gutiérrez mentions the hurried, incorrect handwriting and spelling of the original as showing under what strains the author was writing, and constantly refers to the story as a 'sketch' or a 'rough drawing'.[6] In the preface to the 1851 edition of *Facundo*, Sarmiento speaks longingly of the day when the struggle is over and he can dedicate himself to more dispassionate work: 'I would gladly throw into the fire all those hurried pages which I have let fall in the combat.'[7] The authors of both *El matadero* and *Facundo* thus have to be justified for not putting their work into a more orthodox literary form.

This problem, of finding forms in which to express American experience, has remained a perennial one. Indeed, the only Latin-American work before 1880 which succeeded in fulfilling the criterion of originality was the poem of gaucho life, *Martín Fierro* (the first part of which was published in 1872) by José Hernández (Argentina, 1834–86) – 'perhaps the most important book we Argentinians have produced in a hundred and fifty years of literature', according to the contemporary writer, Jorge Luis Borges.[8] Like *El matadero* and *Facundo*, the work arose out of a need to protest against a social injustice; but, whereas the first two held up 'barbarism' to shame from the authors' standpoint of European civilization, *Martín Fierro* attacked the Europeanized government of Buenos Aires for destroying the traditional American way of life of the gaucho. Specifically, the author protests against the sending of gauchos as conscripts to the frontier. Yet the poem transcends this limited, local issue. As the poet began to write, says Borges, 'something mysterious, something magical happened': Martín Fierro became, not only a victim of conscription, but a lonely outlaw against society, a man whose human condition is solitude and who incarnates the qualities of pampa life. But, even more important than the fact that Hernández was able to unite national and universal themes with a local issue, is the way he presented his material, for he attempted to work within an existing Argentine tradition of popular ballad poetry, drawing heavily on proverbs and folk imagery. In this way he broke across the barriers that traditionally divided the literate from the illiterate. Hernández wrote a poem with an outlaw hero with whom the country-dwellers could identify themselves, in language which was familiar to them and using a verse form that could be easily memorized. As a result, the poem was immensely popular among ordinary people; men were paid for reciting it in remote farmhouses, and there was an enormous number of editions. *Martín Fierro* thus indicated one way out of the difficulty of writing a poem that was effective as social protest. Hernández ensured himself a mass audience by writing in an existing tradition rather than by borrowing a European form, and he ensured a lasting interest by developing from the local issue a universal 'outsider' theme. Even so, the poem was to remain unique and unappreciated by the more sophisticated public and by Europeanized writers who disdained this native product.

In the nineteenth century, literature was conceived of as being not only an instrument for social protest, but also a way of shaping national consciousness and giving a sense of tradition. Here again, the writer's desire to show the originality of his own culture often conflicted with the European standards he unconsciously accepted. No less a person than Andrés Bello recognized this difficulty when he declared that Spanish-American civilization was 'an exotic plant which still does not take its nourishment from the soil which sustains it'. Bello was alarmed at the rejection of Spanish culture by the writers of the new republics, for he believed that their cultures should stem from the Hispanic tradition. His views were not generally accepted, however. Yet, though writers set out to create a Latin-American literature somewhat deliberately and *ab ovo*, they often had a very superficial vision of what 'Latin-American reality' was. The use of local place names in the numerous imitations of Byron which appeared did not make them any less of an imitation. Similarly, the historical novel – which might have been an important genre, and which could have illuminated the present through an understanding of the past – remained very superficial in its approach, being concerned more with historical trappings than with history. Only *Enriquillo* (1882) by Manuel de Jesús Galván (Dominican Republic, 1834–1911), which deals with the extermination of the Indians of Santo Domingo soon after the Conquest, achieves a significant vision of the past. Perhaps one reason for the failure of the nineteenth-century historical novel (apart from the sheer inability of writers) was the difficulty of finding a key period of which to write. The pre-Columban, Colonial and Independence periods were so disparate that to chose any one single period was to leave out certain important factors in national life. No doubt the difficulty could have been overcome by a writer with real historical imagination; the fact remains, however, that the most successful effort to make an imaginative re-creation of the past is one which broke out of the limits of the historical novel to invent a new genre: the 'tradition'. This work, the *Tradiciones peruanas* by Ricardo Palma (Peru, 1833–1919) consists of a series of stories, published intermittently between 1872 and 1910, covering every aspect of Peru's past – from the pre-Conquest world to the colony and the republic – and also embracing all the regions of the country. The *Tradiciones* were the first successful attempt to synthesize South American national reality and give the people a sense of continuity and tradition. But, as with the social protest type of literature, the *Tradiciones* demonstrate that a successful work of art could emerge only when the European mould was abandoned or transformed.

The real change in the Latin-American artistic scene began to occur in mid-century with the emergence of literary groups and circles founded to promote the publication of poems and novels, to offer encouragement and criticism, and to provide a public – however small – for the aspiring writer. Some of the best novels of the nineteenth century were written directly as a result of the encouragement of such literary groups. In Cuba, for instance, where the home of Domingo Delmonte (1804–53) provided a meeting place for writers, a school of national literature began to emerge which placed an emphasis on national and social themes. Out of this group came Cirilo Villaverde (1812–94) who, in 1882, published the definitive version of *Cecilia Valdés*: a novel with a mulatto heroine. In Colombia, the literary group 'El Mosaico' financed the publication of *María* (1867) – the best romantic novel of Latin America – by Jorge Isaacs (1837–95). In Peru, just after the Peruvian-Chilean war, Manuel González Prada formed a literary circle in order to invigorate Peru's intellectual life. A member of this Peruvian circle, Clorinda Matto de Turner (1854–1909) wrote the first novel to expose the sufferings of the modern Indian, *Aves sin nido* (Birds Without a Nest, 1889). In Mexico, literary discussions were held in a secondary school, the Liceo Hidalgo; at one of the meetings Ignacio Altamirano (1834–93), a writer of Indian origin, read chapters from his novel *El Zarco* * (published posthumously in 1901). Even in Brazil, where literary life had had a more settled and peaceful development, the literary group was important as a stimulus.[9]

Not only did the literary circles help to prepare the ground for a national literature by encouraging the writing of novels and poems on national themes; they also helped to rehabilitate the national writer, for long depreciated by comparison with the foreign writer. In this respect, literature was in advance of the other arts which depended much more directly on public taste and which were in no position to affect that taste. It is not until well into the twentieth century that there develops any significant stimulating demand for native plays, paintings or music. Literature was fortunate in that even the small stimulus provided by a literary circle could often have a decisive effect. A second factor with a decisive effect on the arts was the prosperity which reached the upper classes of Latin America at the end of the nineteenth century as a result of increased trade (for instance, meat exportation from Argentina), foreign investments and improved communications. One of the first effects of this prosperity was to encourage the buying of more European prestige

* *Zarco* means blue-eyed. This is the nickname of the bandit villain of the novel.

art products – paintings, European-designed houses and public buildings, imported books and furniture. Here, France was the important source of supply, partly because French civilization was generally regarded as setting the highest standard of elegance, and also because a large number of wealthy Latin Americans lived in Paris for shorter or longer periods and hence adopted French values. However, whilst the first effect of increased prosperity was simply to spread this French-style elegance more widely, none the less the Latin-American arts indirectly benefited from the emergence of new wealthy classes who provided a potential market and from the larger number of newspapers and periodicals which could now be financed. Studies on the sociology of the arts in Latin America are, unfortunately, almost entirely lacking; however, in the case of Venezuela, there is some evidence to suppose that the emergence of a native middle class had a direct effect on stimulating a school of Venezuelan writing.*

The 1880s also saw the emergence of a new dominant ideology – Positivism. Latin-American adherents of the French philosopher, Auguste Comte (1798–1857), or the British thinker, Herbert Spencer (1820–1903), believed Positivism to be the instrument by which Latin Americans could emancipate themselves intellectually from the 'retrograde' influence of Spain. They also believed that Positivism would provide the intellectual training which Latin Americans needed if their countries were to become modern industrial states. As one critic has commented:

Between 1880 and 1900, a new Hispanic America seemed to arise. It was a Hispanic America that apparently no longer resembled in any way the Hispanic America of the first fifty years following its political independence. A new order arose in each country . . . an order based upon science, an order concerned with the education of its citizens and the attainment for them of the greatest material comfort.[10]

*For instance, *El cojo ilustrado* (1892–1915), a periodical which became the chief patron of new Venezuelan writing, began as the trade paper of a tobacco company. In Chile, *Pluma y lápiz* (1900–1904) carried publicity articles on big companies (which helped to finance the magazine) as well as printing new Chilean writing.

But what Latin-American Positivists failed to perceive was that no imported system could transform Latin America into a modern state so long as the social structure was feudal or oligarchic. Moreover, the financial boom of the 1880s ended in a series of financial crises which were particularly serious in Chile and Argentina. In the latter country, feverish speculation ended in a spectacular financial crash of 1890.*

It is precisely at this period, when the evils as well as the advantages of the new industrial and financial age were apparent, when society was in a state of flux with fortunes made and lost, that the Spanish-American Modernist movement has its beginning. The Modernist poets were the first group of Latin-American artists to regard themselves as separated from the rest of society, and to justify this isolation on the grounds that modern society was base and materialistic, ignorant of the true values which they, as seers and prophets, glimpsed. This affirmation of their isolation was by no means rhetorical, as the fate of many minor Modernist poets in countries like Ecuador, Nicaragua and Honduras shows (see chapter 8, page 263). Their significance is that, unlike previous generations of poets, they tried to dedicate themselves wholly to art. The Modernists were thus the first generation of professional writers in Spanish America.†

* The speculation fever of the period has been described by Julián Martel (pseudonym of José Miró, 1868–96) in his novel *La bolsa* (1891).

† The situation in Brazil was better than in Spanish America. There were writers from humble backgrounds (e.g. Machado de Assis) who were able to maintain themselves in civil service posts or journalism. See Antônio Candido, 'O Escritor e o Público', *Literatura e Sociedade*, São Paulo 1965, pp. 87–104.

1

A Symbolic Revolt:
The Modernist Movement

'Art is a religion, the poet a worshipper of the eternal ideal.' This summary of the Modernist * creed appears to have little connexion with social conscience. Yet the appearance of this group of poets, writing at the end of the nineteenth century, had a deep significance, for two reasons. First, because the Modernists regarded the artist – and the poet in particular – as standing in a special relationship to society, and were therefore the first Spanish Americans to consider themselves professional writers. Second, because they made a symbolic revolt against the society of their time.[1]

The most influential representative of this 'new spirit' was Rubén Darío (1867–1916), a prodigy from the small town of Metapa, Nicaragua, whose talents soon raised him out of his provincial background. Invited to Managua, the Nicaraguan capital, while still an adolescent, he was quickly launched on a career which took him to other Central American countries, and thence to Chile where, in the library of the president's son, Pedro Balmaceda Toro, he read those contemporary French poets whose styles and rhythms he was to incorporate brilliantly into Spanish. He spent many years in Buenos Aires and later lived in Paris and Madrid. A powerful personality, his presence galvanized literary life. Both in Santiago and Buenos Aires he was at the centre of literary discussions in the cafés. He helped to start literary reviews, like the Argentinian *Revista de América*, founded in 1894, and he was an indefatigable contributor to little magazines. He it was who gave the name 'Modernism' to the urge for literary revival which was evident all over Latin

---

* Spanish-American Modernismo, which reached its height in the 1890s, is translated as Modernism; to avoid confusion, when the quite different Brazilian movement of the 1920s, also known as Modernismo (the Modernista group), is referred to in the text, the Portuguese words are retained.

America.[2] The name caught on and came to characterize a broad movement whose aim was to revolutionize the form and content of poetry and prose. Moreover, two of his own publications – *Azul* (Azure), which first appeared in Chile in 1888, and *Prosas profanas* (Profane Prose, 1896) – had a far-reaching influence in the whole of the Spanish-speaking world.[3]

Darío was not a lone figure by any means, nor even the pioneer of the literary renewal to which he gave a name. All the most vigorous poetic talents of the time were united in a common desire to change the literary language. Among them we may mention José Asunción Silva (Colombia, 1865–96) and José Martí (Cuba, 1853–95) as examples of poets who had either started to experiment in poetic form before Darío or who stood outside the Modernist movement proper. A rebellion against a literary heritage, the invention of new forms of expression – these are seldom gratuitous exercises. They usually indicate a deep discontent with existing interpretations of experience and a disparity between the artist's attitudes and those expressed in his literary tradition. There is a gulf between experience and existing forms, and only the invention of new forms can bridge this gulf. For the Modernists, Spanish language and poetic form were inadequate for the expression of their new sensibility. But they were not the only ones to feel this inadequacy. The late nineteenth century was a period of lively polemic in many countries of Spanish America between intellectuals who wished to defend the purity of Castilian and revolutionary intellectuals who wanted a literary language that corresponded in some way to the language actually spoken in America.[4] For the Modernists, however, the conflict was not so much between pure Castilian and American Spanish as an ideological conflict between a language that had failed to develop with the modern world and their own spiritual and aesthetic experience. Darío's strictures on the Spanish language are significant in this respect. Spanish, he declared, was walled in by tradition; his own mission was to bring the language up to date, and for this the introduction of non-Spanish vocabulary was necessary.* Pedro Emilio Coll

* Darío was very conscious of a mission in this respect, as his prefaces to his collections show: see, for example, *Poesías completas*, p. 703.

(Venezuela, 1872–1947) also emphasized this mission of the Modernist poet. Rubén Darío and others, he said, 'are giving life to our Castilian tongue and sending warmth and blood through the veins of our language which was dying of anaemia and which seemed destined to expire like a decrepit and worn-out old man.'[5]

There was some justification in these strictures. In Spain, there was no Baudelaire, no Rimbaud and no Victor Hugo. Spanish culture lacked that brilliant and subversive strand of post-Romantic poetry with its challenge to conventional values. The poet, who, by his very profession, was aware of an invisible world beyond the world of appearances, was gravely frustrated by the irksome restrictions of a language which as yet had no names for his experiences. In attacking Castilian, therefore, the Modernist was also attacking Spanish values. Pedro Emilio Coll pointed out that the technical developments made by the Modernists went hand in hand with an 'evolution in sensibility'.*[6] Manuel González Prada (Peru, 1848–1918) felt that the Spanish example could no longer be of value to the New World, for 'the sick man who wants better blood transfused into his veins would rather choose that of a strong young friend than that of his aged and tired grandfather'.[7] Rubén Darío believed that Spain was responsible for the feeling of rebellion everywhere apparent in its former colonies. The metropolitan culture had provided no intellectual stimulus, and its writers treated those of the New World with condescension. Hence Spanish-American writers had come to feel stronger links with the culture of other European countries than with that of Spain. A cosmopolitan and polyglot city like Buenos Aires, he observed, could no longer feel that it belonged solely to Castilian tradition when it was open to influences from all over the world.[8] In short, Modernism arose at a moment of crisis, when traditional religious beliefs and moral conventions were being challenged.

---

*In most European countries, Romanticism had been a major evolution in sensibility, whereas in Spain it had remained a largely literary movement. There is some reason to suppose that Modernism is the Hispanic equivalent to the evolution in sensibility signalled by Romanticism in England, France and Germany.

'Works of art no longer fit in the moulds that are worn out with so many centuries of use.'[9] What more natural than that the Modernist should look for inspiration to a language and a culture that were capable of expressing this new sensibility: the language and culture of France.

France indeed supplied all that Spain lacked: a literature that opened up new vistas of experience; a language flexible enough to express this; an environment that offered encouragement to the artist. France represented the topmost height of artistic consciousness, and it was therefore with the French contemporary artist that the Modernist most ardently wished to identify himself. Darío, for instance, arriving at the Gare Saint Lazare, felt as if he were treading on holy ground. On one occasion, he stated that his dream had been to write in French.[10] On the publication of *Azul* in 1888, he was congratulated by his friend Julián del Casal (Cuba, 1863–93) for writing 'like a French artist'. Julián del Casal, who was to die young of tuberculosis, was another admirer of France, but of a France that was perhaps legendary. He declared that he hated the Paris which 'celebrates the fourteenth of July every year, the Paris that shows itself off at the Opera' – in other words, the bourgeois Paris. On the other hand: 'I love the strange, exotic, delicate, sensitive, brilliant and artificial Paris. . . .' This Paris, he goes on to say, is the Paris that pays tribute to the artist: 'theosophical, magic, satanic and occult Paris'; 'the Paris which foreigners do not know and whose existence they are not even aware of'.[11] Similarly, when the Mexican Manuel Gutiérrez Nájera (1859–95) who, like Casal, had never been to Paris, writes of his mistress, he praises her because she is like the 'grisette of Paul de Kock'.[12] The Modernists had this tendency to measure all things with a French metre stick.

It would be tempting to regard Modernism as a substitution of French for Spanish influences, accentuating a trend that was by no means new in Spanish America. Imported French translations had been the favourite reading of the Spanish-American literary elite for years; in painting and architecture, French influence was paramount, as many buildings in Buenos Aires and Mexico City testify to this date. The Modernists themselves

were the first to proclaim their debt to France. Salvador Díaz
Mirón (Mexico, 1853–1928) acknowledged himself a disciple of
Hugo; Darío freely acknowledged the influence on his verse and
prose of writers as diverse as Leconte de Lisle, Catulle Mendès,
Alphonse Daudet, Hugo and Banville. Julián del Casal dedicated a series of poems to the French painter Gustave Moreau.
The three important volumes of poems which mark the height
of the Modernist movement all bear the traces of French influence: Darío's *Prosas profanas*; *Las montañas del oro* by
Leopoldo Lugones (Argentina, 1874–1938); and *Castalia
bárbara* by the Bolivian Ricardo Jaimes Freyre (1868–1933).[13]

Yet Modernism is much more than the substitution of influences. The spiritual flight to France indicated defects in the
poet's own environment. France offered that communion with
like minds which did not exist in the barbarous wastes of Spanish
America. To whom could the American writer address himself
in his own country? As Amado Nervo (Mexico, 1870–1919)
complained:

> In Mexico, people write for those who write. The literary man has
> a circle of the chosen few who read him and who become his only
> public. The 'gros public', as the French say, neither pay nor under-
> stand, however simply he writes. What more natural than that he
> should write for those who, even if they do not pay him, at least buy
> his books?[14]

And at the other end of America, in Chile, Antonio Bórquez
Solar (1873–1938) was complaining equally bitterly. He felt
that, in the future, the period in which he lived would be looked
upon as a barbarous period, one in which there was 'an absolute
lack of high thinking, a spirit that is hostile and refractory to the
beautiful things of poetry and art'. He believed that poetry was
an intellectual luxury which the masses could not attain. For
this reason those who raised themselves above the general
mediocrity were insulted and regarded as decadent; for people
could not understand why some should want to cultivate roses
when the majority were content to live on cabbage.[15]

The Uruguayan poet, Julio Herrera y Reissig (1875–1910),
cursed the 'implacable stupidity' of his country. Darío's friend

the Argentinian Luis Berisso (1866–1944), complained that his country's upper class appreciated only sport and horse-racing, and cared nothing for literature. Outside politics, he wrote, 'there is nothing that breaks through the thick layer of indifference which covers everything'. He added that, among the many factors militating against the artist – the unsettled political state, anarchist attacks, an unstable economic situation – the most serious was lack of an appreciative public.

> It is not enough to have an Ateneo and an Academy. An artistic public is indispensable, a public which loves learning, poetry, art and the beautiful things of the spirit.
> It is really a shame that, in a city of 600,000 inhabitants like Buenos Aires, books by native authors should not find a hundred readers.[16]

Against this dismal environment, the Modernist poet could at least protect himself in the warmth of friendship with other poets. Across national and continental frontiers, French, Spanish and Spanish-American poets could communicate their sense of solidarity against an uncomprehending world.

Lack of an understanding public in their own countries was not the only fault that the Modernists found there. Pedro Emilio Coll, speaking of the 'new sensibility' of contemporary Spanish-American art, saw this as reflecting 'the disturbed and twilight states of the spirit which have their roots in deep social factors, in education, in the anguished historical moment whose air we are breathing'.[17] The poet's 'new sensibility' clashed with the social norm, and hence he felt very deeply that his position was one of an outsider from society.

THE POET AS OUTSIDER

The outsider position was often dramatically underlined by the events of the poets' lives. Long before writing, many of the Modernists had already had proof in the hard arena of experience of the cruelties and dangers of a world in which money or force ruled. The Spanish-American economy was highly unstable at the end of the nineteenth century. Civil war, inflation and political disturbance all contributed to this instability. The wheel of fortune spun erratically and in its course left many of their families ruined. José Asunción Silva of Colombia spent much of his adult life trying to refloat the family business which had been ruined after a civil war. Leopoldo Lugones's parents were forced to abandon their family estate and settle in Córdoba after landing themselves in financial difficulties. By the age of twenty, Julio Herrera y Reissig had seen his family lose wealth and political influence. The family of Julián del Casal was forced out of its small sugar-holding by the development in Cuba of the big competitive companies. It would be absurd to suggest that these men became poets because their families lost their money (indeed, there were also wealthy dilettantes among the Modernists, such as the Venezuelan Manuel Díaz Rodríguez (1871–1927), but these reversals almost certainly hardened that hatred of contemporary society which is one of the constants of their writing. It is little wonder that many of them viewed with sympathy the nascent socialist and anarchist movements since they themselves felt so bitter, not only about their own societies but about society as a whole. A projected novel by Julián del Casal epitomized their attitude. He planned a story in which the hero would travel from place to place, finding each nation intolerable. So he will go from country to country until he finally comes to believe that '... the civilized world is impossible to live in because men are the same everywhere'.[18] Similarly, we find José Asunción Silva deploring the utilitarian basis of contemporary society.[19]

The type of society the Modernists hated above all was contemporary bourgeois society. This may seem strange, since Spanish America was only at the margin of industrial and capital expansion. Yet the poets did not have to see 'dark satanic mills' on their doorsteps to realize that a new and disturbing force was looming over them. In a short sketch, 'Father León's Umbrella', José Asunción Silva contrasted colonial Bogotá – whose presence still lingered in buildings and atmosphere – with Bogotá of the new era, represented by a rich man dashing about in his fast carriage.[20] The cash nexus, destructive of all other human relations, was what the artist most feared. Indeed, many of the prose pieces written by the Modernists are in the nature of allegories about the relation of the artist to a materialist society. For example, the Venezuelan Manuel Díaz Rodríguez, in one of his *Cuentos de color* (Coloured Stories, 1899), wrote of the downfall of Psyche who was honoured only as long as she was richly dressed; in modern times only the poet could see her, the rest of society being blinded by a golden veil.[21] Darío's story, 'El rey burgués' (The Bourgeois King), told of the fate of the poet condemned to play a barrel organ in the snow because he had proclaimed his defiance of bourgeois values. The poet represented the voice of the 'fertile jungle' in a world of convention with which he could not compromise. 'Art does not wear trousers, or speak middle-class language, or dot all its i's.' In another of Darío's stories, a poet, a sculptor, a musician and a painter compare the sorry lot of the modern artist with that of artists of former times. 'The lunatic's cell' and the 'mocking crowd' are all they can expect from society; hence their need for 'Queen Mab's veil': the veil of illusion which will help them live in the modern world. In a prose poem, the 'Canción de Oro' (Song of Gold), a beggar who is also a poet sings ironically his song in praise of the Golden Calf whom everybody now worships.[22]

The condemnation of gold is frequently on the lips of the poets of the time, from Asunción Silva to the Cuban José Martí, whose work in many ways diverges from that of the Modernists. Yet even Martí had this hatred of materialism, in common with others of his generation. One of his poems contrasts the ephemeral beauty of gold and the real pleasures of the countryside.

> Yo he visto el oro hecho tierra
> Barbullendo en la redoma
> Prefiero estar en la sierra
> Cuando vuela una paloma.[23]

> I have seen gold turned to dross
> And bubbling in the flask
> But I would rather be in the hills
> When the dove takes wing and flies.

REAL AND SYMBOLIC REBELLION

The poet's hatred of the materialism of his age was often to remain verbal. Yet to condemn this generation, as some critics do, because of its ivory tower attitude is too simple-minded. There were many shades of social involvement between Herrera y Reissig's lonely attic and the militancy of José Martí. But, whether the poet chose inactivity or death in battle, his poetry invariably showed a nonconformity with the bourgeois values of his time.

However, it must be admitted that Martí's direct involvement in the Cuban independence movement does mark him off from the other poets of his time who preferred a more symbolic form of revolt. Born in Cuba in 1853, Martí was, by the age of seventeen, already in conflict with the Spanish authorities and was sentenced to six years' imprisonment: a sentence that was later commuted to exile. After visiting many countries of Europe and America, he returned to Havana in 1878, only to be exiled once again. In 1881 he founded the *Revista Venezolana* in Caracas, but neither in Caracas nor in any Spanish-American country could he find the political conditions he wanted and he finally settled in New York. He was killed while on a liberation expedition to Cuba in 1895. Martí composed three volumes of poems: *Ismaelillo*, dedicated to his son, was published in 1882; *Versos libres* (Free Verses) were written soon after *Ismaelillo* but not published until 1919, long after his death; *Versos sencillos* (Simple Verses) appeared in 1891. These titles are significant, for they reveal a view of poetry which had more in common with Wordsworth than with Darío. Nothing could be further from an elite attitude than these words of Martí:

Poetry is the work both of the bard and of the people who inspire him. . . . Poetry is durable when it is the work of all. Those who understand it are as much its authors as those who make it. To thrill all hearts by the vibrations of your own, you must have the germs and inspirations of humanity. To walk among the multitudes who suffer, with love in your heart and song on your lips, you must hear all the groans, witness all the agonies, feel all the joys and be inspired with

33

the passions common to all. Above all, you must live among a suffering people.[24]

Compare this with Darío who, in his poem 'Torres de Diós: Poetas' (Towers of God: Poets), describes the poet as a 'tower', a 'lightning conductor', a 'breakwater', because he stands apart and above the rest of the world. But for Martí isolation was 'frightful'. 'Man needs to go outside himself,' he wrote, 'in order to find repose and renew himself.'[25]

The difference between Martí's thoroughly committed attitude and the symbolic revolt of his contemporaries is best seen by comparing attitudes to the past. Where Darío saw the past as a lost Golden Age in which the artist was honoured, and had nothing but contempt for modern society, for Martí the past was a constant challenge to the present. This is well expressed in one of his most famous poems, 'Los héroes'.

Sueño con claustros de mármol	I dream of marble cloisters
donde en silencio divino	where in silence divine
los héroes, de pie, reposan;	heroes stand at rest.
¡de noche, a la luz del alma,	At night, in the soul's light,
hablo con ellos: de noche!	I speak to them. At night!
Están en fila; paseo	They stand in rows; I walk
entre las filas: las manos	between the rows; their hands
de piedra les beso: abren	of stone I kiss; they open
los ojos de piedra: mueven	their hands of stone; they move
los labios de piedra: tiemblan	their lips of stone; they shake
las barbas de piedra: empuñan	their beards of stone and grip
la espada de piedra: lloran:	the sword of stone. They weep.
¡vibra la espada en la vaina!	The sword shivers in its sheath.
Mudo, les beso la mano.	Silent, I kiss their hands.
¡Hablo con ellos, de noche!	At night I speak to them.
Están en fila: paseo	They stand in rows. I walk
entre las filas: lloroso	between the rows and, weeping,
me abrazo a un mármol: '¡Oh mármol,	I embrace a stone: 'O stone,
dicen que beben tus hijos	they tell me your sons are shamed
su propia sangre en las copas	and drink from the poisoned cup

venenosas de sus dueños!	where the masters have poured their blood.
¡Que hablan la lengua podrida	I hear them speak the degenerate tongue
de sus rufianes! ¡Que comen juntos el pan del oprobio, en la mesa ensangrentada! ¡Que pierden en lengua inútil el último fuego! ¡Dicen, oh, mármol, mármol dormido, que ya se ha muerto tu raza!'	of their pimps and watch them eat together the bread of shame, at the blood-stained table. Hear them waste in useless talk their final spark. They say, O stone! O sleeping stone! that your race is already dead.'
Echame en tierra de un bote el héroe que abrazo: me ase del cuello: barre la tierra con mi cabeza: levanta	The hero I had embraced fells me to earth with a blow. He grasps my neck with his hand and my head he drags to the ground.
el brazo: ¡el brazo le luce lo mismo que un sol! resuena la piedra: buscan el cinto las manos blancas: ¡del soclo	His arms are raised on high, arms that shine like the sun. The stone reverberates. White hands fly to waists. From their plinths
saltan los hombres de mármol!²⁶	Leap the men of stone.

In this poem, Martí represents the past as a standard of achievement, not as a dead hand on the present or a lost Paradise. It is of a piece with his whole attitude to life.

How does it come about that Martí stands so far apart from the other poets of his time, managing as he did to combine political action and the writing of poetry? Certainly one difference was the fact that his goal was different from theirs. Whereas the Modernists appealed to a posterity which would understand their verse, Martí looked to a posterity that would understand and approve his actions. His letters show a continual awareness that the eyes of the future were upon him. That is why he could not commit a cowardly, evil or corrupt action for eventually he would face the scrutiny of history. Literary fame was of secondary importance to him, therefore. Another factor that accounts for the difference between Martí and his contemporaries was the fact that he worked with people from many different countries on political issues and thus came to understand some of the far-reaching problems that faced the Americas – problems such as racialism and the imbalance of power between the U.S. and the rest of the continent. He saw that it was no use dividing Latin America into the 'civilized' and the 'barbarians' as Sarmiento had done and then proceeding to exclude the barbarians from society. In a famous essay, 'Our America', he showed that the 'barbarians' had an authenticity and spontaneity which would finally be more valuable to the continent than the borrowed fineries of the civilized.

Despite the fact that the Modernists generally rejected social or political action, many, as has been noted, were drawn through their hatred of contemporary society to nascent socialist and anarchist movements. In the Plate region in particular, the nineties were years of great activity in the formation of socialist parties. Both Leopoldo Lugones and Ricardo Jaimes Freyre were early socialists, although Lugones in later life became a right-wing nationalist. Rubén Darío was drawn towards 'artistic socialism'; and, in his early years, during his stay in Chile, he had addressed a poem 'To the Worker', intended to be read at the birthday celebrations of a Workers' League in Valparaiso.[27] The poem is, however, devoid of any political content; it simply exalts the glory of work, and exhorts the workers to imitate the bee and the beaver. More revealing is a poem (probably written between 1888–9 and addressed to Mother Spain) from 'El salmo de la pluma' in which Darío predicts the downfall of tyrants and the rise of the working masses.[28] The root of whatever sympathy Darío had for socialism is clearly revealed in a letter he wrote to the Chilean poet, Emilio Rodríguez Mendoza: 'The path of artistic socialism does not displease me because it represents the reaction against the oppression of modern life. But you don't forget, and you are right, that art is essentially aristocratic.'[29]

Nevertheless, not all Darío's contemporaries disdained the use of poetry as an instrument for arousing humanity's conscience. Chilean Modernism was decidedly humanitarian in tone;[30] and in Mexico Salvador Díaz Mirón, inspired by Victor Hugo, wrote bitter and powerful verses on behalf of the oppressed. His poem 'Los parias' (The Outcasts) described the tribulations of those whose hard lives are lived to no purpose:

> Mas, ay ¿qué logra con su heroísmo?
> ¿Cuál es el premio, cuál su laurel?
> El desdichado recoge ortigas
> y apura el cáliz hasta la hez.[31]

> But, Oh, what win they with their noble courage?
> What is the prize and where the laurel crown?
> The unhappy pauper reaps only the nettle
> and must drain his wine glass down unto the lees.

Such complete identification with the poor was rare. The poet saw himself not as one of the masses, but as their leader. As the Chilean Bórquez Solar so naïvely declared: 'I called for justice in prose, verse, in the press and public meetings. I dreamed of making myself heard. I wanted – oh madness – to be like a prophet and so attain immortality through fame.'[32] In one of his youthful poems Darío spoke of the poet as 'less sublime than God and more than humanity'. Despite some early humanitarian sympathy, the aristocratic view was to prevail in Darío. 'I am not a poet for the masses,' he was to say in 1905 when he wrote his preface to *Cantos de vida y esperanza* (Songs of Life and Hope). Yet in the same preface he remarks: 'I know that I must inevitably go to them.' Behind Darío's poetry there lurks his view of the poet's mission as a prophet.

One has not to look far for the origin of this view. The shadow of Victor Hugo looms over the whole generation, whose members were naturally drawn to a poetic creed which raised the poet to a semi-divine status. The many tributes paid to Hugo by the poets of the period betray in their very language the enormous attraction his example had for them. Salvador Díaz Mirón described him as an 'Atlas holding up the Heavens, The seer who explores the infinite'; and as the 'column guiding mankind across the desert to Eden'.[33] Many of Darío's early poems are extravagant in their praise of Hugo: 'Immortal genius ... prophet at whose voice oppressors tremble on their thrones.'[34] Other poems echo Hugo in their exaltation of the poet. In 'A un poeta' (To a poet), Darío declared that the poet's talent was God-given and it is to God that the poet must answer.[35] Leopoldo Lugones's *Las montañas del oro* (The Mountains of Gold, 1897) is even more exaggerated in its claims for the poet: 'The tree still sleeps in the seed but the seed vegetates in the heart of the future. From it, there rises this atom, this sun. A poet. A poet? It must be. God does not work in vain.'[36] Sometimes the poet's own self-exaltation reaches comic dimensions. The Peruvian José Santos Chocano (1875–1934) had printed in red ink his *Iras santas* (Holy Wrath), written in prison between 1893 and 1895, and boasted that he would enclose the corrupt in the 'prison of my verses'.[37]

Sometimes the poet's view of himself as 'above the battle' was accepted by his own society. José Santos Chocano, for instance, was appointed to delicate diplomatic missions and became a close friend and adviser to the Guatemalan dictator, Estrada Cabrera. Rubén Darío was appointed to represent Nicaragua in Madrid, and Ricardo Jaimes Freyre served Bolivia, not only as a diplomatist, but also as Minister of Education and Foreign Minister in the twenties.

But there was a dark side to the poet myth. Nonconformity with society could be paid for in suffering and death. José Asunción Silva shot himself when he was thirty-one. The Uruguayan poetess Delmira Agustini (1886–1914) was murdered at the age of twenty-eight and Julio Herrera y Reissig died in poverty at a relatively early age. Darío, who survived to middle age, spent the last years an unhappy dipsomaniac.

The Modernists also played to the hilt the part of the poet as bohemian and eccentric. This attitude followed on their view that the poet was semi-divine and therefore not subject to the ordinary rules of social behaviour. Like the English and French aesthetes, Asunción Silva and Julián del Casal dressed and behaved in a way calculated to outrage society. Asunción Silva would meet his friends in a study full of books, flasks of perfume, Egyptian cigarettes and vases of flowers. On his table there was a picture of his sister Elvira, who had died in 1891 and with whom he had supposedly been in love. He cultivated his reputation as a drug addict. In Havana, Julián del Casal received his friends dressed as a mandarin in a room full of Chinese and Japanese knick-knacks. Here he would offer them tea, while fumes of sandal-wood and incense arose in front of an image of the Buddha. In Montevideo, Herrera y Reissig called his attic room the Tower of Panoramas and lived there in bohemian disorder, surrounded by portraits of the great men he admired.

ESCAPE – OR THE ASSERTION OF TRUE VALUES?

In 1882, Oscar Wilde lectured in North America and urged his audience to cultivate beauty and shun the material values of their age. He declared that, when men were united in common intellectual pursuits, war and strife would disappear. The lecture was attended by José Martí, who admired the courage of Wilde in upholding aestheticism in the face of a hostile society. Nevertheless, Martí did not believe Wilde's analysis to be right. It was not lack of beauty that was wrong with society, but its concentration on purely material ends. Darío and his generation would perhaps have agreed with Martí that materialism was the evil of the age, but they would also have agreed with Wilde that the poet's task was to cultivate beauty and thus set an example to the rest of mankind.[38] This dedication to non-personal values was what set the Modernists apart from others and sustained their belief in their superiority as the true aristocrats of society. Gutiérrez Nájera signed himself 'Duke Job'; Julián del Casal wrote under the pseudonym 'Count de Camors'. Darío boasted that, if he had Indian blood in his veins, it was the blood of an Indian princess. These 'aristocrats' had their communion of saints. Two influential books which appeared in the 1890s – *Literatura extranjera* (Foreign Literature, 1895) by Enrique Gómez Carrillo (Guatemala, 1873–1927) and Rubén Darío's *Los raros* (The Eccentrics, 1896) – were collections of essays dealing with their heroes, Verlaine, Baudelaire, Poe: men who had suffered and were sometimes martyred in the pursuit of 'true' values.

It followed that poetry was always spoken of in terms of the utmost reverence. Gutiérrez Nájera stressed the immortality it conferred.[39] Julián del Casal was sustained in the difficulties of existence by his pride in being a poet who could 'extract a golden atom from the pestilential depths of the mire'.[40] For Asunción Silva, verse was a 'holy vessel' and only pure thoughts should be poured into it.[41] Darío spoke in glowing terms of him 'who dares to proclaim the triumph of Harmony and the Idea in the face of the Barbarians; . . . who, among human glories, prefers that of worshipper and priest of the eternal ideal'.[42] The *eternal* ideal. The aesthetic creed of this generation was based on the assumption that there were eternal Platonic ideas. Like Blake, they believed that: 'This world of the Imagination is the world of Eternity; it is the divine bosom into which we shall all go after the death of the Vegetated body. This world of the Imagination is Infinite and Eternal, whereas the world of Generation or Vegetation is Finite and Temporal.' Darío was to say much the same in other terms: 'The poet has a direct, introspective vision of life, a super vision which goes beyond all that is subject to the laws of general knowledge. . . . It is Art which conquers time and space.'[43] It was this vision of an unchanging and eternal world that, as José Asunción Silva recognized, sustained the poet in his lonely battle against a society almost totally preoccupied with day-to-day politics and money. Asunción Silva's happiest moments were those when he was able to lose his sense of individuality and separation, and this could be done only through a process akin to mysticism, which he described as follows:

In the first hour of pensive quietude, scenes from the past came to my mind, ghosts of dead years, memories of distant readings: then the particular gave way to the universal; general ideas like processions of muses bearing in their hands the formulae of the universe passed across my inner field of vision. Then four grandiose entities, Love, Art, Death, Science, rose into my imagination, suspended between the two infinities of water and sky; then these last expressions of the human melted into the black immensity and oblivion of self, of life and death; the sublime spectacle entered my being, so to speak, and I was dispersed into the starry dome, into the tranquil ocean as if I was one with them in a pantheistic ecstasy of sublime adoration.[44]

The constant preoccupation of Asunción Silva is the contrast between the world of eternity, which is also the world of the dead, and the shifting world of time and appearance. His poem

'Día de Difuntos' (Day of the Dead), contrasts the tinkling sound of a bell that marks the time and the grave deep notes of the church bells tolling for the dead. In the sound of the bells, time and eternity mingle. In his most famous poem, 'Nocturno', he describes a moonlight walk with his beloved during which he watched the shadows lengthen and finally merge.

> Y tu sombra
> Fina y lánguida
> Y mi sombra
> Por los rayos de la luna proyectada
> Sobre las arenas tristes
> De la senda se juntaban
> Y eran una
> Y eran una
> ¡Y eran una sola sombra larga!
> ¡Y eran una sola sombra larga!
> ¡Y eran una sola sombra larga![45]

> And your shadow
> slender, languid
> And my shadow
> cast by the rays of the moon
> upon the melancholy sand
> of the path were joined
> and they were one
> and they were one
> and they were one long shadow
> and they were one long shadow
> and they were one long shadow.

But this union is in time and is ephemeral. The poet's beloved dies, and the poem evokes the sense of separation which is overcome only when the poet, walking in the moonlight, imagines that the shadows are once again joined. The poem hovers over the limits between life and death, communicating the shadowy nature of existence. The fact that it was written for Asunción Silva's sister, Elvira, adds significance, not because of the supposed incest motif, but because the sister represented, even more than a mistress, a sense of wholeness and completion. Elvira served as a symbol for all that represents perfect communion and yet, at the same time, she represents a double unattainability, for she is dead and she is a sister. Yet the poet's vision overcomes this limitation and the shadows are joined in the world of imagination.

'FREEZING' TIME

The Modernists lived in a period of rapid change, and undoubtedly their yearning for 'eternity' was associated with subconscious fears of the transformations taking place around them. Many of them deliberately tried to achieve a static effect in their verses, as if they wanted to stop all time and movement. Such an effect was attained by Julio Herrera y Reissig, the Uruguayan poet. In the poems of *Los éxtasis de la montaña* (The Ecstasies of the Mountain, 1904), he created a pastoral world in which by avoiding precise place-names, by using verbs in the present tense, and by depicting eternal pastoral types and activities, he conveyed a sense of changelessness. His choice of a pastoral setting is deliberate, for peasant life is slow to change. But in choosing the pastoral form, he also betrayed his nostalgia for an ordered and guiltless society. His frequent use of the word 'cándido' is significant in this respect. 'Cándido' translates as both white and ingenuous and has connotations with the purity and innocence associated with childhood. In fact Herrera y Reissig's poetry attempted to create a world in which humanity was still in its infancy, a world without conflict or change or unpleasantness. His *Sonetos Vascos* (Basque Sonnets, 1906) were set in the Basque country which he had never visited but which symbolized for him the ordered patriarchal communities that were the very antithesis of the brash and impatient New World.

Darío, too, has his special vocabulary of 'princesses', 'marchionesses', 'swans', 'roses', which raised his poetry above the commonplace into a realm of eternal beauty. Yet Darío, unlike some of his followers and contemporaries, realized the difficulty of 'freezing' time through the medium of language: a medium closely bound up with temporality. One of his best poems expresses this conflict.

Yo persigo una forma que no encuentra mi estilo,
botón de pensamiento que busca ser la rosa;
se anuncia con un beso que en mis labios se posa
al abrazo imposible de la Venus de Milo.

Adornan verdes palmas el blanco peristilo;
los astros me han predicho la visión de la Diosa;
y en mi alma reposa la luz, como reposa
el ave de la luna sobre un lago tranquilo.

Y no hallo sino la palabra que huye,
la iniciación melódica que de la flauta fluye
y la barca del sueño que en el espacio boga;

y bajo la ventana de mi Bella-Durmiente,
el sollozo contínuo del chorro de la fuente
y el cuello del gran cisne blanco que me interroga.[46]

My style has never found the form I seek.
It is the bud of thought which wants to be a rose.
It is heralded by a kiss which on my lips bestows
Venus de Milo, whom one cannot embrace.

Green palms adorn the white column;
stars have foretold my vision of the Goddess.
On my soul light rests, like the bird of the moon
resting on a tranquil lake.

But I hold nothing but the fleeting word,
the opening phrase that flows from a flute,
a bark of dreams floating in space.

And under the window of my Sleeping Beauty
the perpetual sigh of a fountain flowing
and the neck of the great white swan that questions me.

Here is described Darío's vision of eternal beauty, symbolized by Venus de Milo: a vision which remains in his soul, but which can be expressed only in the 'fleeting word'. The flowing fountain of time, the white swan with its reminder of the enigma of death, express the unresolved conflict in Darío's mind between his vision of the eternal and the claims of the temporal.

Darío is often rightly praised for the musicality of his verse which is yet another indication of his imperative desire to purify words of immediate ephemeral associations and make them reflect archetypal patterns of experience. Words thus take on a magical property which allows the poet to convey root experiences. But, unfortunately, in many of his poems Darío did not go deeply enough. He took the trappings of the literary and humanistic culture that, at the end of the nineteenth century, still formed the basis of middle-class and upper-class education. This education gave these classes a common body of knowledge and literary experience derived from classical poets and their mythology. In the sense that this was common to the cultivated minority of most Western countries, it could be regarded as a universal tradition. Darío could assume that his allusions to centaurs, to Venus and to Leda, would be readily understandable both because of the classical education of his readers and also because of the continued use of these myths and symbols in Western literary tradition. What he could not know was that this common body of knowledge was not to endure long in the twentieth century.[47] Yet, perhaps as much as in the actual myth-potential of the Greek gods and goddesses, Darío was interested in their sculptural and pictorial representation. Sculpture and painting have an advantage over words in that they are not as subject to the laws of time as the word with its shifting values. Darío's poems are full of marble statues and sculptures, as if these alone will help his verse endure. At other times, he pours jewels and precious stones into his verse, or he tries to impart a heraldic quality to his poems. And sometimes he was directly inspired by a particular painter. One of his poems, 'El reino interior' (The Kingdom Within), was inspired by a painting by Dante Gabriel Rossetti which depicted the seven virtues and the seven deadly sins.[48]

Julián del Casal, in an attempt to find images of beauty 'cold as virgins' and 'whiter than swans', turned to the paintings of Gustave Moreau – one of the most popular artists among the aesthetes of the late nineteenth century. In his poems, 'Prometeo' and 'Salome', Casal attempted to put into words the 'frozen moment' which Moreau had expressed in his painting. So Prometheus lies on his rock 'marmoreal, indifferent and solitary'; Salome dances before the Tetrarch, attired in brocade, glittering with jewels, her hand forever raised and grasping the occult symbol of the white lotus with its golden pistils.[49]

SENSUALITY AS A FORM OF PROTEST

The figure of Salome was particularly significant at this period, symbolizing as she did a sexuality charged with ambiguous implications. As Mario Praz has pointed out, Salome was both 'sexless and lascivious', an androgyne type who, he believed, indicated 'a turbid confusion of function and ideal'. The triumph of sensuality in the poetry of the period was another assertion of what the poets regarded as 'true' values against the false restrictions of society and convention. But it also brought the Modernists up against society's traditional moral code. Sometimes the conflict found expression in a strange violence, as in the first line of one of Casal's poems,

> Like a torn stomach, the twilight bleeds . . .

In Darío, the expression of sensuality gave rise to a dramatic conflict which ran through his life and poetry. A man of ardent temperament, his life was a stormy series of marital adventures and passionate affairs, interspersed with guilt-ridden remorse when he longed for the tranquil harbour of religion. Towards the end of his life, when he was very ill, he drew nearer to the church. Even so, the old sensuality would break out again and again. In his poetry, the conflict between the sensuality of his nature and his religious belief was so strong as to wreck some of his poems. Indeed the Nicaraguan poet's tragic life and his verse symbolize the generational conflict between tradition and a new set of values. Catholicism, with its doctrine of original sin and evil, was itself in conflict with the optimistic belief in progress and perfectibility. Darío's early poems showed a great preoccupation with the idea of progress and with Hugo's optimistic religious beliefs which united the idea of progress and perfectibility with an acknowledgement of evil. But Hugo's evil was redeemable. In the 'Fin de Satan', he had forecast the reconciliation of Satan and God. Many of Darío's poems seem like a dialogue with the French poet, whose religious beliefs he would like to have shared but which could not altogether convince him. So in 'Zoilo', written in 1886, he exclaims, 'Great Hugo, Evil exists!' Such poems can be divided into two categories. In some, sensual love is guiltless, a source of joy, part of the rhythm of nature. In others, there is a consciousness of guilt and a desire to return to the surety of religious belief.[50]

In Darío's collection *Azul*, sensuality is uppermost. Four poems, set in the four seasons, deal with different aspects of love. In the first, 'Primaveral' (Springtime), love is associated with the rhythm of nature, with a guiltless pagan world where naked nymphs bathe in 'serene' water and the air is 'crystalline'. Here, sensuality is associated with serenity and purity. Darío presents us with a world that antedates original sin. Although sin does enter *Azul*, it is in the form of cruelty, not of sexual love. In one poem, a tiger – a symbol of the beauty, strength and fertility of nature – is wantonly killed by a huntsman. In another, a dove who feels herself part of the harmony of nature is killed by a hawk. In his next volume of poems, *Prosas profanas*, Darío resolves the conflict between sensuality and guilt by sublimating them into myth. He evokes the paintings of Watteau, the fairy-tale world of princesses waiting for lovers, and the carnival gaiety of Pierrot and Columbine. In this way he attempts to pass off sensuality as something beautiful, gay or nostalgic – but not sinful. His most ambitious attempt at reconciling his conflicts through myth is in the poem 'El coloquio de los centauros', in which the centaurs symbolize the mingling of animal, human and divine. His centaurs meditate on the conflicting aspects of life, of love and of death. The assumption behind the poem is that the contradictory elements of existence, irreconcilable in life, can be resolved through art, which restores the wholeness and integrity that is the truth of creation.[51]

The task of the poet is, therefore, not only to keep people constantly aware of 'true' values, but also to remind them of the unity and wholeness that have been refracted through temporality and extension. In Darío, this wholeness is most often suggested through complex myth figures or symbols such as the centaur or the swan. In his 'Leda', the swan, with its classical associations as an incarnation of Jupiter, is identified with the divine. In the form of a swan, Jupiter ravished Leda, who gave birth to Helen of Troy; so the swan comes to stand for that union of animal and divine which gives birth to beauty and poetry. In artistic creation, all ugliness and all evil are sublimated; hence, the rape of Leda by the swan, the supreme creative act, comes to have the significance of the annunciation.

> ¡Antes de todo, gloria a tí, Leda!
> Tu dulce vientre cubrió de seda
> el Dios. ¡Miel y oro sobre la brisa!
> Sonaban alternativamente
> flauta y cristales, Pan y la fuente.
> ¡Tierra era canto; Cielo, sonrisa!

> Glory above all to thee, O Leda!
> Thy sweet womb was covered with silk
> by the God. Honey and gold on the breeze!
> And now the sound of flute, now that
> of crystal water. Pan and the fountain.
> Earth was song, the sky a smile!

The musical accompaniment of flute and water, both symbols of time, underlines the beauty and harmony of the act. How different from Yeats's poem on Leda, where violence is uppermost.

> A sudden blow: the great wings beating still
> Above the staggering girl; her thighs caressed
> By the dark webs, her nape caught in his bill,
> He holds her helpless breast upon his breast.

> How can those terrified vague fingers push
> The feathered glory from her loosening thighs?

Yeats's poem looks forward to an era of cataclysmic destruction.

> . . . the broken wall, the burning roof and tower
> And Agamemnon dead.

Contrast this 'terrible knowledge' with Darío's poem, which ends on a note of gentle melancholy. Jupiter here cannot but feel the sadness of the flesh for, in the act of rape, he had partaken of temporality. He had made love 'by the fountain in the trees'

> with shining neck outstretched
> between Leda's white thighs.

The difference between the two poems is instructive. Darío's is all harmony; Yeats glimpses the abyss. The one moves in a closed, complete world; the other on to future destruction.[52]

Darío would have liked to live forever in his 'ideal wood' where 'the body burns and lives and Psyche flies': a wood with a place both for satyr and nightingale. Yet as he grew older, his wood was increasingly darkened by guilt. His eyes began to turn towards Bethlehem, and many poems in *Cantos de vida y esperanza* and *El canto errante* show nostalgia for the simple religious beliefs of his childhood.[53]

Darío's conflict – which ended in death – was the most dramatic of his time; but it was a conflict common enough among the poets of a generation that was making sorties into a no-man's-land without religion. Most of Darío's contemporaries tended to make a choice rather than remain torn by the conflict as he had been. Delmira Agustini, the Uruguayan woman poet, boldly dedicated her verse to Eros. The Mexicans Amado Nervo and Enrique González Martínez (1871–1952), on the other hand, turned increasingly to recording their own inner religious and philosophical experiences. But perhaps the only poet, apart from Darío and Asunción Silva, really to find the 'objective correlative' for his inner preoccupations was the Bolivian Ricardo Jaimes Freyre. In the snow-bound world of Norse mythology, Jaimes Freyre found the language of symbol and myth to fit his own spiritual mists and solitudes. His 'El canto del Mal' (Song of Evil) strikingly foreshadows his twentieth-century interpretation of evil as separation.

> Canta Lok en la obscura región desolada
> y hay vapores de sangre en el canto de Lok.
> El Pastor apacienta su enorme rebaño de hielo,
> que obedece – gigantes que tiemblan – la voz del Pastor.
> Canta Lok a los vientos helados que pasan,
> y hay vapores de sangre en el canto de Lok.

Densa bruma se cierne. Las olas se rompen
en las rocas abruptas, con sordo fragor.
En su dorso sombrío se mece la barca salvaje
del guerrero de rojos cabellos huraño y feroz.
Canta Lok a las olas rugientes que pasan,
y hay vapores de sangre en el canto de Lok.

Cuando el himno de hierro se eleva al espacio
y a sus ecos responde siniestro clamor,
y en el foso, sagrado y profundo, la víctima busca,
con sus rígidos brazos tendidos, la sombra del Dios.
Canta Lok en la pálida Muerte que pasa,
y hay vapores de sangre en el canto de Lok.[54]

Lok sings in the dark and desolate region
and clouds of blood are in the song of Lok.
The Shepherd grazes his great flocks of ice
which, like trembling giants, obey the Shepherd's voice.
Lok sings in the icy winds that blow,
and clouds of blood are in the song of Lok.

Dense mists arise. The waves are breaking
on the steep cliffs with deafening roar.
On their dark peaks, wild and fierce,
the red-headed warrior rocks in his boat.
Lok sings to the roaring waves that pass,
and clouds of blood are in the song of Lok.

A hymn of iron soars into the air
and there echoes in answer a sinister roar,
and in the holy depths of the pit, the victim seeks
the shadow of God, his rigid arms upstretched.
Lok sings in the pale shade of Death as he passes,
and clouds of blood are in the song of Lok.

In this icy, snow-bound world, God hardly exists. The victim's
arms are upstretched in vain. Lok, or evil, triumphs in a cold and
sinister world in which only the sound of storms and the
'hymn of iron' are heard. Although of the same generation,
Jaimes Freyre's poem is a century removed from the 'Nocturno' of Asunción Silva. The latter is still living in the Romantic era: Jaimes Freyre has discerned the lonely world of modern
man.

THE MODERNIST REVOLT

Can one speak of Modernism as a revolt? At first sight, the movement appears more of a flight from reality; and certainly the Modernist poets appeared to expect little from their own societies, tending to seek recognition from abroad. Nevertheless, despite the seemingly negative characteristics of the movement, the Modernists achieved certain positive results. First of all, by their very existence, they justified the pursuit of art. For the first time the artist began to exist as a separate and distinct member of Spanish-American society. Secondly, they asserted values which were in opposition to the values of the societies in which they lived. They explored taboo areas of feeling, and brought to the forefront that dialogue between sensuality and religious belief which corresponds to a polarity in human experience between the affirmation of individuality and the need to transcend personal limitation. But, above all, it was by asserting a need to dedicate themselves to non-personal ends that they defied their more conventional contemporaries. The movement helped to give voice to the dissatisfaction of a whole class of intellectuals with the backwardness of their culture. Against the prevailing crudity and vulgarity of their environment, they asserted the value of a humanistic and cultured tradition. If their influence did not spread throughout the whole of society, on the cultured elite it was decisive.

This is not to deny the negative aspects of the movement. Fear of change was deep-rooted among the Modernists; hence the reassurance they found in the realm of eternal values. A return to Platonism, with its emphasis on permanence and absolutes in a world of appearance and fragmentation, often occurs in periods of rapid change. Like many poets before them, the Modernists considered beauty to be one of the permanent values. They did not realize that their standards of beauty were as relative as their culture. That is why, in many respects, they seem to be not so much rebels as men at the end of a tradition that was already doomed. That is also why, into the serene and closed world of their paganism, there break whirlwinds of doubt and anguish. The change they feared was already upon them, and the eternal values on which they rested their aesthetic creed were already undermined.

Modernism was a Spanish-American phenomenon. Certainly, there were poets in Brazil – notably the Parnassian Raimundo Correia (1869–1911), and the Symbolist João Cruz e Sousa (1861–98) – who shared many of the attitudes of the Spanish-Americans towards poetry and beauty. The poetry of Cruz e Sousa, in particular, was very close to that of Jaimes Freyre and he was praised by both Jaimes Freyre and Darío. The Modernist's hatred of materialism was shared by the poet Joaquim de Sousa Andrade – Sousândrade – (see chapter 2, p. 61), and there is some similarity between the conception of art of the great novelist Machado de Assis, who saw it as a way of rising above the flux and agitation of everyday life (see chapter 2, pp. 69–70), and that of the Modernists. Nevertheless, for various reasons, the 1890s was a period in which Brazilian intellectuals turned increasingly to the national scene rather than to Europe. The abolition of slavery in 1888, the proclamation of the republic in 1889, heralded a new epoch of national life which was reflected in an increased preoccupation with a truly national culture. This ferment was not, however, reflected in poetry; indeed, there were many complaints in the nineties at the poverty of Brazilian literature, and there were already voices raised against the importation of literature from abroad which, it was said, was 'alien to our nature'. As Raimundo Correia declared in 1890:

We must set up an artistic and literary nationalism; we must have less contempt for what is national, native and our own. Poets and writers must cooperate in the great task of reconstruction.[55]

2

The Select Minority:
Arielism and Criollismo, 1900–1918

The year 1898 was a dramatic one for Latin America. Cuba and
Puerto Rico, the last remaining Spanish colonies in the New
World, gained their independence, as did Spain's Asian colony
of the Philippines. Far more significant than the defeat of Spain
was the rise of a new world power, and one with an increasingly
marked interest in Latin America. Having consolidated its own
territory, the United States now sought a sphere of influence
south of its own borders. In 1895, the then American Secretary
of State, Richard Olney, had declared that the United States was
'practically sovereign on this continent', and that 'its fiat is law
upon the subjects to which it confines its interposition.'[1]

'The subjects to which it confines its interposition' proved to
be numerous. In consequence of the Spanish-American War,
Puerto Rico and the Philippines were annexed and Cuba was
occupied. Although the Cuban occupation ended in 1904, United
States influence continued to be exerted over the island by virtue
of the Platt Amendment, which sanctioned intervention in
Cuba's internal affairs. During the early years of the twentieth
century, United States interests established a commercial hold
over the Central American 'banana republics'. In 1903, using
the excuse of a minor uprising in Panama City (then part of
Colombia), the North Americans helped to create the independent republic of Panama, which allowed them to secure a favourable treaty for the canal across the isthmus of Panama. The 'safe-
guarding of North American interests' justified the occupation of
Nicaragua in 1912. The Latin-American republics were in no
position to compete either politically or commercially with the
United States. They were divided among themselves, absorbed
in border rivalries. Wealth was in the hands of the few. And
though there were strong dictatorships – such as those of Porfirio
Díaz in Mexico and Estrada Cabrera in Guatemala – these did

not stand up against foreign influence but ceded huge concessions to monopoly interests and so compromised the future of their countries. Chile, almost alone among Latin-American countries, had made important steps on the road to democracy, but even Chilean society was marked by social injustice and great poverty among the lower classes. Politically, socially and economically, Latin America was weak.

This contrast between the weak and divided republics and the powerful United States was undoubtedly one of the factors which led Latin-American intellectuals to look at their own society and its own culture in a new and critical light. Hitherto many intellectuals had been concerned to see the flowering of a great national culture; after 1898, more and more intellectuals began to stress the common racial and cultural bonds of Latin America and the great difference between the Mediterranean and Latin tradition in which it had its roots and the Anglo-Saxon tradition from which the culture of the United States stemmed. The stress on Latin America as an identity, rather than on narrow nationalism, is one of the main features of intellectual life after 1900, finding expression is such movements as 'New Worldism' and 'Literary Americanism'.*2 This did not prevent a continuing interest in the development of a national culture. In the novel, the short story and poetry, writers increasingly depicted the landscape and people of their native country, especially those of the rural areas where manners were most different from those of Europe. This movement is generally known as 'Criollismo'.† Many factors contributed to this increased interest in the national scene, not least the appearance of newspapers and periodicals, such as *Caras y caretas* (Argentina, founded 1898), *El cojo ilustrado* (Venezuela, 1892–1915), *Pluma y lápiz* (Chile, 1900–1904), in which short stories with a native setting could appear. A further factor is the appearance on the literary scene of writers,

*'Mundonovismo' was a term coined by the Chilean critic, Francisco Contreras; 'Americanismo literario' was used by F. García Godoy in a collection of essays published in 1917.

†'Criollo' (anglicized in this book as 'Creole', but not to be confused with the 'Creoles' of other areas) is an American of Spanish descent. 'Criollismo' is a broad term, referring to a literature on Spanish-American themes and especially on life in the rural areas.

like Mariano Latorre (Chile, 1886–1955), Baldomero Lillo (Chile, 1867–1923), Roberto J. Payró (Argentina, 1867–1928) and José Rafael Pocaterra (Venezuela, 1889–1955), who had not been educated in Europe or in a very Europeanized environment. These writers were concerned with incorporating into Spanish-American literature those areas of the countryside and the life of its people which had hitherto been neglected.

But, on turning for material to their own hemisphere, writers soon found themselves in difficulties. In the first place, very little was known about their area; primary works on the history and geography of Latin America scarcely existed. Secondly, if any part of Latin America could be regarded as having an original culture, it was the rural areas with their rich oral traditions, their music, dances and dialects; a true national culture could not ignore the rural areas, the indigenous population and the American landscape. Yet it was precisely these areas which were most unfamiliar to the intellectual. The writer had somehow to encompass this reality, a task which proved rather more difficult than would first seem possible. Not only was the Latin-American landscape something very different from the European garden; there was also the difficult problem of the inhabitants – rude, primitive and, for the most part, illiterate peoples who were often cruelly exploited. The intellectual who explored the countryside, far from finding himself in a rural Arcadia, found himself at the centre of the knottiest national problem. There was often a real dilemma between the demands of a literature dominated by the example of Zola and Gorky, and the intellectual's own upbringing, which tended to subdue his sympathies for farm labourers or serfs. Most writers and artists still belonged to the upper or middle classes: most were White, and many belonged to landowning families, accustomed to regarding peasants as their inferiors. The Venezuelan writer and politician, Rufino Blanco Fombona (1874–1944), expresses what must have been a common opinion among his contemporaries of the intelligentsia:

I am leading a new life, a bucolic Arcadian life. But I am getting tired of it. The slowness and rusticity of the peasants exasperate me. They are always wrong and it is impossible that they should ever be rescued from their sad condition of inferior beings except through a persistent educational programme. . . . I cannot talk to any of them for more than five minutes at a time. I can find nothing to say to them. They give me the impression of speaking another language than mine and I feel that I cannot talk to them, not because I have nothing to say, but because I do not know their language.[3]

Communication was only one difficulty. Far more serious, perhaps, were the racial differences that divided the elite from the Mestizo, Mulatto, Negro, or Indian country-dwellers.* In Uruguay, Argentina and Chile, it is true, the Indian had almost disappeared, but there were gauchos of Mestizo descent. None of the Latin-American countries could regard itself as wholly White, and in most of them the Whites were a minority, sometimes a very tiny minority. Hence, no White elite could possibly regard itself as representative of the nation or the subcontinent. The racial question was difficult to evade. Yet it was precisely the problem of race that revealed the generation's greatest failings: the tendency of its members to feel themselves as belonging to a superior caste, and their unwillingness to surrender this superiority. Though the backwardness of the non-White and mixed races was clearly a corollary of economic slavery, few writers of the period appeared to envisage the ending of economic serfdom, nor did they understand that major changes in the social structure might be necessary if other members of the population were to progress. Instead, they put their faith in solutions more flattering to their self-esteem, such as immigration from Europe (which would alter the racial composition of Latin America) or education, in which they would be mentors.

THE RACIAL OBSTACLE

Attitudes to race in Latin America at this time were greatly influenced by determinism in philosophy and by European racial theories. The geographical determinism of Buckle and Taine stressed the influence of physical environment on the formation of national character; the racial theories of de Gobineau and

*Mestizo: half-caste of Spanish or Portuguese and Indian; Mulatto: offspring of European and Negro.

Demolins attributed superiority, respectively, to the Teutonic and Anglo-Saxon races.[4] When Latin Americans of this period turned to the examination of their countries, they tended to concentrate on the defects, on the backwardness and lack of culture. Geographical determinism and 'racially inferior' stock were usually put forward to explain these defects.

In Spanish America, the first social study of this time was by an Argentinian, Carlos Octavio Bunge (1875–1918), whose *Nuestra América* was published in 1903. Bunge had nothing good to say about any of the racial elements in Spanish-American society. The Spaniard was 'arrogant', indolent, lacked a practical spirit, was 'verbose and uniform'. Negroes had a slave mentality and were soft. Indians were characterized by their resignation, their passivity and their vindictiveness. Equally gloomy were Alcides Arguedas (1879–1946) when discussing Indian, Mestizo and White character in his study of Bolivia, *Pueblo enfermo* (The Sick Nation, 1909),[5] and Francisco García Calderón (1883–1953) in his study of Peru, *Le Pérou contemporain*.[6]

In Brazil, which was entering a new period of national life with the ending of slavery and the proclamation of the republic, it was natural that consideration of racial questions should be in the minds of writers and intellectuals. Some saw Brazil as the potential rival of the United States in America; at the same time, it was obvious that the South American state had not the sense of identity and mission which the northern power had. José Veríssimo (1857–1916), the prominent literary critic, was one of many who raised the question of Brazil's identity in the 1890s and he perceived that, in considering Brazil's role in the future, he must also face the problem of the racial composition of the country. He seems to have believed that the Mulatto woman was responsible for a certain softness of character, and he came to the conclusion that large-scale immigration from Europe would help to invigorate the country.[7] Many of the doubts felt by Brazilians concerning race were expressed in two works which appeared in 1902. The first was *Os Sertões* by Euclydes da Cunha (1866–1909), a sociological study of the drought-ridden, rocky, cattle country or *sertão*; the second was a novel, *Canãa* by José Pereira de Graça Aranha (1868–1931). In both of these works, the authors' humanitarian and liberal outlook is distorted by their acceptance of contemporary deterministic racial theories.

Os Sertões (translated into English as *Revolt in the Backlands*) was written as the result of a government military campaign in north-eastern Brazil against a group of separatist religious fanatics under their leader, Antonio 'The Counsellor', a campaign in which da Cunha took part as official reporter. The attack ran into unexpected difficulties because 'The Counsellor' and his followers knew the terrain much better than their attackers, and were incredibly tenacious in their resistance to the government forces. Their heroic courage aroused not only da Cunha's sympathy and admiration but also his curiosity. He found an explanation for their courage and their ferocious desire for independence in the constant struggle they waged against the natural environment. Yet, how could this be reconciled with the fact that the *sertanejos*, or inhabitants of the *sertão*, were racially mixed descendants of Portuguese and Indian, and therefore presumably degenerate? Da Cunha could only conclude that the struggle with the environment had offset their racial defects. He assumed the superiority of the European way of life and the desirability of bringing the *sertanejos* into an up-to-date nation pledged to 'progress'. His policy for integrating the dissidents into the new Brazil consisted of a vigorous educational policy: education being, along with immigration, one of the two great 'solutions' favoured by the intellectuals of the period.[8]

Graça Aranha's *Canãa* is even more ambivalent in its attitude to race. The novel tells the story of two German immigrants to Brazil, Lenz and Milkau, who go to live in a pioneer community which is opening up the interior. Lenz and Milkau represent two different concepts of the immigrant. Lenz believes firmly in European superiority and thinks that Brazil's future lies in being a White-dominated nation. Milkau does not doubt Europe's present superiority, but believes that European civilization is in decline and that perhaps new civilizations are destined to replace it:

Africa's time will come. Races become civilized through fusion; it is in the meeting between the advanced races and the virgin savage races that is to be found . . . the miracle of civilization's renewal.[9]

Graça Aranha's ambivalence is, however, not about the future but about the present. His picture of both Brazilians and the run-of-the-mill German immigrant is disheartening, for the Brazilians in the novel are venal and lascivious, and the Germans uncharitable and harsh. It is obvious that his real faith is in an 'aristocracy' of the intellect, consisting of men like Milkau who transcend the pettiness of their contemporaries. His views are thus very much in harmony with those of his Spanish-American contemporaries.

In the Andean republics and in Mexico, the Indian was regarded by many intellectuals as a serious obstacle to progress. In Peru this was perhaps surprising, for one of the outstanding figures of the period, Manuel González Prada (1848–1918), had again and again warned his contemporaries that the concept of Peruvian nationality must be extended beyond the White majority to include the Indian masses. 'Our type of government is nothing but a great lie because a state in which two or three million individuals live outside the law is not worthy of the name of a democratic republic.'[10] González Prada's ideas inspired the first Peruvian novel to deal sympathetically with the problems of present-day Indians: *Aves sin nido* (Birds Without a Nest, 1889) by Clorinda Matto de Turner (1854–1909). However, despite this example, there were those who hankered for an immigration policy to make Peru into a more European-type nation. For instance, Francisco García Calderón believed that the Indians could be brought into national life only 'by wise tutelage'. Their traditional patterns of life must be broken down by bringing in European immigrants, by teaching the Indians Spanish and by the education of Indian cadres.[11] In Bolivia, Alcides Arguedas – a man who felt great sympathy for the Indians and who rejected the easy solution of immigration – was profoundly conscious of the sadness and sordidness of the Indian's life; he put his trust in education.[12]

The unhappy effects of applying Darwinist theories to racial questions were illustrated in Mexico where, during this period, there was considerable discussion on the place of the Indian and the Mestizo in national life. The dictatorship of Porfirio Díaz favoured the White Mexican and the foreigner; yet Mexico's racial composition was such that the presence of the Indian could scarcely be ignored. The more level-headed intellectuals – like Justo Sierra, who had considerable influence on intellectual life – generally trusted to education to bring the Indian into the nation. Sierra roundly asserted his belief in the Mestizo as a dynamic factor in Mexican history and also in the educability of the Indian. But his views were not shared by all contemporary thinkers. Indeed, a modern critic has noted that 'fear of the Indian . . . was rather widespread during the early years of the Díaz regime', and he refers to newspaper articles which expressed apprehension that the Indian was becoming too militant and that his militancy might culminate in race war.*[13] One of the most curious analyses of the racial problem put forward in Mexico at this time was that of Francisco Bulnes (1847–1924) in his *El porvenir de las naciones latino-americanas* (The Future of the Latin-American Nations, 1899) which suggested the theory that Indians, Africans and Asians were condemned by environment to inferiority because of their poor diets of rice or maize. Though Bulnes suggests a policy of White immigration into the tropics to hasten the amalgamation of races, he can see no way out of the difficulty arising from the fact that tropical diet and environment produce inferior races.[14] Thus, even in Mexico where Mestizo and Indian had played an active part in national life, these early twentieth-century thinkers were dominated by deterministic and Darwinistic thinking on racial matters.

In Venezuela, a country with a racially mixed population, some members of the elite favoured immigration in order to make the racial composition more European,[15] and even in Argentina and Uruguay – countries where race was not so important a factor – the laziness and inferiority of the racially mixed gaucho was taken for granted. The most vigorous intellectuals in Argentina –

---

*This fear may have been provoked in part by uprisings such as the one described by Heriberto Frías in his novel *Tomóchic*, which was written under circumstances rather similar to those of *Os Sertões*. The author helped to crush an uprising of Indians who were also in revolt against the government through the influence of a religous mystic. Like da Cunha, Frías, whose novel is based on his experience as an officer in the Mexican army, came to feel sympathy and admiration for the people he had been sent to fight.

men like Carlos Octavio Bunge and José Ingenieros (1877–1925) – favoured the European immigrants, who formed an increasing section of the population, against the Indo-Hispanic stock, whom they regarded as lazy. Ingenieros, whose father was born in Italy, in one essay hailed 'the advent of a White Argentine race that will soon allow us to erase the stigma of inferiority with which the Europeans have always branded the South Americans'.[16] The lazy, degenerate Creole is a stock figure in the short stories of the Uruguayan writer Javier de Viana (1868–1926), and the clash between the unenterprising, lazy Creoles and the hard-working, money-grabbing Italians dominates the action of *La gringa* (1904),* a play by his compatriot, Florencio Sánchez (1875–1910).

Few essayists or novelists came anywhere near the intuitive sympathy with the Indian shown by two poets of the Modernist generation, José Santos Chocano of Peru and Rubén Darío of Nicaragua. Admittedly, their sympathetic regard for the Indian was for the aristocratic Indian of Inca times and was associated with the cult of the exotic. Yet it would be a grave mistake to brush aside the Indian poems of Darío and Santos Chocano as representing mere exoticism. Certainly, we find Darío writing in the introduction to *Prosas profanas*: 'If there is any poetry in our America, it is in the old things; in Palenque and Utatlán and in the legendary Indian and the sensual, refined Inca and in the great Moctezuma of the golden throne.'[17] But his poem 'Tutecozimi', written as early as 1890, is an evocation of pre-Columban Mexico of great sensitivity. Its message is the triumph of a chief who sings of 'peace and work' over the cruel warrior chief, and it reveals a high appreciation of the beauty of Indian legend. Darío was one of the first to appreciate the aesthetic possibilities of Indian legend and of folklore. This was one way of coming to a deeper understanding of the Indian.[18] Similarly with the poetry of Santos Chocano: his loud proclamations of pride in his mixed blood and his Inca past was a step in the right direction. To recognize the glories of the Inca was an indirect way of rehabilitating the contemporary Indian, and certainly, in

* *Gringa* is the term used in the Plate region to designate an immigrant Italian woman.

Chocano's case, there are poems which show that he was by no means indifferent to the modern Indian.

> Indio que labras con fatiga
> tierras que de otros dueños son:
> ¿ignoras tú que deben tuyas
> ser, por tu sangre y tu sudor?[19]

> Indian who sweats and labours
> on lands that others own:
> Do you know that they should be yours
> by right of your blood and sweat?

One of his poems, 'Ahí no más' (Just There), praises the race which 'is strong in its sadness', which always finds what it wants 'just there', and whose wise irony about distances communicates a 'flavour of eternity'. Hence Chocano's 'escape' into the Inca past did in fact lead him to see virtues in Indian attitudes which many of his contemporaries, firmly convinced of European superiority, did not perceive.[20]

ARIELISM AND THE LATIN RACE

As early as 1877, there appeared an attack on North American materialism, inserted in the middle of a long Romantic poem by the Brazilian poet Joaquim de Sousa Andrade, or Sousândrade, as he liked to be called (1833–1902). This strange poem, *O Guesa Errante*, tells of the wanderings of a modern bard who at one stage of his journey visits New York. In Canto X, 'O Inferno de Wall Street', written in a strange mixture of English and Portuguese, the poet witnesses a *Walpurgisnacht* of stockbrokers, politicians and corrupt businessmen. The combination of Bible and dollar, puritanism and materialism, is satirized, and the canto ends in a verse in which Stock Exchange 'bears' and Mammon, Pegasus and Parnassus, are chanted in an almost incoherent hymn:

> Bear, bear, its ber-beri, Bear . . . Bear.
> Mammumma, mammumma, Mammon
> Bear, bear, ber' . . . Pegasus
>   Parnassus
> Mammumma, mammumma, Mammon.[21]

Indeed, it was in Brazil that fear of the Northern American power seems to have been first felt.* The literary critic, José Veríssimo, for instance, published in 1890 a treatise on national education, in which he attacked the materialism of the United States. The aim of the treatise was the reform of Brazilian education on more practical and nationalistic lines in order to give Brazilians some sense of national identity. In it, Veríssimo stated that, while he believed Brazil could equal the United States in material wealth and power, his native land should be superior in its conception of a national destiny. 'I admire but do not esteem it' was his judgement on the United States which, he said, had a mediocre culture and too utilitarian an approach to science.[22]

These words were echoed almost literally in a work that was to wield a vast influence over the whole of Latin America: the essay *Ariel* by the Uruguayan thinker, José Enrique Rodó (1871–1917).[23] Conceived in 1898 and published in 1900 – that is, in the immediate aftermath of the Spanish-American War – *Ariel*'s enormous popularity arose from the fact that it expressed views which Latin Americans wanted to hear. Deriving the symbolism from Shakespeare's *Tempest*, Rodó represents Ariel as the 'noble and winged part of the spirit', with Caliban typifying sensuality and grossness. This symbolism had already been used by Ernest Renan in his 'drame philosophique', *Caliban*, in which the aristocratic culture represented by Prospero is overthrown when Caliban (the masses) comes to power. The work expressed the French Positivist thinker's fear that, with the coming of democracy, 'Ariel', or the spirit, would disappear.[24] Rodó, however, did not accept Renan's conclusions about democracy. He believed that, provided there was equal opportunity for education, a natural aristocracy of the best – i.e., men and women prepared to follow a disinterested ideal – would emerge to lead society. A really great civilization could arise in a society only when its members pursued some non-personal goal. The Greek ideal of beauty and the Christian ideal of charity were two such ideals for a worthy modern society to combine. Such a society, based on a democratic system enabling 'the best' to rise to the top as leaders, would inevitably produce a superior civilization. On the other

*And also in Cuba through the writing of Martí.

hand, a power whose only concerns are material was doomed to mediocrity. Such a power, affirmed Rodó, was the United States, whose 'great prosperity is matched by its equally great failure to satisfy the most modest conception of human destiny'.[25]

But how were Latin Americans to resist North American influence? Mainly by virtue of 'the genius of the race' which clearly differentiated the Latin Americans from their neighbours in the North. For the rest, salvation must depend on the young intellectual who, by cultivating 'the disinterested ideal', would help to raise his society above the level of materialistic North America. Rodó thus gave a cultural solution to difficulties that were economic and political. He did not deny that a working democracy must be based on an adequate standard of living for all and on equality of educational opportunity, but for him these were the prerequisites for something greater. Unless individuals dedicated themselves to the pursuit of non-personal ends, society was bound to be vulgarly materialistic. The idealistic nature of this solution appealed to the Latin-American intellectual, and editions of *Ariel* quickly appeared all over the sub-continent. It was published in the Dominican Republic in 1901, in Cuba in 1905, in Mexico in 1908. *Ariel* was followed by *Los Motivos de Proteo* (Motives of Proteus, 1909): a rather verbose work in which Rodó examined more fully the nature of 'vocation' and of individual ideals as the motivating force in human life.

Ariel's influence had negative and positive aspects. On the negative side, the essay created a comforting myth: the myth that the United States had no culture and that its inhabitants were wholly materialistic in outlook. The view was repeated *ad nauseam*, notably by Manuel Ugarte (Argentina, 1878–1951) in his *El porvenir de la América latina* (The Future of Latin America, 1911) and in other essays, by Carlos Arturo Torres (Colombia, 1867–1911), and by Blanco Fombona. The counterpart of this myth was that of Latin America's superior 'spirituality'. Both these myths were attacked by a Cuban disciple of Rodó's, Jesús Castellanos (1879–1912), who, in 1910, pointed out that, whereas since their emancipation the Cubans seemed wholly preoccupied with material interests, in the United States idealism was triumphing over materialism.[26]

The positive contribution of *Ariel* to the ideology of the post-1898 generation was two-fold. In the first place, by stressing the power of ideals and of ideas in the shaping of societies, Rodó gave an impulse to educational theory and reform. The intellectuals of the new era saw it as their task to educate the masses to their level, and in this way bring about the gradual transformation of the political and social life of Latin America. Secondly – and it is to this that we shall give immediate attention – a 'Latin-American ideal' gave intellectuals a higher sense of purpose than narrow nationalism could ever have done, enabling them to see beyond their frustrating and limited national situations.

For Rodó, the ideal of Latin America provided a supranational ideal that could bring the separate nations together and inspire individuals with a higher sense of purpose than mere national aims.[27] Whereas a single country might have little in the way of cultural tradition, Latin America, taken as a whole, had an impressive tradition. Moreover, though nations were separated by differences, Rodó discovered among them a cultural unity. The concept of a Latin-American identity arising from the cultural unity of the sub-continent was perhaps Rodó's most important contribution to the ideology of his day and was to be taken up by his contemporaries. Blanco Fombona, for instance, found in the literature of the separate republics a 'family resemblance' which demonstrated the cultural unity of Latin America.[28] Manuel Ugarte felt that, though 'we call ourselves Argentinians, Uruguayans and Chileans ... we are above all Spanish-speaking Americans'.[29] Down to the present, this ideal of the cultural unity of Latin America has attracted leading writers and thinkers, including men like José Vasconcelos (1882–1959)* who, as Mexican Minister of Education in the 1920s, was to give practical impulse to the concept by inviting artists from all over Latin America to share in the new Mexican society. Ventures such as the *Revista de América*, founded in Paris in 1909, and the publishing house *América*, founded by Blanco Fombona in Madrid in 1914, were practical offshoots of Arielism.

With the concept of a united 'Latin' America, many writers

*Though many works of reference give Vasconcelos' birth date as 1881, the edition of his *Obras completas* gives 1882.

came to look more kindly on the former 'mother country', Spain, no longer a threat since its defeat in 1898. The Arielist generation was to contribute some outstanding scholars in Hispanic studies, such as the Dominican Pedro Henríquez Ureña (1884–1946) and the Mexican Alfonso Reyes (1889–1959).* Two novels of the period stress the common Hispanic heritage: *El embrujo de Sevilla* (The Magic of Seville, 1922) by Carlos Reyles (Uruguay, 1868–1938), and *La gloria de Don Ramiro* (Don Ramiro's Glory, 1908) by Enrique Larreta (Argentina, 1875–1961), a skilful historical reconstruction of Spanish life in the time of Philip II. In poetry, the ideal of the unity of the Latin race was sung by Darío in many of the poems included in his *Cantos de vida y esperanza*, the first of which was dedicated to Rodó. The best known of these, his 'Salutación del optimista' is a tub-thumping effort in Virgilian hexameter, warning darkly of threats from the North but envisaging the dawn of a glorious 'Latin' era. Less polemical and more nostalgic in tone, the poems of Santos Chocano's *Alma América* (1906) stress the spiritual affinities between America and Spain. 'O mother Spain,' Chocano wrote, 'welcome me to your arms.' Elsewhere he writes nostalgically of the Peru of the viceroys, a gracious Peru that has now disappeared.[30]

THE POWER OF THE IDEA

'The warm America of Spanish origin' and the 'cold America of the North' were irreconcilable, according to Manuel Ugarte.[31] Rodó's picture of a utilitarian North gave rise to a parallel myth: that of a spontaneous and idealistic South. At a philosophical congress held in Heidelberg in 1908, Francisco García Calderón maintained that there was a 'real idealism of race' in Latin America, and cited the many philosophers teaching and working in Latin America whose views reflected some form of idealism.[32] García Calderón's observation was correct. The predominantly

---

*This rapprochement was actively encouraged by certain sectors in Spain, especially intellectuals. The historian, Rafael Altamira, made a tour of Latin America sponsored by Oviedo University, and on his return suggested an extensive programme of cultural exchange. See R. Altamira, *Mi viaje a América* (1911).

The Modern Culture of Latin America

Positivist teaching of many Latin-American universities * had begun to be displaced by other methods and other systems. He was wrong, however, in attributing this to some innate idealism in the Latin-American mind. It was, rather, a natural reaction from a Positivism which had failed to provide the hoped-for panacea to the problems of Latin America and which had, in Mexico at least, become an unimaginative conformism.

Mexico was, indeed, instructive in this respect. There, a group of *científicos* ('scientific thinkers') had provided the ideological backbone of the Díaz regime whose emblem was 'Order and Progress'. But order was equated with oppression, and progress with the well-being of a few at the expense of a poverty-stricken rural population. The first rebellion against this state of affairs was not political, but an intellectual revolt against the stuffy authoritarianism of the Díaz regime. It began with the inauguration of a lecture society in 1907, a society which became the *Ateneo de Juventud* and later the *Ateneo de México* (1909–14). The group included José Vasconcelos, Pedro Henríquez Ureña, Martín Luis Guzmán, Alfonso Reyes, who was later to become a distinguished man of letters, and Antonio Caso, a distinguished thinker. All these men were, in later life, to recognize the importance of the *Ateneo* in changing the intellectual atmosphere of the Díaz regime, and all agreed that this change came about with the abandonment of Positivism, the exploration of other contemporary streams of thought, such as Bergsonism, and the return to metaphysical speculation which Positivism had condemned as fruitless.[33] One of the lectures given in 1910 was on the work of Rodó; indeed, the whole generation of the *Ateneo* were to carry Arielism into practical effect when, after the revolution of 1910, they shared in the task of forging a new type of Mexican culture.

Rodó had been emphatic on the importance of the idea in guiding societies: 'It is enough that the idea should insist on *being* for the propagation to be inevitable and for its triumph to be certain.'[34] But such guiding ideas, it was argued, could come only from an intellectual elite. According to Rómulo Gallegos (Venezuela, 1884–1969), they could not come from below because the inferior could not give rise to the superior.[35] In Carlos

* See Introduction, p. 22–3.

Reyles's view, it was the lack of guiding ideas that had led to the anarchical political situation in Latin America.[36] Francisco García Calderón believed that reforms, if they came, would be set in motion by an elite that would act as an oligarchy until the rest of the nation could think for itself.[37] The notion of a select minority that would guide its country's destinies or, at the very least, create a worthy example, was closely bound up with the function of the moral fitness of the ruling elite. There is no doubt that many of Rodó's disciples believed that intellectuals who had sacrificed personal ambitions for the 'disinterested ideal' would make the best rulers. A real democracy, said Rodó, would allow those with really superior qualities to rise to the top; and those superior qualities must be qualities of virtue, character and spirit.[38] This high moral tone was shared by Manuel Ugarte and Rómulo Gallegos, and is revealed in *Idola fori* by Arturo Torres. C. Vaz Ferreira (1873–1958), the Uruguayan thinker and writer, in his *Moral para intelectuales* (Moral Code for Intellectuals, 1908), took the high-minded view that the intellectual should set the example. He counselled his readers to devote half an hour a day to meditating on matters of no immediate personal relevance, as a sort of spiritual exercise.[39] Not that the elevating effect of education was to be limited to the intellectuals; the education of other sections of the community was also regarded as important. Certainly, some writers set greatest store by the enlightenment of the upper classes; for example, the Peruvian Alejandro O. Deústua (1849–1945) believed that his country would be transformed by the right moral training of the governing elite, whose members must learn to act for the common good rather than out of self-interest.[40] But, on the whole, the generation was also aware that education must be spread over the whole population. José Veríssimo, Manuel Ugarte and Rómulo Gallegos were all agreed in giving a place of special importance to civic training, and in stressing the necessity of teaching the masses about their own country.

The didacticism of the essayists is matched by novelists and short-story writers. Indeed, one of the striking features of the creative writing of the period is its strong moral tone and its concentration on exposing moral weaknesses. Sometimes, however, the concern with 'conformist' moral problems, such as adultery or prostitution, led to the writer's evading larger problems. This was the case with Federico Gamboa (Mexico, 1864–1939) who, at the height of the Díaz regime, wrote novels on problems of behaviour that concerned a very small section of the urban middle class. Blanco Fombona's *El hombre de hierro* (The Man of Iron, 1907) is centred on the selfish ambitions of the arriviste society of Caracas. Even so, the novels of this period did, at times, plumb deeper levels. In *A la costa* (To the Coast, 1904), the Ecuadorian novelist, Luis Martínez (1869–1909), attacks the false values of the Quito middle class whose members want their sons to swell the professions when there are more productive occupations. The Argentinian novelist, Roberto Payró, in his *Divertidas aventuras del nieto de Juan Moreira* (The Amusing Adventures of Juan Moreira's Grandson, 1910), attacks the political bosses who control the rural areas. Descended from the old gaucho stock, the new generation of bosses, though they no longer wear the poncho, still retain the traditional disrespect of their forebears for centralized government and law. But, in discarding the poncho, they have also lost 'the virtues that went with it', according to Payró, 'retaining only a certain personal valour'. The best way of fighting the evil of *caciquismo* (or political bosses), Payró believes, is by making the type known, 'warts and all'.[41]

Such a view is very typical of this generation's concept of literature as an *instrument*, a concept which is associated with their faith in the power of the written word and in education as a social panacea. It is not, however, a view which produced entertaining writing, since the authors were more concerned with depicting types and characteristic abuses (prostitution, for instance*) than in the portrayal of individuals. Only one or two writers withstood the temptation of didacticism and concerned themselves with human beings as they were. It is interesting that two of the best writers of the time were men with no desire to reform the world, men who put their art before any pedagogical or reforming function. These writers were the Colombian short-

---

*A vast number of novels have been written about prostitution: e.g., *Santa* (1903) by Federico Gamboa, *Juana Lucero* (1902) by Augusto d'Halmar (Chile, 1882–1950), *Nacha Regules* (1919) by Manuel Gálvez.

story writer and novelist, Tomás Carrasquilla (1858–1940) and the Brazilian novelist, Machado de Assis (1839–1908).

For Carrasquilla, the novel was a description of 'man in his environment'. He took his material from experience, 'without idealizing the reality of life'. Hence, when political issues and social reality enter his novels, these are included, not because they are evils or abuses in the system, but simply as part of the environment in which the characters develop. One of Carrasquilla's best stories, 'El Padre Casafús', is about a grumpy, bad-tempered priest who refuses to curry favour with the most powerful lady of the parish. Because of the priest's uncompromising character, her hatred for him grows and she spreads with such vigour the rumour that he is a liberal and a heretic that he is suspended by the bishop and brought to the verge of starvation. Political and religious controversies are thus germane to the story, but only in so far as they are also part of the story of the priest.[42]

Machado de Assis's stories are even further from any didacticism. His best novels, *Memórias Póstumas de Brás Cubas* (translated as *Epitaph of a Small Winner*, 1881), *Quincas Borba* (translated as *The Heritage of Quincas Borba*, 1891), *Dom Casmurro* (1899) and *Esaú e Jacob* (*Esau and Jacob*, 1904), reveal a 'bitter and harsh sentiment' which owes much to his Schopenhaueran view of life. He sees man as torn by all the passions, 'agitated as if he were a bell until the passions destroyed him like a rag'.[43] Each of his major novels shows a human life wasted. In *Quincas Borba*, for instance, Rubião, the protagonist, inherits a fortune at the outset of the novel and wastes this and the rest of his life pursuing a married woman whose husband cynically fleeces him, leaving him mad, poor and friendless. In *Esaú e Jacob*, although there is a political theme, politics are held up as a slightly absurd game. The novel is in fact an allegory. The main characters, Pedro and Paulo, represent the warring factions in Brazilian political life. They are twins, born in the year of the Republican Manifesto, who quarrel from the womb and who are rivals for the love of Flora and for the love of their mother, Natividade, a woman – representing Brazil itself – who is married, significantly, to a prosperous banker. All through the novel, the frivolity and senselessness of political partisanship is brought out and the momentous events of contemporary history are treated in a light-hearted way. The passing of the empire is described through the reactions of the confectioner who is afraid he may lose business if he does not change the name of his 'Imperial' pastry shop. Machado de Assis saw a sacrifice of principles as one of the inevit-able consequences of living in society. In many of his short stories, he expounded the view that human beings have two selves, a public self and a private self, and that the public self may flourish at the expense of the private one. In his story *O Espelho* (The Looking Glass, 1882), the reflected image of the narrator is dim until he puts on his lieutenant's dress uniform, when the outlines of his reflection become sharp and clear.[44] Machado de Assis's approach to politics and society was, of course, based on a deep conviction of the unchangeability of man: a view which was not shared by the majority of the intellectuals at this time.

THE WRITER AND TRADITION

The most urgent task of the writer, in the view of Rodó and many of his disciples, was that of creating an original culture, of keeping alive whatever American tradition existed. There was therefore a determined effort to revive the memory of the heroes of the past. As the *Revista de América* stated: 'Remembering past glories, studying the work of the masters, noting and discussing in-fluences, let us confess that the ideas and forms have not arisen suddenly in a land without history.'[45]

Several essays on America's great men were published during the period. One of the first, by Luis Berisso – the friend of Rubén Darío – was *El pensamiento de América* (1898): a collection of thirty-five essays on Spanish-American writers and intellectuals, including many Modernists. Rodó's *El Mirador de Próspero* (Pros-pero's Belvedere, 1913) included essays on prominent Latin-American celebrities, like Bolívar and Montalvo. Blanco Fom-bona's *Letras y letrados de América* (1908) and his *Grandes escritores de América* (1917) were written with a similar didactic intention. Writers did not confine themselves to persuading their own countrymen that they possessed a noble tradition: they also carried on propaganda from the more pleasant surroundings of the Paris boulevards. *Les Démocraties Latines de l'Amérique* (1912) by Francisco García Calderón, and *Les Écrivains contemporains de l'Amérique espagnole* (1920) by Francisco Contreras (Chile, 1877–1933), were both written for a foreign public. García Calderón and Contreras lived for long periods of their life in Paris, but continued to carry on active propaganda on behalf of Latin-American culture.

Besides stressing the common Latin-American tradition, writers also began to publish works designed to stimulate a sense of their nation's history and traditions. The cultural nationalism of the 1920s, indeed, has its roots in the 'Latin-American ideal' formulated in the two previous decades. One of the pioneers was the Argentinian poet, Leopoldo Lugones (1874–1938), who moved from a socialist to a nationalist position. Lugones – along with the literary historian, Ricardo Rojas (1882–1957) – was among the first Argentinian writers to take José Hernández's *Martín Fierro* as a serious literary work. This narrative poem of the 1870s, long popular among the country people, had hitherto been scorned by the cultured section of the population; but Lugones, in *El payador* (The Gaucho Minstrel, 1916), raised *Martín Fierro* to the rank of epic. Not only that: he made it *the* epic of Argentina, giving it a vital national significance.

> To produce an epic poem is for any nation the greatest proof of its vitality, because such a creation expresses the heroic life of its people. This life is the epitome of supreme human achievement and represents the greatest heights that the race can attain: the affirmation of its identity with the rest of the world.[46]

The contribution of the gaucho was just as great, Lugones asserted, in the history of the nation. His historical novel, *La guerra gaucha* (The Gaucho War, 1905), described episodically the heroic part the anonymous country dwellers had played in the wars of independence.

It is to be noted that Lugones's estimation of the gaucho departs from the view – held by such Argentinian thinkers as Ingenieros and Bunge – of the inferiority of the Indo-Hispanic elements. It can, in fact, be argued that Lugones's views represent those of a section of the community that was beginning, for socio-political reasons, to turn to a concept of a traditional Argentinian culture, for this concept to a large degree embodied the reaction of the old landowning elite against the immigrant invasion.*

INTELLECTUALS AND RURAL LATIN AMERICA

The select minority aspired to be the creators of an original Latin-American culture. The fact could hardly escape them, however, that whatever originality Latin America possessed was in the rural areas, among the Mestizo or indigenous masses who had evolved special ways of life. Costume, speech, traditions, oral culture and popular art – all these were free from recent European influence. Critics, from José Veríssimo to Francisco García Calderón, urged writers to concentrate on these differences. They waxed eloquent on the beauties of the American landscape. 'The age-old trees are entwined with uncountable lianas. An insatiable vegetation covers its harsh nakedness. An immense parasitic world ferments upon the damp earth.'[47] Manuel Ugarte, in his *El porvenir de la América Latina*, wrote:

When literature, painting, sculpture and music arise from our national ideas and embrace the spirit of the whole area, uniting contradictory influences and mingling them with the primitive element which the land and atavisms impose, then the masses will welcome with ecstasy the moral synthesis that has finally emerged from them.[48]

And he added that artists should forget models and learn to *see* America. García Calderón was firmly convinced that originality in art was as important as economic independence. To achieve such originality, artists and writers must submit themselves 'to the influence of the land'. Artists and writers did, in fact, turn their eyes eagerly to the rural hinterland to discover the originality Calderón yearned for. Many of these writers were the sons of landowners or were city-educated intellectuals, and they there-

* Adolfo Prieto, in his *Literatura autobiográfica argentina* (1962), stresses this return to the land as a defence-mechanism on the part of certain Argentinians against the threat of the immigrants.

fore had to make a real leap of the imagination in order to identify themselves with the humbler elements of the population. Mariano Latorre, a Chilean writer of French immigrant stock, described how his eyes had suddenly been opened to the 'unpublished' world about him, a world which had as yet been unrecorded. Latorre's literary vocation was awakened by the gap he felt between the world of his experience and his education, which left him in ignorance about the geography and the history of his native land.[49]

In Chile, more than in any other part of Latin America at this period, there was a determined effort on the part of intellectuals and writers to close the gap that divided them from the countryside and its inhabitants. Chile was one of the most politically advanced countries of the sub-continent, and yet it was harassed by great social problems and by a lack of any sense of national identity. Writers felt more than an urge to teach and guide their fellows, the need to identify themselves with the poor and break down the barriers between them. This is strikingly illustrated by the pathetic attempts of two writers, Augusto d'Halmar and Fernando Santiván (b. 1886), to start a Tolstoyan colony and to work on the land, despite their total ignorance of agriculture.[50] Even more striking, however, were the efforts of a schoolteacher, Alejandro Venegas (died 1922), who used to disguise himself and dye his hair blonde before making sorties among the poor. The fact that he needed to disguise himself illustrates the gulf that existed between the middle-class intellectual and the rest of the community.

So I learned of the life of the inhabitants of our countryside; I visited the mines of Lota, Coronel and Curanilahue to observe the life of those who extract coal; I penetrated into the Araucanian region to learn of the situation of our indigenous population; I travelled the provinces of Coquimbo and Atacama to get an idea of legendary miners; finally, in Tarapacá and Antofagasta, I ate at the same table and slept under the same roof as the workers in the nitrate fields in order to be able to write conscientiously of their necessities and miseries.[51]

The kind of spirit that animated Venegas is also reflected in the poetry of Carlos Pezoa Véliz (Chile, 1879–1908) which captures the sadness of the countryside, the loneliness and the anonymity of the inhabitants.[52] Sympathy for the fishermen, for the country people and even for the Indian is expressed in Mariano Latorre's work. Occasionally stories which expressed these humanitarian feelings could rise to considerable heights, as the collections of Baldomero Lillo, *Sub terra* (1904) and *Sub sole* (1907), illustrate. Lillo was spurred to writing by the indignation he felt at the conditions in which the miners had to work. One of his stories, 'La compuerta número 12' (Gate Number 12), is an indictment of child labour in the mines. Yet Lillo does not make the mistake of many of his contemporaries of using the story to preach. He simply presents a situation in all its brutality. The father taking the child down the mine; the child half-afraid, half-fascinated by what he sees. Only when he realizes that he must stay down the mine to work does the child rebel. The father, torn between his fatherly feelings and his need for money, finally ties the child to a rock and goes to work.

The cutting edges of coal shot out, wounding his face, his neck and his bare chest. Threads of blood were mixed with the copious sweat which bathed his body, the body which like a wedge pressed into the open breach, widening it with the fury of the convict who breaks the wall which shuts him in; but without the hope that animates and strengthens the prisoner – that of finding at the end of the day a new life full of sun, air and liberty.[53]

Like Machado de Assis in his story of slavery, *Pai contra mãe* (Father Against Mother, 1906), Lillo brings out the cruel inhumanity of a system in which the economic need drives out all feeling for others and destroys the closest relationships. A deeply felt indignation of this type could produce excellent writing as long as it was expressed through a situation and not in the form of speeches or comments by the author.

Apart from artistic failings, what weakens many stories of country or humble life written during this period is the writer's ambivalence of feeling. This was patently not true of Baldomero Lillo, but in many other writers 'realism' (that is, their portrayal of the humble as they saw them) came into conflict with their humanitarian sympathies. For what the writer saw was often sordid and brutal. Mariano Latorre, for instance, is evidently aroused by man's fierce struggle with nature; yet he often portrays people who are animal-like in their moral indifference.[54] This ambivalence becomes even more marked in certain writers from other parts of Latin America. In Rufino Blanco Fombona's most famous story, 'El catire', (*catire* is a Venezuelan word for a blonde person), a sadistic farm labourer tortures a donkey until it runs away and then he watches indifferently when an alligator kills it as it attempts to swim across the river.[55] Even more interesting is the case of the Uruguayan Javier de Viana, who wrote innumerable stories of gaucho life. Viana was of a landowning family of Spanish descent and, though he regarded his early years on a farm as the most valuable part of his education, he had no illusions about the peasants. He often stresses the indolence of gaucho women, their 'laziness', 'inertia' and 'animal indifference'. In one story, typical of many, he tells of a bandit's daughter with whom two men are in love. When the man she loves begins to avoid her after he finds out that there is a rival, the father decides to simplify matters by removing the rival from the scene. In the dark, he kills the wrong man and, unknowingly, takes the head home to his daughter who, on recognizing it, exclaims in a nonchalant manner: 'But that's the one I liked best.'[56] It is true that this is not Viana at his best and that his stories do indeed faithfully reflect the proletarianization of the Uruguayan labourers and their increasing poverty, owing to developments in the cattle industry. Yet there is also a big difference between his attitude and that of Lillo: in 'La compuerta número 12', it is the system that is condemned, not the miner. In Viana's stories, on the other hand, the characters often fail to arouse our sympathy and their defects appear to be inherent. Javier de Viana's stories, therefore, tend to confirm thinkers like Ingenieros and Bunge in their belief that the mixed stock is inferior. It is the opposite view to that of Lugones, who recognizes the virtues of gaucho life. The two points of view correspond to a conflict in Argentinian and Uruguayan life at this period between the old and the new, between the traditional inhabitants of the land and the 'new' Argentinians from Europe. The conflict was brought to the stage in the works of the Uruguayan playwright, Florencio Sánchez: one of the first modern Latin-American dramatists of any worth. In addition to *La gringa* (1904), already mentioned, he wrote two other major dramas of rural life: *M'hijo el dotor* (My Son, the Doctor, 1903) and *Barranca abajo* (Downhill, 1905). In *M'hijo el dotor*, Sánchez presents the clash between the generations, which is also a clash between modernity and tradition. In *La gringa*, as we have seen, he dramatizes the conflict between the immigrant and the Creole. *Barranca abajo* treats of the decline of a Creole family of the old type.

RURAL ARCADIA

Not all writers portrayed life in the countryside as nasty, brutish and short. There were those who saw that the land was the basis of economic life and that any raising of material standards must come from the country areas. In their view, if country people were backward and ignorant, this was partly the fault of absentee landlords and of a ruling elite that was ignorant of its own country; a wise elite, firmly based on the land, was the best guarantee for the nation's future. Three important novels of the period convey this message: *La parcela* (The Plot of Land, 1898) by José López Portillo y Rojas (Mexico, 1850–1923); *A la costa* by Luis A. Martínez; and *El terruño* (The Native Soil, 1916) by Carlos Reyles.

La parcela centres on a dispute between two rival landowners for a plot of land. Don Miguel is grasping, selfish and does not scruple to overturn law and justice to get what he wants. Don Pedro is the ideal type of landowner: humane towards peasants, with a thorough knowledge of all land questions, an upholder of justice and a believer in hard work on the land as a training for life. Don Pedro's moral superiority triumphs. The paternalistic landowner with the right moral standards, it is to be concluded, is the backbone of the life of the country. A similar type of good landowner appears in *A la costa* (discussed on p. 68 in connexion with false middle-class values). Salvador, the hero of Luis Martínez's story, is a poor law student whose studies are interrupted by civil war and who afterwards scrapes a living as shop assistant and at various other jobs. His friend Luciano Pérez, son of a landowner, abandons his legal studies to work on his father's farm. Life on the land gives Luciano a 'double moral energy' that he has never had before. He begins to feel 'the dignity and energy that only come from money earned in the daily task and without fear of political catastrophe and changes of fortune'. The healthy life of the land is contrasted with Salvador's frustrations in Quito, frustrations which finally drive him, like Luciano, to the land. He gradually wins self-respect and the respect of others as the foreman of a banana plantation in the tropics. *El terruño* likewise depicts a good landowner and illustrates the Uruguayan author's belief that a wise landowning class is the proper basis of a sound state. In an earlier novel, *Beba* (1894), Carlos Reyles had portrayed a landowner who had tried to improve his cattle estates by applying modern stock-breeding methods, but who failed in an environment hostile to new ideas. *El terruño*, written much later, after Reyles had suffered some disillusionments in the political field, contrasts the clever but impractical intellectual, Tocles, with his mother-in-law, Mamagela, a woman of great practical genius who runs her farm and looks after the labourers despite civil war and disturbances. Tocles is forced to admit that Mamagela's practical egotism is far more effective and, in the long run, far more beneficial to national life than his own sorry intellectual efforts.

These novels by Carlos Reyles and Luis Martínez have more than an immediate social message. They imply that the land offers a permanence and security against the fluctuations and change of the rest of society, and that it is the duty of the intellectual to go back to the land. Indeed, rural life was regarded by some writers as the true life for mankind, the only form of life that gives him a sense of identity and worth. Such a view is expressed in *Los gauchos judíos* (The Jewish Gauchos) by Alberto Gerchunoff (1884–1950) which appeared in 1910. This is a series of episodes describing life in a community in Argentina founded by Jews who had been forced to leave pogrom-haunted Russia. The book is prefaced by a quotation: 'The greatest and strongest men of Judea worked the soil; when the chosen people fell into captivity, they dedicated themselves to vile and dangerous employments and thus lost the grace of God.'[57] The rural life, then, was just as likely to be idealized by men like Gerchunoff, who hated 'the vile and dangerous employments' associated with capitalism, as by the representatives of the old landowning class. Roberto Payró, an anarchist by conviction, appears also to have cherished an ideal society based on small holdings.

The rural ideal was often the subject of poetry. Leopoldo Lugones, after his early Socialism, began to turn increasingly to a nationalism which he indentified with the landscape and scenes he had known as a child. His *Odas seculares*, published in 1910 to mark the anniversary of Argentinian independence, are deliberately reminiscent of Virgil's *Georgics*, for they extol 'the cattle and the corn'. He believed that the country-dweller had a sense of purposeful endeavour and the certainty of being a human being which were lacking in the city-dweller.

THE NOVEL OF DESPAIR

None of this generation was happy, none of them attained the tranquillity necessary to undertake a really lasting work. But in this setback to the first true germination of a continental idea, there remains something more than a memory of a sacrifice.[58]

So wrote Manuel Ugarte. The sense of frustration was reflected in many novels of despair. The select minority had turned its eyes from Europe to America, but only to encounter vast problems of race, education, and environment. Even the writers who were most vocal in proclaiming the 'continental ideal' were also eloquent in their criticisms of the American environment. Rodó, for instance, expressed to Unamuno, the great Spanish writer, his longing to be in Europe where it was really possible to live the life of the spirit.[59] The intellectual or the artist broken by his environment, or ruined by faulty education, is one of the constant themes of the novel of the period. It occurs in *Idolos rotos* (Broken Idols, 1901) by Manuel Díaz Rodríguez (Venezuela, 1871–1927), in *Un perdido* (A Failure, 1917–18) by Eduardo Barrios (Chile, 1884–1963), in *El mal metafísico* (The Metaphysical Sickness, 1916) by Manuel Gálvez (Argentina, 1882–1962), in *Triste Fim de Policarpo Quaresma* (The Sad End of Policarpo Quaresma, 1915) by the Brazilian novelist Lima Barreto (1881–1922) and in the first novel of Rómulo Gallegos, *Reinaldo Solar* (1920), which was first published with the title *El último Solar* (The Last of the Solars).

The common characteristic of all these novelists is that they present situations in which the intellectual meets with failure. In Gálvez's *El mal metafísico*, for instance, the hero, Carlos Riga, gives up his studies to devote himself to literature. He dies a failure, without having made his mark on the life of his country, because, as one of his friends remarked, 'he was unable to adapt himself to the stupidity, banality and baseness of modern life.' [60] The eponymous heroes of Rómulo Gallegos's *Reinaldo Solar* and Lima Barreto's *Quaresma* are both eager to realize national as well as personal ambitions, and both reach the end of their lives frustrated in all their plans and endeavours. All these novels are intensely pessimistic. The feeble efforts of the heroes to act on their surroundings are insignificant compared with the magnitude of the task of bringing any measure of order or civilization or culture to their countries. This despair is in part attributable to the frustrated position of the writer and the intellectual of the Arielist generation. They placed their trust in educational reform and in the effectiveness of the printed word, but these tools were puny compared with the magnitude of the social and economic problems that faced them. The optimism of *Ariel* was like whistling in the dark; a confidence-seeking optimism hid, for a time, the real hopelessness which many intellectuals (including Rodó himself, in other moods) felt. A striking illustration of the writer's sense of helplessness is to be found in some of the stories of Baldomero Lillo. Lillo obviously hated the system which allowed miners to be treated inhumanely, but in his stories he could do no more than show them eternally imprisoned – or alternatively depict some cataclysmic destruction which would ruin the mine. [61]

The combination of revolutionary doctrines and deteriorating labour conditions between 1900 and 1920 undoubtedly caused apprehension among the middle class. Sometimes their very humanitarianism, their concern for the underdog, is a mark of their fears of what may happen if the situation does not improve. Alejandro Venegas, for instance, explicitly warns of a catastrophe if the Chilean ruling class do not take more interest in the workers and peasants.[62] But the most striking evidence of this fear of the oppressed is to be found in two novels: *Los de abajo* (The Underdogs, 1916)* by Mariano Azuela (Mexico, 1873–1952), and *Raza de bronce* (Race of Bronze, 1919) by Alcides Arguedas. Azuela's *Los de abajo* tells the story of the rise of a peasant, Demetrio Macías, who, through cold-blooded courage, becomes a self-styled general during the Mexican revolution. Macías represents the blind, destructive force which the revolution has unleashed: a force which cannot be stopped and which is utterly barbaric. A medical student, Luis Cervantes, who joins the revolutionary army is, however, even worse than the peasants, since his superior cunning enables him to profit from the revolution. The revolutionaries have neither idealism nor even sympathy for their fellows; they are simply destructive. The novel thus reflects the author's own fears that culture will be swept aside when the masses triumph. Alcides Arguedas's *Raza de bronce* is written about the Bolivian Indians. Although he deals with a situation in which the underdog is far from threatening the ruling elite, in the description of the sufferings of an Indian community near Lake Titicaca under the tyranny of a landowner and his agents, Arguedas betrays a certain apprehension. He shows the Indians bearing injustice with resignation until, after the mass rape of an Indian girl by white men and *ladinos*,† they finally lose patience and rebel. The landowner's house is set alight and destroyed. The message that comes through is, again, that the ruling elite must develop a more humanitarian attitude or perish.

Even before the outbreak of the Mexican revolution of 1910 and the Russian revolution of 1917, many writers and intellectuals felt that a great social transformation was at hand and that their place was not above the workers but alongside them. As early as 1904, González Prada had warned the intellectuals against the select minority attitude and against their setting them-

---

* Los de abajo was first published as a newspaper serial in El Paso, Texas, in 1915 and was published in book form in 1916.

† *Ladino*: someone who speaks Castilian as opposed to those who speak an Indo-American language. This usually implies a class and racial difference.

selves up as *lazarillos*, or leaders of the blind. Many of them joined Socialist or Anarchist movements – among them Roberto Payró, Florencio Sánchez, Alberto Ghiraldo (Argentina, 1874–1946), José Ingenieros and Manuel Ugarte. Symptomatic of the new current in intellectual circles is the statement of the Brazilian poet, Olavo Bilac (1865–1918). He welcomed the Russian 'Duma Revolution' of 1905, affirming that the triumph of the Russian people was at hand and that at last they had achieved 'the right to be treated like men and not like miserable beasts'. These words show that the poet had descended from Parnassus.[63]

3

Back to the Roots:
1. Cultural Nationalism

The Arielist generation had believed itself to be a select minority fit to guide its fellows towards a European standard of civilization. By 1918, however, belief in the superiority of European cultural and social systems was shattered. The spectacle of the great powers dedicating the resources of science and industry to the task of exterminating one another seemed a mockery to those Latin Americans for whom Europe had been equated with the highest human values. The overbearing influence of the United States had, after 1898, made the Latin-American intellectual examine the deficiencies of his own part of the continent; but now, after 1918, the failure of Europe as an ideal led him to look for Utopia in the American hemisphere. In the 1920s, musicians, writers, painters and sculptors were to 'retrace lost steps' in an effort to find in their land and in their indigenous peoples those qualities which Europe had either lost or all along lacked. Many Europeans themselves believed that their civilization was in decline, and looked outside Europe for a new age. Oswald Spengler, in *The Decline of the West*, declared that Europe was not the highest culture achieved by man, but simply one out of many civilizations which, like others before it – Egyptian, Greek, Roman – was destined to fade away.* At the beginning of the First World War, because of their traditional admiration for France, many Latin-American intellectuals had supported the Allies, but, as the war went on, many began to realize that the significance of the war lay not in the victory of one side or the other but in the new kind of world that would emerge. Hence we

---

* Spengler's celebrated work began to appear in 1918. It was widely discussed throughout Latin America in the 1920s, and references to it are frequent in reviews and articles of the period. Unfortunately, no study has yet been made of the effect of Spenglerian ideas on Latin America. For further discussion of Spengler's influence, see below, pp. 118–19.

find Alberto de Oliveira (1857–1937), a Brazilian writer, looking forward to the 'new ideas' that would emerge in a 'new social period, with a new and perhaps better humanity'.[1] The Argentinian socialist, José Ingenieros, viewed the war as a struggle between the reactionary forces whose destruction would herald a new era of social justice.[2] In 1917, with the Bolshevik revolution in Russia, Ingenieros and many others saw the first signs of this new age.

The post-war period, both in Europe and Latin America, was a period of social ferment. In Peru, Chile and Brazil, there was unrest among the working classes, to whose cause many writers and intellectuals rallied. A university reform movement, which began in Argentina and quickly spread to Chile, Uruguay and Peru, rallied students in an attack on the old teaching systems and on the elite position of the intellectuals. The development of new radical movements coincided with the ending of the old order in many countries. Mexico had undergone a great social revolution. In 1920, the Guatemalan dictator, Estrada Cabrera, fell after twenty-two years in power. In Chile, the government of Alessandri came into power, pledged to a programme of social reform. In Uruguay, the government of Batlle y Ordóñez had adopted an intensive reform policy. In Brazil, there was a cycle of revolutions in 1922, 1924 and 1925 which kept the country in a ferment. Though the risings were all crushed, the definitive revolution seemed at hand. The heroic march of Luis Carlos Prestes and his column across the unknown interior of Brazil between 1925 and 1927 was a dramatic example of how to spread the revolutionary message. This former army officer was not concerned with teaching or leading the forgotten population of Brazil's interior but with getting them to fight in the common cause of social justice. The 1920s, then, were a time of hope in Latin America – hope that was kept alive by the radical détente that had taken place in the sub-continent itself: the Mexican revolution.

MEXICAN CULTURAL NATIONALISM

The effect of the Russian revolution on Latin-American art probably reached its peak in the 1930s. In the 1920s it was the Mexican revolution that provided a new ideal. Unlike Russia's, Mexico's revolution had been inspired by no definite ideology; it was a national revolution which altered the structure of the country by removing many of the old landowning elite. New elements – peasants and workers – had been brought into national life. The programme which emerged from the revolution was a broad one of social reform designed to remove grave injustices and diminish the foreign stranglehold on Mexico's economy. In executing the programme, it was intended to allow Mexico to develop in its own special and original way. Thus, Mexico did not set itself up as a pattern to be followed, but as an example of a new type of nationalism based on an equitable social structure. The immediate result of the revolution was the release of powerful new energies, as Pedro Henríquez Ureña pointed out in a speech to Argentinian students:

This Mexico is at present in one of those active periods of national life, a period of crisis and creation. . . . Mexico is creating a new life, affirming its own character and declaring itself fit to found its own type of civilization.[3]

Mexico's new civilization, Henríquez Ureña said, was to be forged by the twin instruments of culture and nationalism. He declared, however, that 'culture and nationalism are not to be understood . . . in the nineteenth-century sense.' In place of the old elite interpretations of these concepts were totally new concepts: 'Culture is conceived of as social, offered and really given to all and founded on work; learning is not only learning to know but learning to do.'[4] Nationalism was not the old political nationalism but a 'spiritual' nationalism which allowed the originality of the nation to be expressed in art and in ideas. In other words, the impulse behind cultural nationalism was two-fold. First, there was the desire to bring all sections of the community into national life. Secondly, the elite now sought, in folk culture, in the indigenous peoples and the environment, the values they had previously accepted from Europe.

One of the architects of Mexican cultural nationalism was José Vasconcelos (1882–1959), the philosopher and writer who had belonged to the *Ateneo* group. Vasconcelos had joined the revolution as a supporter of Francisco Madero and had little sympathy for the peasant leaders, Villa and Zapata.[5] All his efforts had gone into furthering the more moderate elements whom he felt, after Madero's assassination, could carry on this leader's policy. In 1914, he became Minister of Education in the short-lived government of Eulalio Gutiérrez. His first appearance at the Ministry was refreshingly vigorous: 'The elderly janitor proving too slow for my impatience, I rushed up, taking the stairs two by two, and proceeded to force an entrance with kicks and blows.'[6] But he had hardly time to take office before the government evacuated the capital. In 1921, the revolution over, Vasconcelos had a second opportunity when Obregón made him Minister of Education once more. This time he remained in power for three years, and in this period implemented a far-reaching programme that transformed educational and cultural life. His resignation came about in 1924, when he was squeezed out by two rising forces: that of the left-wing and trade union movement, and that of the strong man, Plutarco Elías Calles (in office, 1924–8). After his resignation in 1924, he led a campaign against the 'barbarian' Calles and his followers, which ended in his own electoral defeat and exile. The year of his defeat, 1929, marks a new era in Mexican life, for thenceforward the intellectual was faced with the choice of aligning himself with the government or working in isolation.

Despite Vasconcelos's defeat, the effects of his programme of cultural nationalism were long-lasting and, indeed, changed the face of Mexico. This programme was shaped according to his own philosophy, which put art and aesthetic appreciation and creativity at the peak of human achievement. In a series of essays – *Pitágoras* (1916), *La raza cósmica* (1925), *Indología* (1927) – he developed a theory of human and social evolution. Humanity, he believed, progressed through a series of stages – a materialist stage, an intellectual or rationalist phase and an aesthetic phase. Aesthetic activity was superior to rational knowledge because the artist, through his perception, sensed the rhythms which united all elements in the universe. But this perception could be achieved only in a state of disinterestedness when ego drives were forgotten. 'What is aesthetics unless a road by which man reaches the divine world of disinterested processes?' he asked.[7]

Vasconcelos believed that society was progressing towards a fusion of races; a fusion which was destined to be first achieved in Latin America since here the beginnings of a 'cosmic race' were already apparent. In some future era, Latin America would be the leading civilization of the world; Latin Americans, therefore, should work to hasten the advent of this era, and this they could do by putting racial interests before narrow nationalisms.[8] In a speech read in Washington, Vasconcelos gave his vision of the future:

I imagine a near future in which the nations will be merged into four great ethnic federations. The world will then be divided into four or five great powers who will collaborate in all that is good and beautiful, but they will express the good and the beautiful each in its own way. . . . That is why in Mexico we teach not only Mexican patriotism but Latin-American patriotism, for here is a vast continent open to all races and all colours of skin, to all humanity, so that they may organize a new experiment in collective living: an experiment founded not only on utility but above all on beauty, on that beauty which our southern races instinctively seek, as if in it they had discovered the supreme divine law.[9]

This ideal of Latin-America unity was furthered by Vasconcelos in a practical way. He gave work to the exiled Peruvian, Victor Raúl Haya de la Torre (b. 1895), then a student leader, and invited the Chilean poetess, Gabriela Mistral (1889–1957), to teach in Mexico. He visited Argentina and also Brazil, where he presented a statue of Cuauhtémoc to the country. On this occasion, he stressed that Latin Americans should get away from the idea that they were the 'spiritual serfs' of Europe though, at the same time, they ought not to reject all European ideas. He declared that, while the introduction of European ideas had been important in the past, this was no longer necessary. The vision of Cuauhtémoc was an anticipation of the flowering of a Latin-American culture.[10]

In the national scene, Vasconcelos was no less active. In his Ministry, he set up three departments dealing with schools, libraries and the fine arts; through them, he conducted his campaign against ignorance and barbarism. Schools were founded throughout the land and, in the campaign against illiteracy, the Indian was not forgotten. Indians were to be trained for entry into the state school system and eventually were to be integrated into national life. Masses of books were published and distributed to further popular education – a bizarre collection, in truth, embracing Spanish dictionaries, *Don Quixote*, Greek classics, Dante and Goethe. In an illiterate country, the publication of Greek classics on a grand scale might well seem absurd, but the enterprise was not altogether a vain one. It meant that the government went in for large-scale publishing, something hitherto unheard of; up to this time in Mexico even commercial publishers seldom thought in terms of editions of more than five hundred or a thousand.[11] Vasconcelos also gave active support to musicians, like Julián Carrillo (1875–1965) whose musical experiments have had influence outside Mexico, and to Joaquín Beristaín (1878–1948) who organized orchestras and folk-singing groups. He also commissioned native artists to decorate the walls of public buildings and was thus the promoter of Mexico's famous school of mural painters.[12] Nowhere was Vasconcelos's programme of cultural nationalism more effective than in the field of painting, for Mexican murals soon began to attract the attention of the rest of the world. Yet the achievements of the muralists were in many ways quite different from Vasconcelos's own concept of what mural painting should represent. He gave the initial inspiration, but others – more in tune with the times – were responsible for its development.

Indeed, the first efforts to find some national expression were extremely tentative. Vasconcelos expected the muralists to produce paintings on literary themes and with a symbolic content. His first commission was for a stained-glass window, perhaps because stained glass symbolized for him the integrated culture of the Middle Ages, while the first mural he commissioned had the typically Vasconcelan theme: 'Action is Mightier than Fate. Conquer!' There was nothing original or particularly Mexican about this mural, which depicts twelve allegorical females, 'meant to be Hours, capering decorously around an armoured knight who leans against a Persian tree of life gay with giant blooms and chirping birds on a gold background'.[13] A mural executed by the fiery revolutionary Dr Atl (1875–1964),* a teacher of painting who had served with Obregón and had enthusiastically helped to sack churches, portrayed quite tame and unrevolutionary scenes, mostly seascapes. True, a North American critic described the mural as 'flaming depictions of Mexican scenery' but a fellow artist, Diego Rivera (1887–1957), was less certain of their national content. 'Shapes and lines depicted by an undiluted Yankee taste of the fiftieth category', was his verdict.[14] But Rivera himself had little right to criticize since his own first murals still owed much to the European art he had initially been schooled in. His colleague, David Alfaro Siqueiros (b. 1898), who had been recalled from Europe by Vasconcelos and was later to become a leading Communist, executed his first mural on the surprising (for him) theme of 'The Spirit of the Occident or European Culture Alighting upon Mexico'. The mural was exactly what one would expect from such a title: 'The winged female, fairly realistic and deeply modelled, hovered against a web of diagonal lines, over which a scattering of seashells alternated with abstract forms.'[15] The third painter who, with Rivera and Siqueiros, formed the trilogy of great Mexican muralists, was José Clemente Orozco (1883–1949), an artist who was already established as a lithographer and caricaturist. His first mural was hardly more 'Mexican' than those of the others, though one of the panels did depict an Aztec deity, and another, 'Man strangling a gorilla', obviously represented a striving towards a new form of symbolism.[16]

For Diego Rivera, the decisive point seems to have been a visit to Tehuantepec, with its wealth of folk art and its tropical scenery. From this point onwards, his murals became increasingly Mexican in the use of Mexican folk-motif, in their background of Mexican fruits and flowers, in the depiction of scenes from national life, and even, he claimed, in the revival of ancient pre-Columban techniques. About the latter, there is some doubt.

*His real name was Gerardo Murillo.

Although Rivera announced that his murals were painted with a preparation mixed with nopal (cactus) juice, an assistant disclosed: 'It consisted, in practice, of slices of nopal leaf left to rot in the bucket of water in which we dipped our brushes. A cynical attitude towards the secret of the Mexicans and an abhorrence of the stink of the decomposed nopal stumps kept but few leaves in our two buckets, enough for inspection, and made us change our water surreptitiously.'[17]

Rivera was not the first to claim that his techniques were derived from pre-Columban sources. One of the teachers employed by Vasconcelos was Adolfo Best Maugard (1891–1964) who drew up a drawing manual and created a new teaching system for drawing based on the 'seven lineal elements of Mexican indigenous and popular arts'.[18] Even so, Diego Rivera's murals in the Ministry of Education and in the Agricultural School of Chapingo were the first major achievements of the new movement. He declared:

I had the ambition to reflect the genuine essential expression of the land. I wanted my pictures to mirror the social life of Mexico as I saw it and through the reality and arrangement of the present, the masses were to be shown the possibilities of the future. I sought to be . . . a condenser of the striving and longing of the masses and a transmitter providing for the masses a synthesis of their wishes so as to serve them as an organizer of consciousness and aid their social organization.[19]

The Ministry of Education murals became, as he painted, increasingly revolutionary in content. Over the mural at the Chapingo Agricultural School he painted the inscription 'Here it is taught to exploit the land, not man'. The revolutionary content of Rivera's murals did not please Vasconcelos, whose portrait came to be included in the Ministry of Education murals among the 'false mystifiers'. Indeed, it gradually became obvious that Vasconcelos's brand of cultural nationalism belonged to another era. Rivera represented the new spirit, which identified the nation with the common people, whose heroes were the anonymous masses of the fighters against oppression. A new iconography appeared, together with an idealization of Indians and peasants who, in Rivera's murals, were associated with flowers, fruit, earth and the rhythms of nature. They were depicted with gently flowing lines, while the 'villains', the oppressors – often encased in armour or ugly suits – were depicted in harsh colours and angular lines.

The development of this revolutionary art will be described elsewhere (see below, pp. 158–62), for the class struggle became an increasingly important theme. From the point of view of cultural nationalism, perhaps the most important aspect of the muralist was the almost complete identification made between national and Indian. The Whites were nearly always foreign exploiters, either Spaniards or Yankee businessmen. Possibly pictorial reasons may have dictated this identification in the early murals, but very soon the myth heroes of this movement were almost invariably Indian or very dark Mestizos – from the Aztec prince, Cuauhtémoc, to the nineteenth-century hero, Benito Juárez. The authentic Mexico thus came to be identified with an indigenous Mexico whose traditions derived from pre-Columban times. The Spanish contribution and subsequent European influences came to be considered essentially foreign and 'un-Mexican'. This radical attitude was later to have a deleterious effect on Mexican art. The initial freshness of the murals and the discovery of the pictorial value of aspects of national life were replaced by a facile formalism or a polemical type of painting. The return to indigenous techniques proved an exaggerated form of national 'purity'. One young muralist, Amado de la Cueva (1891–1926), prematurely killed in an accident in 1926, attempted to go back to the spatial and perspective conventions of pre-Hispanic painting. The result would certainly have been a kind of pictorial archaism. Another tendency of the muralists – their abuse of folk-art motif – was criticized by José Clemente Orozco (Mexico, 1883–1949), who gave a timely reminder that national art was not necessarily folk art:

The essential difference between painting at its noblest and painting as a minor folk art is this: the former is rooted in universal permanent traditions from which it cannot be torn apart, no matter what the pretext, the place, or the time, while folk arts have strictly local traditions that vary according to the customs, changes, agitations and convulsions suffered by each country, each race, each nationality, each class, even each family or tribe. . . . Such thoughts led me to eschew once and for all the painting of Indian sandals and dirty clothes. From the bottom of my heart I do wish that those who wear them would discard such outfits and get civilized. But to glorify them would be like glorifying illiteracy, drunkenness, or the mounds of garbage that 'beautify' our streets, and that I refuse to do.[20]

Perhaps the most complete expression of this type of cultural nationalism is to be found in the architecture and decoration of the National Autonomous University which was begun in the forties and completed in the fifties, and to which Diego Rivera, Alfaro Siqueiros and many others contributed.* Certain of the buildings, particularly the *frontones* and the library, show attempts to reproduce indigenous architectural forms; the mosaic on the university library building is made from coloured Mexican stones and some of the motifs are pre-Columban.

That the concept of Mexican art eventually proved too narrow has been shown by a recent revolt among some of the younger painters who have resented the imputation that learning or using techniques from abroad is unpatriotic.[21] All the same, the enormous stimulus that the Mexican muralist movement, at its best, has had on the whole of artistic and intellectual life cannot be denied. From the muralists, there spread a widening circle of interest in folk art, in native dress, dance, music and language. Perhaps their most valuable contribution came about through the reputations they achieved abroad. Through this foreign recognition, they helped to make Mexican art respectable among their own people and thus created an interest in native productions that was to have beneficial results in all fields of artistic creation.

Closely linked with cultural nationalism in painting was the introduction of national themes into music. Vasconcelos, as we have seen, had been greatly interested in developing musical taste in Mexico, and consequently had encouraged the formation of orchestras, the teaching of music and the engagement of native musicians. Three outstanding composers emerged during this

* Rivera did a mosaic mural for the stadium; Siqueiros contributed murals; Juan O'Gorman executed the mosaic murals on the library.

period: Manuel Ponce (1882–1948), Silvestre Revueltas (1889–1940) and Carlos Chávez (b. 1899). One of the latter's compositions, the tone-poem *Xochipilli-Macuilxochitl*, scored for indigenous pre-Columban instruments, demonstrates the application to music of the 'back to the roots' principles of the muralists. In 1938, Chávez completed a *Sinfonia india*.[22]

Music and painting received government sponsorship, both while Vasconcelos was at the Ministry and afterwards. Dance, especially folk dance, also received encouragement, although the *Ballet folklórico de Mexico* was not officially recognized as a national company until 1959. Vasconcelos was also one of the first to acknowledge the value of the cinema in forming a national consciousness. His own project for a film on the life of Bolívar, however, came to nothing; early Mexican films were often sentimental love stories with a western or revolutionary background and, in general, the cinema failed to become the cultural weapon that Vasconcelos had hoped.[23]

The whole atmosphere of Mexico in the 1920s, when artists were torn between the claims of avant-garde experiment, the claims of the revolution and the desire to produce a national art, has been described in a novel published in 1959, *La creación* by Agustín Yañez (b. 1904). Mural paintings always had a public, even if it were a dissenting one. In poetry and the novel, Mexican writers were faced with the difficulties of communicating with an illiterate public, or else of remaining in a position of isolation. This isolation, it is true, had its advantages, in that writers were able to deal freely with themes that had little reference to immediate social reality; and, as literature was less directly identified with the government than were the plastic arts, they tended to be more critical of the new era. Whereas the painters became the iconographers of the revolution, the writers remained aloof. Ramón López Velarde (1888–1921), the major poet of the post-Modernist period in Mexico, identified the happiness of childhood with the Eden of pre-revolutionary Mexico.

> It will be better not to go back to the village,
> to that shattered Eden, silent
> in the destruction of the guns.[24]

Nevertheless, although the revolution had its darker side, it also brought a great widening of horizons and possibilities for the writer. The novelist now had a world that had never previously been described in Mexican literature: a world of the peasants and the Indians. Above all, there was the rich material afforded by the revolution itself.

For the writer, then, cultural nationalism was seen primarily as a question of subject matter, the introduction into the novel and short story of Mexican reality. Yet the new literature was slow to appear, as a newspaper critic impatiently remarked in 1924. His article on 'The Effeminacy of Mexican Literature' complained of the absence of a 'literature of the revolution'. The nearness of grim events, the inadequacy of the publishing trade, and the lack of a responsive public – these factors, in varying degrees, help to explain the curious absence of revolutionary novels in the 1920s. Possibly another factor was the ambivalence of the middle-class writer towards the revolution.[25] Indeed, out of the mass of novels of the revolution which eventually appeared after the first hiatus, the most interesting and the best written are almost invariably critical, not of the revolution itself, but of the barbarism that it unleashed.

The pioneer writer of the revolution was Mariano Azuela, who – in *Los de abajo*, (1916), *Los caciques* (1917) and *Las moscas* (1918) – covered several major aspects of the struggle. In *Los caciques* (The Bosses), he describes the exploiters whose heartless treatment of the poor helped to bring about the revolution. *Los de abajo* (The Underdogs) deals, as we have already mentioned (p. 80 above), with the rise of a peasant who becomes a general during the revolutionary fighting. In *Las moscas* (The Flies), Azuela describes the flight by train of a group of opportunists and members of the old order as revolutionary forces enter Mexico City. The author shows himself uncompromisingly against the evils of the old order, mercilessly exposing the selfish, jostling parasites whose talent for survival is as great as their cynicism. On the other hand, the structure of *Los de abajo* reveals the author's pessimism for the future. The novel's climax is the battle of Zacatecas in which, for the last time, the revolutionary forces fought together against the common enemy, the Federalists. After the battle, the Revolution breaks up into inter-warring factions only actuated by self-interest or, as in the case of the protagonist, Demetrio, by negative factors. He is unable to stop fighting because he has no goal except destruction of the enemy and once that is accomplished, he can only repeat the same behaviourist pattern. The circular structure of the novel in which Demetrio dies fighting on the site of his first battle reinforces the pessimistic impression.

Azuela was a pioneer of the revolutionary novel in another respect. He was the first Latin-American novelist to use the masses as the protagonist, and to find techniques for showing the mass in action. *Las moscas* is an excellent example of a novel with a multiple protagonist. Since nearly all the action takes place on a train, the setting provides a tight container, a unity of place. Within this unity, he is able to show the milling crowd with its conflicting impulses and fears. In *Los de abajo*, also, there is a mass protagonist: 'the underdogs'. Here, Azuela again skilfully conveys the impression of a mass by concentrating on the ad-ventures of one guerrilla band, that of Demetrio Macías. This technique was to be used with great effect by other writers of novels of the Mexican revolution, notably by Gregorio López y Fuentes (b. 1897) in *Campamento* (Bivouac, 1931). In this novel, the author simply presents an anonymous group of men who bivouac before going into action, recording their thoughts and memories during the pause in the fighting. At the end of the novel, they are moving into action.[26]

The other type of writing that emerged from the revolution was the eye-witness account. A great many Mexican writers had per-sonally been involved in the revolution. Very often their works consist of crudely novelized accounts of their adventures, but in two writers – Martín Luis Guzmán (b. 1887) and José Rubén Romero (1890–1952) – the eye-witness account has more than an immediate, topical interest. Personal reminiscence forms the backbone of Martín Luis Guzmán's *El águila y la serpiente* (The Eagle and the Serpent, 1928), which is autobiography rather than novel. Its main interest lies in the author's vivid descriptions of Pancho Villa and the other major revolutionary leaders, whom Guzmán had met in the hope of finding one who would fulfil his own ideal of the man who could guide Mexico after the revolution. The novel is a record of his failure to find such a man, and the scene at the end, in which he and Villa say good-bye, is not only powerfully written; it also underlines implicitly the discrepancies between the 'barbarian' peasant leader and the 'civilized' intellectual. Rubén Romero is a novelist of the provinces, of the slow life of the small town, observing its characters and idiosyncrasies. In one of his major works, *La vida inútil de Pito Pérez* (The Useless Life of Pito Pérez 1938), he uses a literary archetype, the small-town drunkard and 'philosopher'; but in two early autobiographical novels – *Apuntes de un lugareño* (Provincial Sketches, 1932) and *Desbandada* (Flight, 1934) – he recounts anecdotes of life in a provincial town which the revolution, except for one or two incidents, largely passes by. The swift, breath-taking brutality of these incidents as he describes them is the more shocking for being set within a picture of a provincial backwater. Like López Velarde, the impression Romero gives is of a 'shattered Eden'.[27] And from *La vida inútil de Pito Pérez*, it is clear that Romero did not believe that the Revolution had caused disaster in itself. Rather, the failure of any social ideal was the fault of human beings who possess neither courage nor charity. The drunkard, Pito Pérez, is outrageous, dirty and defiant but does not merit the cruel treatment he gets from the town jokers who have him play Christ and then leave him crucified. When he dies, his testament is a bitter outcry against humanity. A novel which dealt directly with the Revolution, *Mi caballo, mi perro y mi rifle* (1936), portrays a poor youth of the lower middle class who has always hated the landowners and the bosses, and joins the Revolution where he becomes the proud possessor of a horse, a dog and a gun, only to find at the Revolution's end that the same men are still in power and his own loot has disappeared.

Despite the critical attitude maintained by the novelists, the net effect of the revolution on artistic activity was, as we have noted, an enormous widening of horizons, affording the writer the opportunity to exploit new material and develop a new concept of nationalism – a concept in which, according to Pedro Henríquez Ureña, all sections of the community were invited to share. For perhaps the first time in Latin America since independence, the government, peoples and artists of a nation – the Mexican – were all inspired by the same fundamental desire to create a new society. But though no other Latin-American country went through a social revolution during this period, all over the sub-continent a new type of nationalist fervour infected artists and intellectuals. They believed that social revolution was imminent, that all classes and races must be brought into national life, and that genuinely original political, social and artistic forms must take the place of the old elite cultures and societies. If the new age had not dawned in 1918, it seemed very near.

POLITICS AND CULTURE IN PERU

Of all Spanish-American countries, Peru seemed most likely to follow Mexico and develop an original form of society and culture. It is true that a strong dictatorship under President Leguía came into power in 1919 and was destined to stay until 1930. Nevertheless, during the Leguía regime, new political parties were founded and their programmes of social reform were framed to suit Peru's special needs as a country with a large indigenous population. One of these parties was APRA (Alianza Popular Revolucionaria Americana), founded by Haya de la Torre, who had cut his political teeth in the University Reform Movement and had spent a period of exile in Mexico as Vasconcelos's secretary. APRA was pledged to an anti-imperialistic programme which included the rejection of any political, social or economic structure based on foreign models. One of the members of APRA, Antenor Orrego, was later to build a political philosophy which took as its thesis the idea that all European patterns were bound to be shattered when parties or governments tried to impose themselves upon Latin America. The destruction of these patterns would cause a state of chaos, but it was from this chaos that the new and original society would emerge.[28]

Shortly after the foundation of APRA, a second political party emerged with a policy of constructing a Socialist society on original Peruvian lines. The founder, José Carlos Mariátegui (1895–1930) – a brilliant journalist and writer who had, early in his career, defended the workers' cause in a magazine, *La Razón* – was at first associated with Haya de la Torre in the APRA movement.[29] In the early 1920s, however, he spent three years in Europe, where he met Henri Barbusse and came into contact with Italian Socialists. When he returned to Peru, he founded an influential review, *Amauta*, in which he expounded his own political and social theories, and published stories, verse and articles by Peru's progressive young writers. In 1928, APRA was condemned by Moscow because its existence hindered the formation of a Communist Party. Mariátegui accordingly formed a new party on Marxist lines: the Peruvian Socialist Party, which attempted to formulate a Socialist policy corresponding to Peruvian reality.* Peru was only part-European; a large proportion of its population – the Indians – still lived in communes which were part of their pre-Columban social structure. These communes, or *ayllu*, could form the basis for future collectivization. Peruvian Socialism also departed from the European model in the importance it gave to the land problem, the basic problem of the country. Mariátegui's Socialist Party was thus an example of the way the European theory of Socialism could be transformed into a national programme.

But 'Aprismo' and Mariátegui's theories were to have repercussions in the artistic field. Included in Mariátegui's *Siete ensayos de interpretación de la realidad peruana* (Seven Interpretative Essays on Peruvian Reality, 1928) was a survey which considered Peruvian literature, for the first time, from the point of its effectiveness as an expression of the national spirit. This essay was also the first in Latin-American critical writing to tackle the problem of incorporating the Indian into literature.[30]

One of the outstanding Peruvian writers to accept the cultural nationalism of Haya de la Torre and Mariátegui was the young avant-garde poet, César Vallejo (1892–1938). He had left Peru in 1923, after a short term in prison for a political offence, to go and live in Paris.† In a number of articles written for Peruvian news-

* See chapter 5, pp. 50–51.

† He was probably not guilty of the offence for which he was imprisoned. See Juan Espejo Asturrizaga, *César Vallejo*.

papers, Vallejo warned against the adoption in America of 'universal' theories, such as Marxism, arguing that history had shown the fallacy of trying to introduce European political systems to that continent. Vallejo was to become a militant Communist after a second visit to Russia in 1929, but before this date his articles clearly reflect the influence of Haya de la Torre whom, indeed, he quotes in support of his views.[31] At the same time, he sees that the attempt to go back to indigenous forms might also have its dangers.[32] Certainly, in his own poetry he did not subordinate to any 'nationalist' sentiment his central preoccupation with the human condition.

In prose writing, cultural nationalism was most clearly reflected in the attempt by several writers to deal with the Indian, for it was the indigenous population and the Incaic past that most clearly marked Peru off as a distinctive national society. In 1924, there appeared a collection of short stories, *La venganza del cóndor* (The Condor's Revenge),[33] portraying the Andean Indians. The author, Ventura García Calderón (1888–1959), belonged to the Arielist generation and saw the Indians from the point of view of a European tourist, marvelling at their strangeness and not a little afraid of what might happen if ever they lost their patience and turned against the white oppressors. Nevertheless, a new spirit was already informing literary circles. The stories by Abraham Valdelomar (1888–1919) in *Los hijos del sol* (Children of the Sun, 1921) remind readers of the greatness of the Indians' past civilization. And the realistic stories of Enrique López Albújar (b. 1872), *Cuentos andinos* (Tales of the Andes, 1920), portray the Indian, not as a passive and exotic creature, but as a human personality whose poverty and ignorance arise from the feudal oppression he has to suffer. López Albújar had, indeed, particular reason for writing about 'inferior' races; he is a Mulatto and therefore could enter sympathetically into his Indian characters' sense of inferiority.

I learned to hold my mouth ready for the wounding reply, to receive and return insinuating remarks, to give back with my fists or any other weapon the blows that I received from my cousins, to look back proudly at those people who observed me maliciously – in a word, to defend myself.[34]

López Albújar's governing interest in the question of colour, and in the problems of breaking down a prejudice that had its origins in the social structure, is clearly manifested in a letter he wrote to the Spanish writer Ramiro de Maeztu, after a criticism that the latter had levelled against his novel *Matalaché* (1928). *Matalaché* deals with the passionate love of the white daughter of a plantation owner for a black slave, and the barbarous punishment inflicted on the latter for this reason. Maeztu had hinted that such a love affair, anywhere but in the tropics, would seem monstrous: a criticism that Albújar answers by showing that it is based on a 'reflex act of repulsion . . . which every white man . . . feels for the colour of a race which symbolizes a long past history of inferiority and servitude'.

In the literature of the twenties, then, Peruvian nationalism was reflected in this determination of writers to awaken public awareness to the plight of the Indian, and other oppressed sectors of the community. And Mariátegui's magazine, *Amauta*, became one of the important organs for the transmission of this literature, encouraging a generation of social realist prose writers such as César Falcón.

THE NOVEL AND NATIONAL REGENERATION

Colombia and Venezuela are countries with populations of mixed origin; both include not only a variety of races and racial mixtures, but also an enormous geographical disparity between high mountain areas and tropical jungles. For years, cultural life had been confined to a small circle of town-dwellers; Bogotá, Medellín and Caracas boasted their literary circles, but these tiny groups were surrounded by vast rural areas about which the intellectuals knew and cared little. By the 1920s, however, in both countries new elements were appearing on the literary and political scene to bring a fresh vision of national reality: writers like the Colombian José Eustasio Rivera (1888–1928), and the Venezuelan Rómulo Gallegos. Rivera came from a provincial Colombian family of modest means. One of the first graduates of a newly founded teachers' college, he was also a law graduate, and his legal work took him into the Colombian hinterland, first to the plains, and then, as a member of a boundary commission, to the Amazon region.[35] Rómulo Gallegos was of even humbler stock; he was born in the provinces, not far from Caracas, and, because of his poverty, he had difficulty in completing his education. For many years he worked as a teacher. Rivera and Gallegos, then, represent a new type in their countries' literature, which had hitherto been dominated by aristocratic or wealthy men, of whom Asunción Silva and Blanco Fombona offer typical examples.

Rivera's one novel, *La vorágine* (The Vortex, 1924), can be considered in many ways: as a romantic allegory, as an urban intellectual's frightened vision of the barbarism of his country, as a novel of protest. Yet at the same time it is an intensely national novel: the first Colombian novel to describe the reality of life among the cow-herders of the plains and the rubber-workers of the jungle. The protagonist, Arturo Cova, is a poet who has to leave Bogotá after seducing and eloping with a girl friend, Alicia. He is a sensitive, literary, city-bred man who is horrified at the brutal reality of the cow-herders' life, with its physical dangers and background of lawlessness. In the plains, there is no national justice – only the law of the strongest, to which even representatives of the state must bow. But there is worse. Beyond the plains exists the lawless world of the jungle to which Arturo Cova flees in pursuit of Alicia, who has joined a group of rubber-workers in search of easy money. In the jungle the ferocity of nature is matched by the ferocity of the escaped convicts who have set up an empire of enslaved rubber-workers. Arturo Cova leaves the world of society and convention to find himself in a world which antedates any human society: a world ruled by the natural law of 'survival of the fittest'. *La vorágine* thus contains a profoundly national lesson, for the novel shows how thin was the civilized veneer of Colombian society, how near to the surface the law of the jungle. If Colombian nationality was to mean anything, it had to be extended to protect the cowboys and rubber-workers for whom there was no law. At one dramatic point in the novel, when Arturo Cova is about to kill a man he thinks is a spy, the word 'Colombian' transforms the situation. The unfortunate victim appeals to the one concept which can save him from the execution of this jungle law.

Rómulo Gallegos, like Eustasio Rivera, was a member of a newly educated class that had sprung from the lower levels of the population. During most of his childhood and much of his adult life, Venezuela was dominated by two strong dictators: Cipriano Castro and Vicente Gómez, both of whom kept an iron hand on the country and thus helped to protect the feudal interests of the estate holders. Gallegos grew up in a generation which placed its belief in education and literary culture as a way of combating barbarism. In his youth, his main preoccupation was social and political rather than literary and this was readily understandable in a period of which one of his friends wrote: 'The years of our apprenticeship seemed dark to our young minds: years of disaster, dark years in which we only wanted to think of our country.'[36]

Gallegos's first novel, *Reinaldo Solar*, did not appear until 1920. It has already been mentioned in chapter 2 as an example of the pessimistic aspect of the Arielist generation that witnessed the frustration of its hopes of saving the country through literature and education. But with his second novel, *La trepadora* (The Climber, 1925), Gallegos's mood changed. 'My first optimistic book', he called it; '*La trepadora* represents a desire for improvement, and as such implies confidence in the future.'[37] This confidence did not spring from anything in the political situation, which was still dark, but arose from the conviction that the great social revolution that had already begun elsewhere in the subcontinent must soon extend to Venezuela. In Gallegos's hands, the novel was to become an instrument of national regeneration through the exposure of the country's weaknesses and the indication of the way to future development. *La trepadora*, the first of his 'regenerative' novels, deals with the theme of race. In it, Gallegos describes the rise to riches and eminence of Hilario, a Mulatto, son of a Negress and a White landowner. Hilario's success enables him to marry into the White aristocracy. His daughter by this marriage, Victoria, symbolizes the fusion of the two essential elements of Venezuelan life: the energetic, rising Mulatto and the cultivated but declining elite of European origin. Gallegos implies that, in the new Venezuela, both these elements must be used.

In a series of novels written during the twenties and thirties, Gallegos was to cover all aspects of Venezuelan life and to set his novels in many different regions – plains, jungles, plantations. But in all of them he had the two-fold aim of describing the unknown life of the hinterland and of showing how the tragic disorder and division of the country might be overcome. During a period of self-exile in Europe, he completed two novels set in the plains, *Doña Bárbara* (1929) and *Cantaclaro* (1934), and a novel of the jungle, *Canaima* (1935). All the protagonists of these novels symbolize aspects of Venezuelan life; the eponymous heroine of *Doña Bárbara*, for instance, incarnates the barbaric lawlessness and independent courage of the inhabitants of those areas to which the rule of law did not extend. In this novel, Doña Bárbara is eventually vanquished by Santos Luzardo, the city-educated man who is himself eventually forced to adopt violent methods to defeat Bárbara. Santos Luzardo's marriage with Bárbara's daughter, Marisela, is symbolic of this 'taming of the frontier' by civilization, which is also the theme of the whole novel. In *Cantaclaro*, this optimistic note is less in evidence, although the cowboy singer who is the protagonist and who disappears into the plains at the end of the novel does incarnate a 'spirit of the plains' which civil war and injustice cannot quench.

Both *Cantaclaro* and *Canaima* illustrate the problem of writing an optimistic and 'national' work when the national political and social scene is so dark. The desired-for changes must always be left for the future unless the present is to be falsified. In *Canaima*, a novel set in the jungle regions around Ciudad Bolívar, Gallegos solves this problem through the character of his hero, Marcos Vargas, who, in the course of his development, experiences all the illusions common to the inhabitants of these tropical areas of Venezuela – the lure of easy riches from gold or rubber, the temptation of political power exercised by virtue of superior physical strength. Vargas gradually discards these false goals and gives up a promising career in order to learn the lore of the region from its original inhabitants, the Indians. His son, the fruit of a union with an Indian woman, symbolizes the hope in the future when indigenous and European civilizations are really fused. By incarnating the virtues and vices of his countrymen in certain characters, Gallegos criticizes the root weaknesses of the nation and at the same time is able to show national virtues which could be exploited when these weaknesses are overcome. He anticipates more recent novelists in attributing many of Venezuela's difficulties to psychological weaknesses.

NATIONALISM AND THE IMMIGRANT

In Venezuela and Colombia, the threat to national unity came from within, from their own internal variety. In several other countries – notably Argentina, Uruguay and Chile – and in regions of Brazil, the threat came from without, from the immigrant. Cultural nationalism was stimulated by a desire to preserve national traditions in the face of a flood of newcomers who had no concept of either Iberian or indigenous cultures, and with an imperfect grasp of either the Spanish or the Portuguese language. From Rodó onwards, intellectuals had been aware of the threat of the immigrant to cultural standards, but it was in Argentina, with the concept of *argentinidad*, that there developed the most determined attempt to resist this threat.

As early as 1910, the anniversary date of Argentinian independence, Ricardo Rojas (1882–1957) – a liberal writer and critic lately returned from Europe – published an essay, *La restauración nacionalista* (The Nationalist Revival), in which he preached a return to the true Indo-Hispanic tradition that had been swept aside by the immigratory currents of the latter half of the nineteenth century. As has been noted in chapter 2, Rojas, in order to inculcate a sense of Argentinian tradition, embarked on the mammoth task of writing the lives of his country's great men, and of compiling a vast history of its literature – in which the late nineteenth-century poem, *Martín Fierro*, was given a high place. Rojas, a humanist and scholar, did not interpret nationalism in a chauvinistic sense; for him, it was self-evident that the spirit of a nation must spring from its past history, out of the nature of the land and society. He identified the authentic national spirit with the autochthonous and the traditional, contrasting these elements with the exoticism and cosmopolitanism of the big city. He believed that European culture should not be rejected but be absorbed and adapted to meet Argentinian conditions.[38]

Rojas was a life-long Liberal and, like cultural nationalists in other parts of the sub-continent, he was primarily concerned with amplifying the concept of nationalism and in closing the gap between the two cultures of Latin America. He was not a nationalist who used 'tradition' as an antidote to modernity. In contrast, the poet Leopoldo Lugones, who had been associated with Rojas, began in the 1920s to preach a right-wing cultural nationalism in which the calm and stability of rural life were set up as an ideal against the fragmentation of city life. Lugones was actuated by a deep-seated fear of modernity: a fear which led him to demand a strong-man government and to work for this end. Always a prolific writer, he published three volumes of poems on themes of rural life. In *El libro de los paisajes* (The Book of Landscapes, 1917) are poems describing his native land. *Poemas solariegos* (Homestead Poems, 1927) include nostalgic evocations of Argentinian pastoral life. The posthumous collection, *Romances del Río Seco* (1938), comprises ballad poems set in the area in which he spent his childhood. His concept of nationalism is reflected in the poems in which he praises the patriarchal values of 'love and duty', the ordered calm of the rural family, and the peaceful and harmonious existence of those who live close to nature.

Whether or not as a direct result of the great social transformations and the unrest that threatened national life, a new attitude developed towards the gauchos, the country-dwellers and the land itself among writers of the Plate region. At the turn of the century, Javier de Viana and Florencio Sánchez wrote of the degeneracy or decline of the country-dweller; but, beginning in the 1920s, writers began to bring a new approach to the traditional gaucho theme. In the novels of Ricardo Güiraldes (1886–1927) and Benito Lynch (1885–1952), the gaucho takes on a new and unexpected dignity.

Ricardo Güiraldes's *Don Segundo Sombra* (1926) – one of the masterpieces of Latin-American literature – presents the gaucho in his own right.[39] The author does not measure him according to a European standard of values, but views him as a man adapted to the circumstances of life in the pampa and able to develop into a full and balanced human being within the terms of pampa life. The countryman, Güiraldes believes, does not need to have culture brought to him from the outside world in order to become a civilized human being. Similarly, in the rural tragedies of Benito Lynch, the gaucho women have deep and noble emotions. In two novels – *Los caranchos de la Florida* (The Vultures of Florida Farm, 1916)* and *El inglés de los güesos* (The Englishman of the Bones, 1924) – tragedy strikes a gaucho community when a man comes from the outside world, from Europe, to shatter for a girl the rough but effective conventions she has hitherto known. Whether intentionally or not, Lynch's stories appear to be an allegory of European influence on his native land. Europe is attractive, but the union of the gaucho girl and the European or Western-educated man leads to tragedy. By contrast, in *Don Segundo Sombra*, Europe scarcely intrudes. The pampa itself is sufficient to educate and bring to maturity the wild young adolescent who is the protagonist of the story.

THE CULTURAL NATIONALISM OF THE AVANT-GARDE

The 1920s was a period of revolution in the creative arts. In poetry, the theatre and the novel, the old conventions tumbled. Rhyme and regular metre in poetry, colour and perspective conventions in painting, had been disappearing for some time. But after 1918 the whole concept of art changed. Art was no longer a sacred pursuit but a game or a practical joke on the bourgeois world. The avant-garde turned the heavy guns of ridicule against society, logic, reason, the ideal of progress – all the assumptions, in fact, of the nineteenth-century mind. And they attempted to find new poetic and artistic codes to interpret the fragmented post-war world. As if to illustrate the non-transcendental nature of all artistic values, avant-garde movements, like Futurism, Cubism and Dadaism, flourished and declined with great rapidity. This spirit of revolt quickly communicated itself to Latin America where there had already been some poetic experiment

* *Carancho* is a bird of the vulture family, native to the Plate region.

by the Chilean Pedro Prado (1886–1952) in his *Flores de cardo* (Thistle Flowers, 1908), and by Leopoldo Lugones in his *Lunario sentimental* (Sentimental Lunarium, 1909). In the latter, Lugones had practised grotesque, humorous distortions of the traditional romantic moonlight scene:

> En las piscinas
> los sauces con poéticos desmayos
> echan sus anzuelos de seda negra a tus rayos
> convertidos en relumbrantes sardinas.[40]

> In the ponds,
> willow-trees poetically swoon,
> casting black silk fishing-lines towards your rays
> which shimmer like sardines.

As in Europe, the avant-garde was revolutionary not only in poetry but also in politics, often being associated with left-wing or Socialist movements. Some poets believed that their all-out attack on the bourgeoisie helped to hasten the process of disintegration of capitalist society: an attitude expressed in Latin America by the Cuban magazine *Avance*, which defended itself against an attack by Diego Rivera on the grounds that the avant-garde represented the first symptoms of the revolution. In Mexico, some of the *estridentistas* preached the destruction of the capitalist world. In two countries of Latin America, avant-garde movements were associated not so much with social revolution as with the attempt to revitalize their national cultures: such were the 'Martinfierrista' in Argentina and Brazilian 'Modernismo'. In both these movements, national culture was identified with the avant-garde culture of the modern city rather than with the folk culture of the backlands.

The outstanding writer of the group which founded *Martín Fierro* in Buenos Aires was Jorge Luis Borges (b. 1899), a young man who had returned to his native city in 1921 after a long stay in Europe.* While in Spain, he had contributed to avant-garde periodicals there; on his return, he found his own country back-

---

* *Martín Fierro* was only one – although the most significant – of the avant-garde magazines in which Borges collaborated. Others were *Prisma* and *Proa*.

ward and arid in the literary field, and quite ignorant of contemporary trends. The foundation of *Martín Fierro* provided an instrument through which the Argentine public could be educated in the new European writing: a role that was to be taken up in the thirties by the periodical *Sur* (South). But *Martín Fierro* had another role. Its writers made fun of the older generation, and satirized the establishment mercilessly, as if determined to shatter forever the old image of Argentina. And this, in fact, was their intention. For them, a big modern city like Buenos Aires should take its place in the literary avant-garde; its writers should proclaim their modernity and identify themselves with the new and create new values.[41]

Indeed, Buenos Aires became something of a cult in the twenties, as if its writers wished consciously to put it on the map among the other great capitals of the world. Some of Jorge Luis Borges's early poems, included in the collection *Fervor de Buenos Aires* (1923), convey this spirit in a rather self-conscious manner. In his poem, 'Arrabal' (Suburb), for instance, the poet feels 'the houses imprisoned in blocks/different and the same'. He watches the 'bill post of the West/in its daily failure' and concludes:

> I felt Buenos Aires:
> this city that I thought my past
> is my future, my present;
> the years I lived in Europe are illusory,
> I have always been (and will be) in Buenos Aires.[42]

Despite the transient nature of *Martín Fierro*, many of Borges's later attitudes on Argentinian language and tradition stem logically from the cosmopolitan and eclectic outlook of this review. Two of his later essays, for instance, with a direct bearing on cultural nationalism – *El idioma de los argentinos* (1928) and *El escritor argentino y la tradición* (1957)* – both identify Argentine culture with Western culture as a whole and not with a narrow local or regional culture. In the first of these two essays, Borges defends a generally intelligible Spanish against the degeneration of the language produced in Buenos Aires as a result of the influx of foreign immigrants. In the second essay, in defining Argentinian tradition, he roundly declares: 'I believe that our tradition

* Included in the second edition of *Discusión*.

is all Western culture.'[43] Borges thus realizes the absurdity of basing any concept of Argentine nationalism on a non-European tradition. Such a tradition was non-existent, for whatever culture Argentina had was an eclectic one. Hence, his affirmation: 'I believe that we Argentinians, and South Americans in general, can deal with all European themes, without having blind faith in them and with an irreverence which may have, and already has had, fortunate consequences.'[44] Both the irreverence and the eclecticism which Borges claims as part of the Argentine tradition were first championed by the *Martín Fierro* review, from which we may therefore trace the emergence of a new spirit, one which looked forward to a sophisticated urban society and not to a rural past.

In Brazil, the avant-garde movement known as Modernismo (which has no connexion with Spanish-American Modernism)* reflected the new nationalism of the sophisticated urbanite. The movement stemmed from the 'Semana de Arte Moderna', a cultural gathering in São Paulo in 1922 in which artists and writers of the younger generation manifested their desire for an entirely new and unconventional approach to art. The movement had the support of Graça Aranha, a writer of the older generation recently returned from Europe, who lent his voice to the attack on the old order. The year marked by this artistic revolution was also one of political revolution, for in 1922 there occurred the rising of a group of idealistic army officers in the Copacabana barracks. This rising failed, but out of it arose the 'Lieutenants' Party' and, with it, the widespread expectation that a new social order was on the way. Hence, 1922 was a year of national ferment at all levels. Little wonder that the critic, Wilson Martins, maintains that it marked the beginning of the Brazilian twentieth century. He goes on to observe:

The twenty years of Brazilian life which stretch between 1920 and 1940 are years of political nationalism, of revolution inspired by ideas of social reform, and of a frantic investigation of Brazilian reality. Modernismo was very largely a response to these preoccupations while at the same time it helped to stimulate them.[45]

*See note, p. 25.

Although the 'Modern Art Week' is generally taken to signal the beginning of Modernismo in Brazil, the ground had been well prepared.

From the year 1912, when Oswald de Andrade (1890–1954) – a young poet and critic – returned from Europe, there was a gradual build-up, particularly in São Paulo, of the elements that were to explode into Brazilian Modernismo. Oswald de Andrade's first task was to publicize the work of the European avant-garde, and to urge that Brazilian artists should develop their own styles and stop copying those from abroad. Shortly afterwards, writers and painters of a new type began to emerge. Among the painters of the São Paulo school, the initiators of new trends were the Latvian-born Lasar Segal (1891–1957) and Anita Malfatti (b. 1896) who had studied in Europe and North America. Anita Malfatti held two exhibitions showing works that reflected the most advanced trends in contemporary paintings and which caused a furore. Two talented poets emerged: Mário de Andrade (1893–1945), whose *Há uma Gôta de Sangue em cada Poema* (In Each Poem a Drop of Blood) appeared under a pseudonym in 1917; and Manuel Bandeira (b. 1886) whose *A Cinza das Horas* (The Cinder of the Hours) also appeared in 1917. The same year saw the publication of *Juca Mulato* (Juca, the Mulatto), a poem by Paulo Menotti del Picchia (b. 1892) which dealt with the love of a young Mulatto for the daughter of his master, but also expressed love of his native land. Also before 1922, there appeared many of the avant-garde São Paulo poems of Mário de Andrade, later published under the title *Paulicea Desvairada* (1922).

These symptoms of literary change were accompanied by a feeling of intense nationalistic awareness, which extended to writers and journalists who were not directly connected with the São Paulo movement.[46] This feeling, like the nationalism of the Buenos Aires avant-garde, was stimulated by the belief that their countries would soon be in the vanguard of civilization. As one critic stated: 'America will inevitably take on leadership of the universe. Civilization shifts according to inevitable sociological laws; Brazil must, from now on, prepare herself so that her mission in this near future will not be a secondary one.'[47]

How was Brazil to prepare? For the São Paulo Modernistas, cultural leadership could be seized only by those who were in the avant-garde, those who had, in their art, comprehended or interpreted the modern world. Since the modern world was a world of the city and the machine, the Italian Futurists – who had preached the beauty of the machine and the technological era – were eagerly read and imitated by the Modernistas, for whom the word 'Future' had special magic and promise. Oswald de Andrade, for instance, declared:

> The São Paulo question is a Futurist question. Never was any human conglomeration so irrevocably bound to Futurism of action, industry, history and art as São Paulo. What are we, inevitably and unavoidably, if not Futurists – this people of a thousand origins, carried here with their failures and hopes in a thousand ships?[48]

Hence, the Modernistas refused to look to the past, which they associated with rural backwardness, with old-fashioned conventions and academicism, and with the servile imitation of European models. The past was to be ruthlessly destroyed, and many of the first literary productions of the movement parody or satirize the old values. Characteristic of this spirit is *Memórias Sentimentais de João Miramar* (1924) by Oswald de Andrade: a novel written in a cinematographic technique which the author employs to present a kaleidoscope of São Paulo. There are glimpses of café life, snatches of conversation, parodies of official speeches and of newspaper reports and obituaries.

This tendency to parody was common to most of the Modernista writers, for it represented a destructive attack on the old that must be done away with so that a new creative literature could arise. We find the critic Ronald de Carvalho (1893–1935) asserting the importance of avoiding all preconceived ideas so that the writer can be really free to see the 'great virgin world, full of exciting promise', which is around him.

> To organize this material, to give it form, to reduce it to its true human expression, should be [the writer's] basic preoccupation. A direct, pure art, deeply rooted in the national structure, an art which fixes all the tumult of a people in gestation – this is what the modern Brazilian should attempt.[49]

Meanwhile, the poets Mário de Andrade, Manuel Bandeira and Carlos Drummond de Andrade (b. 1902) were launching their attack on conventional verse-forms. In his 'Poética' Manuel Bandeira declared himself in favour of:

> All words and especially universal barbarisms,
> All constructions, especially the exceptions to the rule,
> All rhythms, especially those which cannot be measured.[50]

Similarly, in one chapter of his novel *Mucanaíma* (1928), Mário de Andrade parodied the type of Brazilian who insisted on writing 'correct Portuguese'. As the author explains:

> Now the occasion was propitious for satirizing our columnists and the present urban, intellectual, political and psychological state of São Paulo. ... I did all that in a pretentious style, satirizing our Portuguese, and surreptitiously pleading for the clear, natural, simple language [that I had used] in the other chapters.[51]

Though the Modernistas attacked the establishment, they were no less critical of a type of literature which had identified Brazilian reality with the lazy and backward peasants of the interior. The following attack by a young Modernista critic is probably partly directed against the writer José Benito Monteiro Lobato (1882–1948) who created in Jeca Tatu a 'national type', but one in whose lazy carefree attitudes many people saw only a caricature.

> It will be marvellous for the foreigner who, to his great delight, will see a Brazil according to his own wishes and liking ... a Brazil of savage cannibals, of the Aimoré Indians – all feathers and human teeth; the Brazil of the miserable Mestizo, inept and indifferent to everything – to the state of his people and the integrity of his country.[52]

And Oswald de Andrade warned against sentimental attitudes towards backward elements in society; it was São Paulo's new art, industry and commerce which were really representative of the future.

At the same time, the primitivism fashionable in contemporary Europe was not entirely absent from Brazilian Modernismo. Many of the paintings shown in the 'Semana de Arte Moderna' were fauviste in inspiration, and both *Macunaíma*, by Mário de Andrade, and *Cobra Norato* (1931), by Raul Bopp (b. 1898), are set in the Amazon. However, though 'primitive', *Macunaíma* is not regional; the hero, though an Amazonian 'king', has none of the characteristics of a particular region. He is described as a man 'without a character'. The author shows no respect for correct geographical details and even the language is an attempt at creating a composite Brazilian which is not tied to any one regional dialect. Hence the nationalism of the Modernistas was very much associated with a vision of an integrated and modern Brazil whose distinctive form of civilization and culture would not be a mere regional folk-culture.

BRAZILIAN REGIONALISM

Mucanaíma appeared in 1928, a year which also saw the publication of a new type of regional novel, *A Bagaceira* (Cane Trash) by José Américo de Almeida (b. 1887). *Mucanaíma* had been de-regionalized; *A Bagaceira* was firmly rooted in the distinctive way of life of north-eastern Brazil. The former was a product of a São Paulo literary movement, the latter sprang from a regionalist movement which started in Recife and owed much of its impetus to the work of Gilberto Freyre (b. 1900), a young scholar who, in 1923, had returned from studying in Europe and the United States. Freyre's years of study abroad had given him the conviction that Brazil's future lay not in centralization but in healthy, distinctive regional cultures. In 1926, a Regionalist Congress was held in Recife to which writers, scientists and foreign delegates came. To these Freyre addressed a 'Regionalist Manifesto', in which he emphasized that his view of regionalism did not imply separatism or localism. He appealed to his country to create 'a new flexible system in which the regions . . . are complemented and integrated actively and creatively in a true national organization'.[53]

The aim of the Congress was the rehabilitation of the traditions and values of north-eastern Brazil, a vast area in which had grown up several distinctive forms of society, including that of the fierce, independent cattlemen inhabiting the *sertão* (or drought-ridden backlands) and the 'big house' society of the sugar plantations with their colonies of Negro workers. In the north-east, there had been a fusion of many races, many religions, many cultures. Freyre called for an active defence of a regional culture – which he interpreted widely, to include not only art and architecture but also cooking – before it disappeared beneath a wave of bad cosmopolitanism and false modernism. One of Gilberto Freyre's friends was a young man who became one of Brazil's most talented novelists: José Lins do Rêgo (1901–57). Both he and Freyre were critical of São Paulo Modernismo, primarily because of the way the Modernistas tried to sweep away all that had gone before. This, according to José Lins do Rêgo, was a cardinal error: 'There was a land, a people, there was a whole typical Brazil, in the North-East, in Rio Grande do Sul, in São Paulo and Minas Gerais. Why pull up roots which were so well planted into the earth and why despise our native feelings and values?'[54] Lins do Rêgo did not believe that being a regionalist implied a cultural impoverishment. On the contrary, to be rooted in one's native soil was to be at the deepest source of humanity:

We might call this regionalism organic, profoundly human. To be of one's region, of one's piece of earth, is to be more of a person, a living creature more bound to reality. To be at home is to be entirely human. For this reason, the regionalism of the Recife Congress deserved to be spread throughout Brazil because it was essentially a consciousness of, and a stimulus to, Brazilian character and human personality. With such regionalism as this, we can strengthen Brazilian unity even more. Because by cultivating what is most personal and unique in each person, we give more life to the political group, forming a nation which will not be a uniform and colourless mass.[55]

The regionalist movement of the north-east helped to give birth to a great literary revival, particularly in the novel.[56] From the publication of *A Bagaceira* in 1928 until the 1950s, the stream of novels of north-eastern life continued to flow. Four great names dominated the Brazilian scene during this period: Graciliano Ramos (1892–1953), Rachel de Queirós (b. 1910), Jorge Amado (b. 1912), and Lins do Rêgo.

Although the novelists of the north-east are often classed together, there are significant differences among them. The novels of Rachel de Queirós, for instance, deal not only with north-eastern themes but also with the position of Brazilian women.

Those of Jorge Amado are interpretations of the society and history of the north-east in terms of the class struggle. Graciliano Ramos's novels attempt a psychological study of certain of the region's types, while Américo de Almeida and José Lins do Rêgo are nearer in spirit to Gilberto Freyre's regionalism. But, whether the emphasis is on social protest or on the chronicling of life, the achievement of the north-eastern novel is the illumination of every aspect of life in the region. The sugar cane plantations are described by Lins do Rêgo and Américo de Almeida; the life of the cattlemen of the *sertão* and their constant fight against drought are the subject of Almeida's *A Bagaceira*, of Rachel de Queirós's *O Quinze* (The Year Fifteen, 1930) and of Graciliano Ramos's *Vidas Sêcas* (Parched Lives, 1938). Jorge Amado describes life among the cocoa planters, and novels by him and by Lins do Rego portray the lives and characters of the fishermen of the region. Even town life is not forgotten; in Lins do Rêgo's *O Moleque Ricardo* (The Kid Ricardo, 1935), the protagonist works in a bakery in the city of Recife.

After the 1930s, no one could pretend that São Paulo and Rio de Janeiro were the essence of Brazil. The north-east had asserted its separate existence, had called attention to its special problems and its unique way of life. Not only was every aspect of life in the region illuminated by these novels, but also every human type therein: types like the boy protagonist of Lins do Rêgo's *Menino de Engenho* (Plantation Lad, 1932), the Negro plantation workers, the hardy, independent men of the backlands and their women-folk, the landowning political bosses who controlled the country-side – not to mention prostitutes and criminals. Other aspects of these novels, notably their social protest and their concern with the struggle of man against nature, are dealt with in later chapters. The two authors who best reflect the aspect now under consideration – the regionalist approach to Brazil's national problem – are José Américo de Almeida and Lins do Rêgo.

Américo de Almeida was a Liberal politician, a supporter of the idealistic 'Lieutenants' Party' that emerged after the Copacabana defeat, and later leader of the Liberal opposition against Getúlio Vargas. The action of his novel *A Bagaceira* is set on a sugar plantation which gives shelter to some *sertanejos* who are fleeing from drought. The plantation owner, Dagoberto, represents the landowner of the old type: domineering, narrow and lascivious. His son Lúcio represents the more human and enlightened attitude of the educated younger generation. The conflict between the generations is exacerbated by the rivalry of father and son over the beautiful daughter of one of the refugees. But, as well as a clash between the generations, there is also a clash between the two north-easts: between the men of the cattle lands and the plantation workers. The novel reveals the complexity of Brazil's problems, its inner conflicts and disunity, and the insuperable hazard of natural disasters. Although Lúcio inherits the plantation and initiates reforms, the deep-seated problems of drought in the *sertão* and the problem of rivalry between the inhabitants of the cattle lands and those of the plantations continue unresolved at the end of the novel.

One of the greatest Brazilian works of this century is undoubtedly Lins do Rêgo's *Ciclo da Cana de Açucar* (Sugar Cane Cycle) a series of novels which he began in 1932 with the publication of *Menino de Engenho*, the story of the childhood of Carlos, a planter's grandson, his relations with the slaves and with the other landowning families of the region. *Doidinho* (Little Fool, 1933) relates the boy's schooldays, and *Bangüê* (1934) shows the plantation in decline; the vigorous old grandfather lies dying, and the young Carlos – now a writer and intellectual – is unable to assume responsibility and continue the grandfather's tradition. *O Moleque Ricardo* follows the adventures of a black boy, Ricardo, who leaves the plantation to go and work in Recife. Here he becomes involved in a strike and is deported as a prisoner to a penal colony. *Usina* (Factory, 1936) marks the virtual end of the plantation. The new owner, an uncle of Carlos, has taken over; he makes money and becomes too ambitious. He starts a factory on the estate but is unable to stand up to the big monopolies. The factory fails, and he and his family are reduced to beggary.

Lins do Rêgo's cycle of novels fulfilled his own demand for a literature which would be deeply rooted in a region and yet say something significant on the universal and the national plane. The history of sugar cane was a vital part of Brazilian history.

Through his own personal experience and his childhood spent on the plantation, he was able to give artistic expression to a significant national theme.

AMERICA AS THE AVANT-GARDE

Except for the attitude of writers, like Lugones, whose nationalism was backward looking, all forms of cultural nationalism – from the Mexican muralists to the Brazilian avant-garde – had the common aim of wresting the lead from Europe. In the 1920s change seemed very near. Mexico found itself on the road to a complete social transformation, and other countries seemed about to follow the Mexican lead. Yet this lead could not be taken so long as Latin-American countries were in a state of political or economic subservience to external powers and interests. 'Liberty' and 'anti-imperialism' were the slogans of the age – and by liberty people meant economic and political, as well as literary and artistic, liberty. Literature and art took on a prophetic tone, pointing to a new age; art became a banner for the slogans of the future.

And these slogans were no longer carried by lonely outcasts. Slowly, artists and writers were conquering a public – often a small public, it is true, but there had begun to exist groups of people who wanted to read about their own countries and to buy national paintings. European recognition of musicians, like Heitor Vila-Lôbos (Brazil, 1887–1959), whose music was inspired by national themes, and North American recognition of the Mexican muralists undoubtedly gave some initial stimulus, but the interest was already there. Novels began to appear in more than one edition and to be printed in Latin America rather than abroad. Though writers, artists and musicians continued to flock to Paris, they also returned to their own countries to make their reputation at home. Europe could still teach them techniques, but they began to realize that it could no longer offer them values, for Europe itself was casting about wildly in an effort to find artistic stimulus in other cultures. For the first time, the Latin-American artist found that he had on his doorstep something that fascinated Europe: the Indian, the Negro and the Land.

4

Back to the Roots:
2. The Indian, the Negro, the Land

After the 1914–18 war, the Spanish-American intellectuals began to seek in the cultures of the Indian and the Negro, and in the land itself, alternative values to those of a European culture which seemed on the verge of disintegration. This attempt to find roots in native culture was related to the rejection not only of European cultural values but also of the rational, intellectual and scientific assumptions on which modern European civilization was based.

In Europe, the 1920s had seen an increasing awareness of the irrational forces in human nature, a recognition of unconscious motivations that were now acknowledged as being more powerful, and perhaps more basic, than conscious behaviour. Much nineteenth-century art had been preoccupied with an exploration of the darker, unconscious aspect of human existence; in the twentieth century, this exploration turned into an assault on reason. The world of logic, of concepts, came under attack because rational structures seemed to ignore the fundamental and unconscious aspects of experience. Reason, in categorizing experience, fragmented it. Similarly, conventional language structures and literary and artistic forms placed a false order on the world of experience, ignoring such factors as constantly changing relationships, the relativity of points of view, the factor of time, or the shifting perspectives of reader or onlooker towards the work of art.

From 1907 onwards, the spearhead of the attack was the Cubist movement, which revolutionized painting. The painter was now able to break away from representational limitations and could transfer to canvas the vast complexity of the human figure and the landscape, exploring in the process a whole range of relationships between the observer and reality. 'An art of dynamic liberation from all static categories', the movement has been called. But beneath the complexity there was an underlying similarity of phenomena: the cubes and geometric shapes out of which the picture was composed. The Cubists were thus at once able to suggest the complexity of reality and the basic similarity and interconnexion of all phenomena. Cubism was important in two other respects. It drew attention to the fragmented nature of urban life and its domination by the geometric shapes of man-made objects. Secondly, it aroused an interest in non-European artistic conventions, especially those of Negro art. The pioneer movement of the Cubists was followed by a number of avant-garde 'isms' – Dadaism and Surrealism in France and parallel movements elsewhere – all of which had in common an anti-rational, anti-intellectual attitude. These were also associated with the cult of the primitive: the 'backward' peoples of Africa had expressed, not repressed, their instincts, and were therefore deemed to be 'healthier' than the decadent European who had lost all spontaneous feeling. It was this exaltation of instinct which drew the attention of the Peruvian poet, César Vallejo; he commented on the success of the African ballet company in Paris: 'The seven Catholic brakes on our civilization are not enough to check the mysterious anguish of the animal who turns his back on man. Dance of the jungle, in the face of whose almost purely zoological crudity there is no possible criticism.'[1]

The extent of the anti-rationalism of this period can be gauged by the incredible respect paid to the views of Oswald Spengler, D. H. Lawrence and Count Hermann Keyserling. Spengler's *Decline of the West*, as has been mentioned in chapter 3, made a deep impression on Latin Americans, particularly because of the suggestion that Western civilization, now in its death throes, had been only one among many world civilizations, and perhaps not even the greatest of these. The implications of this theory were that American indigenous cultures might have been the equals or superiors of European culture; and that, further, there was no reason why a new civilization, more advanced than that of Europe, should not develop in the New World. Spengler's theories were speedily absorbed by Latin Americans; he had a direct influence, for instance, on Caribbean writing,[2] and he probably helped to make

Latin Americans feel both an increased respect for the cultures of the past and more confidence in the future. D. H. Lawrence's influence is less easy to determine, but *The Plumed Serpent*, in particular, was symptomatic of a cult of the instinctual, of the 'blood', which was to have its reflection in Latin-American art. In Mexico, Lawrence had discovered 'a mysterious hot-blooded soft-footed humanity with a strange civilization of its own'.

> The Mexicans were still this. That which is aboriginal in America still belongs to the way of the world before the Flood, before the mental-spiritual world came into being. In America, therefore, the mental-spiritual life of white people suddenly flourishes like a great weed let loose in virgin soil. Probably it will as quickly wither. A great death comes. And after that, the living results will be a great germ, a new conception of human life that will arise from the fusion of the old blood-and-vertebrate consciousness with the white man's present mental-spiritual consciousness.[3]

How close this is to Keyserling, who declared that Latin America would create

> a culture of great depth in the sense of nearness to earth. Even that part of South America which is of European blood is not Christian in its deeps. It is determined by primordial life, not by spirit. . . . South America's true life . . . is nought but darkness of the netherworld. No art of life beautifies and adorns its actual facts: no genuine faith of the spirit redeems life from reality. Thus, the original heaviness of earth completely dominates the atmosphere of the continent. South American joy is the voluptuousness of the Night of Creation. Its suffering is abysmal pain. . . . Its death is the simple and unquestioning home-coming of the womb of Earth.[4]

Of these three apostles, Keyserling – whose theories were partly drawn from reading Latin-American novels such as *La vorágine* and *Don Segundo Sombra* – was probably the most directly influential. And though his view of America as a 'pure teluric force' was probably more harmful than helpful, he had a virtue unusual in European visitors to the continent. He declared, on arriving in Argentina, that he had come not to teach but to learn.

In the twenties, everything tended to make the Latin-American artist look for values in his own land and its peoples and often his personal experience reinforced this trend. Many 'Indianist' writers, many who adopted Negro themes in their art, were in Paris at this time; when they returned to their own countries, they brought a totally new outlook on their indigenous culture. Diego Rivera, Miguel Angel Asturias, Rómulo Gallegos, Ricardo Güiraldes, Jorge Luis Borges, José Carlos Mariátegui – all spent periods in Paris before embarking on their major work. And it was in Paris that one of the poets of the Afro-Cuban movement, Alejo Carpentier (Cuba, b. 1904), presented his *Passion noire*, and that Heitor Vila-Lôbos had his works on Brazilian themes performed. There is thus a clear connexion between the European avant-garde and the Latin-American intellectual's return to his native roots.

THE INDIAN

Of all the writers of the time, probably José Carlos Mariátegui realized more clearly than any other the connexion between Indianism and the European fashion for exotic art. In one of his *Siete ensayos* (1928), he associated Indianism in Latin-American literature with the European cult of the exotic, which he declared was a sign of decadence. However, he was far from condemning Latin-American Indianism merely because it had received its first impetus from a declining Europe. He believed that, in Peru, the movement was a healthy one for it meant that, at last, novelists and short-story writers were undertaking the rein-statement of the Indian. At the same time, he was the first to point out that an Indianist literature written by Whites or Mestizos could hardly be authentic. A true literature of the Indian could come only from the Indians themselves.[5]

Indianist literature in Latin America was to have two distinct functions. One was to fulfil a direct social purpose by arousing a general awareness of the plight of submerged sections of the population. The other – and this is the one with which this chapter is concerned – was to set up the values of Indian culture and civilization as an alternative to European values.

For obvious reasons, it was in Mexico that this cult of Indian values went furthest. The revolution not only changed people's attitudes to the Indian: it also accorded to him a prominent place in the new revolutionary mythology. The Indian represented the national, the patently non-foreign. Uncorrupted by imperialist pretensions, he was a symbol of suffering and purity. So much is obvious from Diego Rivera's Chapingo, Cuernavaca, National Palace and Ministry of Education murals.★

It is quite clear that, particularly in the early stages of Mexican muralism, the adoption of so-called pre-Columban techniques, the imitation of their spatial and perspective conventions, was mainly a gesture of defiance against Europe. The symbolic act of Gerardo Murillo, who changed his Spanish to an Aztec name, Dr Atl, could not be more revealing. But later on, there was a conscious attempt to revive certain mythological or historical figures, such as Cuauhtémoc, and invest them with significance for the modern Mexican. Cuauhtémoc, who was hanged by Cortés, became the new Mexican Christ-figure: a Mexico trampled on by the European. The muralists were undoubtedly at the forefront of this myth creation, which has been only partly successful. After all, the painters themselves had no living experience of Indian belief or tradition, and their revival of pre-Columban myths and symbols was largely an archaistic movement in which these symbols were divorced from their social and religious structure and used as decorative motifs. An example of the meaningless use of symbols is the library building of the National University. The University was constructed in the 1940s, but the decoration was entrusted to a generation of artists – Siqueiros, Juan O'Gorman, Diego Rivera – who had formed the backbone of the muralist movement. The library building, executed by O'Gorman in a mosaic of native stone, is covered with stylistic symbols of Mexican culture: a hotch-potch of figures and symbols. In front of the library is a pool backed by a bas-relief showing two serpents. The effect of the stone is pleasant, but the serpent motif is an archaism: neither for the sculptor nor for the students at the University could the symbol have any meaning, for there is no living tradition to connect the serpent with the modern Mexican. This backward-

★e.g. 'Before the Conquest' (on the right wall of the stairway in the National Palace) and 'Betrayal of Cuernavaca' at Cuernavaca.

looking and rather narrow concept of what a genuine Mexican art should be has been condemned by a younger generation of artists who, according to one of them (José Luis Cuevas), are looking for 'broad highways leading out to the rest of the world rather than narrow trails connecting one adobe village with another'.

Yet despite the tendency to restrict Mexican culture to an Indian heritage, and despite the archaizing tendency, Indianism in Mexico has produced some fruitful results in the field of scholarship. A vast impetus was given to archaeological and anthropological research, to the restoration of archaeological sites. Scholars began to study pre-Columban languages. A literature in *náhuatl* was rediscovered,* and texts (such as the prophetic book, *Chilam Balam*,[6] and the Maya 'Bible', *Popul Vuh*) were reissued in Spanish translations. The results of these investigations have been far-reaching. The oversimplified picture of the Indian and of Indian culture has been gradually replaced by a picture of vast complexity. As new sites are uncovered, pre-Columban civilizations have been found to be more varied, to go back further in time, and to be more complex than had hitherto been believed; while a great understanding of the religious and social structures of pre-Columban societies has enabled scholars to put Indian art and literature into a total social pattern.

For many reasons, the Indianism of Mexican muralists was not translated into literature. As was pointed out in chapter 3, the painters were the iconographers of the revolution, employed by the government and with a mission to communicate directly with the illiterate Indians, whereas the writers had no such immediate public and no mission to fulfil except their own. The nearest that Mexican writers come to an idealization of the Indian is in their reconstruction of the historical past. Francisco Monterde (b. 1894), for instance, writes of the period of the Conquest in *Moctezuma, el de la silla de oro* (Moctezuma, He of the Golden Throne, 1945) and *Moctezuma II, señor de Anáhuac*

Náhuatl was the language of Náhua, a pre-Aztec culture whose literature survived into Aztec times. Some of this was recorded in post-Conquest records. See Irene Nicholson, *Firefly in the Night*.

(Moctezuma II, Lord of Anahuac, 1947). Ermilio Abreu Gómez (b. 1894) in *Quetzalcóatl, sueño y vigilia* (Quetzalcoatl, the Dream and the Awakening, 1947) relates stories of pre-Columban gods and heroes.

But the Indian of the present is a different matter. Even as hero of a social protest novel, he has seldom been depicted in ideal terms by Mexican writers. Both *El indio* (The Indian, 1935) by Gregorio López y Fuentes (b. 1897) and *El resplandor* (Sunburst, 1937) by Mauricio Magdaleno (b. 1906) are primarily novels of protest about the way the Indian was treated after the revolution. Both novels clearly illustrate the great gulf between White society and Indian society: a gulf not to be bridged in a single generation. In *El indio*, Gregorio López y Fuentes describes the daily life and customs of a remote Indian village whose inhabitants have always had a well-founded suspicion of the Whites. The White Man has never appeared in the village except to exploit or cheat. The revolution comes, with its promise of land distribution and education, but the mutual distrust is still there. At the end of the novel, the village hunchback watches the road along which he expects the 'civilized' men to approach and attack the village. Nothing has changed. The Indians are still outsiders, and the 'leaders' who had promised to help them are still cheats and exploiters. In *El resplandor*, Mauricio Magdaleno tells the story of Saturnino Herrera, an Indian from a village who becomes a post-revolutionary leader, only to exploit the villagers in his turn.

Along with the social protest Indian novel, there is also a type of Mexican novel which documents Indian life and customs, often with great detail and accuracy. Gregorio López y Fuentes's *El indio* includes extensive descriptions of feast days and marriage ceremonies. Ramón Rubín (b. 1912) is the author of a series of novels documenting Indian life, of which *El callado dolor de los tzotziles* (The Silent Grief of the Tzotziles, 1949) is the best. *El diosero* (The God-Maker, 1952) by Francisco Rojas González (1903–51), a short-story writer, includes a number of tales that show first-hand knowledge of Indian religious beliefs and attitudes. The most valuable of this document-type literature is the novel *Juan Pérez Jolote* (1952), in which Ricardo

Pozas (b. 1910), a trained anthropologist, describes life in a Chamula community over the period of a generation. Through the adventures of a central character, he shows us the social transformation that occurs in the community with increased contact with the outside world, and the modifications which this brings to the Indian way of life. The documentary type of writing about the Indian helped to show that the concept of the 'primitive' Indian was quite inadequate. Indian attitudes were complex; their rites and beliefs were closely connected with the rhythm of nature: a nature which they had come to understand better, perhaps, than the White Man. The publication of the prophetic *Book of Chilam Balam* made writers aware that the Indian attitude to land exploitation was totally different from that of the European, that they regarded all natural things – plants and animals – as sacred and would not wilfully destroy them. Thus, in some ways, Indian attitudes could really be considered superior to those of the destructive and perverse European.

This contrast of attitudes has been brought out by a woman novelist, Rosario Castellanos, born in 1925 in Chiapas, a region inhabited very largely by Maya-descended Indians. Unlike many previous novelists of Indian life, Rosario Castellanos was brought up by an Indian nurse and therefore from childhood she absorbed the legends and beliefs of these people. In *Balún Canán* (1957) she adopts the expedient of presenting a conflict between Indian and White partly through the eyes of a White child who has a special sympathy for her Indian nurse. In this way, Rosario Castellanos gives us a sharp insight into the clash between two utterly opposing cultures: one which regards the land as sacred and one which regards it as an object to be exploited. The novel is set during the presidency of Lázaro Cárdenas (1934–40), whose announcement that land will be confiscated from the large landowners for redistribution causes the Indians on a Chiapas estate to become restless and rebellious. The course of their development, from timid serfs to men and women aware of their rights and able to fight for them, is traced in the novel, which culminates in the destruction of the sugar mill – symbol of the White Man's exploitation. The clash, however, is more fundamental than a fight between exploiter and exploited. The novelist suggests that, although the White Man exploits his land, he is not a part of it. Once he leaves, his influence disappears, as if he had never lived there. No mark of his presence remains. This is not so with the Indians who, even in their defeat, profoundly influence the White inhabitants. Their legends, their beliefs, their presence in the land, are indestructible because they are truly a part of it. Their beliefs spring from the nature of the land itself and therefore cannot be destroyed, as can the influence of Christianity. Indian 'superstitions' even invade the White Man's consciousness and prove stronger than his European religion because they are more intimately a part of the land. Rosario Castellanos thus suggests that Indian values are the natural values for their environment, and therefore more permanent and more effective.

A similar picture of the Indian had already been given by the Guatemalan novelist, Miguel Angel Asturias (b. 1899). Like Rosario Castellanos, Asturias writes with an intimate knowledge of the Central-American descendants of the Mayas. He studied Maya religion and society at the Musée de l'Homme in Paris and also helped to translate the Maya sacred book, the *Popul Vuh*. His first creative work, *Leyendas de Guatemala* (Guatemalan Legends, 1930) is a poetic transcription of the stories – both of Indian and Spanish origin – which he had heard as a child. His *Hombres de maíz* (Men of Maize, 1949) represents the most ambitious attempt so far made by a Spanish-American writer to penetrate the mind of the Indian and write a novel informed by Indian psychology.[7] *Hombres de maíz* covers a long period of history in which the Indian lands are confiscated and converted into estates on which maize is grown for profit. This does violence to the Indian's deepest attitudes to the land, which for him is sacred and should be made to yield only enough for immediate needs. Asturias shows that the Indian does not feel himself separate from nature or the land which the bones of his dead help to feed, in which his own umbilical cord was buried at birth. Trees and plants – even fire and the elements – are not objects but sacred manifestations of life, like man himself. Hence the Indian burns only as much of the virgin bush as is necessary to plant enough corn for his needs. Asturias's novel describes the coming of the White Man, the expulsion of the Indian, the burning of the land and the slow degeneration of the surviving Indians after contact with commercialized White civilization. The plot is presented, not as an orthodox novel, but as the Indian would experience reality: in terms of myth. The early myths in the book are heroic, relating the struggle between Indian and White; then comes the myth of the blind Indian whose wife runs away, symbolizing the feeling of separation and loss when the Indian has been deprived of his land. There is a myth of a postman who turns into a coyote, which symbolizes the Indians' rejection of White government and civilization. At the end of the novel, there are no longer any myths, for the Indians have been reduced to the state of ants in a commercialized world in which their identity has been forever lost.

Hombres de maíz thus enters deeply into Indian attitudes, as this extract from the opening paragraph illustrates.

Gaspar Ilóm is letting them rob the sleep from the eyes of the land of Ilóm . . .

Gaspar Ilóm moved his head from side to side. He wanted to crush the accusation of the earth on which he was sleeping along with his mat, his shadow and his wife, and in which he was buried with his dead and his umbilical cord; from this snake of six hundred thousand circles of mud, moon, woods, rainstorms, birds and echoes which he felt around his body, he was unable to free himself.

At the same time, remarkable as it is in its penetrating insight into the Indian mind, the novel does illustrate the paradox of the Indianist writer, for it presents tremendous difficulties to the reader whose knowledge of Guatemalan Indian psychology is non-existent. On the other hand, the novel cannot communicate to the Indian himself, since most Indians are illiterate. Even if the Indian were to learn to read, he would then almost certainly adopt European ways of thought and would no longer look at experience through the eyes of Gaspar Ilóm.

Writers of the Andean republics face exactly the same problem as

Mexicans and Central Americans when writing about the Indian. Here, too, Indianist novels are either of the social-protest type – such as those of Jorge Icaza (Ecuador, b. 1906) and Adolfo Costa du Rels (Bolivia, b. 1891) – or they attempt to exalt Indian values.[8]

In Bolivia, an Indianist novelist, Jaime Mendoza (1874–1939) was also the author of *La tesis andina* (The Andean Thesis, 1920) and of *El macizo boliviano* (The Bolivian Massif, 1935) in which he developed the argument, first put forward by Arguedas, that the territory had an effect on the character of the inhabitants, on the creation of their aesthetic attitudes.

However, it was in Peru that the Indianist novel developed along the most original lines. Already in the twenties, López Albújar in his series of stories, *Cuentos andinos* (1920), had depicted a militant and defiant Indian, not the submissive and exploited slave of many social protest novels. A later story, 'Hayna-Pishtanag',* describes an Indian couple of great dignity and pride who defy to the death a bestial major-domo's attempt to seduce the wife. López Albújar was, however, mainly concerned with restoring a sense of dignity to the Indian. It is in the novels of Ciro Alegría (1909–67) and José María Arguedas (1911–69) that the most ambitious attempts have been made so far to penetrate the mind of the Peruvian Indian.

The three main works of Ciro Alegría are: *La serpiente de oro* (The Golden Serpent, 1935), a novel about a community on the river Marañón; *Los perros hambrientos* (Hungry Dogs, 1939), which deals with the fight of an Andean Indian community against hunger; and *El mundo es ancho y ajeno* (Broad and Alien is the World, 1941), wherein he describes an Indian community's defiance of a landowner who seeks to encroach on their land. Already in Alegría's first novel, the men who take their rafts down the rapids of the river Marañón are shown as being in tune with nature.

If we die, what does it matter? We were born here and feel in our veins the violent magnificent pulse of the earth. In the forest, the wind sings a hymn to fruitful existence.[9]

*Included in *Nuevos cuentos andinos* (1937).

El mundo es ancho y ajeno is a political novel, illustrating the thesis that the Indian *ayllu*, or commune, can form the basis for a Socialist community. Rosendo Maquí, head of an Indian village, is versed in all the traditional lore. So long as the Indians live in isolation, his wisdom serves to guide the community and to make it prosper; but when the clash comes with the unscrupulous *ladino* * landowner, Alvaro – who can use all the forces of the police state and the twentieth-century legal system to confiscate the Indians' land – Rosendo's wisdom is inadequate. He is taken prisoner on a trumped-up charge and beaten to death. The community is left leaderless. At this point, a new man arrives: Benito, a Mestizo, a man who was born in the commune but who has since spent most of his life in the outside world, where he has learned about Socialism and become a militant. He returns to the commune in order to reorganize it on Socialist lines. His effort fails because the time is not ripe, and government troops are able to crush the nascent Socialist community. Alegría does not attempt to enter into Indian psychology in the way that Miguel Angel Asturias does. The Indian is always seen through the novelist's eyes, and his beliefs are explained rather than transmitted directly through the language and the narrative. Throughout *El mundo . . .*, Alegría seems to demonstrate that the Indians' communal form of living is in many ways superior to the brutal and greedy behaviour of the private landowner. The message is that, potentially, the Indians are the best part of Peru, but they have to be educated out of their superstitions before they can really make any headway.

José María Arguedas, the greatest Peruvian interpreter of the Indian in the novel, owes his penetration of the Indian mind to the circumstances of his upbringing. He spent much of his child-hood in villages with predominantly Indian populations and where there was only a small ruling minority of priests and government officials. He spoke Quechua before he spoke Spanish, and grew to manhood with a deep sympathy and admiration for the Indian. For Arguedas, the true artistic expression of Peru is to be found in the Indian songs and dances. In the Andean villages, he declares, the great church feasts are

* See note, p. 80.

prepared entirely by Indians, and even the White and Mestizo inhabitants of such places prefer Indian music and dances, which communicate to their deepest sensibility, rather than foreign imported tangos or jazz. 'And this art moves them because it is the most exact expression of their own feelings.'[10]

But while the Mestizo is moved by Indian art, Arguedas argued, he is also ashamed of it. Why this shame? The *wayno* * is art both as music and as poetry.

... The indigenous is not inferior. And the day on which the people of the highlands who still feel ashamed of the Indian discover of their own accord the great creative possibilities of their Indian spirit, on that day, confident of their own values, the Mestizo and Indian peoples will definitely prove the equality of their own creative ability with that of the European art which now displaces and puts it to shame.[11]

The egotism of the landowner, he contends, is to blame for the wall of suspicion that separates Mestizo and Indian, and it is this that prevents the Indian from developing. Only when the Indian is accepted and the value of his culture appreciated can Peru prosper as a nation. And only then can Peru have an art which is at once national and universal.

For Arguedas, then, the development of an original Peruvian art depends on the recognition that the Indian is the truest and most important element in national life. But this recognition also implies a complete transformation of an economic system which relies on prejudice and the myth of the Indian's inferiority to keep it in existence. He also states explicitly that no Peruvian literature, painting or music which does not come out of the artist's deep knowledge of Indian life can ever be successful. Although he hails the increased interest in the Indian on the part of artists and writers, he does not believe that their music, painting or literature could be authentic until the artist has lived on close terms with the people.

When José María Arguedas began to write, he was faced with the problem of language. Quechua seemed to him a patently better instrument for expressing Indian attitudes than Castilian

Wayno: Andean Indian song.

and he tried, in his early collection of stories, *Agua* (Water, 1935), to convey a Quechua flavour while writing in Spanish. He has three novels: *Yawar Fiesta* (1941), which relates the story of the expulsion of Indians from their communal lands, *Los ríos profundos* (The Deep Rivers, 1958), which is closely based on his own childhood experiences, and *Todas las Sangres* (All the Bloods, 1964). In *Los ríos profundos*, he tells the story of a boy who travels the Indian villages with his lawyer father until the father decides to put him into a boarding school run by friars. The harsh, alien discipline of the school, the savagery of the boys and the religious creed which is used to keep the Indians in check alienate the child, whose sympathies and love go entirely to the Indians and their beliefs. Whenever possible, the boy escapes from school. On one such occasion, he finds himself in a procession of rioting Indian women; on another he befriends an Indian harp player whom the soldiers arrest for playing subversive songs. All the deepest experiences of the child are thus associated with the Indians, with the ordinary people from whom he is cut off by inhuman social and religious codes. Arguedas's novel thus shows us the Indian problem in the deepest and most searching manner, revealing that it is not only the Indians who suffer but also the Whites, who become alienated by loss of contact with the real culture of the country.

It is no coincidence that the most outstanding representatives of Indianism in the Latin-American novel have been intimately connected with Indian life, either by upbringing or education. In the writings of José María Arguedas and of Miguel Angel Asturias, we are given a profound insight, not only into another mind and culture, but also into the relation of Latin Americans of European origin to that culture. At its most serious, the Indianist novel suggests that native ways of life and attitudes, evolved by the Indians over thousands of years of living in the American continent, may be a more significant expression of the land than the imported adaptations of Western culture, and that perhaps the White and the Mestizo shut out this knowledge at their peril.

THE NEGRO

The Indian, it could be claimed, had evolved a culture more suited to the environment than the Europeans, who had come to Latin America to impose their own structures. But what of the Negro? He was the most recent arrival of the three races in the Latin-American sub-continent; in the slave societies of which he formed the base, any original culture he possessed must have been destroyed or severely altered. Nevertheless, like the Indian, the Negro has mixed with the conquerors. Negroes and Mulattos form part of the population of Brazil, the Caribbean islands, and the coastal areas of Mexico, Central America, Venezuela, Colombia, Peru and Ecuador.

Although there was an extensive literature on Negro themes in the nineteenth century, it was not until the 1920s that a literature ascribing to the Negro values superior to those of the White made its appearance in Latin America. Two factors account for the new dignity accorded to the hitherto despised Negro. In the first place, in newly independent Cuba, there was a search for national identity in which these previously ignored aspects of Cuban culture began to be investigated and brought to the fore. The first studies of Negro culture came from the Cuban scholar, Fernando Ortiz (1881–1969), who in his *Hampa Afrocubana: los negros brujos* (Afro-Cuban Underworld: Negro Sorcerers, 1906) and his *Hampa Afrocubana: los negros esclavos* (Afro-Cuban Underworld: Negro Slaves, 1916) published his investigations of Negro society,[12] and a woman writer, Lidia Cabrera, published collections of Cuban Negro stories and collected information from members of seret santería lodges. The second factor accounting for the reinstatement of the Negro was the European fashion for Negro art, which the avant-garde introduced into Cuba. This fashion was associated, in part, with the prevalent anti-rationalism. The Negro was a type of man who had not made intellectual progress at the expense of emotional repression and whose art was a spontaneous expression of the instinctual drives that Europeans had forgotten. In one of his poems the Cuban Mulatto poet, Nicolás Guillén (b. 1902), poked fun at the fashion – though he points out that the cult has its advantages as far as the Negro is concerned.

> Es bueno . . .
> y ahora que Europa se desnuda
> para tostar su carne al sol,
> y busca en Harlem y en La Habana
> jazz y son,
> lucirse negro mientras aplaude el bulevar,
> y frente a la envidia de los blancos
> hablar en negro de verdad.[13]

> It's great . . .
> now that Europe is stripping
> to toast itself in the sun
> and finds in Harlem and Havana
> the music of jazz and the 'son',
> you can be proud of being Negro, (while the
>   boulevard applauds),
> and, in the face of the White man's envy,
> you can talk real Negro too.

The fashion for 'talking real Negro' spread throughout Latin America and even to countries with no Negro populations. The avant-garde poets who introduced the fashion were usually White writers who enjoyed playing with these new poetic rhythms, much as Edith Sitwell did in England. In countries with Negro populations, Afro-Hispanic poetry became more than a fashion because poets could draw on popular legends and folk-forms. As with Indianism, rejection of Europe and the assertion of a 'national' type of art were important factors. In Puerto Rico, for instance, the poet Luis Palés Matos (1898–1959), in revolt against Western intellectual tradition, declared that he wanted to create an art that was as little art as possible – an art in which the technical realization would be subordinate to 'the beat of blood and instinct'.[14] In 1937, he published his *Tuntún de pasa y grifería* (the 'nonsense' title is difficult to translate), in which, by the liberal use of African words and place names, he managed to imitate Negro rhythms. Palés Matos's poems are amusing and playful, and evoke a lazy tropical and sensual atmosphere in which the Negro song is an invitation to curl up in the womb and dream.

> Al rumor de su canto
> todo se va extinguiendo,
> y sólo queda en mi alma
> la ú profunda del díptongo fiero,
> en cuya curva maternal se esconde
> la armonía prolífera del sexo.[15]

> At the sound of her song,
> everything slowly dies
> and there remains in my soul
> only the deep U of the savage diphthong
> in whose maternal curve is hidden
> the proliferous harmony of sex.

In Matos's 'Ñam-ñam', Asia dreams its 'nirvana'.

> America dances to jazz
> Europe plays and theorizes
> Africa grunts: Nyam-nyam.[16]

This sensual Negro is the subject of much of the verse written by Afro-Cuban poets.

The movement of Afro-Cubanism began in 1928 with the publication of two poems in rumba-rhythm, one by José Zacarías Tallet (b. 1893) and the other by Ramón Guirao (1908–49). The movement was not confined to poetry: Amadeo Roldán (b. 1900) wrote a Negro ballet, *La Rebambaramba* (1928), and a *Poema negro* (1930) for string quartet, and Alejo Carpentier wrote a *Passion Noire* which, as has been mentioned earlier, was performed in Paris. Two of the outstanding figures of the Afro-Cuban movement, Alejo Carpentier and Emilio Ballagas (1908–54) – both White men – did much to make Negro art respected in Latin America. Ballagas had considerable influence through his anthology of Negro poetry, *Mapa de la poesía negra*, published in 1946. Carpentier, a trained musician as well as a poet, is also a novelist. His *Ecué-Yamba-O* (1933) described the adventures of a Negro boy who, after killing a man, drifts to Havana and joins a *santería* cult. The novel served the dual function of exposing the conditions of the Negroes in the Cuban countryside and towns, and of documenting their customs. Carpentier even included photographs, to give authenticity to his account.

The first examples of Afro-Cuban poetry – the rumba-verse of Tallet, for instance – did little more than exploit the exoticism of African dancing, emphasizing its animal sexuality. They imitated the rhythms of the African dance with some success by the use of onomatopoeia and verbal repetition on the pattern of the voodoo and santería ceremonies, in which repetition of sounds is used to help induce a trance-like state in the initiates. A poem such as Emilio Ballagas's 'Solo de maracas' depends entirely on sonic effects and the words have little, if any, connotative and expressive value:

> Cáscara y chácara,
> Cascára y máscara.
> Máscara y gárgara
> Maraca . . .[17]

But though Afro-Cubanism started by emphasizing external characteristics, some writers soon began to give the Negro a national significance. Juan Marinello (b. 1898), explaining that the indigenism to be found elsewhere in Latin America can have no roots in Cuba where Indians had long disappeared, declares that it is the Negro who can be the source of Cuban culture.

His participation in Cuban life was decisive in the revolution against Spain; his social tragedy, a new slavery, makes him the object of meditation and hope. His physical characteristics, enriched and multiplied in his mixing with the White and the Yellow man, his dances of a subtle and enchanting primitivism, make him the object of the greatest artistic potentialities.[18]

Negro art, Marinello declares in another essay, is something distinctively Cuban. 'Here the Negro is marrow, and root, the breath of the people. . . . He may, in these times of change, be the touchstone of our poetry.'[19]

As with Indianism in Spanish America, the Afro-Cuban poetry movement had the effect of stimulating research into Negro life and art. The *Revista de Estudios Afro-Cubanos* (1937–

41) in particular, devoted its numbers to serious studies of these subjects.

The outstanding poet of the Afro-Cuban movement was a Mulatto, Nicolás Guillén, whose first two volumes of poems – *Motivos de son* (Themes of the 'Son', 1930) and *Sóngoro cosongo* (1931) – used Hispanic and African folk themes and rhythms. Guillén takes us right away from the Afro-Cuban cliché figure of the sensual rumba dancer. He introduces us more directly to the African world and its beliefs, and to the New World Negro with his dialects and attitudes. Some of Guillén's poems evoke a world of African folklore.

> ¡Ñeque que se vaya el ñeque!
> ¡Güije, que se vaya el güije!
>
> Las turbias aguas del río
> son hondas y tienen muertos;
> carapachos de tortuga,
> cabezas de niños negros.
> De noche saca sus brazos
> el río, y rasga el silencio
> con sus uñas, que son uñas
> de cocodrilo frenético.[20]
>
> Ñeque go away ñeque!
> Güije go away Güije!
>
> The dark waters of the river
> are deep and have dead in them –
> turtle shells,
> heads of black children.
> By night the river lifts
> its arms and tears the silence
> with its nails, which are the nails
> of a furious crocodile.

Or, as in 'Sensemayá' (Song for killing a snake), he imitates an African ritual dance and song.

> ¡Mayombe-bombe-mayombé!
> ¡Mayombe-bombe-mayombé!
> ¡Mayombe-bombe-mayombé!

La culebra tiene los ojos de vidrio;
la culebra viene y se enreda en un palo;
con sus ojos de vidrio, en un palo
con sus ojos de vidrio.
La culebra camina sin patas;
la culebra se esconde en la hierba;
¡caminando se esconde en la hierba!
¡Caminando sin patas!

¡Mayombe-bombe-mayombé!
¡Mayombe-bombe-mayombé![21]

¡Mayombe-bombe-mayombé!
¡Mayombe-bombe-mayombé!
¡Mayombe-bombe-mayombé!

The snake has eyes of glass.
The snake comes and curls round a stick
with its eyes of glass, on a stick
with its eyes of glass.
The snake walks without feet,
The snake hides in the grass,
walking it hides in the grass,
walking without feet.

¡Mayombe-bombe-mayombé!
¡Mayombe-bombe-mayombé!

Guillén has many charming witty poems in which the verse is spoken by a Negro or Negress, characters who comment in Cuban slang on their lovers or their friends.

All that English you used to know,
See, Manuel,
All that English, and you can't say
Yeah.[22]

Guillén differs from a poet such as Luis Palés Matos in that his use of African and popular themes has little to do with a rejection of European values. Guillén does not exalt the African at the expense of the European but is concerned with restoring the dignity that the Negro lost with slavery. He seeks to give his fellows a sense of pride, yet at the same time he recognizes that the main struggle is not between White and Negro but between oppressors and oppressed. In Cuba, Negro culture is important, but so is European culture. His poem, 'Balada de los dos abuelos' (Ballad of the Two Grandfathers), shows that he appreciates both the 'white anguish' and the 'black anguish'. For Nicolás Guillén, as for the scholar of Negro culture, Fernando Ortiz, Afro-Cubanism is thus more than a fashion: it is a way of reintegrating the Negro into national life, and the preliminary step towards forging a truly national culture.

Afro-Cubanism aroused great interest throughout the Spanish-American world, and the Negro became the theme of novels and poems. But obviously such a movement could have a significance only in countries where the Negro formed a substantial element, or at least a significant minority, in the life of the nation. In Venezuela there was no need to follow the Cuban example, since the theme of the Negro had already appeared in literature in Rómulo Gallegos's *La trepadora* (1925), discussed in chapter 3. However, it is significant that in Gallegos's other novel on a Negro theme, *Pobre negro* (Poor Negro, 1937), African dances, folk tales and songs are interwoven somewhat in the Afro-Cuban manner, into the tale of the Negro rebel, Pedro Miguel Candelas.

That a literary fashion can eventually give genuine artistic expression to a hitherto silent section of a community is illustrated by the career of the Ecuadorian writer, Adalberto Ortiz (b. 1914). In an introduction to his collection of poems, *El animal herido* (The Wounded Beast, 1959), Ortiz – a Mulatto – relates how he had little interest in literature until he came across Emilio Ballagas's *Antología de la poesía negra hispanoamericana*. 'I was dazzled by the Negro rhythms which, unknown to me, were beating in my own blood. . . . On finding myself, I exclaimed "Anch'io sono poeta".'[23] And in one of his poems Ortiz declares:

> I still remember your fraternal voice saying
> I don't want to be Negro
> I don't want to be White;
> This is my silent cry
> I want to be more Black than White.[24]

Adalberto Ortiz also wrote a novel of Negro life, *Juyungo* (1943), set in the river area dividing Ecuador and Colombia. The novel is a picaresque account of the adventures of a poor Negro who runs away from his home to travel the rivers of his native country. In common with many Indianist novels, *Juyungo* documents the life of a hitherto unknown area, and arouses awareness of the human condition of its inhabitants.

Of all Latin-American countries, it is surely from Brazil that one would expect the most dynamic Negro literature. Yet, perhaps because the country is so rich and varied, no Afro-Brazilian movement has ever become the predominant literary fashion. Possibly one reason has been the healthy influence of Gilberto Freyre's outstanding sociological study, *Casa Grande e Senzala* (1933; English translation *The Masters and the Slaves*). From this remarkably rich and fascinating book, one important lesson emerges: Brazil's culture is not Negro or White or Indian, but an immensely complex culture in which all three racial elements have made a contribution and have mutually influenced one another. The Modernista as well as the north-east regionalist writers were more concerned with the total Brazilian phenomenon. And it must be remembered that the Negro had figured prominently in nineteenth-century literature and had given rise to a literature of documentary and humanitarian interest rather similar to many of the works on the Indian.[25] After the 1920s the Negro figured in art less as an object of humanitarian sentiment than as a figure in his own right, whose culture had a intrinsic value. Negro folk-themes made their appearance in art and painting and literature, but as only one part of the variegated Brazilian scene.

The outstanding fictional presentation of the life of a Brazilian Negro is the novel by Lins do Rêgo, *O Moleque Ricardo* (1935) earlier discussed in the context of regionalism. Not only does the prose of this novel capture the psychology of the character in a remarkable way, but it does so without having recourse to dialect or falling into incomprehensibility. Ricardo is not a 'type', not 'The Negro', but an individual who happens to be Black. The novel is thus not really a novel about colour but simply the story of a young man and his life, first on a plantation, then in town where he works in a bakery and is caught up in a strike movement. There is never any suggestion that any of Ricardo's attitudes stem from the fact that he is Black, or that any of his difficulties arise from his colour. It is not the colour that is important so much as Ricardo's position in a changing social structure.

Jorge Amado wrote a novel of Negro life, *Jubiabá* (1935), set in Bahia, which is much closer in spirit to Afro-Cubanism than *O Moleque Ricardo*. The hero, Antônio Balduino, is a picaresque character, a street boy who 'knew only the law of the instincts', and who in the course of his life becomes a musician, a boxer and a woman-chaser. Although the novel has a political message and Antônio ends as a labour organizer, having learned the joys of human solidarity, one cannot escape the feeling that the political message is incidental to the portrayal of the picturesqueness and colour of Negro life.

It is in the poetry rather than the novel of Brazil that Negro values are set against the White. Jorge de Lima (1893–1953), a writer from the north-east whose poetic career was to develop through many different manners and stages, published in 1928 his poem 'Essa Negra Fulô' (That Negro Girl, Fulô), which evokes a world of master and slave which anticipates Freyre's description in *Casa Grande e Senzala*. In Jorge de Lima's poem, folk-rhythms are skilfully used to present an archetypal situation, as in traditional ballads. This tale of a Negress, a servant in the big house who steals the love of its master, evokes not only the attraction of the Negress but the whole complexity of the White-Negro symbiosis in Brazil. Like Guillén's poems, those of Lima often develop into protests against the sufferings of the Negro, in whom he sees a moral superiority.

> ¡Olá Negro! Olá Negro!
> A raça que te enforca, enforca-se de tédio negro!
> E és tu que a alegras ainda com os teus jazzes,
> com os teus *songs*, com os teus lundus.
> Os poetas, os libertadores, os que derramaram
> babosas torrentes de falsa piedade
> não compreendiam que tu ias rir!
> E o teu riso, e a tua virgindade e os teus mêdos e a tua
>   bondade
> mudariam a alma branca cansada de tôdas as ferocidades![26]

Hey, Negro, hey Negro!
The race that browbeats you, does it out of boredom, Negro.
And it is you that has to liven them with your jazz,
with your songs and your dances.
The poets, the emancipators who dripped
slimy torrents of false pity,
did not understand that you would laugh!
And that your laughter and your virginity and your fears and your
   goodness
Would change the white soul, tired of all its cruelties.

This suggestion of the moral superiority of Negro and Indian,
together with the view that their cultures bore more relation to
the environment than did the imposed culture of the West, is
characteristic of the indigenist art produced after the 1914–18
war. At its most superficial, this movement was a mere gesture
of defiance towards Europe; at its best, it did justice to hitherto
mute sections of the community.

THE LAND

The land is the third member of the trinity to which artists
turned in their search for roots. Indeed, it was the very closeness
of the Negro and the Indian to natural life that attracted the
intellectual to them. Close to the surface of their cultures was
the land itself. But the return to nature could not be made on
European terms. Here was no Arcadia but a hostile environment
with nothing in common with the European garden. Man's life
in the jungles or mountain regions was a dramatic struggle.
The first lesson the artist learned when he looked at his own
hinterland was that it was not a place where men could have a
sense of personal importance, but an environment which
demolished the individual.

One of the first important novels to bring out the contrast between European and Latin-American man's relations with
nature was José Eustasio Rivera's *La vorágine*, published in
1924. (See page 100 above for an earlier discussion of this
Colombian novel.) The protagonist, Arturo Cova, is a cultured,
city-educated man who flies into the wilderness, very much in

the spirit of the European Romantic who wished to escape from society. But there the resemblance to Europe ends. *La vorágine* turns into a cry of horror and surprise at the hostile world that Arturo Cova finds outside the civilized fringe of urban society. Time and time again in this novel, the natural idyll is shattered. Arturo Cova camps by a water-hole and gives himself over to romantic meditations, only to come upon a hideous water-snake. A round-up of cattle stops abruptly when one of the cowboys is gored and left headless. When Cova reaches the jungle, he finds that the human personality breaks down completely. Man is reduced to a tiny element in an implacable natural cycle in which plant feeds on plant and animal on animal. The human carnage that goes on in the jungle is simply a repetition of nature's law. Eustasio Rivera's novel thus deliberately sets out to destroy the European concept of a tamed nature.

Not all writers, however, were to view the natural landscape with such horror. With the rejection of European values in the twenties and the return to the indigenous, many artists found in the land a source of true national values. This was particularly the case in Argentina and Uruguay, where there were no Indian or Negro populations who could provide an indigenous culture. The part played by the land in the formation of a culture was first put forward as a serious thesis by the Argentinian writer, Ricardo Rojas, in *Blasón de plata* (Silver Shield, 1909), in which he suggested that the *fuerza territorial* (the pull of the land) had a profound influence in shaping the character of the people. Rojas believed that, even in Argentina, the Indian was important because he had made a key contribution to the formation of the nation and its culture. He believed too that there was something about the Argentine soil which had a beneficent influence on people and which would transform even the immigrants into true Argentinians.[27] Though not expressed so explicitly, this concept of the land as a formative and beneficent force is reflected in the verse of two women poets: Gabriela Mistral (Chile, 1889–1957) and Juana de Ibarbourou (Uruguay, b. 1895). However, it was in the novel and the short story that the mystique of the land and its influence on the formation of a culture and a way of life received its fullest development, and especially in the works of Horacio Quiroga of Uruguay (1878–1937), Ricardo Güiraldes of Argentina and Rómulo Gallegos of Venezuela (1884–1969). It is interesting to note that, in the first two, the exaltation of nature, or of man formed in contact with nature, implies a condemnation of society.

Horacio Quiroga began writing at the turn of the century under the influence of the Modernists and of Edgar Allan Poe. The turning-point of his career was a visit under the auspices of the Argentine government to Misiones in northern Argentina. Misiones was a tropical region that had been in decline since the expulsion of the Jesuits in the eighteenth century and was occupied largely by hardy pioneers. Quiroga was so enchanted by the life of the region that he spent the larger part of his life living either there or in other remote regions as a pioneer farmer. His best stories, in *Cuentos de amor, de locura y de muerte* (Tales of Love, Madness and Death, 1917), *Cuentos de la selva* (Tales of the Jungle, 1918), *Anaconda* (1921) and *Los desterrados* (The Exiles, 1926), were set in these regions.

Nature never appears merely as a background in Quiroga's stories. The river Paraná, the jungles, the natural hazards of heat and flood – these are all part of man's existence, obstacles against which he has to fight, dangers which must be overcome. There is no reward for the fight, no Heaven to come. The quality of man's life is in the struggle, and this alone is the meaning of existence. People may be banal, ordinary and acting for the most trivial of motives – as in 'En la noche' (In the Night), in which a shop-keeper and his wife row across the Paraná when it is dangerously high. The man is stung by a ray and the woman has to row alone through the night, performing an incredible feat of endurance. In such an environment, the slightest defect of character becomes fatal. In 'La miel silvestre' (Wild Honey), a greedy young man on a visit from the city takes a stroll in the jungle as if it were a lark. He eats some wild honey, is stricken with paralysis and eaten by ants. The greed which would hardly have been noticed in the city is fatal in the jungle. But, though life in the jungle is subject to great natural hazards, the quality of that life is exhibited as being infinitely superior to life in society. Indeed, Quiroga's stories are an implicit condemnation of society; the majority of his characters live quite alone, isolated from all but the minimal human contacts. In an allegorical tale, 'La patria', the jungle animals are perfectly happy until the bees, aspiring to intellectual superiority, read a human book and try to live according to human law. They make a nation with frontiers and a flag, from which all foreigners are expelled. A wall is erected round the jungle and a net put across the sky. Man returns to the jungle, disillusioned by war; when he finds what the bees have done, he preaches to the animals: 'The worth of your country comes from your own worth. A piece of earth has no more value than the man who treads it at this moment.'

Quiroga's scornful attitude to the machinery of society is illustrated by 'El techo de incienso' (The Incense Roof), in which a character, closely based on himself, is supposed to act as registrar for a remote district of Misiones, but he allows the birth and death records to get into hopeless confusion because he spends nearly all his time mending the roof of the bungalow. In both this story and 'La patria', Quiroga seems to imply that man can do perfectly well without the machinery of nationality and society and, indeed, that social organization increases rather than lessens difficulty and strife. Many of Quiroga's stories have animal protagonists, and in one of his most famous stories, 'Anaconda', the heroine is a boa-constrictor. In all such stories, the author shows great insight into animal behaviour which, by contrast, shows up man's ineptitude. In 'La insolación' (Sun-Stroke), two dogs lying in the shade during a dangerous heat-wave watch in astonishment as their master drives himself on, working in a heat that has already killed a horse. The dogs' prudence contrasts favourably with man's senseless drive, which finally destroys him. In 'El alambre de púa' (The Barbed Wire Fence), two freedom-loving horses cannot understand man's anxiety to fence in his lands or the heartless vengeance which one man takes on a bull which has knocked down his fence. In many of Quiroga's stories, man destroys animals or misuses them because he has lost his understanding of nature and natural life.

One of Quiroga's finest stories, 'El hombre muerto' (The Dead Man), drives home the tenuousness of human links with the land. The story is in the form of a brief meditation, during the few seconds before his death, of a man who has just wounded himself with a machete. The dying man observes the banana plantation he has been clearing and the banana leaves, motionless in the sun, until the concept of the 'I' slowly begins to disappear. Nothing fundamental has changed. The plantation, the banana leaves are still there, but the living being who had regarded them as part of 'his' possessions is no longer on the scene. For Quiroga, then, the significance of the land is that it shows up the triviality of human society and civilization and the ephemeral and puny nature of human beings.

This sort of lesson is developed by Ricardo Güiraldes in his *Don Segundo Sombra* (1926), where the humility and patience that man learns in contact with nature help to educate him as a human being. The story (previously discussed on pp. 104–5 above) tells of a young boy, Guacho, who runs wild in a provincial town where he lives in the charge of uncomprehending aunts. Because of his admiration for a cow-herder, Don Segundo Sombra – a man who is brave, independent, mature and just – he leaves home to work on a ranch. Don Segundo Sombra takes charge of the boy, accompanies him across country with a herd of cattle and teaches him the skills of the cowboy life. The boy learns that, in the life of the cowboy, there is no room for individual whims, for egotism or bravado. The physical hazards prove a man's quality, and any weaknesses of character are soon apparent. Within a year or two, Guacho has been transformed from a delinquent boy into a mature and capable human being able to take on responsibilities as a ranch owner. When this happens, Don Segundo Sombra, his duty done, rides away. The name 'Sombra' (shadow) is partly symbolic, for Sombra is intended to be the pampa itself. The lessons Guacho learns are the lessons taught by contact with nature.

Both Quiroga and Güiraldes contrast 'natural values' and social values: both situate their characters outside society and allow them to develop in contact with nature alone. Neither sentimentalizes nature nor underestimates its potential dangers, but both implicitly suggest that human civilization and society have failed to develop truly moral qualities in man.

Rómulo Gallegos's novel *Canaima* (1935) also contrasts the influence of nature with that of human society, although Gallegos condemns not society itself but only that particular sort of society which had developed in Venezuela. (The novel's 'national regeneration' significance is discussed on pp. 102–3 above.) Through the character of a mysterious huntsman, Juan Solito – a man who has learnt to control nature, and who believes that wisdom must come from 'below', not from above – Gallegos drives home the point that the land, not the European values of material wealth or power, is the educative force that should be allowed to form the Venezuelan character.

PRIMITIVISM AND THE AVANT-GARDE IN PAINTING

Avant-garde and primitivism were not as contradictory as they first appeared. The exploration of the subconscious and the irrational was accompanied by an interest in primitive rhythms and art forms. The *fauviste* movement of the early twentieth century in Europe had its counterpart in Latin America in the twenties. In Brazil, some of the paintings exhibited in the *Semana de Arte Moderna* were *fauviste* in inspiration. In the Plate Region, the Uruguayan painter Pedro Figari (1861–1938) became famous in the twenties (he had only been a Sunday painter before this) with his 'naïve' scenes of creole life. And in Cuba, some of the early paintings of Wifredo Lam use diagrammatic elements drawn from santería cults practised among the Negroes of the island.

There was also something of this primitivism in the work of Diego Rivera.

Though this primitivism was very much in tune with the mood of the avant-garde of the twenties, it was not destined to bear very great fruit in the plastic arts, apart from the isolated example of Figari. In 1924, an exhibition was held in which Emilio Pettoruti (b. 1892) showed semi-abstract paintings in Buenos Aires and this, in fact, was to be the pointer for the avant-garde of the future.

RETRACING LOST STEPS

The rejection of European values induced Latin Americans to turn to the Indian, the Negro and the land in a search for roots. In many ways, the movement was healthy. Novels, poems and paintings of enormous power and originality were produced by artists who discovered indigenous values. The poetry of Nicolás Guillén, Gabriela Mistral and Jorge Lima; the novels of Miguel Angel Asturias, Rómulo Gallegos and José María Arguedas; the stories of Horacio Quiroga; the paintings of Diego Rivera – all opened up new areas of experience. But, ultimately, the vein of experience from which they sprang proved too narrow to be exploited further.

In 1953, there appeared a novel that is in the nature of an allegory of the Latin-American artists' search and a warning for the future: *Los pasos perdidos* (The Lost Steps) by Alejo Carpentier. Carpentier had been a poet of the Afro-Cuban movement and therefore knew what he was talking about. In *Los pasos perdidos* his protagonist is a musician, a man who composes music for films and works in a big cosmopolitan modern city: he is married to an actress who is performing in a play with a never-ending run. The two of them are artists who have been staled by commercial, urban civilization. But the musician gets a second chance when he is sent on an expedition to collect primitive musical instruments from the Orinoco jungle region. The musician's journey proves to be a pilgrimage to retrace his own 'lost steps': that is, his own cultural roots and those of his sub-continent. He joins an expedition of people who are fleeing from modern life in order to found a new community far from civilization. He accompanies them into the heart of the jungle, coming upon more and more primitive communities until, at last, he reaches a region in which man has not settled. For a time, the musician is tempted to settle in this new Eden, but he finds that he cannot reconcile this existence with his musician's craft. He returns temporarily to civilization; when he attempts to go back to the jungle community, he finds that he can no longer find the way.

Carpentier's novel thus makes the point that, while the artist can and should trace lost steps to his own cultural roots, he must not stay in the past. The author states explicitly at the end of the novel that no artist can afford to go back, since this is to deny his justification as a man whose task is 'Adam's task of naming things'. Whether Carpentier intended this as a comment on his own career, or as a comment on the cultural nationalism of his time, is immaterial. The validity of his point is demonstrated by the fact that the artists themselves have found that indigenous peoples and the telluric force of nature are only, after all, aspects of a vastly complex Latin-American reality, much of which still remains unexplored.

5

Art and the Political Struggle

In the 1920s, the world gradually began to divide into the hostile political camps of Communism and Fascism. Political concern was almost unavoidable; whether such concern could be reconciled with the pursuit of art was another matter. This chapter proposes to examine the diverse ways in which artists faced the sometimes incompatible demands of politics and art. Some became militants and abandoned their painting or poetry; some put their art to the service of a message. A few – and these were a minority – attempted to find a form of art which could universalize the political preoccupation. Some, but not all, of these artists were members of the Communist Party, although it should be borne in mind that these did not always conform to party aesthetic requirements, and, conversely, that many who were not Communists felt called upon to write about the political struggle.

It is important to recall that, in Latin America, many Communist and Socialist parties were founded and run by artists and intellectuals. The most outstanding example was the Mexican Communist Party which had, at one time, no less than three painters – Diego Rivera, Siqueiros and Xavier Guerrero – on its executive committee. In Peru, the Socialist Party* was founded by the intellectual, José Carlos Mariátegui; in Cuba, one of the outstanding Communist militants of the 1920s was an avant-garde poet, Rubén Martínez Villena.

Nor is it surprising that, among these first Communist or near-Communist militants, the name of the novelist, Henri Barbusse, was as important as that of Lenin. Far greater than the direct impact of the Russian revolution – news of which, in

---

*This Socialist Party was a Marxist party and part of the Communist International. On Mariátegui's death it was reorganized and renamed the Peruvian Communist Party.

any case, was distorted and inadequate – was the impact of the French intellectual left and particularly of the *Clarté* movement. Barbusse, author of a best-selling anti-war novel, *Le feu* (1917), had founded *Clarté* in 1919: a periodical rallying outstanding intellectuals of the period 'in the struggle against ignorance and against those who direct it like an industry'. The intellectuals of *Clarté* were pacifist and opposed to intervention against the newly formed Soviet Union.[1] The *Clarté* movement quickly became international, and there were soon branches in Latin America. In Peru, Haya de la Torre and Mariátegui were both associated with a *Claridad* magazine.[2] On his visit to Europe in the early twenties, Mariátegui visited the *Clarté* offices and there he met Barbusse. An essay, 'La revolución de la inteligencia', written on his return, describes the work of Barbusse and those associated with him. In Argentina, a *Claridad* magazine was founded in 1922 and its publishing house brought out translations of Marx and Barbusse, and published Argentinian contemporary novels and classics. In Chile, the students published a *Claridad* magazine in which some of Pablo Neruda's first poems appeared.[3] In Brazil, a *Claridad* magazine was founded in Rio de Janeiro, and in São Paulo there emerged the 'Zumbi Group': a short-lived association of 'young petty-bourgeois and working-class writers'.[4] Students formed another revolutionary section among the intellectuals. The University Reform Movement in Argentina expressed its faith in a Socialist future; Haya de la Torre began his political career as a militant in the student movement. In Cuba, militant students in 1923 held the Primer Congreso Revolucionario de Estudiantes (The First Revolutionary Students' Congress), out of which emerged a 'Popular University'.[5] The militancy of students and intellectuals in these early years of the Communist movement is not in doubt. The more convinced among them – Diego Rivera, César Vallejo, Rubén Martínez Villena – visited the Soviet Union. And, apart from working in or with the Communist Party, intellectuals at this period were associated with the trade union movement and with the anti-imperialist leagues. Writers were attracted to the left not only because of French influence or because of a desire for social justice; there was another, perhaps even stronger, appeal: that of belonging to the force which would inevitably triumph in the future. In Argentina, José Ingenieros, a veteran Socialist doctor, was quick to see the Russian revolution as the harbinger of a new era.* The laziness, corruption and immorality of the dying bourgeois class was manifest, but this class would be replaced by the workers with their new and superior moral conscience. Thus, Ingenieros was convinced that he was throwing in his lot with the forces of the future.[6]

However, influential intellectuals soon began to argue that sympathy for the new forces was not enough. There must also be active participation in the political battle. In Paris, Henri Barbusse's *Manifeste aux intellectuels* (1927) argued that intellectuals should do everything possible to help the birth of the new society. In the present period of crisis, social considerations must take precedence; intellectuals should, therefore, 'take on the social role that is incumbent upon them'.[7] Certain Latin-American intellectuals shared this view, notably José Carlos Mariátegui. In an essay exploring the problem of the intellectual and the revolutionary movement, he pointed out that, in the past, intellectuals had been dubious allies in a political movement:

Intellectuals are generally averse to discipline, to programmes and systems. Their psychology is individualist and their thought heterodox. In them, more than in anybody, the sense of individualism is excessive and overweening. The intelligence of the intellectual always considers itself above ordinary rules.[8]

Further, he said, intellectuals are often conservative since they have an aversion to change. For Mariátegui, Barbusse represented a new type of intellectual, one who had joined the progressive forces of the world, and who had thus broken with the traditional image of an unreliable and disloyal ally.

In the late twenties and the early thirties, these initial broad enthusiasms gave way to a more rigid line. A stricter adhesion to Moscow policy began to be demanded. The Comintern was formed. Movements, such as the Peruvian Alianza Popular Revolucionaria Americana (APRA), based on a union of the

* Though he himself never joined the Communist Party, remaining a member of the Argentinian Socialist Party.

middle class and workers, were condemned. Mariátegui's Peruvian Socialist Party also came under criticism, and was re-organized on his death to become the Peruvian Communist Party. Certain unorthodox members of the Communist parties began to be weeded out. Diego Rivera was expelled in 1929 (and was only readmitted just before his death). In Latin America this 'hardening' of the left occurred at a time when – with the exception of Mexico – optimistic hopes of social revolution had begun to fade. In Brazil, for instance, a revolution of 1930, which seemed to be the first stage towards the implementation of social reform, brought in Getúlio D. Vargas (1930–45) who, after promising change, introduced a corporative state on Fascist lines, crushing all opposition and in particular persecuting members of the Communist-led Aliança Nacional Libertadora.[9] In Argentina, too, right-wing landowners regained control in 1930. In Chile, Arturo Alessandri was re-elected in 1934 as a reformer, but came to represent the interests of the landed oligarchy. As might be expected, the effects of the depression were felt acutely in many Latin-American countries, such as Brazil and Chile, where the economy was heavily dependent on the export of primary products.

Undoubtedly, the depression, combined with the activities of the right-wing, helped to crystallize the opinion of many intellectuals who had hitherto not been actively involved in politics. In 1936, the outbreak of the Spanish Civil War drew many more hitherto non-militant writers and artists into the left-wing ranks, and prompted idealistic middle-class intellectuals to join with workers and peasants. Neruda joined the Communist Party in 1939 after being in Spain during the war. Octavio Paz (b.1914) was profoundly influenced by his experiences of Spain during the Civil War; and his fellow-countryman, David Alfaro Siqueiros (b. 1898) – long a member of the Mexican Communist Party – was at the Spanish front.

For the Brazilian novelist Graciliano Ramos, the example of Prestes, and particularly his spectacular march through the interior of Brazil between 1925 and 1927, was one of the decisive factors in deciding his sympathies. 'This purposeless rebellion was not without significance in a country of conformism and usury in which the bureaucrat sticks to his position like an oyster, and tradesman and industrialist pitilessly gnaw at the prostrate consumer.'[10] Although he believed that many points in the left-wing programmes were absurd – the redistribution of land, for instance, was nonsense in the Brazilian north-east – he recognized the quality of self-sacrifice and heroism in the better militants. Graciliano Ramos was far too honest to believe that belonging to the Communist Party made a man good, and far too clear-eyed about himself to hide the fact of his own doubts and hesitations. One of the most interesting of the revelations in his *Memórias do Cárcere* (Prison Memoirs, 1954) is the account he gives of his difficulties when he has to forgo his privileged position and live in the mass. He is not used to having strangers address him as 'tu', to being dirty and unwashed and indistinguishable from the proletariat. Nevertheless, when the authorities of the penal colony try to put him in charge of a group or to distinguish him in any way, he will not allow it.

Graciliano Ramos constantly speaks scathingly of his literary efforts. Far from feeling himself a privileged member of a select minority, he does everything possible to reveal his ordinariness, even his inferiority in some respects to men he believed more courageous or militant than himself. Other writers pushed this attitude even further, and abandoned artistic activity to become militants or trade union leaders; for instance, David Alfaro Siqueiros, the Mexican muralist, became a trade union organizer and was a delegate to the first Latin American Trade Union Congress in 1928. At intervals in his life he was to abandon his art in order to carry on the political struggle and also to go to Spain during the Civil War.[11] Perhaps the two most interesting examples of conversions from intellectuals to militants are those of two avant-garde poets: the Cuban, Rubén Martínez Villena (1899–1934), and the Peruvian, César Vallejo (1892–1938).

Martínez Villena was a law graduate whose first political campaigns were fought in the university. When the dictator Machado came to power in 1925, the political struggle intensified. After the 1930 general strike Martínez Villena was sentenced to death, but he succeeded in getting out of the country. It was a year or two before this, after joining the Communist

Party, that the change in his attitude to poetry came about. He told Raúl Roa: 'I shan't write another poem like the ones I have written so far. I do not need to. Why should I? I no longer feel my personal tragedy. I no longer belong to myself. I belong to them and to the party.'[12] When a colleague proposed to publish his verses, Villena answered roundly: 'I am not a poet (although I have written verses). Do not consider me as such. . . . I destroy my verses, despise them, give them away, forget them; they interest me as much as social justice interests the majority of our writers.'[13] In the same letter quoted here, he declared that he might have consented to publication if his book had been one of protest 'showing the absorption of our land by United States capitalism or the miserable conditions of the life of the wage-earner in Cuba' – instead of being just a book of poems.

The case of César Vallejo is less clear-cut. In 1923, this author of two remarkable volumes of verse – *Los heraldos negros* (The Black Heralds, 1918) and *Trilce** (1922) – left Peru, where his poems had failed to cause any stir, for Paris. He lived there almost continuously, in extreme hardship, until his death in 1938. In his early days in Paris, his sympathies were with APRA. When Haya de la Torre visited Paris, he was met at the station by Vallejo who seemed to have joined the APRA cell established in the French capital. Articles that Vallejo wrote from Paris at this time clearly reflect the APRA views on art and ideas. He stated that both art and ideology must spring naturally from the national reality and not follow foreign models. As late as 1929, we find him attacking Marxism for its excessive rigidity: 'There are men who create a theory or borrow one from their neighbour in order to force and push their life into this framework. In such a case, life comes to serve a doctrine instead of vice versa.'[14] There was a danger of a theory like Marxism pushing the vital flow 'into tight slippers' and thus falsifying experience. In an article 'El apostolado como oficio' (The Career Apostles), he spoke ironically of Barbusse and Romain Rolland, and complained that everyone and everything at the time was aspiring to be revolutionary when what was needed was a 'dynamic equilibrium'.[15]

* *Trilce* is an invented word, made up of *triste* (sad) and *dulce* (sweet).

Nevertheless, despite doubts about Marxism and the rigidity of the party line, both Vallejo's poetry and his articles reveal a distrust of the intellectual and an admiration of ordinary suffering humanity which was to be decisive. In June 1928, for instance, in an article on 'manual and intellectual' workers, there was already a distinct change of tone. The article commented on a questionnaire sent to leading French intellectuals, asking them why they had chosen their particular career. Vallejo used the questionnaire as the starting-point for an attack on intellectuals, arguing that they were, by the very nature of their calling, dishonest. 'Thought is the faculty which most easily lends itself to the devices of fraud and bad faith, of sham and tricks.'[16] The intellect, he said, was a source of evil, for it was a rationalizing faculty 'at the conscious or unconscious service of one or other of the passions or interests'. Intellect was anti-life. 'Life presupposes honour, cleanliness, health. Fraud, the ugly dialectic expedient, is opposed to life.' It is interesting that, in this argument, Vallejo contrasts the intellect with the vital forces. Indeed, the basis of his thought seems to have been a Bergsonian view of a life-flow which reason falsifies. The intellect is thus the villain.*

In contrast to the intellectual, the manual worker lives more simply and honestly. His psychological state is one of natural saintliness and of 'evident wisdom that arises from the simple fact that his intellect is not so systematized nor does it function with such formalist complexity as in the writer'. The worker therefore acts naturally according to a vital, and not an artificial, dialectic. From this position, Vallejo gradually developed a certainty that the artist must join the political battle on the side of the workers. For this reason, he condemned the Surrealists who refused to take this step, deploring the fact that Surrealism, which could have developed into an important and positive movement, had failed to do so. 'Pessimism and despair must be means, not ends. In order to move and fertilize the spirit, they

---

* The superiority of the worker over the artist or intellectual was, of course, part of current Communist ideology. It is the detail of Vallejo's argument which is interesting, for it is similar to the argument he used against Marxism.

should develop and transform themselves into constructive forces.'[17]

Like Martínez Villena, Vallejo became a militant. He carried on intense journalistic activity, made two journeys to Russia, and became very interested in genres such as the theatre and the novel which he felt reached a wider public. However he continued to write poetry with increasing intensity until he died. Though documentation on this period of his life is scarce, it is clear from passages in his novel *Tungsteno* (Tungsten, 1931) that he regarded the intellectual as inferior to the militant worker.

The intellectuals never do anything good. Those who are intellectuals and who are not with the workers and the poor know only how to climb up and get into the government and make themselves rich, and they do not remember the needy and the workers any more.

And a character in the novel, Huanca (a trade-union leader), says to the intellectual: 'The only thing you can do for us is to do what we say and listen to us and put yourselves at our orders and at the service of our interests.'[18]

For Siqueiros, Martínez Villena and Vallejo, then, membership of the Communist Party meant that artistic creation was subordinate to party activities.

TOWARDS A COMMUNIST AESTHETIC

The avant-garde's attack on bourgeois art and values seemed revolutionary enough in the early twenties. It was not necessary to be a member of the Communist Party to hail the Russian revolution or prognosticate the decline of Western civilization. Vicente Huidobro (1893–1948) – a Chilean writer who initiated Latin-American avant-gardism with his 'creacionismo' (creationism) – wrote poetry that used daring typographical devices and had a free form. In these verses he attacked the world of death-dealing machines and inhuman poverty:

> In a thick and vegetable fog.
> the beggars of the London streets
> are stuck like posters
> to the cold walls.[19]

In Mexico, the 'Estridentistas' (Stridentists) hailed the Russian revolution. 'Urbe' (1924) by Manuel Maples Arce (b. 1898) is dedicated to 'the workers of Mexico'. In it the poet declares:

> The lungs of Russia
> breathe in our direction
> the wind of social revolution.

And elsewhere he describes in lurid terms the guilty fears of the capitalists:

> And now the thieving bourgeoisie began to tremble
> for the fortunes
> they had robbed from the people
> and under their dreams somebody had hidden
> the spiritual pentagram of explosives.[20]

The main function of left-wing poetry at this time seems to have been prophetic – the proclamation of the coming apocalypse, as in the poem which Diego Rivera included in his Education Building mural. The author of the poem looked to the Golden Age:

> When the people overturned their kings
> and the mercenary bourgeois governments
> and installed their councils and their laws
> and founded the proletarian powers.[21]

In the early 1920s, no conflict was apparent between avant-garde technique and the new revolutionary content. But gradually, beginning with painting, artists began to realize that a revolutionary commitment meant a change in the attitude of the artist to his art. This was manifest in external matters rather than in the painting itself. In Mexico, a trade union of painters was formed, calling itself 'El sindicato revolucionario de obreros técnicos y plásticos' (Revolutionary Union of Technical and Plastic Workers). Then there was the virtual replacement of canvas work by mural painting. As one critic has remarked: 'Here the division between physical and spiritual labour, so crippling and dehumanizing to both poles of separation, was bridged over.'[22] José Clemente Orozco, not himself a Communist, undoubtedly points to one important advantage of the

mural over other forms of painting: 'It is . . . the most disinterested form, for it cannot be made a matter of private gain:
it cannot be hidden away for the benefit of a certain privileged
few. It is for the people.'[23] The painters stressed the manual and
craft aspects of painting; they wore worker's overalls, and we
find Siqueiros urging that they should use Duco and industrial
paints and paint-sprays instead of brushes. The organ of the
painters' union, later to become the official Communist Party
paper, was *El machete*, whose slogan was:

> The machete is used to cut cane,
> to open up paths in the dark woods,
> to behead snakes, to cut all weeds
> and to humble the pride of the impious rich.

Another aspect of fresco painting was to have an appeal for the
left: namely, the fact that it was a cooperative or team effort.
Obviously, it was hard to transfer this team spirit to the other
arts but perhaps the nearest approach was the Brazilian composite novel, *Brandão entre o mar e o amor* (Brandão between the
Sea and Love), published in 1942 with parts written by Jorge
Amado, José Lins do Rêgo, Aníbal Machado, Raquel de Queirós
and Graciliano Ramos.*

The demand for 'Socialist realism' in literature and for a
figurative technique in painting, the appeal to a mass rather than
to a select public, only gradually became rigid requirements for
the left-wing artist. Nevertheless, that there was a big gap
between the people's taste and that of the artist was exemplified
by the reception accorded to the first Mexican murals. Although
they were figurative, even poster-like in some cases, the people
seemed to have found them too stylized and 'ugly'.[24] In literature in the early twenties, even in Russia, there was considerable freedom of technique and it was not until the Russian
Association of Proletarian Writers began to make headway that
there was any attack on avant-garde writing. In 1934, the First
All-Union Congress of Soviet Writers, attended by foreign
intellectuals, officially decreed that literature should undertake
'the ideological remoulding and education of the toiling people

* The author has not been able to see a copy of this work.

in the spirit of Socialism'. Henceforth, Communist writers were to try to portray the class struggle. Since the message of Communism was a messianic one, they were to portray not only the misery of the workers but 'the solutions to the misery'. The imposition of 'Socialist realism' on writers tended to cause a split between those who defended the avant-garde's right to experiment and those who believed art should have a more direct social function.

In Latin America, the attack on the avant-garde had already begun in the twenties. The conflict between the extremes was most bitter in Argentina, Cuba and Mexico. In Argentina, the left-wing *Boedo* group (a group of writers who took the name from the street where they met) accused the Martinfierrist avant-garde of cosmopolitanism. From Mexico, Diego Rivera launched an attack on both the Mexican *Contemporáneos* review and on the *Revista de Avance* of Cuba, accusing them of 'aristocratism and excessive departure from vital currents'.* The term 'cosmopolitanism' implied neglect of native values and needs whilst aristocratism was an accusation that implied exclusivism on the part of the avant-garde. Both literary experimentation and experiments in painting, because they were aimed at an elite, came to be considered reactionary and symptomatic of decadence. When New York became the avant-garde centre of abstractionism, abstract painting was often identified with 'imperialism' by some of the left-wing figurative painters, particularly in Mexico, and recently a similar identification has been made by a Cuban critic.[25]

REVOLUTION AND PAINTING

In 1947, José Clemente Orozco, the Mexican mural painter, gave a scathing description of the stages through which the Mexican mural movement passed after the revolution. He distinguished three currents. First, a 'nativist' current 'in its two forms: archaic and picturesque, and folkloric – the Toltec or Aztec Olympus, and the types and customs of the modern native'. Secondly, 'murals with historical content'. He pointed out that

*See chapter 6, pp. 212–15.

such murals often showed contradictory attitudes, the heroes of one mural being the villains of another. Thirdly, a current of 'revolutionary and Socialist propaganda in which there appears, with curious persistence, Christian iconography with its interminable martyrs, persecutions, miracles, prophets, saints, fathers, evangelists'. This iconography, Orozco declared, had been 'brought up to date in a superficial fashion; rifles and machine-guns instead of bows and arrows; flying or atomic bombs instead of the divine wrath and a confused and fantastic Paradise in a rather indistinct future'. He added that the Christian imagery was hopelessly mixed up with a nineteenth-century symbolism of Freedom, Democracy and Peace.[26]

Orozco's attack is directed at those who adopt an over-simplified solution to the problems of revolutionary painting. Among the more outstanding muralists there was a genuine attempt to deal with the problem at a fundamental level. Orozco himself, despite his non-allegiance to a definite political ideology, was drawn to express revolutionary ideas in paint, as the titles he gave his murals show. His first murals in the Escuela Nacional Preparatoria have titles such as 'The Bourgeoisie Sowing Hate among the Workers' and 'Destruction of the Old Order'. In the Government Palace of Guadalajara, he painted a mural on the subject of 'Social Struggle, Criollo Rule and Hate'. In the Assembly Hall at Guadalajara University, his murals depict different types of creative man: the Worker, the Rebel, the Philosopher, the Man of Science. Yet, when we come to examine Orozco's work, we find that the attack on the corrupt rich is more religious than political, and that it has its roots in Mexican and medieval tradition.[27] His non-caricaturesque works – 'Soldaderas' (Camp Followers), the oil painting 'La Trinchera'; the magnificent 'Fire', painted on the cupola of the orphanage at Guadalajara; 'Christ Destroying the Cross' – all dwell on human suffering and anguish, not in anecdotal fashion. In the lithograph 'Soldaderas', two retreating revolutionary soldiers fade into the blackness of a wall. The whole curve of their shoulders under the guns, the bowed heads, the sloping figure of the white-clad woman that follows, express resignation. The sadness of war, not its glory, is conveyed. Similarly, in 'La

Trinchera', the figure of a wounded or dying man slopes back-
wards across the painting, in a posture of helpless despair;
human bodies in this picture are bowed, suffering or defeated,
surrounded by a frame of sharp, teeth-like bullets, a knife, a
pointing gun. In 'Fire' in the Guadalajara cupola★ and in the
painting 'Christ Destroying the Cross' – two works of enormous
power – there is a sense of struggle, effort and anguish. In the
cupola painting, man emerges from whirling tongues of fire and
appears consumed by it. Here, the Heraclitean whirl is expressed
in paint. In 'Christ Destroying the Cross', the figure of Christ
wielding an axe is almost lost in the hard diagonal lines of stone
and cross.[28] Orozco thus uses paint to tell us about human
anguish and struggle on a universal level.

The two other outstanding Mexican muralists, Rivera and
Siqueiros – both members of the Communist Party (Rivera until
his expulsion in 1929) – also attempted to translate the revolutionary ideology into paint. Rivera's first murals are predominantly decorative. In the Ministry of Education building, the
murals show the landscape and people of the Isthmus of
Tehuantepec: the people from the north, miners, peasants,
pottery workers and so on. Festivals of the people are shown,
their dances and ceremonies. But even here the use of colour
reveals by implication the painter's outlook. A critic has
declared: 'On the second floor, in *grey monochromes*, there are
intellectual symbols. In the corridor of the third floor, in *warmer
tones* . . . the spiritual life of the people is shown.'[29] [Our italics.]
Rivera, thus, equates 'the good' with warmth, earth, the natural
rhythms of existence; cold colours are reserved for anti-life
intellectual symbols or for the oppressors of the people. He
hereby reveals a naturalist outlook that finds its most complete
expression in the murals of the Agricultural School at Chapingo,
which are dominated by the huge naked figure of a woman,
representing the Earth. In contrast to the broken lines and
slashing diagonals of Orozco's paintings, Rivera's tenderest
works have womb-like shapes and soft curves, especially when he
is painting nature or men and women who are symbolic of
natural goodness. Curiously enough, Rivera's most controversial

★ i.e., 'Man of Fire'; see Plate 6.

and polemical murals belong to the period after his expulsion from the Communist Party. His murals for the Palacio Nacional, for instance, showing the history of Mexico, portray Cortés as a ferocious and degenerate-looking beast. Even more outright were the Hotel Reforma panels which satirized dictatorship in a poster-like manner.

In the murals and easel paintings of the third painter of the Mexican trio, David Alfaro Siqueiros, an extraordinary 'close-up' technique is used to emphasize certain human features, particularly the arm and the fist. One of his self-portraits has a giant thumb in the foreground. A picture of a woman crying has the face almost obscured by two great hands which dig into the eyesockets. 'La obrera' (The Working Woman) emphasizes the sturdy arms and hands in contrast to the face, which is blurred and indistinct. A mural executed for the National Autonomous University shows a huge arm terminating in a clenched fist. The arm and the hand, for Siqueiros, symbolize the dignity of manual work; they are the worker's chief instrument. This glorification of the manual worker, as opposed to the intellectual or the aristocrat, is also a characteristic of his portraits in which strong, coarse-featured men and women are painted in vigorous lines. They are the very antithesis of the refined eighteenth-century aristocratic portraits – of a Gainsborough, for instance.[30]

The fourth painter to adopt the mural form and to try to bring a new and revolutionary spirit into painting was Cándido Portinari of Brazil (b. 1903). Like Orozco, Portinari has refused to mix politics and painting; nevertheless, both in his easel painting and in his murals, he brings the manual worker to the fore. Portinari studied in Europe between 1928 and 1931, and his first important paintings executed after this date – for instance, 'Woman of Bahia with Child' – are very reminiscent of the monumental women painted by Picasso in the early twenties. Indeed, the monumental torso of the worker and the working-class woman became for Portinari what the hand and arm are for Siqueiros. A series of murals for the Ministry of Education buildings in Rio show different aspects of manual labour: Tobacco, Cotton, Rubber, Cattle. In all these, emphasis is on the worker's body rather than the face.

In short, this new school of painting has come to express new values by breaking with the aristocratic conventions and portraying a different physical type, in which pictorial emphasis is placed on bodies and limbs or on coarse, honest features, rather than on aristocratic features or soft, reclining nudes.

THE PROBLEM OF POETRY

Painting is a form of art that can speak directly to the masses. For this reason, Orozco has called the mural 'the highest, the most logical, the purest and strongest form of painting'.[31] How could poetry – the most private of arts – be made accessible to the people? Perhaps it could not. César Vallejo seemed to have his doubts for, soon after his second visit to Russia in 1929, he turned to the drama and wrote a series of plays: *Mampar*, *Entre las dos orillas corre el río* (The river flows between the banks), *Lock-out* and *Piedra cansada* (Tired stone); none of these has yet been published. The fact that he made these attempts to write plays and that he temporarily neglected the writing of poetry seems to show an attempt to reach a public which poetry could never attain.

Apart from folk poetry, which was still a living tradition in some parts of Latin America, poetry from Modernism onwards was addressed primarily to an elite. Even after the Modernists, the predominant tradition in Mexico, Chile, Argentina, Uruguay and Colombia was of a poetry that reflected inner spiritual conflicts. This was still the case in the twenties and thirties when poetry movements, such as the Contemporáneos in Mexico and Piedra y Cielo in Colombia, produced poetry that was primarily concerned with private anguish and metaphysical questions or with technical perfection. The adherence to the Communist Party in the twenties and thirties of three outstanding poets and some lesser poets (César Vallejo, Nicolas Guillén and Pablo Neruda) meant the emergence of a type of poetry in which the individual's conflicts and anguish gave way to a more communal theme. This implied also a new type of poet who would not only be concerned about the masses but would also communicate with them.

The evolution of this new type of poetry was gradual. In the twenties – with the Estridentista movement, for instance – it was enough for the revolutionary poet to describe revolution in the free form of avant-garde verse. Sometimes this revolution was associated with the machine-age through the influence of the Italian Futurists – in other words, it was an industrial as much as a political revolution the poet looked to. But in 'Salutación fraternal al taller mecánico' (Fraternal Greeting to the Mechanic's Shop), the Cuban poet, Regino Pedroso (b. 1896) saw the machine both as the instrument of oppression and as a 'psalm of hope'.

> ¡Oh, taller resonante de fiebre creadora!
> ¡Ubre que a la riqueza y la miseria amamanta!
> ¡Fragua que miro a diario forjar propias cadenas
> sobre los yunques de tus ansias!
> Esclavo del Progreso,
> que en tu liturgia nueva y bárbara
> elevas al futuro, con tus voces de hierro,
> tu inmenso salmo de esperanza.[32]

> O workshop resounding with creative fever,
> Udder on which riches and poverty feed,
> Iron that I see daily forging chains
> Upon the anvil of your cares.
> Slave of Progress
> who with your new and barbarous liturgy
> raise to the future, in voices of iron,
> your mighty psalm of hope.

The poet sees a future in which:

> each instrument of work will be like a weapon
> – a saw, a spanner, a hammer, a sickle.
> We will occupy the land like an army on the march
> greeting life with our unanimous song.

Like the machine, the city with its clamour, noise and smoke – the 'incense of work', according to Rubén Martínez Villena – also makes an appearance in poems. At a deeper level, the Communist poet could express the suffering of alienation, or those conflicts which had made him a revolutionary. The loss of religious belief, the realization that man was only a temporary machine, were often the starting-points for an anguished search that led to an assertion of human solidarity in suffering. Often the poet's anguish was translated into an ironic attack on the romantic cliché of the past, like the following attack on the heart by Martínez Villena.

> Corazón: – los poetas – rubios de candideces –
> te rellenaron firme de goces y pesares
>
> ... Tú apenas responsable de una inquietud antáxica
> pues isócronamente, un día y otro día,
> preso en la celda ósea de la jaula torácica
> mueves tu mecanismo vil de relojería.[33]
>
> Heart – the poets, blonde with innocence,
> filled you full of joys and sorrows.
>
> ... You are scarcely responsible for an antaxic worry
> since isochronically from day to day
> caught in the oseous cell of the thoracic cage
> you move your vile clockwork mechanism.

The early poems of Pablo Neruda and César Vallejo, written before they became active militants, centre on personal pre-occupations of love, death, the inexorability of time. But in Vallejo's poems from the collections *Los heraldos negros* and *Trilce*, the concern is less for the sufferings of the self than for the inability to transcend this self. Many of the poems of *Trilce* were written in prison but they are without self-pity. The four walls of the cell hem in the poet but his thoughts reach out in space and time; infinities of distance and memory contrast with the cell-like limitations of the self.

> En la celda, en lo sólido, también
> se acurrucan los rincones.
>
> Arreglo los desnudos que se ajan,
> se doblan, se harapan.
>
> Apeóme del caballo jadeante, bufando
> líneas de bofetadas y de horizontes;
> espumoso pie contra tres cascos.
> Y le ayudo: Anda, animal!

Se tomaría menos, siempre menos, de lo
que me tocase erogar,
en la celda, en lo líquido.

El compañero de prisión comía el trigo
de las lomas, con mi propia cuchara,
cuando, a la mesa de mis padres, niño
me quedaba dormido masticando.

... En la celda, en el gas ilimitado
hasta redondearse en la condensación,
¿quién tropieza por afuera? [34]

In my cell, in solidity, even
the corners are crouching.

I care for the naked who are crushed,
bowed down, covered in rags.

I get down from my horse which is panting, snorting out
lines of blows and horizons;
one foaming foot against three hooves
and I help him. Giddy up, animal.

Less, always less will be taken of that
which I had to give
in the cell, in liquidity.

My cell-mate ate the wheat
of the hills with my own spoon
when, at my parents' table as a child,
I fell asleep as I chewed.

... In the cell, in the gas which is limitless
until rounded off in condensation,
who stumbles outside?

The extraordinary inventiveness of Vallejo's verse, his use of a syntax in which prepositions, verbs and nouns are wrenched from their normal structures, represented a genuine search for expression. The poem just quoted uses a cinematic technique which, within the limits of the cell, can yet take the reader out to the hills or back to the poet's childhood. The poet is able at once to suggest human limits and the breaking down of limitations. Vallejo himself 'assumed complete responsibility for its aesthetic'; it arose, he said, out of his need for the freest possible form. 'God knows how I have suffered so that the rhythm should not go beyond this freedom and fall into licence.' But, though the rhythms are free and syntax contorted, much of Vallejo's imagery is familiar, for it is the traditional imagery of suffering, sin and guilt – albeit a suffering felt both on an individual and on a communal level. It was undoubtedly his deeply felt tragedy of separation from his fellows and a sense of the common suffering of all humanity that led Vallejo to accept Communism. For many years after joining the party, his main energies were devoted to journalism and party work. In 1936, he was in Spain to attend the sessions of the Congress of Revolutionary Writers, held in various cities of that country during the Civil War. Almost all the contents of his last two works – the posthumously published *Poemas humanos* (Human Poems, 1939), and *España, aparta de mí este cáliz* (Spain, Remove this Chalice from Me: Fifteen Poems on the Civil War, 1938) – were written just before, during and after the visit to Spain. He died on Good Friday, 15 April 1938.

It might be expected that the poems of these last two volumes should show some development, both of content and form, in the direction of a Communist poetry. In fact, the techniques of the later poems are not substantially different from those of *Trilce*; and, though the Peruvian edition of the Spanish Civil War poems states that these were first printed during the war by troops of the republican government, and were therefore intended for popular consumption, the verse is almost as difficult as poetry written without this aim in mind.* In fact, it is clear that what Vallejo sought in Communism was something which transcended individual limitation and therefore transcended death and suffering. He looked forward to an era of justice and love and of comradeship between men when 'only death will die'. In a Civil War poem, 'Masa' (Mass, meaning the multitude), he stated his belief that universal love is the true resurrection.

---

* The first Mexican edition of Vallejo's Civil War poems, published in 1940 with a preface by Juan Larrea, includes a note to the effect that the first edition had been set up and published by republican troops, but had been lost in the Catalonian débâcle.

Al fin de la batalla,
y muerto el combatiente, vino hacia él un hombre
y le dijo: '¡No mueras; te amo tanto!'
Pero el cadáver ¡ay! siguió muriendo.

Se la acercaron dos y repitiéronle:
'¡No nos dejes! ¡Valor! ¡Vuelve a la vida!'
Pero el cadáver ¡ay! siguió muriendo.

Acudieron a él veinte, cien, mil, quinientos mil,
clamando: '¡Tanto amor, y no poder nada contra la muerte!'
Pero el cadáver¡ ay! siguió muriendo.

Le rodearon millones de individuos,
con un ruego común: '¡Quédate hermano!'
Pero el cadáver ¡ay! siguió muriendo.

Entonces todos los hombres de la tierra
le rodearon: les vio el cadáver triste, emocionado:
incorporóse lentamente,
abrazó al primer hombre: echóse a andar . . .[35]

At the end of the battle
when the soldier had died, there came to him a man
and said to him 'Do not die. I love you very much.'
But oh, the body went on dying!

And two came up to him and said again,
'Do not leave us. Courage. Back to life!'
But oh, the body went on dying!

There came to him twenty, a hundred, a thousand, five hundred
thousand,
crying 'So much love. Does it avail nothing against death!'
But oh, the body went on dying!

And thousands surrounded him
with the common cry: 'Stay brother!'
But, oh, the body went on dying!

Then all the men of the world
surrounded him; the body watched them, sad and moved,
and slowly rose
and embraced the first man, then began to walk.

The Christian imagery of resurrection in this poem runs through many of Vallejo's poems, as do the images of communion bread, the good thief, crucifixion, paradise and hell. They throw into relief the faithless loneliness of modern man, the pathetic hope of human solidarity as a bulwark against death. They throw into relief, too, man's sense of worthlessness, his lack of dignity which was certainly increased by the hunger and horror of economic crisis which looms in *Poemas humanos*. Vallejo's originality lies in the fact that man in general, rather than his own personal fate, arouses his greatest concern: a concern that is not only about death (which makes existence seem absurd) but also for the fact that this absurdity also involves so much suffering.

> And unfortunately
> suffering increases in the world at every moment
> it increases at thirty minutes the second, step by step.[36]

The whole machinery of the world has come to a halt in a giant depression crisis:

> También parado el hierro frente al horno
> paradas las semillas con sus sumisas síntesis al aire,
> parados los petróleos conexos,
> ... y hasta la tierra misma, parada de estupor ante este paro.[37]

> The iron has stopped in front of the oven,
> the seeds have stopped with their submissive synthesis exposed,
> stopped are the linked petroleums,
> ... and even the very earth has stopped in amazement at this
>   stoppage.

But the social situation is not the only culprit. Suffering is the essence of human life itself:

> I do not suffer this pain as César Vallejo. I do not suffer as an artist, as a man, nor even as a simple living thing. I do not suffer this pain as a Catholic, as a Mohammedan or as an atheist. I simply suffer. If I were not called César Vallejo, I would still suffer this same pain. If I were not an artist, I would still suffer. If I were not a man, not even a living thing, I would still suffer. If I were not a Catholic, atheist or

Mohammedan, I would still suffer. Today I suffer on a lower plane. I simply suffer.[38]

Vallejo's militant life and early death, his self-imposed asceticism, his deep sense of guilt and horror at the tragedy of the depression have certain similarities with the experience of two other writers of the period, George Orwell and Simone Weil. All three attempted to live lives of poverty and to break down their sense of separation from the workers and the poor. For Vallejo commitment meant suffering as the worker suffers; at the same time, the bread he asked for was not only material.

> ¿Un pedazo de pan, tampoco habrá ahora para mí?
> Ya no más he de ser lo que siempre he de ser,
> pero dadme
> una piedra en que sentarme,
> pero dadme
> por favor, un pedazo de pan en que sentarme,
> pero dadme
> en español!
> algo, en fin, de beber, de comer, de vivir, de reposarse,
> y después me iré. . . .
> Hallo una extraña forma, está muy rota
> y sucia mi camisa
> y ya no tengo nada, esto es horrendo.[39]

> Will there not be a piece of bread for me too?
> I am no longer to be what I have always to be,
> but give me
> a stone on which to sit,
> but give me
> please a piece of bread on which to sit,
> but give me
> in Spanish
> something, finally, to drink and eat, to live and rest on
> and afterwards I shall go away. . . .
> I find a strange form:
> my shirt is very torn and dirty.
> And I have nothing left. This is horrible.

Vallejo's Communism was thus a metaphysical need.[40]

With Nicolás Guillén and Pablo Neruda, it was otherwise.

Guillén's early poems were very much influenced by those of the Spanish poet, Federico García Lorca, whose *Romancero Gitano* (Gypsy Ballad Book, 1928) had been a great success in the Spanish-speaking world. Guillén was to adopt the ballad, which was still a living form in Spanish-speaking countries, in some of the poems of *Motivos de son* (1930) and *Sóngoro cosongo* (1931). An example is the following:

> In this mulatto land
> of Africa and Spain,
> Saint Barbara's at one hand
> and at the other is Changó.[41]

But Guillén draws from many popular sources, not only from the ballad. His poems are often entitled 'son', the name of a popular dance, and from his association with the Afro-Cuban movement he brought a rich variety of African words and rhythms. Often his poems are written in the stylized pronunciation of the lower classes, and many are in dialogue form:

> – ¿Qué bala lo mataría?
> – Nadie lo sabe.
> – ¿En qué pueblo nacería?
> – En Jovellanos dijeron.
> – ¿Cómo fué que lo trajeron?
> – Estaba muerto en la vía,
> y otros soldados lo vieron.
> ¡Qué bala lo mataría!
>
> La novia viene, y lo besa;
> llorando, la madre viene.
> Cuando llega el capitán
> sólo dice:
> > Que lo entierren![42]

> – What bullet was it that killed him?
> – Nobody knows.
> – What village was it he was born in?
> – In Jovellanos, they say.
> – How was it that they brought him?
> – He was dead on the way,
> and other soldiers saw him.
> What a bullet it was that killed him!

The fiancée comes to kiss him;
weeping, his mother comes too.
When the captain sees him
he only says:
     Bury him then!

The tragedy of the anonymous soldier lifts him for a moment out of the crowd, whose comments fill the first lines of the poem. He achieves singularity by being dead, only to be thrust back into anonymity by the harsh words of the captain, whose thoughts are explicitly stated at the conclusion of the poem:

The soldier is the least of our cares
We always have more soldiers.

Guillén draws heavily, then, on folk tradition and especially on ballad tradition, in order to give the masses a voice in his poems, and particularly those masses who had scarcely been heard hitherto in Latin-American poetry: Negro boxers, conscript soldiers, the bar-room singer. But he has also another style, an apocalyptic or prophetic tone which is a characteristic of much Communist art. In one poem, he envisages the entry of the masses into the city of the rich:

¡Eh, compañeros, aquí estamos!
La ciudad nos espera con sus palacios, tenues
como panales de abejas silvestres;

¡Eh compañeros, aquí estamos!
Bajo el sol
nuestra piel sudorosa reflejará los rostros húmedos de los vencidos
y en la noche, mientras los astros ardan en la punta de nuestras
    llamas
nuestra risa madrugará sobre los ríos y los pájaros.[43]

Ah comrades, here we are!
The city awaits us with its palaces, delicate
as honeycombs of woodland bees.

Well, comrades, here we are!
Under the sun
Our sweating skin will reflect the damp faces of the conquered,
and at night, while the stars shine on the tip of our flames,
our laughter will dawn over rivers and birds.

The city waits to be plundered by humble men who are neither White nor Black but 'sweating'. They are workers, who are identified with nature (the birds and rivers) and with devouring flames. In his 'Song of Lost Men', the humble wander through the city like 'abandoned dogs' until the time comes for 'white dog' and 'black dog' to march against the common enemy. Guillén's poetry captures folk language and poetic forms and even folk psychology. In one poem, a Mulatto woman tells her man to go out and earn money; in another a bar-singer insults the tourists and promises to sing them songs 'they can't dance to'.[44]

Of the three major poets, it is undoubtedly Pablo Neruda who has made the most thorough-going attempt to forge a new technique after joining the Communist Party. Born in Chile in 1904, Neruda was a boy prodigy whose second volume of poems, *Veinte poemas de amor y una canción desesperada* (Twenty Poems of Love and a Song of Despair, 1924), won him a justly earned reputation and revealed a fertile creative imagination. In the twenties he was highly praised and honoured: he was appointed Chilean consul, first in Rangoon and later in Colombo and Java. Between 1933 and 1937, he published his *Residencia en la tierra* (Residence on Earth), three volumes of poems nearly all of which deal with death and the passage of time. These poems take us into a Heraclitean flux with no stability but that of oblivion.

It is apparent from many poems in *Residencia en la tierra* that Neruda was seeking something outside his own personal anguish and that the world of material objects offered him a certain re-assurance, even though their wearing away reminded him of the passing of time. It was through these ordinary things that Neruda was able to reach out and come into contact with other human beings, as he explained in a characteristically-worded editorial for the first issue (October 1935) of the Madrid magazine, *Caballo verde para la poesía* (Green Horse for Poetry), of which he was editor. Here he attacks pure poetry and dwells lovingly on the 'impurity' of 'wheels which have travel-led long, dusty distances', of 'coal sacks, barrels, baskets':

They evoke the contact of man and earth and are a lesson to the tormented lyric poet. . . . The confused impurity of human beings can be seen in them, the collecting of things, the use and neglect of them, the marks of feet and fingers, the evidence of a human presence invading them from inside and out.

Poetry should be impure in this way, 'corroded as if by an acid, by the toil of the hand, impregnated with sweat and smoke, smelling of urine and lilies'.

Neruda's attack on purity was an implicit attack on elitism and on any separation of poetry from ordinary life. This attitude was to become yet more explicit in the third volume of his *Residencia en la tierra*, written at the beginning of the Spanish Civil War. In the poem 'Reunion under new flags', he declares that henceforth he will unite his 'lone wolf's walk' to the 'walk of man'. During the Civil War, he had attended the Writers' Congress in Spain and, at the end of the war, joined the Communist Party. In 1943 he returned to Chile, and stood for election as a senator in 1945. The change of political creed is matched by a change in poetic style: 'The world has changed and my poetry has changed,' he wrote in 1939.[45] His new creed makes him seek a form which will express not simply a personal theme but a collective experience. Further, the poetry must now communicate to people outside the narrow circle of poetry lovers and critics. The first poem written according to this new canon was his *Canto general*, published in 1950. During the writing of the poem, he made one of his few statements of his literary intentions to a writers' congress in Santiago. In this statement, he condemns obscure writing and the tendency of many poets to cultivate obscurity rather than clarity. He attributes this to a class feeling on their part, a desire to keep their distance from the less cultivated. The problem in America, Neruda believes, is to reach the immense majority of illiterate or semi-literate people.

Canto general is a giant epic which covers the whole cultural, geographical and historical development of Chile, the American continent and the world class-struggle. 'My first project,' Neruda wrote, '. . . was simply a Chilean song, a poem dedicated to Chile. I wanted to expand it into the geography, the human life of my country, to define its men and its products and its living nature. But very soon I found the subject becoming involved, because the roots of all Chileans plunge beneath the earth and extend to other regions.'[46] The poem depends on the devices of oratory – repetition, and long litany-like passages – intended to be read aloud and thus reach an uneducated public.

> Escribo para el pueblo aunque no pueda
> leer mi poesía con sus ojos rurales.
> Vendrá el instante en que una línea, el aire
> que removió mi vida, llegará a sus orejas,
> y entonces el labriego levantará los ojos,
> el minero sonreirá rompiendo piedras,
> . . . y ellos dirán tal vez: 'Fue un camarada.'[47]

> I write for the people though their
> rustic eyes cannot read my poetry.
> A moment will come when a line, when the breeze
> which stirred my life, will reach their ears,
> and then the labourer will lift his eyes,
> the miner will smile as he breaks his stones
> . . . and perhaps they will say: 'He was a comrade.'

In this poem, Neruda's previous preoccupation with death is left behind with the words, 'Let others worry about the ossuaries.' This new strength derives from his membership of the Communist Party.

> Me hiciste construir sobre la realidad como sobre
> una roca.
> Me hiciste adversario del malvado y muro del
> frenético.
> Me has hecho ver la claridad del mundo y la
> posibilidad de la alegría,
> Me has hecho indestructible porque contigo no
> termino en mí mismo.[48]

> You made me construct on reality as upon
> a rock,
> You made me an adversary of the wicked and a wall
> for the desperate,
> You made me see the clarity of the world and
> the possibility of happiness,
> You made me indestructible because with you
> I do not end within myself.

The *Canto general* is divided into fifteen sections which cover the geography and the history of America, with its conquerors, its nameless heroes and its dictators, as well as the history of his native Chile. There is an address to the United States which invokes the spirit of Lincoln, and the poem culminates with the poet's own story and with an affirmation of belief in the Communist Party which, by virtue of the very construction of the poem, is presented as the apex of humanity.

But the more revealing section and incidentally some of the best poetry of *Canto general* is *Alturas de Machu Picchu*, a section in which Neruda meditates upon the Inca ruins of the fortress of Machu Picchu and upon the nameless men and women who constructed the fortress out of their suffering and who have now no identity except through the poet's re-creation of their saga. The section, divided into twelve parts, is a Dantean descent into the hell of individual consciousness and then a journey upwards to the paradise of communal consciousness and the brotherhood of man. In climbing the heights of Machu Picchu, Neruda ascends from his own despair into the new consciousness of his true role as the voice of the silent masses, whose forgotten sufferings represent the true passion.

> Dadme el silencio, el agua, la esperanza
> Dadme la lucha, el hierro, los volcanes
> Apegadme los cuerpos como imanes.
> Acudid a mis venas y a mi boca.
> Hablad por mis palabras y mi sangre.

> And give me silence, give me water, hope
> Give me the struggle, the iron, the volcanoes.
> Let bodies cling like magnets to my body.
> Come quickly to my veins and to my mouth.
> Speak through my speech, and through my blood.

The *Canto general* was followed by the three volumes of *Odas elementales* (1954–7) which were short-lined poems – sometimes the lines being only three or four syllables long – about the 'elemental' things; the artichoke, the onion, love, air, crab soup, a flower, the fertility of the earth, a book, a simple man, rain, wood, and so on.

> Ay, de cuanto conozco
> y reconozco
> entre todas las cosas
> es la madera
> mi mejor amiga.
> Yo llevo por el mundo
> en mi cuerpo, en mi ropa,
> aroma
> de aserradero,
> olor de tabla roja.[49]

> Ah, of all that I know
> and know again
> amongst all things
> the best of my friends
> is wood.
> I carry through the world
> in my body and my clothes
> scent
> of sawmill
> smell of red board.

Sometimes this simplicity can fall into superficiality. In the first of the *Odas elementales*, Neruda condemns the poet who makes his meaning obscure, who 'twists and retwists', and contrasts him with the worker who is too busy to speculate in a complex fashion. In another poem, we find him asserting:

> There are no mysterious shadows,
> no shades
> all the world talks to me.

Such a sentiment may indicate wilful ignorance rather than genuine simplicity.*

The attack on the literary is implicit in the title of *Poemas y*

---

*Neruda has, of course, published many volumes of poetry since his *Canto general* and *Odas elementales* but there have been no marked advances in technique. His *Plenos poderes* (Full Powers, 1962) and the five-volume *Memorials de Isla Negra* (Memories of Isla Negra, 1964) do, in fact, show a return to slightly more complex forms and language and are no longer obviously designed for 'simple people'.

antipoemas (1954) by Nicanor Parra (Chile, b. 1914). Parra shares with other left-wing poets a sympathy for the popular. In *La cueca larga* (The Long Cueca, 1955 – the *cueca* is a Chilean dance), he skilfully and amusingly imitates the verse sung during the dance. In *Poemas y antipoemas*, he champions the popular against the 'literary' in another way. These poems use ordinary conversational language; they are nearly all in the form of monologues in which the poet converses in an ironic and self-deprecating manner about existence, its small miseries and absurd pleasures. Absurdity is the main theme. If the poet raises his tone at all, it is to rail against the lack of dignity and nobility in life. One of his finest poems, 'Autoretrato', is put in the mouth of a schoolmaster whose ravaged face and body bear the marks of his joyless years in the profession.

> En materia de ojos, a tres metros
> No reconozco ni a mi propia madre.
> ¿Qué me sucede? ¡Nada!
> Me los he arruinado haciendo clases:
> La mala luz, el sol,
> La venenosa luna miserable.
> Y todo ¡para qué!
> Para ganar un pan imperdonable
> Duro como la cara del burgués
> Y con olor y con sabor a sangre.
> ¡Para qué hemos nacido como hombres
> Si nos dan una muerte de animales! [50]

> As for my eyes, from three yards away
> I can't even tell my own mother.
> What's the matter with me? Nothing.
> I've ruined them teaching:
> The bad light, the sun
> The poisonous, miserable moon.
> And for what?
> To earn unforgivable bread
> Hard as the face of the middle classes
> And tasting and smelling of blood.
> Why were we born men
> If they make us die like animals?

In 'Vices of the Modern World', Parra condemns the whole of modern existence, and suggests that man might as well go back to the cave. But no! Why should he? 'Life has no sense,' he concludes despairingly.[51] The writing of political poetry, particularly since the 1950s, has not been confined to members of the Communist Party. The guerrilla movements, the Cuban Revolution, the revolutionary wing of the Catholic church also have their poets, although here one can point to no definite required line. Nor do many of these poets consciously attempt to break with an elite type of poetry or evolve a new popular poetry. In Cuba, Pablo Armando Fernández published *El libro de los héroes* (The Book of Heroes), a collection of the heroic poetry of the Revolution which somehow combines the dignity of the classical eulogy with a modern idiom. In the following poem, a mythic man comes from the sea and goes to the mountains as Castro had done.

> Cuando llegó al centro de sí mismo, ya no era un hombre,
> era el árbol mayor, sus ramas, múltiples remos,
> su tallo, tantas barcas de fortaleza idéntica
> y juntos una flor redonda de oro.
> Frente a él vio, a sus flancos y espalda
> multiplicarse el monte hasta un número exacto,
> dividido en fragmentos iguales,
> enteros unos y otros, siempre el mismo
> que vino entre las aguas y dos luces.

> When he reached the centre of himself, he did not find a man,
> he was the eldest tree, its branches, a fan of oars,
> its shoot, so many boats straining together
> that they were like a round golden flower.
> Before him he saw and at his sides and shoulders
> the mountain multiplying itself into an exact quantity
> divided into equal fractions
> complete each one, always the same one
> who came between the waters and at night.

This is Castro's landing, his retreat to the mountains where he gathered forces but a landing and a retreat made into myth. This mythic man who embodies all Cuba is compared to a boat and a tree, so that the comparison at once suggests progress and a rooted, organic quality. The universality of the images gives Pablo Armando Fernández's poetry a stately and ritual quality that is very different from the colloquial, even anecdotal poetry written by many of Cuba's younger, post-revolutionary poets.

Outside Cuba, the political poets write more of the conflicts in society than the conflicts within themselves. Ernesto Cardenal (b.1925), a Nicaraguan poet who has had a strange, mixed career as a militant against Somoza, as a theological student, as founder of a contemplative order, writes in a Whitmanesque style. His poems are ironic, denunciatory, pop (he has written a prayer for Marilyn Monroe) and often include collages of advertisements or newspaper headlines. *La hora O* (Zero Hour, 1960) represents the tragedy of Nicaragua as banana republic and dictatorship in which the heroes of resistance are tortured or killed.

It is not easy to appraise the ultimate significance of a school of literature which is still in being, but certain conclusions suggest themselves from this short outline of the work of Latin America's leading Communist poets. Neruda's attempt to break out of the 'aristocratic' or minority tradition has not developed;* so far, his *Canto general* remains the most successful example. Nevertheless, the attempt made by him and by his fellow left-wing poets to write a poetry using the rhythms and vocabulary of ordinary speech has been highly successful. They have brought to verse in the Spanish language a new quality – of directness, simplicity, of reverence for everyday objects – which has had a beneficial influence on modern literature in Latin America.

POLITICS AND THE TECHNIQUE OF THE NOVEL

At a time when painters were calling themselves 'workers', when poets were speaking in the language of the ordinary people or attempting to address them more directly, it was inevitable that the novelist too should try to emphasize the social usefulness of his art. Like the poets, many novelists were to disclaim any attempt to write 'well' or produce fine literature. The quality of the writing, they openly proclaimed, was a matter of indifference. The social worth of the contents was all important.

*Although he has had many imitators.

As Jorge Amado states in his preface to *Cacau* (Cocoa, 1933):
'I tried to relate in this book, with the minimum of literature and
the maximum honesty, the life of the workers on the cocoa
estates south of Bahia. Is it a proletarian novel?' The rhetorical
question goes unanswered but, through the mouth of his
fictitional narrator, he declares: 'It is not a beautiful book, well-
composed without repetition of words.'[52] He makes his narrator
an educated worker who, because of his job as a typesetter, has
learnt something about literature but whose vocabulary is still
small. 'Besides, I never had any literary preoccupation when I
wrote these pages. I tried to tell about the life of the cocoa
workers.'

Roberto Arlt, the Argentinian writer (1900–1942), sprang from
a poor background and his books had to be written whilst he
was carrying on a full-time job. In the preface to his novel *Los
lanzallamas* (The Flamethrowers, 1931), he, like Amado, dis-
claimed any pretensions to 'fine writing'. 'To write with style,
comfort, a private income and a leisurely existence are necessary.
But in general, people who enjoy such benefits always avoid the
bother of literature. Or they approach it as an excellent manner of
distinguishing themselves in the society *salons*.'[53] He disclaims
any interest in what newspaper critics may think of his writing.
Why should he send his book to some 'pompous man' who
would write his article between telephone calls 'to satisfy
respectable people'? And just as the Mexican painters emphasized that they were workmen, so Arlt stresses the labouring side
of his activity. 'We have earned this [the future] with the sweat of
ink and the grinding of teeth before our Underwood which we
hit with tired hand hour after hour, hour after hour.'[54]

Graciliano Ramos's novel, *São Bernardo* (1934), opens with a
comic attempt by the narrator, a farmer, to construct a book 'by
division of labour'. Father Silvester would undertake the moral
side and write the Latin quotations, João Noguer would look
after grammar, punctuation and syntax. A newspaper editor was
put in charge of the literary composition, but his attempts
proved disastrous. 'Nobody speaks like that,' the narrator protests, to which the editor replies: 'That's the way it has always
been done. Literature is literature, Mr Paulo. People discuss,

fight, go about their business naturally, but to compose words with ink is something different. If I were to write the way I spoke, nobody would read me.' The narrator is thus forced to undertake the work himself in his own rough and disordered manner. By implication, Graciliano Ramos is telling us that what is said is more important than the way it is told. By giving his hero a pseudonym and thus assuring him of anonymity, he also seeks to establish the truth and sincerity of the narration.

In the hands of the politically conscious writers of the thirties and forties, then, the novel is often a document in which the true reporting of the facts is regarded as more important than style or form. The narrator of Jorge Amado's *Cacau*, for instance, wonders whether the account of his love affair with the boss's daughter has not ruined the story he was trying to tell. In other novels, almost all personal relationships of this type are suppressed or played down in order to throw into relief the social theme. There is nothing new in this. Before the days of the sociological study, the novel in Latin America and elsewhere has frequently served as a social document and this was indeed a convenient way of publicizing abuses – the Cuban anti-slavery novel is an example. Eustasio Rivera's *La vorágine* (1924) included many pages which were written with the avowed intention of publicizing the condition of the rubber-workers in the Amazonian jungle. *El roto***** by Joaquín Edwards Bello (Chile, b.1887) contained actual statistics on sickness and mortality rates among the Chilean lower classes:

> In seven years, smallpox consumes more than 30,000 Chileans and different types of tuberculosis 60,000 more. Syphilis makes even greater inroads. In 1908, the republican police picked up from roads and waysides 58,000 drunkards; in 1911, they picked up 130,000.[55]

The aim of both Rivera and Edwards Bello in the documentary sections of their novels is to arouse humanitarian feeling. But with the politically conscious novelists, documentation serves rather a different purpose and it is here that the novelists under discussion depart from their predecessors. From 1930 onwards

*El roto is the Chilean term somewhat equivalent to 'teddy-boy' in English.

there appeared a vast number of novels depicting the class struggle in different parts of Latin America among different types of workers and peasants, and in many cases the authors were either members of the Communist Party or Communist sympathizers. Among the best known of such novels are: *Nuestro pan* (Our Bread, 1942) by Enrique Gil Gilbert (Ecuador, b.1912) which deals with the rice-workers, *Viento negro* (Black Wind, 1944) by Juan Marín (Chile, b. 1900) which is about the miners and sailors of Chile; *Cacau*, a documentry novel of the cocoa workers, and *Suor* (Sweat, 1934) a description of the tenements of Bahia, both by Jorge Amado; *Tungsteno*, César Vallejo's study of the Peruvian Indians working in the tungsten mines; *Mamita Yunäi* (Mother Yunai, 1941) by Carlos Luis Fallas (Costa Rica, b. 1909); and *Metal del diablo* (The Devil's Metal, 1946) by Augusto Céspedes (Bolivia, b. 1904). In *Mamita Yunäi* – which appeared originally as newspaper articles – Fallas deals with the American control of the banana plantations, and denounces the exploitation of the workers by the big fruit monopolies. Céspedes's *Metal del diablo* describes the development of tin mining by members of the Patiño family, who became millionaires and controllers of Bolivia's destiny.[56] In addition, many novels about the exploitation of the Indians were published during this period, the most noteworthy being *Huasipungo* (1934) by Jorge Icaza and *El mundo es ancho y ajeno* (1941) by Ciro Alegría.

What these novels and many others written during the period have in common is a clearer emphasis on economic exploitation as a source of evil. In this respect, it is revealing to compare early Indianist novels like Clorinda Matto de Turner's *Aves sin nido* (1889), in which the stress was on the moral weakness of the ruling elite, with novels such as *Huasipungo* or *El mundo es ancho y ajeno*, in which the mainspring of the plot is the expulsion of the Indians from their lands in order to create an easily exploitable proletariat. Economic exploitation, along with political oppression, form the mainspring of most of the novels mentioned above but, as a subject, it involved the writer in difficulties of presentation. If the characters are the dehumanized victims of a dehumanized situation, how can they rouse the reader's sympathy or interest? *Huasipungo* is a good illustration of this paradox. The novel describes the brutal action of a landowner who forces the Indians to work on a road and later expels them from their plots of land (*huasipungos*) in order to prepare the way for the exploitation of the territory by a foreign company. The main theme is the brutal exploitation of man by man, with both exploiter and exploited enmeshed. Priest, landowner and foreigner deny their humanity in order to protect their privileged situation whilst the Indian is reduced to an object. All human elements are excluded; the result is a dehumanization which in the end is fatal to the intentions of the novelist. The whole environment is treated by the author in terms of repulsion. Even the natural landscape is unpleasant. 'The plateau, with its perpetual whiplash of wind and rain, with its solitude that frightens and oppresses, imposed silence [on the travellers].' Human habitations appear abandoned:

... only two black pigs grovelled in the earth floor ... doubtless to hollow out their bed. Beyond, in the street, a few skeletal dogs – the accordion of their ribs half-unfolded – fought over a bone that must have passed through the whole village. ... [57]

Conversation among the Indians is largely limited to grunts and exclamations, while the exploiters make defiant speeches or hurl insults. Not only do the Indians live in animal conditions – they behave like animals, as the following love scene shows:

With a feline leap, he seized hold of the Indian woman by the hair. She dropped the wood she had gathered and crouched under some thorn plants, like a hen waiting for a cock. ... After shaking and mauling her, Andrés Chiliquinga, breathing hard with the effort of possession, dragged his victim into the interior of the hut. [58]

Dehumanization, in order to direct the reader's attention to the situation without involving sentimental responses, has often been used successfully. But in the case of *Huasipungo*, Icaza's attitude is too ambivalent either to arouse the reader's wholehearted sympathy for the characters or to allow him to see the central situation without emotional involvement with the characters. In other words, Icaza seems both to be asking us to sympathize with the Indian and at the same time to be depriving the reader of any desire to sympathize. An example is the brutal beating of the protagonist, Andrés, in which the reader is certainly intended to sympathize with the victim: but the description of the beating is immediately followed by this passage: 'In the solitude of the hut, father and son cured their bruises and wounds with a strange mixture of aguardiente, urine, tobacco and salt.'[59] The 'strange' mixture, the 'urine' which Andrés uses to cure his wounds, immediately distances him from any literate reader. He is no longer a victim but an exotic creature held up as an example of the oddness of primitive behaviour. Thus, the lack of an artistically coherent approach ultimately robs the novel of its value as an account of exploitation.

The problem of writing this sort of novel was recognized by Ciro Alegría, author of *El mundo es ancho y ajeno*, a novel which also deals with the expulsion of Indians from their communal lands. In the prologue to the twentieth edition of this work, he declared his dissatisfaction with the existing Latin-American novel. '. . . The novel of social themes disregarded the individual characters and the novel of individual characters did the opposite.' Alegría attempted to sustain interest in very simple characters in a number of ways. In the first place, he made the protagonist a whole community, thus ensuring variety. Secondly, to replace an interest in developing individual psychology, he showed the development of the community, whose fight against the White exploiter is led first by Rosendo, an old man who is wise in the traditional Indian lore, and then by Benito Castro, a half-caste who was bred among the Indians but who has experience of modern society beyond the community. Benito's experience has made him politically conscious and literate; through him, the author is able to drive home the lesson that the Indian cannot remain in the past but must reorganize his traditional communal way of life, using all the tools that modern society can offer.

Although Alegría recognized the difficulty of presenting character in the social novel, he himself did not attempt to get beneath the skin of a character like Rosendo Maqui but presented him from the outside. To get beneath the skin of an illiterate character requires more than a little ingenuity, especially if the writer also wants to show a high level of political awareness and historical consciousness. Many novelists therefore introduce an educated or a politically aware character who is able to act as a mouthpiece for the 'message'. In Jorge Amado's *Cacau*, the narrator is a labourer but one who was born into an impoverished middle-class family and hence was taught how to read and write. Later he works as a typesetter, which helps to explain how a labourer on a cocoa plantation could write so fluently. Some writers abandoned such devices, since the emphasis on verisimilitude hampered their scope. In *El luto humano* (The Human Struggle, 1943), José Revueltas (Mexico, b. 1914) uses a Faulkner-like interior monologue to express the feelings of poor peasants who were trapped by a flood and doomed to die.

Even more difficult than the psychologically convincing presentation of a simple character is the presentation of the political awakening, especially if this is not to seem fortuitous. In the novels of Jorge Amado, such a conversion often occurs at the end of a series of vicissitudes and adventures. The reader has the best of both worlds in a novel like *Jubiabá* (1935). The picaresque adventures of the hero take us into all the colourful and exciting corners of Bahia Negro society until, in the end, the hero, Balduino, is converted; from a vagrant and adventurer he becomes a political activist. Again, in his *Capitães de areia* (1937),* some of the delinquents whose lives Amado describes with such gusto eventually redeem themselves by defying the police or taking part in the labour movement. Amado's novels make it plain that even a left-wing writer often found that a rascal made more interesting novelistic material than a left-wing saint. In fact, the most successful of Amado's works, *Terras do Sem Fim* (Lands Without End, 1943), chronicles the epic of the cocoa planters, the lawless and ruthless men who cleared the jungle and then fought for political as well as economic empire over their domains. The novel tells of the bloodthirsty struggle between two such planters, a struggle which ends only on the death of one of them. In this way, Amado could take as protagonists for his

**Capitães de areia* – literally, Captains of the Sand – was translated into English as *Beach Waifs*.

novel men who were by no means working-class heroes and yet embodied the historical consciousness of the period in which they lived. Nor was he the only left-wing writer to be attracted by the vigour and courage of the pioneer-patriarch. The Ecuadorian novelist, José de la Cuadra (1903–41), in his novel *Los Sangurimas* (The Sangurima Family, 1934) told a similar vendetta story. Such novels are the Latin-American equivalent of the Western and cover a similar stage in the sub-continent's history.

In a sense, however, the presentation of such characters involved nothing new so long as their development was shown through actions and adventures. The problem of how a simple peasant could change through his ordinary everyday experience, without coming into contact with some politically conscious mentor and without being attributed with an extraordinary awareness, was a different matter. There seems to be only one Latin-American novel, Graciliano Ramos's *Vidas Sêcas* (Parched Lives, 1938), which achieves this. The novel centres on two periods of drought in north-east Brazil and on the flight of a cow-herder, Fabiano, his wife and two children from drought and starvation. The whole development of Fabiano takes place between these two events. After the first flight, they return to the life they have always known but, after the second flight, as a result of his experiences, Fabiano decides to leave the country-side and make for a new life in the city. This uprooting implies a real revolution in the mind of Fabiano and his wife: a revolution which is produced not as a result of a long and conscious process, but as a result of all kinds of contradictory impulses and hesitations. Fabiano is not an ignorant man but one whose learning has come entirely from his experience as a cowherd. Like *Don Segundo Sombra*, he knows his environment perfectly and, in so far as human skills avail him, he can survive in that environment. But, apart from the natural disasters that have to be borne, there are human disasters, such as the boss and government authority in the shape of the 'yellow soldier' who unjustly has Fabiano whipped and put into jail. His countryman's wisdom is not adequate against these forces when they are combined with the hostile environment to keep him down. So, at the end of the

novel, Fabiano leaves the country for ever; the idea of betterment
has begun hesitantly to enter his mind.

Graciliano Ramos presents the development of this man, not
through thoughts nor even stream of consciousness, but
through behaviour. His extraordinary skill and insight are
demonstrated in this scene, in which Fabiano comes upon his
old enemy, 'the yellow soldier', and suppresses his first impulse
to kill him. Fabiano had been cutting his way through the under-
growth and has a knife in his hands:

... he turned and faced the yellow soldier who, a year before, had
carried him off to jail where he had been whipped and shut up for the
night. He lowered his weapon. That lasted a second. Less; it lasted a
fraction of a second. If it had lasted longer, the yellow man would have
fallen sprawling in the dust with his gizzard cut. As the impulse that
moved Fabiano's arm was very strong, the gesture that he made would
have been enough for murder if another impulse had not directed his
arm in the other direction. The blade suddenly stopped, near the head
of the intruder, well above the red cap. At first the cow-herder did not
understand. He only realized that there was an enemy present.
Suddenly he noted that it was a man and, even more serious, a man
of authority. He felt a violent shock, and stood with his arm held
irresolutely, loosely swinging from one side to the other.[60]

Fabiano's conflict is described wholly in terms of behaviour.
Conscious realization comes only after the body has already
reacted in two opposing directions, a conflict which brings
awareness into Fabiano's mind. This observation of the behaviour resulting from conflict is far more perceptive than the
'thought streams' which many novelists put into their characters'
minds.

Graciliano Ramos has made equally acute studies of two other
types of mentality – that of the isolated city-dweller in *Angústia*
(Anguish, 1936) and the mind of the exploiter in *São Bernardo*.
The latter is a subtle consideration of how economic exploitation
eventually affects a man's psychological attitudes. The protagonist, Paulo Honório, is a ruthless go-getter whose behaviour
reflects an inner contradiction between a desire to behave like a
human being and the status of landowner and political boss,
which leads him to ride roughshod over all who come near him.

Only when his wife commits suicide does he realize that he has lived 'like a pig', that his achievements as a farmer are vain, and that all his struggle to enrich himself has merely made him guilty and unhappy. He can only conclude: 'I ruined my life.' As an account of what drives a man to exploiting others, the novel is unrivalled.

Graciliano Ramos's novels attempt to penetrate the motivations of ordinary or humble members of society and, in so far as they attempt to give us something of the texture of living, they may be termed 'realistic'. However, many writers came to believe that the novel, like painting and poetry, must transform its technique in order to reflect a fragmentary and dehumanized world. There were a number of avant-garde novels in which the bourgeois world was shown in a grotesque and distorted manner. In one or two cases, this grotesque distortion was savage in its intensity. The Guatemalan writer, Rafael Arévalo Martínez (b.1884), for instance, tells the strange and farcical adventure of a group of Central Americans in the salmon fisheries of Alaska. Beneath the humour, there is a bitter note of criticism of the crudeness and competitiveness of the work, which by implication is also a criticism of the transformation of fishing from an individual pursuit to an industry.[61] On a far larger and more ambitious scale, the Argentinian novelist, Roberto Arlt, wrote two novels, *Los siete locos* (The Seven Madmen, 1929) and *Los Lanzallamas*, which narrate the adventures of the hero, Erdosain, and a group of madmen who are planning to destroy the capitalist world. The madmen merely carry to absurd but logical conclusions the lessons of the world around them, in which science and industry produce death and destruction. Erdosain and his colleagues – the 'Astrologer', the 'Juggler' and so on – behave in a no less fantastic manner than people in the contemporary world, reports of whose activities are inserted in the novel. Arlt thus exaggerates to the point of absurdity the 'realities' of his society.

Arlt's attack is directed at modern society in general. But there is one type of novel which is political in theme and in which a non-realistic technique is particularly successful: the novel of dictatorship. Indeed, even nineteenth-century novels of this type, such as *Amalia* (1851–5) by José Mármol (Argentina, 1817–71), while apparently 'realistic' in technique, tended to create an impression of nightmare. In the twentieth century, most of the outstanding novels attacking dictatorship have employed the techniques of caricature, of broken time sequence or of expressionism in order to convey the effect of a fragmented, nightmarish and depersonalized world. Novels like *El acoso* (The Pursuit, 1956) by Alejo Carpentier and *La fiesta del rey Acab* (King Ahab's Feast, 1959) by Enrique Lafourcade (Chile, b. 1927) successfully convey horror by such means. Indeed, there is always the difficulty that straightforward reporting of the atrocities of a dictatorship might arouse in the reader revulsion toward the victim, whereas it is the crime and not the mangled body that should repel us.

This is why the masterpiece of the genre, *El Señor Presidente* (Mr President, 1946) by Miguel Angel Asturias, is so much more effective than mere reportage would have been. In any case, Asturias is less concerned with denouncing a political dictatorship than to show the effect of dictatorship on human personality. His novel portrays a society in which fear of the president is the only cohesive force, and in which normal values are reversed: the president, who is the incarnation of evil, is the object of worship while charitable acts are punished. One of the novel's themes is the fall from grace of the president's favourite, 'Angel Face', who, by saving Camila, a disgraced general's daughter, sins against the presidential code. 'Angel Face' falls in love with Camila and from then on, since his loyalties are no longer indistinguishable from those of the president, he is condemned to die. At the end of the novel, tortured, in solitary confinement, his personality is systematically broken down and destroyed. The theme of the effect of dictatorship on the human personality is, in this novel, associated with the theme of the artificiality and depersonalization inherent in modern life. Urban civilization brings the invention of the telephone along with guns, explosives and trains, but all these have become instruments for accomplishing more efficiently the dictator's will. His will is to break the personality of his subjects, to destroy human values and relationships until there is one relationship: that of their dependence on him. In such a society, it is impossible to live a whole life, for the dictator relentlessly hunts down those who, like his favourite, 'Angel Face', attempt to escape. Only a few characters are allowed a glimpse of what a good life may be, and these characters – significantly – are to be found living in the country areas, where nature restores a sense of personality and balance. As with many of the left-wing writers of the period, the basis of Asturias's attitude is naturalistic. Life lived according to nature is the good life; city life, supposedly more civilized, has greater possibilities for evil.

El Señor Presidente and *Huasipungo* form an interesting contrast. By breaking away from a mere reporting of atrocities, Asturias creates the effect of nightmare and therefore effectively communicates the horror of dictatorship. Icaza attempts honest reporting but alienates the sympathy of the reader.

From the discussion in this chapter, it should be evident that, while political commitment does not of itself produce great art, out of political conviction great art can spring. Clemente Orozco's paintings, Vallejo's poems, the novels of Miguel Angel Asturias and of Graciliano Ramos – these achieve universality because they plumb deeper than the local and immediate to the more basic strata of human life and personality. Significantly, all four artists achieve greatness through their intuition of areas of experience in which the individual and the social meet, and in each case they are aware of the immense complexities and ambiguities of such experience. They also have in common the theme of human anguish which cannot be extraneous to the social and political status of the individual.

6

Cosmopolitan or Universal?

Although in Latin America it is difficult to remain outside the political battle, there have always been many writers and artists who have affirmed that art has little to do with national boundaries and that the task of the artist is either the mastery of formal problems or the expression of the supreme interests of man. In many Latin-American countries, where artists feel themselves isolated, this view has a special appeal, for, by participating in avant-garde experiment or pursuing a 'universal' form of art, such men feel themselves in communication with a wider public. As the Mexican writer, Alfonso Reyes (1889–1959), declared in his speech, 'En el Día Americano' (1932): 'Over the interest of class, party and countries are the supreme interests of man and these are the ones which are the responsibility of intellectuals.'[1]

Reyes had his roots deep in the Arielist generation, and his view of the role of the artist is close to that of Rodó; hence he rejects the belief that the artist's expression of the 'supreme interests of man' necessarily implies an indifference to national questions. Indeed, it is precisely the disinterested discipline of the artist that makes him a valuable member of his own society, a potential arbiter.

... the men of spiritual discipline, of cultural and technical knowledge – from the philosopher to the artisan – those who have mortified themselves to acquire a real knowledge or skill, those who have, therefore, been proved morally suitable ... these should one day take the reins of society decisively so that American man can be happier and have a fully responsible order to appeal to in his eternal struggle.[2]

In words which echo those of Rodó, Reyes expresses the hope that, even at the most heated moments of political strife, there may still be a few 'permitted the privilege of isolating themselves and guarding the treasure of acquired culture, saving it whole for the generations of tomorrow'. This 'treasure of acquired culture' is the whole body of Western tradition to which Latin Americans as much as Europeans belong. At the same time, according to Reyes, the Latin American is in a special, and perhaps privileged, position with regard to this tradition. The eclecticism of his culture, the experience of his history, mean that there is already in Latin America 'a practice of international living' not possessed by the European.

> The experience of dealing with American people who are very near to us, and of studying the whole cultural past as if it were our own, is the compensation which is offered in exchange for having arrived late at so-called Western civilization. We are in the position of making a synthesis and of profiting from this, without being limited to narrow cultural spheres.[3]

The European, he concludes, finds it more difficult to have an international vision precisely because it is more difficult for him to see beyond national boundaries.

Reyes's views have had an enormous influence in Spanish America. A similar, though not identical, position is occupied in Brazil by the literary critic, Tristão de Ataíde (b. 1893), who considered that Brazilian culture must be incorporated into Western tradition. Reyes's belief in the potential superiority of Latin America, at the crossroads of cultures in a world in which national cultures are no longer sufficient, has been shared by many of the leading artists and writers in Latin America. It has been fed both by the Arielist stream and also by the influence of European avant-garde movements which, from Dada onwards, have been essentially cosmopolitan in their approach.

The avant-garde artist in the first half of this century regarded himself – like Reyes – as part of an international brotherhood, but whereas Reyes tended to stress the responsibility of the intellectual, the avant-garde stressed artistic freedom, the autonomy of the work of art and the special nature of artistic experience. At first sight, there seemed no connexion between a doctrine of social change and avant-garde experiment. Indeed, their enemies often accused the avant-garde of evading reality

Jose Guadalupe Posada, *Cyclists*. Engraving in type metal.

2. Pedro Figari, *Creole Dance*. Oil on cardboard.

3. Rufino Tamayo, *The Bird Watcher*. Lithograph in colour.

4. José Clemente Orozco, *The Trenches*.

5. David Alfaro Siqueiros standing in front of his mural, *Sacrifice for Liberty*, in the Palacio de Bellas Artes, Mexico City.

6. José Clemente Orozco, *Man of Fire*. Fresco in the cupola of the Hospicio Cabanas, Guadalajara.

7. Diego Rivera, *Scenes of the Conquest*. From a mural in the Palacio de Cortes, Cuernavaca, Mexico.

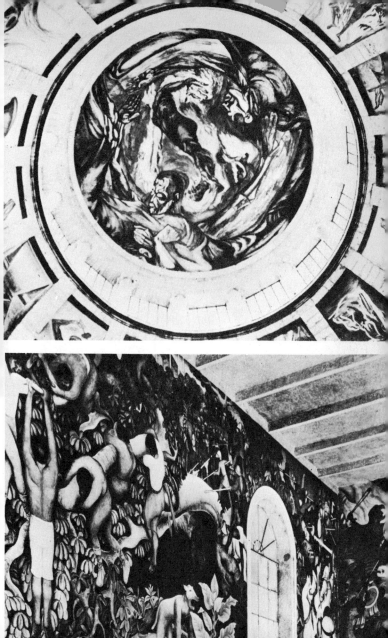

8. José Clemente Orozco, *The Public and the Leaders*.
Fresco in the University of Guadalajara.

9. David Alfaro Siqueiros, *Ethnography*. Duco on composition board.

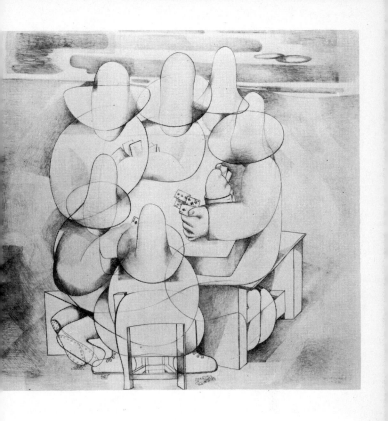

10. Francisco Eppens, *Fire, Earth and Water, Life and Death*.
Glass mural in the Faculty of Medicine, the University,
Mexico City.

11. Amelia Pelaez del Casal, *Card Game*. Pencil.

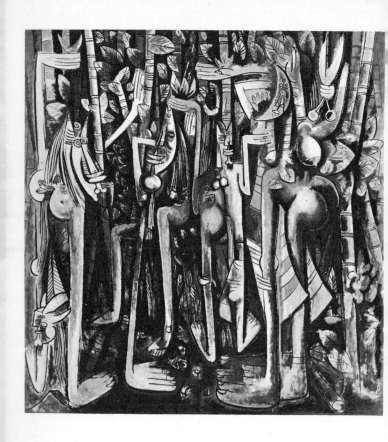

12. Wifredo Lam, *The Jungle*. Gouache on paper mounted on canvas.

13. Sculpture by Jean Arp, *Berger de Nuage*, and ceramic tile mural by Mateo Manaure in the University of Caracas, Venezuela.

14. Auditorium of the University of Caracas, Venezuela, with acoustic ceiling elements by Alexander Calder.

15. Brasilia, the Presidential Palace. The sculpture is by
Alfredo Ceschiati, one of the best contemporary Brazilian sculptors.

16. Brasilia, Chamber of Deputies and Senate.

17. Fernando Botero, *Mona Lisa, Age Twelve*. Oil on canvas.

18. Sebastian Antonio Matta, *The Hanged One*. Oil on canvas.

19. Joaquin Torres Garcia, *Composition*. Oil on canvas.

20. Fernando Botero, *The Presidential Family*. Oil on canvas.

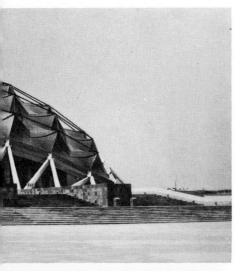

21 and 22. Mexico City,
Olympic Sports Palace.
Architects: Felix Candela,
Antonio Peiry and
Antonio Castañeda.

23. Mexico City, Museum of Anthropology.
Architects: Pedro Ramírez Vázquez and Rafael Mijares.

24. Mexico City, Museum of Modern Art.
Architects: Pedro Ramírez Vázquez and Rafael Mijares.

25. Mexico City, Aztec Stadium.
Architects: Pedro Ramírez Vázquez and Rafael Mijares.

26. Mexico City, Aztec Stadium.

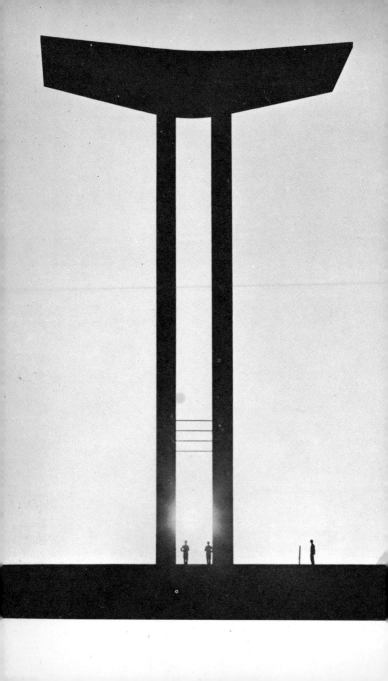

27. Rio de Janeiro, Monument to the Unknown Soldier.

28. Mexico City, Olympic Swimming Pool.
Architects: Antonio Recamier, Javier Valverde Garcés,
Manuel Rosen and Edmundo Gutiérrez Bringas.

29 and 30. Faculty of Architecture of the University
of Caracas, Venezuela.

31. Corridors and entrance to the Aula Magna in the
University of Caracas, Venezuela.

32. Stained glass window at the entrance to the library of the University of Caracas, Venezuela.

and of short-circuiting the problems of art. César Vallejo, for instance, stated:

Almost all avant-garde writers are avant-garde because of cowardice or artistic poverty. They fear that the rhyme will not be right or that it will not come out and, as a last resort, they take refuge in experiment. That is 'the professional secret' which Jean Cocteau defends, and it is the 'kingdom which is not of this world' of the Abbé Brémond.[4]

Despite – or perhaps because of – such criticism, the avant-garde both in Europe and in Latin America tended to stress their revolutionary role. Many argued, indeed, that their freedom from dogma and the restraints of day-to-day political tactics made them more genuine revolutionaries. Others among them argued that their revolution was a more fundamental one than a mere political battle. 'Trenches of ideas are worth more than trenches of stones,' writes the Cuban, Jorge Mañach (b. 1898). Moreover, as he argues on another occasion, there are times when the symbolic rebellion of the artist is the only rebellion possible:

We persisted against capital letters because it was not possible for us to suppress the caudillos who were our capital letters in politics. We deformed images in drawing because the opposite of this deformity was academic art and the academics were the bulwarks of the official, of favouritism, of routine and of the mediocrity of the establishment.[5]

However, the difference between the militant and the man who carried on his revolutionary activities in the avant-garde is more fundamental than this and revolves around the question of 'freedom' as against 'commitment'.

'Freedom' was the essential starting-point of both the Dada movement and Surrealism, and hence of the Latin-American avant-garde which took their cue from these movements. This freedom was itself a radical freedom; it implied a revolt against all accepted forms and ideas, as is clear from the following description of the Dada movement:

Dada not only had no programme, it was against all programmes. Dada's only programme was to have no programme ... and, at that moment in history, it was just this that gave the movement its explosive power to unfold *in all directions*, free of aesthetic or social constraints. . . . These negative definitions of Dada arose from the rejection of what needed to be rejected. This rejection arose from the desire for intellectual and spiritual freedom.[6]

Basic to the Dada position was the notion that in art, or in any other activity, nothing must be 'given'; any activity or creation must arise from spontaneous choice. Indeed, spontaneity was one of the most valued characteristics of Dada art and 'shock' the most desirable reaction on the part of reader or spectator. Chance, too, played a fundamental role. 'Chance appeared to us as a magical procedure by which one could transcend the barriers of causality and conscious volition, and by which the inner eye and ear became more acute, so that new sequences of thoughts and experiences made their appearance.'[7] Chance became the 'voice of the unconscious', a protest against 'the rigidity of straight-line thinking'. 'The realization that reason and anti-reason, sense and nonsense, design and chance, consciousness and unconsciousness belong together as necessary parts of a whole – this was the central message of Dada.'[8]

This attitude often resolved itself into an anarchistic attack, with the artist laughing at society and interested not so much in the future of society as in the liberation of the individual human being: 'We wanted to bring forward a new kind of human being, one whose contemporaries we could wish to be, free from the tyranny of rationality, of banality, of generals, fatherlands, nations, art-dealers, microbes, residence-permits and the past!'[9] This anarchic type of revolt was common in the twenties in Latin America; it was found, for instance, among the Brazilian Modernista and among the Argentinians of the Martín Fierro circle. Very soon, however, another stream of influence came from Europe which introduced a more ambitious concept of artistic freedom. This was Surrealism.

The Surrealists interpreted freedom as a psychological liberation which would permit the artist to grasp intuitively the 'totality of being'. Their theory was fed by the relatively new science of psychology. As one of them stated: 'Freud has shown that there prevails at this unfathomable "depth" a total absence of contradiction, a new mobility of the emotional blocks caused by repression, a timelessness, and a substitution of psychic reality for external reality, all subject to the principle of pleasure alone.'[10] The word 'timelessness' underlines the religious nature of surrealist experience which is confirmed by the words of its pope, André Breton: 'Everything leads us to believe that there exists a spot in the mind for which life and death, the real and the imaginary, the past and the future, the high and the low, the communicable and the incommunicable, would cease to be contradictory.'[11]

The techniques of Surrealism – automatism in writing, the juxtaposition of usually disassociated objects in painting, the importance accorded to elements of shock or chance – were thus primarily intended as a technique for by-passing consciousness and logic in order to penetrate this 'psychic reality'. Hence the importance attached to Hermetism, the cabbala and spiritualism for their value in 'increasing these short-circuits'. 'Their purpose is and never will be anything more than to reproduce artificially that ideal moment when man, under the influence of a psychical emotion, is suddenly possessed by that "stronger than himself" which throws him, despite himself, into the immortal.'[12] Phrases like the 'alchemy of the word', the poet as 'mage', the 'deep true occultism of Surrealism' which are sprinkled through the Surrealist manifestoes bear witness to the fundamentally 'religious' nature of Surrealist art.

Like Dadaism, Surrealism welcomed 'revolution', but stressed an inner rather than a social liberation.

It is not by stereotyped declarations against Fascism and war that we will ever free the spirit of man from the old chains that hinder and the new chains that threaten him. It is by the affirmation of our unshakeable faith in the forces of emancipation of the spirit and man that we have slowly recognized and that we shall struggle to make others recognize. 'To transform the world,' Marx said; 'to change life' said Rimbaud – these two commands are only one for us.[13]

It is clear that Breton regarded the inner spiritual emancipation as primary.

A second major difference between the left-wing militant artist and the Surrealist or Dada avant-garde writer with revolutionary principles was that, whereas the former tended to regard culture as part of a national superstructure, the latter regarded art outside a national context. The Latin-American Surrealists – for example Wifredo Lam (b. 1902) – no longer regarded themselves as imitators of Europe but as part of an international movement.

Nevertheless, in Latin America, the adoption of an avantgarde position tended to define the position of the artist towards his own society, whether he liked this or not. To proclaim an interest in artistic experiment inevitably implied a system of values that was non-national, and indeed it forced artists and writers into stressing their cosmopolitan links. At the same time, the cosmopolitans justified themselves on the grounds that they were putting Latin America on the cultural map. Their reviews thus had the double role of giving information on, or translating the works of, European avant-garde movements, and of providing a mouthpiece for the native avant-garde.

In Argentina, this dual task was performed by the influential magazine *Sur*, founded in 1931 by Victoria Ocampo (and still in being at the time of writing). *Sur* drew on international talent, including the Spanish philosopher Ortega y Gasset, the Argentinian Jorge Luis Borges, the North American Waldo Frank, as well as the most prominent contemporary French and English writers. In Mexico, the much shorter-lived magazine, *Contemporáneos*, had a declared policy of establishing a contact between 'European achievement and American promise', and publicized a wide variety of European writers along with native Mexican poets. More recently, the Mexican magazine *El corno emplumado* – printed in Spanish and English – has performed the same integrating function with regard to North America placing the work of Latin-American and North-American poets side by side. Thus, whereas the committed artist tended to stress the national roots of his art, the avant-garde has generally placed the emphasis on the international nature of art and on Latin America's right to participate in Western culture.

THE LAUGHTER OF THE GODS

Adoption of a 'cosmopolitan' position, however, no longer means that the artist solemnly accepts European values or forms. Indeed, the eclecticism of Latin-American elite culture makes it easy and tempting for the artist to take a sceptical, even an ironical, attitude towards the very ideas and movements which come to him from abroad. After all, the Latin-American artist is not living European or North-American reality. He may share the attitudes of an 'angry young man' or a 'beatnik', but he is not one of them. Such movements come to him divorced from any national context and tend to be more abstract by the time they reach him. Moreover, he may be equally isolated from his own national reality. Lévy-Strauss's comment that, in Brazil, culture tends to be the 'plaything of the rich' is not a generalization that can be applied to the whole of Latin America. Nevertheless, it has remained true for a section of the art world in each country, and it is also true that it is amongst the dilettante upper-class public that an 'international style' is most favoured. Eclecticism and rootlessness, however, though they seem a dubious starting-point, have in fact produced some remarkable work in recent years: work which largely ignores national reality and yet also turns a sceptical eye on Western culture. Within Western culture and yet apart, a group of writers has emerged for whom art represents the laughter of the gods.

This attitude is particularly evident among Argentinian writers and has been so since the days of Roberto Arlt, whose novel *Los siete locos* was an attack on the whole fabric of capitalist society, not simply in Argentina but all over the world. This attack was carried on essentially in the spirit of 'game' or 'play'. And this impression is strengthened by the verbal jokes, the use of phonetic spelling, the tone of parody which run through the whole novel. The air of playing a game is even more apparent in the work of the Argentinian writer, Jorge Luis Borges (b. 1899), although Borges is far from sharing Arlt's political views. Borges's games are, moreover, played not with capitalist society but with 'infinity'. The aim of his work is to shock the individual out of conventional notions of time, space and reality, and so force him to realize their contingency. In spirit, he approaches the Dada movement's anarchist rebellion against all convention and formulae. It is, indeed, of some significance that his formative years were spent in Europe (and in Switzerland) at the height of Dadaism. He himself helped to found a Hispanic avant-garde movement, Ultraism, whose aim was 'to reduce the lyric to its element – the metaphor'.

Borges's characteristic work – a combination of essay and short story which he developed in the thirties, and which he called 'fictions' – arises from a Crocean view of art which considers that 'forms have their virtue within themselves and not in any possible "content"'; and also from a deep-seated scepticism towards all intellectual forms that man puts on experience. The aim of the 'fiction' is to reveal that the form is only a form and merely one possible interpretation of reality. Borges has readily admitted his tendency to 'consider religious and philosophic ideas for their aesthetic values and even for what they contain that is singular and marvellous', and he grants that this is an indication of an 'essential scepticism'.[14] He has also stated that the stories included in his *Historia universal de la infamia* (Universal History of Evil, 1935) are the 'irresponsible games of a timid man who could not pluck up courage to write stories and who distracted himself by falsifying and changing ... other people's stories'.[15] Both the title and the disclaimer are significant. We are far from the view of evil in the social protest novel, where evil was a function of a social situation. Evil, in Borges's work, is universal and eternal: a kind of perversity which possesses man irrespective of the place he is born in or the time in which he lives.

The aim of the 'fiction', then, is to upset the reader's confidence in fact and reality. For this reason, Borges uses the names of real scholars, real authorities, real encyclopedias and real works of reference to construct a scaffolding of 'facts'. In the 'fiction', 'Tlön, Uqbar, Orbis Tertius' (1941), for instance, he tells how he came across references to an imaginary country. Later, he discovered one volume of an encyclopedia which related to the unknown planet, Tlön, 'with its architecture and its playing cards, its mythological terrors and the sound of its dialects, its theological and metaphysical arguments, all clearly stated, coherent, without any apparent dogmatic intention or parodic undertone'. There follows a discussion of the language and philosophy of Tlön. The latter turns out to be an extreme form of idealism. 'The case of a doorway which lasted as long as a beggar visited it and which disappeared at his death is a classic one. Sometimes a few birds or a horse have saved the ruins of an amphitheatre.'[16] In a footnote, Borges reveals that the invention of the unknown planet is a plot thought up by a secret society of idealists who, generation after generation, infiltrate evidence of this unknown world into our planet until we no longer know what is real and what is not. The story thus makes our own 'reality', our 'architecture and playing cards' seem equally fictional. Borges constantly challenges the authority of fact. In the story 'Emma Zunz', for instance, he describes how Emma shoots her employer to avenge her father and how she is able to distort the facts so that it looks as if she had shot him in order to avenge her honour after he had raped her. All the 'facts' which the police learn are 'true', yet they do not know the essential element which would really allow them to understand the crime.

It does not follow that Borges's view is solipsistic. Perhaps the nearest statement of his true position is the following:

Denying the temporal succession, denying the 'I' and denying the astronomical universe are ways of apparent despair and secret consolation. Our destiny ... is frightful not because of its unreality; it is frightful because it is irreversible and composed of iron. Time is a substance of which I am made. Time is a river which drags me away but I am the river; it is the tiger which destroys me, but I am the tiger. ... Unfortunately, the world is real: 'I', unfortunately, am Borges.[17]

'Unfortunately' is perhaps the key word in the sentence. Man's destiny makes life a tragedy, and in this tragedy the only consolation and distraction is human ingenuity in building constructions, in playing games 'with infinity'. Little wonder, then, that Borges's favourite analogies are the labyrinth (at once complex and simple), the book (perhaps, he believes, simply a permutation of a few metaphors), and the library (like the labyrinth, monotonous and yet infinite).

The role of art in this iron-bound destiny is a liberating one. It is a voluntary dream in which man exercises his imaginative freedom and which brings him nearer to the comprehension of reality, complete comprehension being impossible.

> . . . all arts aspire to the condition of music which is nothing but form. Music, states of happiness, mythology, faces worn by time, certain twilights, certain places, try to tell us something, or they said something that we ought not to have lost, or they are about to tell something; this imminence of a revelation which is not produced is, perhaps, the aesthetic act.[18]

Art is a game, and games are important because they rest on chance (a major element of existence) and because they require a ritual, a return to a magic formula which induces a feeling of timelessness.

On the surface, it would seem that Borges's work is quite remote from any sort of 'social consciousness', and that he approaches very near to a theory of art as an escape from the horrors of the human condition. Yet this view is not quite accurate. At various times in his life, Borges has taken a stand on political issues: two notable examples are his attack on Nazism in 1944 and his opposition to Perón (1945–55). Persecuted and humiliated by Perón, he maintained a very consistent and dignified opposition to him. In fact, both Borges's political stand and his pronouncements on Argentine culture and language reveal a remarkable consistency which is in keeping with his views on art and his general attitude towards existence. In every case, his attitude stems from a deep-seated respect for Western culture and a hatred for all forms of barbarism which threaten this culture. Thus he attacks Nazism on these grounds: 'For the Europeans and Americans, there is an order – one single order – possible: that which previously bore the name of Rome and which is now the culture of the West. To be a Nazi . . . is, in the long run, a mental and moral impossibility.'[19] Similarly, his opposition to Perón was based on his profound dislike of a politician who distrusted and persecuted intellectuals. Perón appointed Borges to the post of chicken inspector as an insult but, as one critic pointed out: 'Borges's commentary on that incident defines him aptly, for he was affected basically only by the intellectual implications, which seemed to him the most ominous.'[20]

Borges defends Western culture because this is the one he belongs to, because it *is* a culture, and because its inadequacies arise from human limitations rather than from any inherent defects in the culture itself. For Argentinians and Uruguayans, the Western is the only culture they can claim as their inheritance since they have no indigenous culture. Borges's defence of Western culture also leads him to stress the importance of using a generally comprehensive Spanish, understandable all over the Hispanic world, rather than stressing local differences in the language. 'When I write, I do not think of myself as an Argentine or as a Spaniard: I write in order to be understood. . . . If a word has an archaic flavour about it, I do not use it. If a word is too local and a more general word can be used, I prefer that word.'[21] He declares that Latin-American writers would do better 'not to stress the differences that separate us, but to think of one common language that unites us Spanish-speaking people on both sides of the Atlantic'. He is thus led to a position that is not very far from that of the Arielist generation, seeing himself as the defender of a common culture which unites all intellectuals against barbarism of any time or any place. He has, however, much less faith than the Arielist generation in the power of literature or education to transform mankind, and he has also a faith in Europe itself that is less blind than that of the Arielists. The Latin American, he believes, has no need to feel that he is imitating Europe because he is an heir to European tradition; moreover, since he is an outsider, his manipulation of that tradition is freer. He compares the position of the Latin American towards Europe with that of the Jew: 'Though the Jew lives, let us say, in Western culture, he does not feel bound to it by any particular loyalty and thus he may invent, may change, may become a revolutionary, may be really important. This may be the case, or at least the case in the future, with

Spanish America.'²² So he ends by making a virtue out of eclecticism and cosmopolitanism.

An essential feature of Borges's approach to art is that it is a game which may shock the reader out of normal conventional attitudes. This is also the aim of many of the novels written by his friend and compatriot, Adolfo Bioy Casares (b. 1914), who embodies his idealist view of life in novels that borrow the forms of the detective story or the space-age adventure. *Los que aman, odian* (Those who Love, Hate, 1946),* for instance, is a mocking parody of the detective story with its 'clues' and 'suspects' and the red herrings which lead away from the real criminal. Bioy Casares's major work, *El sueño de los héroes* (Sleep of the Heroes, 1954), is an example of the use of a realistic background – the streets and bars of Buenos Aires – and a real hero, a workman, in order to tell a fantastic story. Indeed, the combination of real setting and universal myth, of Buenos Aires and the Argonaut heroes, reminds one of James Joyce's *Ulysses*. The workman hero, Gauna, gets drunk during the carnival celebrations of 1927, has a knife fight and is saved from death because of the intervention of 'El brujo', a mysterious wizard who declares: 'I defended him against a blind god. I broke the web which was to be woven. Although it is thinner than air, it will be woven again when I am not there to stop it.'²³ Three years later, the same events are repeated; but on this occasion, without the protection of 'El brujo', Gauna is killed. He thus resembles the hero of the ancient myths because he is a prey to forces which he does not understand. All notion of transforming reality is absent from *El sueño de los héroes*, in which man is a tragic prey whose only choice is that of acting out his destiny.

More recently, Julio Cortázar (Argentina, b. 1914) has developed this game theory of art in a brilliant, virtuoso fashion in short stories and novels whose titles underline his intention. One short-story collection is called *Final del juego* (End of the Game, 1956), and one of his novels is called *Rayuela* (Hopscotch, 1963). In this, and in his other works, Cortázar has constructed fictional games which are like life and the theories people weave about life. In *Los premios* (The Prizes, 1960), a

*Written in collaboration with Silvina Ocampo.

group of people from Buenos Aires win a free cruise as a lottery prize. It is a motley collection – teachers, a proof-reader, respectable families, a business tycoon – that embarks on the liner. Once aboard, they are asked to obey a set of rules. They are not allowed to go on to the bridge and are required not to be curious about their destination. Otherwise they are free to enjoy themselves. Very quickly, the passengers divide into two groups: those who accept the rules and are content to abide by them, and the 'rule-breakers' who do everything in their power to get to the bridge and find out about their destination. Finally, one of the 'rule-breakers' is killed. The cruise comes to an abrupt end and both groups return to Buenos Aires, to be absorbed back into city life as though the event had never happened. In a witty postscript, Cortázar discourages the reader from looking for meaning in the novel or trying to see the liner as a symbol. Any interpretation will be valid – but will be no more nor less valid than the next man's different interpretation. Despite this warning, the reader is almost irresistibly drawn to identify himself with the rule-breakers rather than with the characters who uphold convention, since the author presents the former in a much more sympathetic light. We can therefore legitimately conclude that Cortázar himself was more favourably disposed to those who try to defy the 'given' and impose their own order: a view which takes us right back to the avant-garde of the twenties.

In *Rayuela*, Cortázar develops the game imagery further. In this novel, or rather anti-novel, the protagonist is a student called Oliveira. The book is a series of events, episodes, thoughts, reflections and quotations, and each of its sections has two numbers (73, for instance, is also 1). At various points, characters or quotations affirm the need to break with 'literature' since literature is still another conformity.

How many times do I ask myself if this is nothing more than writing, in a time in which we rush mistakenly between infallible equations and the machinery of conventions. But to ask oneself if we can find the other side of convention or if it is better to be carried along by its happy cybernetics, isn't this literature again? . . . The simple fact of asking oneself about possible choice harms and muddies the choice potentiality.[24]

Cortázar sees the novel as something akin to the procedure of Zen, the salutary shock:

> For my nonconformist happily to make a kite and fly it to the joy of the children present is not a minor occupation . . . but a coincidence of pure elements and hence a momentary harmony, a satisfaction which helps to overcome the rest. In the same way, the moments of estrangement, of happy alienation, which precipitate him into the briefest contacts with something which could be his paradise, do not represent for him a better experience than the fact of making a kite; it is like an end but not above or beyond.[25]

And he goes on:

> In a plan of daily events, the attitude of my nonconformist is expressed in his rejection of all that smells of a received idea, of tradition, of gregarious structures based on fear and on falsely reciprocal advantages. . . . He is not a misanthrope but he accepts of men and women only the part which has not been moulded by the social structure; he himself has half his body within the mould and he knows it, but this knowledge is active and not the resignation of the man who marks time. With his free hand he smacks his face most of the day and, in his free moments, he smacks other peoples', and this they return in triplicate.[26]

Cortázar's view of the artistic shock process is not far from Borges's for, as his character Morelli explains, the nonconformist who acts in this way knows intuitively another sort of freedom beyond, a 'more secret and evasive freedom, though only he (and scarcely he) can be aware of its games'.

Whereas Borges accepts destiny but wishes his art game to be a consolation, Cortázar's game is part of a hyperbolic revolt against all convention. His novels move outside any society, social institution or grouping except those which are absurd or subject only to the laws of chance: the Bohemian circles of Paris, for instance, French tramps, a Buenos Aires circus troupe, a mental home. All meetings, activities and events, whether in Paris or Buenos Aires, are chance occurrences. Oliveira and his girl friend Maga prefer to meet by accident, since they believe that people who make dates 'are those who need lined paper to write on and squeeze the toothpaste from the bottom'. Oliveira is constantly inventing his own games – games with words, new systems of communication and meaning – which are symbolic of a private order that he imposes in defiance of the socially accepted order. *Rayuela*, therefore, is a drastic statement of personal anarchy in a world whose order appears absurd. The very form of the novel, in which Buenos Aires and Paris are interchangeable, is an implicit criticism of nationalism, and there is a long passage mocking both action (a moralist illusion) and the cultural approach to national problems:

If he had chosen one thing from his youth onwards, it was not to protect himself through the rapid and anxious accumulation of a 'culture', which was the special gimmick of the Argentine middle class and allowed them to take the substance out of national reality and any other reality and believe themselves saved from the vacuum which surrounded it. ... Besides, it seemed to him deceptive and facile to confuse historical problems like the Argentinian or Eskimo essence with problems such as those of action or renunciation. He had lived long enough to suspect something which is right under people's noses and yet which they usually ignore – the importance of the subjective in the notion of the object.[27]

To have fixed principles is therefore an absurdity. There are simply certain individuals, like Maga who 'was always looking out on to those great timeless terraces which they were all seeking dialectically'. Cortázar's novels then are not concerned with conveying a truth but rather with shocking or surprising the reader into making new explorations. Cortázar, too, would make a distinction between the novel and the short story, the latter being more akin to poetry. His own short stories, he declares, 'write themselves'. Novels, however, are more systematic forms of creation, 'in which poetic alienation only comes in sporadically to carry on an action that has become stranded in thought. But is there sufficient realization that such thought is less akin to logic and more to semantics, that it is not so much dialectical as verbal or imaginative associations?'[28] The title of Cortázar's most recent novel, *62. Novela para armar* (62. A Novel to Put Together, 1968) underlines this insistence on putting an onus of creation and participation upon the reader. But readers and men in general are divided into kinds – *cronopios* and *famas* –

whose characteristics Cortázar has defined in a book, *Historias de cronopios y de famas* (Stories of cronopios and famas, 1962). The *famas* need rules and regulations even for weeping or laughing (what would now be termed 'a high degree of structuralization'). The *cronopios* are those who live spontaneously without needing the props of structuralization. In a book of essays, *La vuelta al día en ochenta mundos* (Around the Day in Eighty Worlds, 1967), he presents us with a *cronopio* composition. Illustrated whimsically with engravings from old editions of Jules Verne, with photographs and old advertisements freely inserted in the texts, the essays are completely remote from anything that might be termed 'criticism'. They are imaginative re-creations of intensely felt experiences – listening to Louis Armstrong or Thelonius Monk or reading the Cuban novelist, Lezama Lima.

Although playing games with serious ideas seems to be most common amongst Argentinian writers (indeed it dates back to the avant-garde of the twenties and the fictional and poetic games of Macedonio Fernández (1874–1952) and Oliverio Girondo (1891–1965), the fictional game is not confined to that country. In Mexico, for instance, *Los albañiles* (The Bricklayers, 1964) by Vicente Leñero (b. 1933) uses the detective story convention, much as Adolfo Bioy Casares does, to cast doubts on conventional notions of right and wrong. In this novel, a night-watchman is killed. Plumbers, bricklayers, the engineer of a building site all appear to confess to the crime, although the author sows doubts in the reader's mind as to whether these confessions are real or imaginary.* At the end of the novel it is clear that all potentially share the guilt, even the police. Thus, like Borges, Leñero uses a structure which seems factual in order to convey a universal message that 'fact' is not 'truth'.

The avant-garde usually tends to be anarchic; it is above all a product of despair.† This is very evident from a number of

---

* Also, finally, one suspects that there was perhaps no murder.

† For the recent upsurge of 'beat' and avant-garde movements, such as 'El techo de la ballena' (Venezuela), 'la generación mufada' (Argentina), the 'Ventana' group (Nicaragua), and the 'Tzántzicos' (Ecuador), see Stefan

avant-garde movements that have emerged in recent years, like the Colombian 'Nadaistas' (from *nada*, nothing). A poem by one of its adherents, J. Mario (b. 1938),* called 'Poeta con Revolver', declares:

> The two demigods of Russia and America might as well let off
>   their megatonic bombs in your face
> so that the earth might go on turning in space
>   empty as a skull
> that the centuries might witness how great was the smallest
>   of God's sons.[29]

The Nadaists are said to have been influenced by Zen Buddhism, but their anarchic attack on an absurd world has its roots in Dada. 'We are shocked at our wickedness and we ask the State to open the lunatic asylums for us because we are geniuses, mad and dangerous men, and we cannot find other more decent places to live in contemporary society.'[30]

As with Dada and Surrealism, the main emphasis of the avant-garde is still on inner liberation, as is shown by a recent editorial in the Mexican magazine, *El corno emplumado*:

> In eight issues, we have published poetry, prose, drama, letters, art-work and talked about a new era peopled by new men. Many still ask us who this new man is and in what new age he lives. One may even feel the change within oneself and be unwilling – as we are, at times – to put a name to it. Pisces/Aquarius. A spiritual revolution, historically comparable to the industrial revolution: a step from the machine to the mind and the heart. It is time for the art of the people which is not an 'art of the people'. A human change no longer hovering in groupism, no longer limited by political or religious answers. An individualism which includes everyone. A slice of bread buttered with vision and divided infinitely. A garland from which every flower plucked unearthed a new bud. A time to look squarely at the sun.[31]

Contributions to the magazine placed the emphasis on 'the agrarian reform of the soul', and Fidel Castro is quoted only for his views on literature. And though the writers stress the

---

Baciu, 'Beatitude South of the Border', *Hispania*, Vol. XLIX, No. 4, December 1966.

  *Pseudonym of J. Mario Arbeláez.

brotherhood of the artist-outcasts, the axis had shifted from Paris to New York, to Zen and Beat rather than Surrealism. The fact that *El corno emplumado* has editorials in English and Spanish – 'when relations between the Americas have never been worse' – is said to reflect the hope that the magazine will be a showcase 'for the fact that WE ARE ALL BROTHERS'.[32]

However, if *El corno emplumado* is prepared to accept the artistic hegemony of the United States, this is not so with another contemporary avant-garde movement: the Brazilian Concrete movement. This movement is concerned with making São Paulo the cultural centre of the world. If one thinks of art as a series of 'technico-formal discoveries', then Concrete poetry has succeeded in imposing itself as a vanguard movement. Concretism began in 1952 with the foundation, by Augusto de Campos, Décio Pignatari and Haroldo de Campos, of the *Noigandres* review. 'Noigandres' is a word used in one of the *Cantos* of Ezra Pound who is, along with Apollinaire, Mallarmé and Cummings, one of the spiritual fathers of the movement. Out of *Noigandres* there developed Concrete poetry, defined as a 'new poetic language, synthetic, substantive, direct and communicative and structurally consequent'. The avatars of this new type of poetry are the Chinese ideogram and the gestalt theory. The experiments of Mallarmé, Pound, Joyce and Cummings are said to converge in 'a new concept of comparison, a new theory of form . . . in which traditional ideas such as beginning-middle-end, syllogism and verse-form tend to disappear and be transcended by a gestalt-poetic, musico-poetic, ideogram-poetic organization of structure.'[33]

The following is an example of a Concrete poem[34] based on the compounds of *se nasce* (one is born) and *morre* (one dies).

```
se
nasce
morre nasce
morre nasce morre
                    renasce remorre  renasce
                          remorre  renasce
                                   remorre
                                   re
```

```
                      re
                  denasce
          desmorre denasce
desmorre  desnasce desmorre
                          nascemorrenasce
                          morrenasce
                          morre
                          se
```

The poem is not to be read as a succession of ideas but to be perceived as a whole, thus 'communicating time and space simultaneously'. The word becomes a gestalt element in the structure.
It follows that Concrete poetry is not 'primarily an intentional
vehicle of meaning'. It is often closer to the visual arts than to
literature in the traditional sense; indeed, according to one
definition, 'it is based on the visual relationships of various
elements and their relationship to the flat two-dimensional space
within which they are contained.' All the same, the ultimate aim
of Concrete poetry is not very different from that of other
avant-garde movements. 'The revolt of Concrete poetry is not
against language. It is against the defunctionalizing and for-
malizing of language. It is against its appropriation for discourse
which converts it into a formula.'[35] Concrete poetry cannot
replace discursive language, 'but it aims at influencing discourse
in as much as it can revivify and galvanize its dead cell, preventing the atrophy of the common organism – language.'

Hence, there is sometimes even an implied social criticism in
Concrete poetry, as in one of Décio Pignatari's poems which
uses the elements of a Coca-Cola advertisement.[36] Concrete
poetry also claims to be a much more up-to-date, direct and
modern form of communication and to have finished with myth,
symbol and metaphor. Its aim is to 'create its own object'.
In theory, it draws on the discoveries of cybernetics and the
language of communication used by advertisers. In the manifestos of the Concrete poets, there is much reference to communications theory and the use of technical terms such as
'feedback'. Unlike much avant-garde writing, Concrete poets
emphasize their wish to provide a more immediate and effective
form of communication. They condemn aristocratic approaches

to art, and emphasize that their poetry speaks the language of the man of today, and that it is a consumer product to be used.

Many Concrete poems are ingenious and amusing, like this one[37] made up of the letters of 'Velocidade' (Speed) by the Brazilian Ronaldo Azeredo:

```
VVVVVVVVVV
VVVVVVVVVE
VVVVVVVVEL
VVVVVVVELO
VVVVVVELOC
VVVVVELOCI
VVVVELOCID
VVVELOCIDA
VVELOCIDAD
VELOCIDADE
```

However, after reading the many manifestos and statements about Concrete poetry, it is impossible to escape from the conviction that the main motivation is much the same as that which built Brasilia and was responsible for the São Paulo Biennale. The desire to make Brazil the cultural capital of the world is explicit. 'On an international plane, it had exported ideas and forms. It is the first Brazilian literary movement to emerge in the vanguard of world artistic experience.'[38] Even more explicit is the statement of Haroldo de Campos that, just as Brazilian industry had advanced from importing foreign products to the manufacture of its own trucks using foreign technical experience, so Concrete poetry has made the same advance in the literary field, 'acquiring creative validity not only in the national sphere but also as a Brazilian export in the field of ideas.'[39]

It is perhaps too early to judge whether the ambitious claims of the Concrete poets are justified. Certainly, they have all the audacity of the men who built Brasilia, but manifestly they impose extreme limitations on themselves by their theory.[40]

In Spanish America, the recent poetry and poetic theories of the Mexican poet, Octavio Paz, have some similarity with Concrete poetry. In one of his essays, he asks, 'Is not the poem that vibrant space on which a handful of signs is projected as in an ideogram which is a fount of associations? Space, projection, ideogram; these three words allude to an operation which consists in revealing a place, a "here" which receives and sustains a writing; fragments which regroup and seek to constitute a figuration, a nucleus of meanings.'[41] The reader participates actively in creation, for his own perceptions are part of the poem. In two recent Paz poems, the reader composes the poem himself: in *Blanco* by choosing which way to read it, and in Paz's latest poem, by twirling a disc which enables the reader to make his own combination of words, his own 'founts of meaning'. Having spent several years as Mexican ambassador in Delhi, Paz has also been influenced by recent Eastern poetry, and some of the poems of *Salamandra* (Salamander) have the compression of the *haiku*.

> Rápidas manos frías
> Retiran una a una
> Las vendas de la sombra
> Abro los ojos
> > Todavía
> Estoy vivo
> > En el centro
> De una herida todavía fresca.

> Cold, swift hands
> Remove one by one
> The bandages of shadow
> I open my eyes
> > Still
> I am alive
> > At the centre
> Of a clean raw wound.

DEATH, SOLITUDE AND UNIVERSALISM

If experiment with language and form has led poets to feel themselves part of a universal brotherhood, this is equally true for those whose art reflects root human experiences. Here, in place of technical experiment for its own sake, there has been an attempt to express significant myths, symbols and archetypes; in this, the influence of Surrealism (condemned by the Concrete poets because it failed to liberate itself from the neo-Aristotelian approach to language) has been decisive. As with the avant-garde experimenters, however, preoccupation with the unconscious and with root experiences has tended to imply cosmopolitanism.

'Root experiences' is of course an intentionally broad term, used to cover all those common aspects of human life from love to death, all that arises from the human condition as such and all that remains unaffected or relatively little affected by the environment. In fact, most Latin-American poetry written over the last sixty years comes into this category. Even Communist poets, like Neruda, or poets who are Socialists, like Jorge Carrera Andrade (Ecuador, b. 1903), have written a poetry about their perception of the material world that deals with experience at a very basic level. Many outstanding contemporary poets – such as João Cabral de Melo Neto (Brazil, b. 1920), and Carlos Drummond de Andrade (Brazil, b. 1902) – have minutely explored phenomenological experience. In the latter two poets, in particular, there is a deliberate acknowledgement of the limits of human knowledge and a consciousness of both the limitations and possibilities of language. In contrast to this type of 'root experience', however, there is another type of Latin-American poetry in which poetry itself becomes a 'spiritual exercise', a way of coming to terms with death and solitude, or even a vehicle through which the poet could establish contact with 'that which is beyond'. This view, which gives to poetry a place previously accorded to religion, has also had many adherents in recent years, although perhaps the most interesting from the social point of view are the poets who wrote for the Mexican magazine, *Contemporáneos* (1928–31), and with whom the themes of death and solitude predominated.

The Contemporáneos group emerged during Mexico's post-revolutionary fervour, and the preoccupation with self of the poets associated with it, together with their interest in such contemporary literary figures as T. S. Eliot, seemed almost counter-revolutionary.[42] The titles of the major collections subsequently published by these poets are significant: *Nostalgia de la muerte* (Nostalgia for Death, 1938) by Xavier Villaurrutia (1903–50);

Muerte sin fin (Death without End, 1939) by José Gorostiza (b. 1901); *Muerte de cielo azul* (Death of the Blue Sky, 1937) by Bernardo Ortiz de Montellano (1899–1949). There can be no doubt as to their main preoccupation. But there is also a special role given to poetry in this death-haunted world. Poetry, says Gorostiza, is 'a game with mirrors in which words, put in front of one another, reflect one another to infinity and recompense one another in a world of pure images where the poet grasps the hidden powers of man and establishes contact with him or with that which is beyond.'[43] This 'contact with that which is beyond' is like Cortázar's 'brief contact', for the moment of perception is only a moment. Poetry does not escape from temporality because it, too, is a part of it. In his *Muerte sin fin*, Gorostiza shows that all must return to primitive chaos:

> In which nothing is and nothing stays,
> Where sleep does not pain;
> In which no thing, no person, ever dies.[44]

The poet's vision of his human destiny inevitably brings him up against society, which tends to deny or ignore the significance of death and time. Salvador Novo (b. 1904), for instance, finds that society and history are 'a repetitive version of the same masquerade'.

> Y yo lloré inconsolablemente
> porque en mi gran sala de baile
> estaban todas las vidas
> de todos los rumbos
> bailando la danza de todos los siglos
> y era sin embargo tan triste
> esa mascarada.

> And I cried inconsolably
> because in my great ballroom
> all lives from every corner
> were dancing
> the dance of all centuries
> and yet so sad
> was that masquerade.

Hence he destroys conventions and preconceived ideas in order to discover 'the real self'.

> Y duró mucho el incendio
> mas vi al fin en mi corazón únicamente
> el confetti de todas las cenizas
> y al removerlo
> encontré
> una criatura sin nombre
> desnuda,
> enteramente, enteramente desnuda,
> sin edad, muda, eterna.[45]

> And the fire lasted long
> but I saw at last in my heart only
> the confetti of all ashes
> and when I stirred them
> I found
> a nameless creature
> naked,
> completely, completely naked,
> aged, dumb, eternal.

It follows that Novo's view of his own society – a post-revolutionary Mexico – can only be critical, as his 'Poemas proletarios' show. These poems are a bitter attack on the weaknesses of the revolution, whose absurd slogans and gestures are contrasted with the ineluctable reality of time.

> Crece el tiempo en silencio
> hojas de hierba, polvo de las tumbas
> que agita apenas la palabra.[46]

> Time grows in silence
> leaves of grass, dust of tombs
> which the word hardly stirs ...

The Contemporáneos group's common vocabulary – 'chance' 'games', 'night', 'dreams', 'death', 'time' – shows that we are in a world not unlike that of Borges.

Nevertheless, Mexican poetry has not remained enclosed within the personal preoccupation. Poets both of the Contemporáneos group and of later groups, such as Taller, have attempted to re-establish communion with others and with society, not by ignoring the themes of death and solitude, but by proclaiming their universality. Torres Bodet (b. 1902), for instance, one of the Contemporáneos poets, while he affirms that poetry is essentially the expression of one man and is personal to him, asserts that the poet, as a man, participates in the sadness of being human. All men form part of a totality and no poet can afford to see only part of this totality. 'I am worth nothing on my own,' Torres Bodet states.

This linking of all human beings through the common tragedy of their destiny has been the subject of much of the writing of Octavio Paz (b. 1914), Mexico's major living poet, whose *El laberinto de la soledad* (The Labyrinth of Solitude, 1950), is a major interpretative essay about the nature of Mexico and the Mexican. Paz cannot be accused of evasion yet his major theme is solitude and man's attempt to break down his solitude through some form of communion. Like Borges, he views poetry as a 'dream' through which man brushes 'the electric frontier of life'. He addresses poetry thus:

> Llévame, solitaria,
> llévame, entre los sueños,
> llévame, madre mía
> despiértame del todo
> hazme soñar tu sueño . . .[47]

> Take me, O solitary one,
> take me, amidst dreams,
> take me, O mother,
> waken me altogether
> make me dream thy dreams . . .

Out of his solitude and anguish, Paz establishes a theory of poetry as communion, as a way of restoring the totality of being: 'The poetic experience is a revelation of our original condition. And that revelation is always resolved in creation – the creation of ourselves.'[48]

The task of creation is a contradiction in a bourgeois society which persists, Paz affirms, in regarding man as merchandise.

Yet the new revolutionary societies are no better since they consider him an instrument. The poet must therefore stand outside society and be in permanent rebellion against its values.

Many contemporary poets, wishing to jump the barrier of emptiness which the modern world erects against them, have tried to find their lost public, have tried to go to the people. But there are no people, only organized masses. And so, 'to go to the people' signifies occupying a place among the 'organizers' of the masses. The poet becomes a functionary.[49]

Such a man cannot, according to Paz, be a real poet since poetry is not an expression of ideas and opinions, but is fed from 'the living language of a community, its myths, its dreams and its passions – that is, on its most secret and powerful tendencies. The poem fuses the nation because the poet goes back up the stream of language and drinks in the original fount. In the poem, society faces the foundations of its being and its original word.'[50] His poem 'Piedra de sol' (Sun Stone, 1957*) is a demonstration of this view of poetry in which the dual nature of experience is expressed partly in terms of myth figures, like Venus and Quetzalcóatl, who bring together 'the two aspects of life':

> arco de sangre, puente de latidos,
> llévame al otro lado de esta noche,
> adonde yo soy tú somos nosotros,
> al reino de pronombres enlazados,
> puerta del ser.[51]

> O arch of blood, bridge of our pulse beating,
> carry me through to the far side of this night,
> the place where I am You equals Ourselves,
> kingdom of persons and pronouns intertwined,
> gateway of being.

Paz is profoundly pessimistic about present-day society in which, he says, the objective conditions for realizing the totality of being are completely unfavourable. Since society 'is far from becoming a poetic community or a living poem which in-

---

*Included in *Libertad bajo palabra*, 1960 edition.

cessantly re-creates itself, the only way of remaining faithful to poetry is to go back to the work. Poetry is realized in the poem and not in life.'[52]

This, however, leads to a new universalism. The poet's feeling of solitude and perplexity is now common to all men. 'The situation is terrible, but it is also propitious to a new attempt at communion. The word of the poet can be a common word because it springs from a situation which affects us all.' Hence Paz believes that the poet's exile has ceased or is about to cease. This conviction that the poet's isolation is now shared by all men has been extended both by Paz and others to apply to the position of Latin America and the Latin American with regard to the rest of the world. He argues that Latin America now forms a bloc along with the underdeveloped countries and that the real 'class' struggle of modern times is between these and the privileged countries.

UNIVERSAL MYTHS AND SYMBOLS IN THE NOVEL

The sense of the Latin American's shared experience with the rest of humanity has helped to change the emphasis of the novel from the expression of purely local phenomena to the expression of more universal themes. The emphasis on discovering distinctively American forms for the novel and on developing a regional literary language has almost disappeared. Novelists, like poets, use the techniques common to Western literature and try to develop these, rather than claim that they are inaugurating a special American tradition.

This 'universalizing' tendency is evident in most contemporary novels. Paradoxically, it often goes with a precise and deep observation of local reality. But the local reality is now linked firmly to universal human experience through the framework of an archetypal situation or of an archetypal myth. Hence the Argentinian family described by Eduardo Mallea (b. 1903) in *Los enemigos del alma* (The Enemies of the Soul, 1950) incarnate the world, the flesh and the devil. Christian symbolism runs through the Paraguayan novel, *Hijo de hombre* (Son of Man 1959) by Augusto Roa Bastos (b. 1917). Even when American

217

myths are used in novels, as they are by Carlos Fuentes (Mexico, b. 1929) and Miguel Angel Asturias, these myths are often the Indo-American version of universal archetypes. One of the most interesting examples of this use of myth is in the Brazilian novel, *Grande Sertão: Veredas*, published in 1956, by João Guimarães Rosa (1908–69); the English-translation title, *The Devil to Pay in the Backlands*, exactly combines the two elements of myth – the devil, the incarnation of evil – and the American setting – in this case, north-east Brazil. The protagonist, Riobaldo, is a bandit who looks back on his stormy life, interpreting all that he does not understand as the work of 'good' or 'evil' forces – though he eventually comes to understand that the 'devil' is simply a name for inner impulses. The novel is in the form of a long monologue whose virtuoso language recalls that of James Joyce.

Another aspect of this universalizing tendency is that, increasingly, writers live in cities whose manners and forms of life resemble those of cities the world over. The titles alone of many recent novels and collections of short stories offer a clear indication of the pervasiveness of this setting: *Montevideanos* (1959) by Mario Benedetti (Uruguay, b. 1920); *En una ciudad llamada San Juan* (In a City called San Juan, 1960) by René Marqués (Puerto Rico, b. 1919); *La ciudad junto al río inmóvil* (The City by the Unmoving River, 1936) by Eduardo Mallea. Unlike the novel of rural life, which tended to dwell on regional differences, the city novel or short story underlines the common problems of all city-dwellers, and particularly their freedom and uprootedness in an environment in which family ties tend to disappear and human contacts to be limited to workmates or chance encounters. In Latin America – especially in those countries with a high proportion of immigrants, such as Argentina, Uruguay and Chile – this loneliness is accentuated by the fact that many of the inhabitants are also newcomers to the country. Not surprisingly, the theme of human solitude and exile is a feature of the Argentinian and Uruguayan novel and is very marked in the work of Eduardo Mallea and Juan Carlos Onetti (Uruguay, b. 1909).

In Onetti's novels and short stories, the universally understandable themes of loneliness, of barriers between human beings, of the impossibility of knowing and communicating with others, of the impermanence of the human personality, its subjection to time and age, are played in an urban no-man's-land which is devoid of local colour. Onetti claims that he 'wants only to express the adventure of man', but it is a singularly disheartening adventure and one in which the modern world plays its part. Onetti's characters lead lives of violent desperation. In *Los adioses*, an ex-cycling champion waits for death in a tuberculosis hospital. Married couples destroy one another with incomprehension as in the story 'Un infierno tan temido' (Hell so feared) or in the short novel, *Tan triste como ella* (As sad as she was). The tragedy of Onetti's characters has little to do with the material miseries of existence. It is the universal tragedy of modern life in which the great emotions of human existence and the rituals of birth, death and marriage have become depersonalized. On the brink of death or of desperate love, man goes on chatting about trivial things, he goes on sleeping and eating, he goes to shops and offices. Tragedy and emotion are somehow out of key with the absurd repetition of day-to-day needs and their satisfaction. His best novel, *El astillero* (The Shipyard, 1961), is about a middle-aged man who places his last hopes in a ruined and deserted shipyard in which there are no boats and no workmen; only a management that goes on working because of some illusory hope. The empty shipyard, the disillusioned protagonist who yet carries on the empty gestures of living, of working, of having (failed) relationships – this is clearly intended to say something about man in general, about the absurdity of the ritual of existence.

The stories of the Uruguayan writer, Mario Benedetti, are much more dependent than Onetti's on the local Montevidean setting, yet he also expresses a universal dilemma: that of man trapped in an impersonal network in which feelings like love or charity or even hope no longer have much meaning. In one of the short stories in *Montevideanos*, for instance, 'Sábado de gloria' (Easter Saturday, or Gloria's Saturday), an office worker awakens on a Saturday afternoon, savouring his temporary freedom, only to discover his wife is ill. Since it is a weekend, he finds it difficult to get a doctor and the wife dies soon after reaching hospital. Benedetti's story reflects the inhumanity of the modern city, the helplessness of its inhabitants when faced with death. The city thus accentuates man's inhumanity, and – as a Chilean writer, Manuel Rojas (b. 1896), shows in *Hijo de ladrón* (The Thief's Son, 1951) – it also accentuates violence. One of the central incidents of this novel, which relates the wanderings of a young delinquent, describes a sudden explosion of rioting when the fauna of the slums turn on the shopkeepers, the tram-cars and all the other symbols of city life in an orgy of destructive violence. No direct explanation is given for this violence; it is just the inevitable product of city-living.*

The predominance of the city setting underlines the modern Latin American's anxiety to share the dilemma of all contemporary human beings and not to feel himself irrevocably separated by culture and nationality. This anxiety corresponds to the Latin-American writer's new situation. Never before, even at the height of the Modernist period, have so many writers lived and travelled abroad; yet never has the question of national identity been posed in a more anguished fashion.

UNIVERSALISM AND COSMOPOLITANISM IN THE PLASTIC ARTS

In literature, the cosmopolitan avant-garde has faced the opposition of an established school of regionalist writers. This has not been the case with the plastic arts. With the exception of Mexico, few countries in Latin America have a strong tradition of native painting. Unhampered by linguistic barriers in their art, painters have generally found it easy to work abroad and develop their painting along lines laid down by foreign masters. A Latin-American critic, Marta Traba, has put the position very clearly with regard to Colombian painting:

I do not believe in 'Colombian art' but in an art which comes from Colombia. The difference between the two is quite obvious. If we say 'Colombian art', we are implying the common denominator

* The works by Onetti and Manuel Rojas which have been discussed above have been chosen merely as representative of the authors' novels. Reference to other novels they have written will be found in the Bibliography.

of a group of works and admitting that they are linked with one another by special aesthetic characteristics, by 'Colombian' characteristics. Yet we know quite well that such characteristics do not exist, nor can they be enunciated in any way.[53]

Marta Traba believes that the arts in Colombia are not the outcome of a national culture nor the reflections of a national spirit, for neither of these exists. This does not mean that they are simply imitations of European art. On the contrary, like Borges, she believes that Latin-American painters have the right to work in Western movements, and – because at the same time they are outsiders – they can handle their material more freely:

The Europeans are too impressed by the force of their great traditions to dare to challenge them. . . . We Latin Americans are, in comparison with these responsible men, like acrobats in a puppet show. . . . But this has its advantages too. There is something in us that is dispersed, wandering, vagabond, that makes us lose gravity and that often leads us into tremendously harsh criticism. We walk illogically through the regions of culture without gravity, relieved of history, but we are motivated by a strange mixture of genuine aesthetic need and our secret glee at seeing how much is to be done.[54]

All this means that developments in painting or sculpture in Latin America are fed, not from a national source, but from the painter's responses to international movements. One tends therefore to think less in terms of Colombian, Venezuelan or Brazilian painting than in terms of schools or movements – expressionism, abstractionism, Concrete painting, etc. At least one critic regards this as a highly desirable state of affairs, and that the next step should be 'the discussion of these artists free from the continental allegiance'.

Then the internationalism which has changed the art of Latin America will have affected the identity of the artists, beyond even their present levels of energy and imagination. For instance, Matta is an artist, not a Chilean artist; Enrique Castro Cid, though born in Chile, declined to participate in 'Magnet – New York' because he wished to exhibit in New York as an artist, not as a national. Presumably this attitude will spread, with the increase of critical consciousness in Latin America, and it is a reminder that national art and continental shows, patriotic or paternal, are interim stages in the development of anybody's art.'[55]

All this may be true; even so, the painter's or sculptor's choice of style often defines him and his relationships with the rest of the world. And even the pursuit of technical objectives may develop into a sort of mystique, as these words of the Uruguayan constructivist, Torres-García, show, when he refers to the essence of art as being 'to construct according to the law of limitations and this law, which governs all things, must inevitably bring us to a concept of the universe'. Many of the 'cosmopolitan' painters then, like many contemporary poets, are concerned in involving the onlooker in a root experience and hence in a universal experience. But having said this, it remains true that the international style in the arts may equally be the reflection of the national situation. There is nothing that illustrates this better than a comparison between three big modern projects in Latin America which combine architecture and the arts: the National University of Mexico, the National University of Caracas, and Brasilia. The first is an attempt to express a national ideal, and therefore its buildings are both ultra-modern (illustrative of the technological age), and yet decorated with pre-Columban motifs, as in the case of the library building, or, in the case of the stadium, deliberately reproducing pre-Columban architectural styles. The university at Caracas, built during the dictatorship of Pérez Jiménez, is a cosmopolitan show-piece, in which the arts and architecture were effectively blended and in which Venezuelan and foreign painters and sculptors, such as Fernand Léger and Alexander Calder, cooperated. Brasilia, on the other hand, although executed in an international style, is the work of national artists and has original Brazilian features.[56] (See Plates 15 and 16.)

In a sense, the international style in the fine arts does provide one answer to the artist's need for a public. The work of the Colombian abstract expressionist, Alejandro Obregón, or the Chilean, Matta (b. 1911) can be shown in any of the big art cities without gloss or explanation. This obviously offers a wider scope. Even in Mexico, hitherto the most 'national' in its approach to art, there are painters whose work has broken with the dominant figurative school. Chief among these is the Guatemalan-born Carlos Mérida who preferred to use geometric patterns which derived from pre-Columban sources. The outstanding Mexican painter, Rufino Tamayo (b. 1899), uses a disturbing personal symbolism and employs colour to give dimensions of dream or nightmare to his paintings. He manages simultaneously to suggest the richness and strangeness of Mexico as well as to appeal to basic human experience. And under the influence of the German-born Mathias Goeritz, there has been an increasing tendency towards abstraction, even in 'public' projects.[57] In Argentina, where abstract painting has flourished since Emilio Pettoruti's 1924 exhibition, there have been a number of important movements such as Otra Figuración and Madi. The latter was formed under the leadership of the European-born sculptor, Gyula Kosice (b. 1924), whose spatial structures include mixtures of perspex, wood and metal. Op art has an outstanding exponent in Julio Le Parc.

In Cuba, the Revolution has not involved any change of style on the part of painters away from the kind of international styles they had adopted before the revolution. The outstanding Cuban painters, Amelia Peláez and Wifredo Lam, have their roots in the art movements of the twenties, Lam in surrealism and Amelia Peláez in a Matisse-like obsession with colour. Just before the Revolution, she was painting interiors which became increasingly vibrant with the years. At the outbreak of the Revolution, a talented group of painters, notably Portocarrero and Mariani, put their talents at the disposition of the Revolution. Whilst continuing to paint in abstract or semi-abstract styles which they had developed before the Revolution, they also decorated buildings, the tops of biscuit tins and designed posters and book covers. In this way, they have succeeded in reconciling revolutionary activity with artistic integrity.

In speaking of an international style in painting, a special word should be said about the influence of surrealism. As in literature, the influence of surrealism in Latin America was intensely creative. Painters originally inspired by European surrealism quickly developed quite personal styles and they include some of the great names among contemporary Latin-

American painters, Botero of Colombia with his strange, monstrous doll-like figures, Matta with his visceral, organic and biological shapes and Tamayo with his personal use of colour.

The tendency towards an international style in all the arts is not confined to Latin America but is observable in most parts of the world. It is, in part, a response to the totally new situation which modern methods of communication have brought about. The artist's approach has thus been modified but, in the case of Latin America, without diminishing the basic preoccupation with the sub-continent, its problems and its future.

7

The Writer as Conscience of his Country

Among the most recent generations of Latin-American writers,
there has been a revival of the belief that the artist has a special
responsibility towards society. At the same time, there is an
insistence on his freedom. 'Freedom' may, of course, mean one
of many things. At its simplest, the writer is stating that he does
not want to belong to any political grouping. Freedom, in this
case, means freedom to take a critical attitude, whoever is in
power: an important privilege in a country like Mexico, where
the government's revolutionary ideals are impeccable while its
practice is totally different. The writer may also use the word
freedom in the avant-garde sense of creative or imaginative
freedom, or he may use it in the existentialist sense of choice.
Associated with these different concepts of freedom, there has
developed an attitude towards society which is neither that of the
'select minority' nor yet that of the militant fighting for a special
class. The writer is increasingly considered as a man with a
conscience; his special sense of awareness makes him testify to
the truth as he sees it, a truth which means facing his own and
his national circumstance with unflinching honesty.

Much of the initial impetus for this self-examination came
from the influence of the Spanish thinker, José Ortega y Gasset,
whose own reassessment of Spanish society served as a method-
ology for Latin Americans. Indeed, according to two modern
Mexican thinkers, Samuel Ramos (1897–1959) and Leopoldo
Zea (b. 1912), Ortega has had a revolutionary effect on Latin-
American ideas. As Ramos declared:

Philosophy did not seem to fit into this ideal framework of nationalism because it attempted to take a universal point of view, in disagree-
ment with the concrete determinations of space and time – in other
words, of history. Ortega y Gasset has helped to solve this problem
by showing the historicity of philosophy in *El tema de nuestro tiempo*.[1]

225

And Leopoldo Zea accounts for Ortega's success in Latin America:

... the philosophy of Ortega found in Spanish America an easy and rapid echo. The Spanish American through the work of Ortega could sustain his already ancient preoccupation with culture and man in this America, and at the same time feel justified as a participant in culture in a more general sense. The Spanish American laid the basis of his task of 'self-appraisal' [*toma de conciencia*] through which he has slowly discovered what his circumstantial characteristics might be as well as his relationship with other peoples and cultures. Ortega offered him a double tool: that of his preoccupation with Spanish circumstance which could also be Spanish American, and that of contemporary philosophy whose methods showed that it was possible to deduce the universal from the circumstantial and concrete, or vice versa.[2]

Ortega's most influential books were *Meditaciones del Quijote* (Meditations on Quixote, 1914), in which he suggested that any discussion of the nature of Spain must start from 'I and my circumstance'; and *El tema de nuestro tiempo* (The Theme of Our Time, 1923), in which he discussed the difficulties of traditional philosophic speculation and the importance of starting from the individual human situation.

Ortega's influence penetrated Latin America primarily through Mexico and Argentina. In Mexico, the Spanish emigré teacher, José Gaos, trained a generation of thinkers who were to approach the problem of 'What is a Mexican?' or 'What is a Latin American?' in an entirely new way, arguing from their own experience and observation. In Argentina, Ortega himself gave lecture courses, and the magazine *Sur* (the title of which was chosen by Ortega) gave great prominence to his ideas. Whether directly through Ortega's influence or not, over the last two or three decades there has appeared in Latin America a vast number of interpretative studies examining the writer's special 'circumstance'. The most outstanding of these are: *El laberinto de la soledad* (1950) by the Mexican writer, Octavio Paz; *Historia de una pasión argentina* (History of an Argentinian Passion, 1937) by Eduardo Mallea; *Guatemala, las líneas de tu mano* (Guatemala, the Lines of Your Hand, 1955) by Luis

Cardoza y Aragón (Guatemala, b. 1904); *Lima la horrible* (Horrible Lima, 1964) by Sebaştián Salazar Bondy (Peru 1924–65); and *Radiografía de la pampa* (X-ray of the Pampa, 1933) by Ezequiel Martínez Estrada (Argentina, b. 1895). In Brazil, the interpretative essay, *Retrato do Brasil* (Portrait of Brazil) by Paulo Prado (1869–1943) appeared as early as 1928, and has been followed by many others, including *Interpretação do Brasil* (1947) by Gilberto Freyre (b. 1900), *Raízes do Brazil* (Roots of Brazil, 1936) by Sérgio Buarque de Holanda (b. 1902), and *A Cultura Brasileira* (1943) by Fernando de Azevedo (b. 1894).

All these studies, and many others too numerous to mention, are interpretations of national reality which reject preconceived formulae, and often begin with a series of personal observations by the author. Octavio Paz begins *El laberinto de la soledad* by recalling his experiences in the United States and his observations of the Mexicans in Los Angeles. Luis Cardoza y Aragón starts his analysis of Guatemala with a description of his return to that country after the revolution which overthrew the dictator Ubico. In *Historia de una pasión argentina*, Eduardo Mallea gives an account of his own search for roots in childhood and adolescence. Even when the author does not start from a personal episode, the essays are the fruits of 'personal' reflection. They do not pretend to be a panacea or a programme but simply the author's way of looking at his country. The emphasis on the personal and the concrete gives the best of the essays a vividness and liveliness lacking in most of the Arielist generation's analyses of its sub-continent.

A second general feature of these essays is the emphasis on the psychological characteristics of certain national types or the prevalence of a national myth. This again marks the modern essayist off from those of the Arielist generation, who had tended to analyse their country or the sub-continent either according to racial characteristics or to environmental influences, or to a combination of the two. The modern essayist tends to take some significant national phenomenon. Octavio Paz, for instance, analyses the character of the *pocho* (the Mexican inhabitant of Los Angeles) as an example of a defensive retention of national identity. Salazar Bondy discusses *viveza criolla* (Creole 'sharpness'), which he interprets as a mixture of unscrupulousness and cynicism. In *Raízes do Brazil*, Sérgio Buarque de Holanda analyses Brazilian types such as the 'genial man' (*o homem cordial*).

Along with this examination of certain significant national characteristics or types goes an examination of attitudes as revealed in local idioms or clichés. Octavio Paz, for instance, discusses the Mexican obscene verb *chingar* (roughly translatable as to rape or violate) and its relation to the Mexican's assertion of masculinity or *machismo*. The Uruguayan writer, Mario Benedetti, in *Literatura uruguaya, siglo xx* (1963) examines the significance of the word *falluto*, with its mixture of the ideas of treachery and hypocrisy. Salazar Bondy analyses the Peruvian words *huachafo* and *huachafería* which mean snobbish, ridiculous and in bad taste. The significance of these clichés is that they reveal the deepest attitudes of the people who use them. Thus, for instance, Octavio Paz on the significance of *chingar*:

The idea of breaking and opening appears again and again in nearly all the expressions. The word is tinged with sexuality but is not synonymous with the sexual act; one can 'violate' a woman without possessing her. And when the sexual act is alluded to, the violation or deceit has a special significance. He who violates never does it with the consent of the violated. In short, to violate is to do violence upon another. It is a masculine, active, cruel word; it pricks, wounds, tears, stains. And it provokes a bitter, malicious satisfaction in the one who does it.[3]

Or Salazar Bondy on *huachafo*:

A judge who is presumptuously concerned with the letter of the law is *huachafo*; the mother who selects her future sons-in-law because of their surnames (without having a good family name herself) is *huachafa*; a man or woman who on any occasion attempts to show off culture or cosmopolitanism is *huachafo*.[4]

Or Mario Benedetti on *falluto*:

The *falluto* is not simply a hypocrite. He is more and less than this. He is the type who fails in giving or receiving a confidence, the individual in whom one cannot trust or believe because – almost unintentionally, simply because of his nature – he says one thing and does another, praises without any immediate reason, lies although it is not necessary, tries to be – just for fun – what he isn't.[5]

All these terms imply some sort of unauthenticity, either on the part of the user or towards what is described. Indeed, in all contemporary essayists, 'unauthenticity' and 'hypocrisy' occur with great frequency. For Eduardo Mallea, the worst type of Argentinian is the one who pretends to be something he is not. The Mexican playwright, Rodolfo Usigli (b. 1905) accompanies the 1944 edition of his play *El gesticulador* (The Gesticulator, 1937) with an essay on Mexican hypocrisy, which he declares had its origins in Mexican colonial times:

The colonial system – which protected hypocrisy and lies in Indians, Mestizos and even in inoculated Creoles, depriving the former of their language and their Gods, and depriving the latter of the best jobs and livings while limiting their commercial transactions – was the first official factory of Mexican hypocrisy.[6]

Lack of authenticity is also found to be at the root of Brazil's troubles. Buarque de Holanda criticizes the Brazilian's inability to come to terms with reality, and Fernando de Azevedo sees in them a too literary approach to reality, which he blames on the inheritance of Jesuit education.[7]

Undoubtedly, this concern for 'authenticity' owes much, either directly or indirectly, to the influence of psychology and to the psychologist's emphasis on coming to terms with self and with self-awareness, which in Spanish is translated by the word *conciencia* (Portuguese *consciencia*). Perhaps more than of Freud, there is here the unacknowledged influence of Jung, who believed that social conflicts and difficulties have their origins in the individual psyche. According to Jung, lack of self-awareness is very dangerous since it leads to neurosis or even psychosis on both the individual and social levels. Societies, like individuals, can go the wrong way, especially when individuals try to resemble 'the collective ideal'. Paz's illumination of the Mexicans' collective ideal clearly has a great deal to do with his conviction that the nation, like the individual, must come to terms with itself and achieve self-awareness. Adler's 'inferiority complex' and his theory of power-drives within individuals have also influenced some writers in their analysis of national character. For example, Samuel Ramos in his *El perfil del hombre y de la cultura en México* (Profile of Man and Culture in Mexico, 1934) found that Mexicans had an inferiority complex which accounted for many of their national characteristics. Less specifically, in other essayists there is the tendency drawn from modern psychology and psychoanalysis to interpret national personality through myths and through collective ideals like the ideal of *machismo*.

Along with this preoccupation with self-awareness, there goes the almost universal implication that Latin Americans are either deliberately deceiving themselves or are setting out to deceive others as to their true nature. 'The mask' is a vital prop which some essayists justify as a way of preserving inner freedom and individuality. Thus, Buarque de Holanda believes that Brazilian *bonhomie*, hospitality and love of social life are 'in a way a defence-mechanism towards society. . . . It is the equivalent of a mask which will allow each person to keep his emotions and sensibility intact'.[8] Luis Cardoza y Aragón sees Guatemalan silence and introspectiveness as a historical heritage. For Rodolfo Usigli, Mexicans lie or act out a part in order to hide their inferiority complex. The crazy taxi-drivers, for instance, illustrate 'the romantic need of the Mexican always to be risking his life – and that of others – in order to overcome his sense of inferiority to discipline'.[9] Usigli also believes that the Mexican is remarkable for his hypocrisy: a characteristic which goes back to colonial times when Mexicans learnt to lie for self-preservation. For Octavio Paz, dissimulation is the essence of Mexican character: 'The Mexican excels in the dissimulation of his passions and of himself. Fearful of the alien glance, he shrinks, lessens, turns into a shadow, a phantom, an echo. He does not walk, he glides; he doesn't suggest, he insinuates; he doesn't reply, he mutters; he doesn't complain, he smiles.'[10] Like Usigli, Paz believes that this is a product of colonial times. The colony has ended, 'but not fear and suspicion'.

The Argentinian, Ezequiel Martínez Estrada, in his *Radiografía de la pampa*, sees Argentina's history as a series of attempts by 'civilizers' to cloak the barbarism of the country – but their attempts are only cloaks and have therefore falsified reality. They introduced 'the evils of appearances, parody which could last a greater or lesser number of years, but which in the end had to fall away like the heroic disguise of the dancer at the end of the show which reveals the goatskin underneath'.[11] Eduardo Mallea discovered two Argentinas: an 'invisible' Argentina and a superficial Argentina of men who had sub-stituted appearances for authenticity. These men were often those who occupied the most important government posts or positions in the social hierarchy:

> For this world the most important thing was the gesture ... even their silence had the value of a great gesture because those who kept silent, those who kept up a game of convenient muteness, reserve, reticence, only wanted to avoid running the risk of exposing a possible personal defect to the criticism of others. Their incredibly developed fear of ridicule had come to constitute an inhibition which took the external form of extreme discretion.[12]

For the Peruvian, Salazar Bondy, the very architecture and plan of the city of Lima reveal a love of externals. The Limeñans themselves have evolved a social code which protects conformity and isolates deviations from the norm: 'To act, to flatter, to please, to conform – these constitute the rules of politeness. Excess, whether positive or negative, and overstatement, even when creative and in the control of genius, are taken as vulgarity or madness.'[13] Mario Benedetti finds the Uruguayans tend to cover up their virtues as if they were ashamed of them:

> They have flexibility of feeling and an ability to listen to others which, in the midst of an international dialogue of deaf men, may mean something constructive. But this same nation ... whether because of an inherited masochism of the tango variety, or because of a certain excessive ritual 'maleness', has come to feel inhibited ... because of its virtues which ... cause it timidity and even shame. This uncertainty, this false pose, seems to me one of the most pathetic and useless Uruguayan traits.[14]

Luis Cardoza y Aragón discovers in the Guatemalan attitude of self-defence a tendency to try to be what one is not. The Guatemalan is a solitary being who does not really communicate with others. 'We do not go out of ourselves and, if we do, it is not to start a dialogue but to explode over our own monologue. We shout, empty revolvers into the air, we relieve our feelings in order to hear ourselves better. We address ourselves. Because of insecurity, we do not accept contradictions or differences.'[15] The Guatemalan prefers not to test his identity in conversation.

These character studies have much in common. In nearly every case the unauthenticity or pose is attributed to fear of exposure, of social censure, and, ultimately, to years of conditioning. The historical roots of these attitudes are therefore important.

History for this modern generation of essayists does not consist of political events or military incidents. They are primarily concerned with the relationship between social structure and attitudes, between society and its culture. Fernando de Azevedo's monumental *A Cultura Brasileira*, for instance, attributes the undue literary emphasis in Brazilian culture to the long-lasting effects of the system of Jesuit education during the colonial period, a system which he describes in detail.[16] Ezequiel Martínez Estrada, in his *Radiografía de la pampa* attributes the lack of authenticity in Argentinian life to the determination of men of the past, like Sarmiento, to impose a European concept of 'progress' on the country.[17] Salazar Bondy finds that Peruvians are alienated because of the excessive weight of the colonial past on the present. 'The past is everywhere, embracing home, school, politics and press, folklore and literature, religion and society.'[18] But this picturesque past is a false past, a deliberately sustained myth which Salazar Bondy shows is part of the Lima aristocracy's machinery of power. Octavio Paz, in his *El laberinto de la soledad*, shows how Mexican creativity was stifled by the imposition of dead forms and alien religious dogma during the colonial period and afterwards. A large part of Cardoza y Aragón's analysis of Guatemala is concerned with the historical basis of the social structure.[19] The Colombian Otto Morales Benítez, (b. 1920) in his *Muchedumbres y banderas* (Masses and Flags, 1962), is concerned with the attitudes and structures inherited from the colony, the tension between the need for freedom and self-expression, and the imposition of 'intellectual, economic and political colonialism'.[20]

It is obvious that the 'unauthenticity' noted by most essayists in the attitudes of certain or all of their countrymen is something bred in them from the past. Again and again, the accusation is made against the colonial elite and the early post-independence politicians and thinkers that they imposed political and intellectual structures upon Latin America which bore no relation to reality. This criticism forms the marrow of many of the studies of Leopoldo Zea, who has made perhaps the most thorough analysis of Mexico's relation with European culture:

> The European who made the discovery, conquest and colonization of Mexico came with a concept of the world and of existence in which there was no place for the concept of the world and existence possessed by the native peoples they met. This world, instead of being understood, was condemned and sacrificed to the so-called universalism which the European had accorded to his own culture, existence and concept of the world. However, a real world like the newly discovered one could not be denied as easily as all that. Despite all the efforts made by the European to deny this reality and substitute his own, it continued alive and throbbing, revealing itself in all its energy on the most unexpected occasions. American man, the result of this union, is a man who has become aware of this dual reality and, with it, aware of his own incontrovertible right to universality as an expression of the human.[21]

Mexican history has been a dialectical struggle between the unauthentic and the real. However, in modern times, European culture can no longer consider itself the only expression of universality. Zea here employs a key concept used by nearly all the essayists writing in the last two or three decades: the concept of *conciencia* (awareness or consciousness). Zea believes that, hitherto, Mexico has been at a stage of development in which there was action but no self-awareness; hence this action was 'spontaneous, concrete and circumstantial'. This was now changing and Mexico was entering into a new stage of awareness of its reality. 'In this new stage, if we are to rise to the circumstances, we shall have to make ourselves aware of the springs which have moved hitherto irrational forces in order to direct them better. In this way, we shall not fall for yet another Utopia.'[22] As a nation, Mexico must now take responsibility in full awareness of its reality.

A very similar analysis of the Argentinian was made in 1936 by Carlos Erro (b.1899) in his *Tiempo lacerado* (Wounded Time), in which he declares that Latin Americans had not hitherto participated in forging the culture which they accepted. But the time of *desengaño* (disillusionment, or opening one's eyes to an unpleasant truth) had arrived. This *desengaño* is the necessary first stage on the road to authenticity. It is clearly a concept similar to the *conciencia* of other writers. Mario Benedetti, speaking of the Uruguayan's tendency to 'evasion', his inability to 'root' himself in reality, also believes that *conciencia* is basic to a change of attitude. Although Benedetti is speaking first of all about writers and literature, he extends his statement to cover Uruguay in general: 'I have the impression that Uruguayans, and in the first place the writers, are learning to look towards Latin America and to feel part of its destiny. . . .'[23] Hitherto the Uruguayans had done little more than look to Europe, only to find that the rich European tradition simply became one more 'influence' on Uruguay. 'People cannot realize what it costs to change one's dreams and recognize one's own frustration. We are doing this now.'[24]

In a sense, Benedetti extrapolates from literature or from artistic life. This is a common feature among the essayists. Octavio Paz, for instance, makes artistic isolation, 'solitude', the basic human condition which all Mexicans must be aware of before they can live authentically: 'Solitude, which is the very condition of our life, is a test and a purgation, at the end of which anguish and instability will disappear. Plenitude and union, which is rest and happiness, harmony with the world – these await us at the end of the labyrinth of solitude.'[25] Eduardo Mallea makes a similar extrapolation in respect to Argentina:

Without exiling oneself, one cannot get anywhere. The path of creation is the path of exile; and there is a time for rejecting this and a time for accepting; there is a time for choosing to remain tied to surrounding fiction and a time for exiling oneself. And such an exile, in our country, means going and living in the invisible nation with its invisible sensibility, living in the heart of the nation.[26]

Both Paz and Mallea are concerned with the idea of 'creativity' as opposed to system and dogma which stifle creation. They see nations and individuals as creative organisms whose true nature can be expressed only when dogmas are rejected, masks flung aside and solitude and anguish fully faced. In Argentina, this emphasis on creativity springs out of the critique of the limitations of rationalism made, not only by Ortega y Gasset, but also by the North-American critic, Waldo Frank, who had an important influence on the *Sur* group and on the essayist, Carlos Erro.

With writers of more decided left-wing sympathies, there is greater emphasis on culture as the reflection of a ruling class ideology. For them, a *toma de conciencia* means recognizing the class origins of certain attitudes. In his *Literatura argentina y realidad política* (1964), for instance, David Viñas (b. 1929) studies Argentinian literature as an expression of class ideology, and Salazar Bondy has studied the city of Lima as an expression of the mind and ideology of the Lima aristocracy.

This striving for authenticity inevitably involves relations with or attitudes to other cultures. But, whereas the nationalists of the twenties had attempted to reject Europe and find values in the land, the Negro or the Indian, artists of the present generation realize the fruitlessness of complete rejection. Whereas nineteenth-century artists had imitated European forms when their own national reality was completely different, those of the present generation are more confident about their own culture, particularly as the European is no longer persuaded that his is the only culture. Leopoldo Zea puts the viewpoint in this way: 'Western man is now realizing the limitations of his own view of what constitutes the human reality. . . . But this is equally being realized by other men who, until recently, had to justify their humanity to a world which begrudged it.'[27] For Octavio Paz there is a common denominator of solitude shared by all modern men. The Argentinian essayist, Hector Murena (b. 1920), believes that America is 'a repetition of the drama of man's exile

235

in the world, and America is the new attempt of man to overcome the silence of the world, to people the inert land of matter with the living word of the spirit. . . . America is the child of Europe and must assassinate her in order to live.'[28] Though there is, perhaps, a closer sense of human identity with Europe, it is clear that the old reverence for Europe has gone, even in writers – like Borges – who are generally regarded as 'Europeanizers'. The modern essayist feels a new freedom towards European culture which is in part the fruit of a self-confidence about America – an America that now includes North America.

The question of the relationship between North and Latin America is obviously the most delicate of all, the point at which the stress on authenticity is apt to slacken. On the one hand, North America is the imperial power par excellence: a fact which recent events in Guatemala, Cuba and the Dominican Republic have confirmed. On the other hand, North-American culture is undoubtedly attractive to Latin Americans. In the first place it is an *American* culture, vigorous, lively and original. The days of Rodó and his view of North America as a purely materialist civilization have long since passed. Furthermore, in many ways the position in his society of the North-American writer is very similar to that of the Latin American; there is the same sense of exile, the same nonconformity, the same fight for the creation of an original yet universal art. And North-American culture undoubtedly gains from the comparative mediocrity of the art being produced in the Soviet Union. The contrast between North-American and Soviet culture tends to strengthen the view of those, like Octavio Paz, who regard art as born out of man's nonconformity with society. Therefore, though essayists still stress differences between North and South America, the gulf has narrowed greatly since the Arielist generation. For instance, the Peruvian Luis Alberto Sánchez (b. 1900) and the Argentinian Hector Murena recognize similarities in North- and Latin-American literature, and stress the differences between this literature and that of Europe.[29] The Colombian Eduardo Caballero Calderón (b. 1910) has gone even further, suggesting in *Americanos y europeos* (1957) that, with the industrialization of Latin America, North and South America will be very similar.

In Mexico, on the other hand, differences between Latin America and North America are still stressed. Octavio Paz's *El laberinto de la soledad* underlines fundamental differences between the Mexican and the North American in their attitude to life. Paz, in fact, sees a world division, not between East and West or Europe and America, but between the underdeveloped and the advanced nations. Here he is perhaps influenced by Toynbee, who has had a considerable impact on Mexico.*

It goes without saying that the artist's own position with regard to his society's *toma de conciencia* is seen as vital. Of all humanity, the artist and intellectual are at the outset the most likely to have a high enough degree of ethic responsibility to achieve self-understanding and hence to be able to understand their own positions as Mexicans or Ecuadorians or Bolivians. As Alfonso Reyes has said, the man who has been able to discipline himself in pursuit of a vocation or craft is the one who should guide American society 'because there is full responsibility only where there is full awareness'.[30] The special importance of the writer is precisely that he works in freedom, without regard to dogma. He is the very one who, according to Octavio Paz, is able to 'invent . . . new words and new ideas for these new and strange realities which have come about'.[31] For Eduardo Mallea, too, national and personal awareness are inextricable: 'With each day, the world, the world of the senses, was my obligation but the world through me and my nation.'[32] According to the Colombian writer, Hernando Téllez (b. 1908), the artist of all men is the one most able to transcend the conditioning of the environment: 'This act of spiritual liberty, thanks to which it has been possibly to swell language with certain meanings and to make a world of beauty gravitate upon living experience, annihilates the servitude of the artist to the powers that surround him.'[33] Hector Murena refers to the 'nonconformism of the artist' which makes him a permanent rebel and therefore an active force in society. For Mario Benedetti, the most creative and vital part of society is the intelligentsia, which he defines in the Oxford Dictionary sense as 'the part of a nation that aspires to

*Leopoldo Zea, for instance, dedicated his *El occidente y la conciencia de México* (1953) to Toynbee.

independent thinking'.[34] For Eduardo Mallea, the act of creation is the most truly spiritual act and is what separates true existence from unauthentic living.[35] The artist pays for freedom and creativity, and the price is his feeling of solitude (according to Octavio Paz) or exile (Eduardo Mallea).

It is tempting to conclude that many of these essayists are merely rationalizing their own isolation. This may be true; yet like all such 'truths', it does not constitute real understanding. However contradictory, vague and self-deceptive some of the attitudes are, they have undoubtedly been very valuable to the artists themselves. The notion of the artist's professional self-discipline, his responsibility to bear witness honestly to his own circumstance and that of his country, has undoubtedly transformed the literary scene, especially in the novel and even in the theatre and the short story. Most valuable of all, the artist's stressing of 'I and my circumstance' has enabled him to by-pass the Scylla and Charybdis of European imitation and regionalism.

THE NOVEL AND THE QUEST FOR AUTHENTICITY

A remarkable development in the Latin-American novel has occurred in the last decade. Not only have a substantial group of novelists such as Julio Cortázar, Mario Vargas Llosa, Gabriel García Márquez and Carlos Fuentes achieved international reputations, but also a new public has appeared, a public that is eager to read novels about its own continent by its own authors. And this emergence of the novel has coincided with the full impact of technical innovations and an emphasis on linguistic inventiveness, which has meant the virtual disappearance of the novel with an obvious didactic message and of the documentary novel concerned with exposing injustice. The place of the latter has been taken by the sociological report (an example being *Los indios de México* by Fernando Benítez). Authenticity now depends not only on the author's own sincerity but on his presentation of the material in a way which allows the reader a freedom of interpretation. However, certain conventional patterns in the Latin-American novel have not entirely disappeared although they have taken on new depths and dimensions in the hands of contemporary writers. For instance, both the quest novel and the historical novel are still found by some writers to be the most suitable vehicles for the expression of their attitudes to Latin America.

The novel in which the intellectual or artistic hero searches for a meaningful life-pattern has long existed in Latin America. In the novels of the Arielist generation, as has been pointed out, the quest nearly always ended in a tragic defeat, owing to the unfavourable environment. In the novel of recent years, however, the quest of the intellectual hero's search for self-fulfilment is generally equated with that of his country.

The link between the two kinds of novel is provided by Rómulo Gallegos. His first novel, *Reinaldo Solar* (1920), is a classic novel of disillusionment; but his *Canaima* (1935) is a new type of quest novel in which the adventures of the hero, Marcos Vargas, are an objectification of the national myths which have to be exploded before a state of authenticity can be reached. At the end of the novel, we find him living close to nature, learning Indian lore among the men of the tribe in which he has gone to live. *Canaima*, therefore, has a lesson: it is only by plunging roots into nature that Venezuelans can develop a sense of national identity. The need to strike roots in the land, however, is not a solution generally put forward by younger writers. Carpentier's novel *Los pasos perdidos* (1953), which is also a quest novel, firmly rejects any solution for the artist or society as a whole which means going back to more primitive ways of existence. The artist's place is on the frontier of the future; he can 'retrace lost steps' but not stay in the past.

Perhaps the classic quest novel of recent times, in which the protagonist represents the author's own search as well as the more authentic aspect of national life, is Eduardo Mallea's *La bahía del silencio* (The Bay of Silence, 1940). In many ways, the events of the novel follow closely the pattern of those adventurous intellectuals of the Arielist era, the main events in whose lives were the founding of a review, the love affair (usually with an intellectual woman), the endless discussions about the future of their country, the visit to Europe, and cognate episodes relating the successes and failures of fellow intellectuals. All these have appeared before in the novels of Gallegos, Reyles and Gálvez. In *La bahía del silencio*, the hero, Tregua, follows this type pattern, and, like those of the intellectuals of the Arielist generation, his successive experiments tend to meet with frustration. He helps to found a magazine, *Basta*, which fails because of divisions among the contributors. The financial backer withdraws his support, advising contributors to go back to their personal isolation. Tregua's experience in Europe leads him to despair of European intellectuals, whom he finds negative: 'I thought of my own country and the breath of its worthy and profound men. They would arise someday but not like these; they would arise, filled with a desire to construct, intelligently and honestly militant.'[36] The third part of the novel deals with Tregua's return to Buenos Aires, and relates his affair with Gloria, a strange tormented girl, and finally his admiration for a married woman, who symbolizes the authenticity of the 'new Argentinian' and for whom he writes the novel. The difference between *La bahía del silencio* and the novels of the Arielist generation is that, in the former, the inevitable frustrations are not seen as failures but as essential experience for those who are to achieve 'priceless awareness'. Of his friends in the novel and of the woman he admires, Tregua says:

You and all of them have reached that place which the sea of fury, persecution and adversity washes without destroying. All of you, and who knows how many others in this world, have reached this bay, this place of waiting, this bay where silence is concentrated and where its fruits are ripened without fear of storm, cyclone and bad weather. How beautiful and deep is the bay. Those are there who have made a triumph of their failure.[37]

The bay of silence is none other than the self-awareness which the essayists had seen as the necessary condition for regeneration.

Mallea is one of the few recent novelists to adopt the situations of the Arielist generation with only slight modifications. Nearly all other novelists have broken away from this comparatively straightforward presentation and prefer to present the quest either in a historical context or through a hero who is a significant national type, or through a combination of these two methods. Indeed, one of the characteristics of the modern Latin-American novel is the enormous attraction of the historical theme. Yet preoccupation with the historical theme is not to be regarded as reflecting an evasion of the present. As with the essayists, it is a way of understanding the origin of national attitudes, and again the main purpose is authenticity. Thus Carlos Droguett (Chile, b. 1915) in *100 gotas de sangre y 200 de sudor* (100 Drops of Blood and 200 of Sweat, 1961) sets about trying to present the Spanish Conquest, not in a romantic idealized light, but as 'a terrible conjunction of Apocalypse and Last Judgement'. Most of the historical novels are fundamentally quest novels in which the choice of historical setting has a special significance in relation to national history.

One of the prototypes of this type of historical novel is *Las lanzas coloradas* (The Coloured Lances) by Arturo Uslar Pietri (Venezuela, b. 1906) which was first published in 1931. Uslar Pietri presents Bolívar's first unsuccessful campaign to liberate South America from Spanish rule through the experiences of Fernando Fonta, a young Creole aristocrat who, almost against his will, finds himself on Bolívar's side. A civilized man, he has little heart for war but dies fighting for his ideals. Against him there fights the former foreman of his estate, Presentación Campos, a man who incarnates the barbarism that, after independence, will dominate Venezuelan life. The novel, therefore, is not merely a historical re-creation but goes back to the origins of the political and social chaos of Venezuelan life. The Cuban novelist, Alejo Carpentier (b. 1904) in *El siglo de las luces***** (1962) also chooses the period of the end of the eighteenth century and the beginning of the nineteenth in which to set his novel. As in Uslar Pietri's *Las lanzas coloradas*, there is a polarity between the aristocratic and intellectual descendants of the Creole aristocracy and the 'new man' – in this case Victor Hugues, a revolutionary from Europe who becomes a cynical dictator in Guiana. *El siglo de las luces* is one of the most ambitious of the 'historical' novels, since Carpentier aims at 'naming' the Caribbean area

*Literally, 'the century of enlightenment'; it was published in English under the title *Explosion in a Cathedral*.

and at presenting it as a unity. The action moves from Cuba to English-speaking and French-speaking islands and to the mainland, and the whole area is seen as a geographical unity: a fact which its post-Conquest history has tragically denied. It is significant that both *El siglo de las luces* and an earlier novel, *El reino de este mundo* (The Kingdom of This World, 1949) are set in the period of the French Revolution. Both have similar themes: the foundering of the ideals of the French Revolution in a Caribbean environment. In *El siglo de las luces*, Carpentier relates the story of the slave risings in Haiti at the end of the eighteenth century and the monarchy of the black emperor, Henri Christophe, whose court was an exact imitation of the courts of the French monarchs before the Revolution. But the reality of Haiti, with the voodoo cults, the belief in magic, the mixture of races and its tropical nature, can never be encompassed in European patterns even when they are supposedly revolutionary. Similarly in *El siglo de las luces*, an orphaned Cuban family adopts Victor Hugues, the revolutionary leader, as a substitute father, and follow his career as an emissary of the French Revolutionary forces, as one of its representatives and finally as a despot in Cayenne. The guillotine which Victor Hugues introduces to the Caribbean is symbolic of the real order he represents. Thus, for Carpentier, the historical past serves as a kind of lesson for the present.

The historical approach has encouraged the writing of the 'roman fleuve'. The Brazilian novelist, Erico Veríssimo (b. 1905), for instance, has covered the history of the province of Rio Grande do Sul in a colossal many-volumed work, *O Tempo e o Vento* (Time and the Wind, 1948–63), which extends from the eighteenth century to the present day. The Ecuadorian novelist, Alfredo Pareja Díez-Canseco (b. 1908) has, on the other hand, in *Los nueve años* (1956) chosen only nine years of his country's history, but he deals in depth with the struggle against, and the ending of, an Ecuadorian dictatorship during the twenties and thirties.

Even novels concerned with denunciation of exploitation, those with an overt political message, have tended in recent years to present their case in a significant historical setting. A notable example of this approach is Miguel Angel Asturias's *Hombres de maíz* (1949) which starts at an indeterminate point in time when the Mestizos begin to take common land from the Indian, and traces the progress of the Indian's degradation down to the present. The Bolivian novelist, Augusto Céspedes, in *Metal del diablo* (1946), presents his country's tragic destiny through the story of the rise of a tin magnate, who is closely modelled on a historical figure, and whose career he follows from 1890 onwards. Another of Céspedes's novels, *Sangre de mestizos* (Blood of Mestizos, 1936), consists of a series of sketches about the Chaco war of the 1930s in which he took part. David Viñas (b. 1929), another novelist of left-wing sympathies, takes a historical incident as the central theme of *Los dueños de la tierra* (The Lords of the Earth, 1958). Like *Metal del diablo*, *Los dueños de la tierra* uses historical characters mixed with fictional ones. The protagonist, Vicente Vera, is a young intellectual, a supporter of Irigoyen, President of the Argentinian Republic, who sends him to Patagonia to mediate in a dispute between the farmowners and their employees. The former are the true 'lords of the earth' and easily obscure the real situation from Vicente, who is both ignorant of the country and unwilling or unable to act decisively. When the army is called in to help the landowners suppress the workers' strike, Vicente remains quite unaware of the real situation; under the most humiliating circumstances, he learns of his impotence and can make only the feeblest of gestures. The novel is thus not only a criticism of Vicente but, through him, of the impotence and limitations of the Irigoyen regime.

Viñas's Vicente symbolizes the kind of middle-class youth for whom the Irigoyen regime acted as spokesman. It is a common device among today's novelists to use such a character in order to expose the unauthenticity or errors of certain periods of the past. This is true of the novels of two Mexican writers, Juan Rulfo (b. 1918) and Carlos Fuentes. Rulfo deals with a Mexico that is now dead, the Mexico of the landowning *cacique*. The eponymous protagonist of *Pedro Páramo* (1955) symbolizes this Mexico which now lives on only through memory. The narrator, one of Páramo's many sons (in a sense all of Mexico is descended from Pedro Páramo), goes to the village of Comala to find Páramo, only to discover that he is dead. His life can be constructed only through memory and through the conversations of the dead which still linger in the air of the village. It is through these that we learn of Páramo's life, of his many affairs, of his domination of the life of the village. The novel ends with his death, which occurs just after the revolution; at that point, with his power gone, he is killed, as the old Mexico he represents has been killed. The technique of the novel, with its use of the strange conversations of dead men, not only gives an air of unreality to the story but also helps to overcome the reader's possible objection to the hero. Páramo is not the villain of the social protest novel; he is a human being of a type that has now disappeared. The novel thus transcends narrow polemic so that the Mexican reader can understand rather than blame the past. A somewhat similar dream-like technique is used by Rulfo's compatriot Elena Garro (b. 1917) in her *Los recuerdos del porvenir* (Memories of the Future, 1963). Here she tries to transcend the divisions of the revolution and show all the elements as human beings.

Carlos Fuentes's novels nearly all deal with the consequences of the revolution. However, their aim is not simply to understand the past but also to point out moral failings on the part of certain classes of Mexican. His novel *Las buenas conciencias* (The Clear Consciences, 1959) traces the history of a middle-class youth, Jaime Ceballos, and his family, from the years that preceded the revolution to just after it. After an initial rebellion, Jaime becomes part of the new establishment.

Such was the order of the world in which he lived. Christ loved the just, he lived in good conscience, he belonged to good men, to the decent people, to good reputation. To the devil with the humble, the sinners, the abandoned, the rebels, and the poor, with all those who remained on the margin of the accepted order.[38]

In *La muerte de Artemio Cruz* (The Death of Artemio Cruz, 1962), Fuentes explores the conscience of one of the new men to emerge from the Mexican revolution. When the novel opens, Cruz is on his death-bed; episodes of his past flash before him in his last moments. The reader is thus given an insight into the moral failure of this man; the illegitimate son of a big house, repudiated by the family, his idealism is destroyed by the revolution, from which he emerges a cynical go-getter who enriches himself by exploiting the failures of a system he knows so well. Artemio Cruz is the incarnation of the hypocritical, deceiving Mexican, the one who, according to Octavio Paz and Samuel Ramos and others, must 'violate'. Fuentes, however, does not condemn him. Cruz has his admirable side just as Mexico, despite the shortcomings of the post-revolutionary era, has its admirable qualities.

The return to the past through a hero or heroine living in the present is made by an Argentinian novelist, Ernesto Sábato (b. 1911) in his novel, *Sobre héroes y tumbas* (On Heroes and Tombs, 1961), which starts from a crime in present-day Buenos Aires. A girl, Alejandra, kills her father and sets fire to herself and the house; through a friend, we learn the history of Alejandra's family, which springs from the heroes of independence days: a family of eccentric individuals, larger than life. The novel covers an enormous range of the social history of Argentina, but it dwells particularly on the twenties and thirties and the years just before Perón came to power. Alejandra's father, the last male descendant of a line of 'heroes', is a mad and degenerate character who has mixed with Anarchists, not from political reasons but to get their help in carrying out robberies. Like *La muerte de Artemio Cruz*, Sábato's novel is a story of the corruption of an ideal: corruption that, in the case of Argentina, goes back to the days of Lavalle and his murder of Dorrego in the early years of the nineteenth century. The real villain is the city of Buenos Aires and the 'unauthentic' values it represents. It is from these that the young man, Martín, escapes at the end of the novel when he goes as lorry-driver's mate to the south; only when he is well away from the city does he feel for the first time 'a very pure peace' entering 'his tormented soul'.

Neither Fuentes nor Sábato writes from a clear-cut point of view; their own torment and confusion about themselves and the state of their countries are reflected in the structures of their novels.

THE GENERATION OF PARRICIDES

For most Latin-American writers, the past is something to be rejected, a period which the present generation must expose and overcome. This attitude is strikingly reflected in the number of modern novels which deal with relations between the generations, and the frequency with which the older generation is held up as an example of inadequacy or failure. Frequently, this is objectified in actual parricide or near-parricide. Ernesto Sábato's *Sobre héroes y tumbas* ends in holocaust, with Alejandra killing her father and then burning herself to death in the same room. The line of 'heroes' is thus wiped out; Martín, the new type of Argentinian, leaves Buenos Aires for the south and starts, it is suggested, a new phase in the story of the nation. In *Gracias por el fuego* (Thanks for the Light, 1964) by Mario Benedetti, the *viejo* (old man) represents the corruption of the Uruguayan establishment. Enormously wealthy, he controls the press and has a ramification of business interests, and he tries to dominate and exploit his family as he has dominated the nation. One of his sons, who represents a more honest and self-aware generation, plans to kill him, but he fails and commits suicide, thus epitomizing the tragic failure of his generation to deal with the evils that beset Uruguayan society. In José María Arguedas's novel of Peruvian life, *Los ríos profundos* (The Deep Rivers, 1958), an old man – this time uncle of the central character – is a corrupt and unscrupulous landowner whose figure overshadows the novel. In Carlos Fuentes's *La muerte de Artemio Cruz*, the corruption of the father is offset by the integrity of a son, who dies fighting in the Spanish Civil War. Pareja Díez-Canseco's novel of Ecuador, *Los nueve años*, begins with the rebellion of a young, soul-searching adolescent, Pablo, against his corrupt army-officer father.

The examples can be multiplied. In nearly every case, the older generation represents corruption, the dead hand on the present. Even when this is not so, as in *El paredón* (The Wall, 1962) by Carlos Martínez Moreno (Uruguay, b. 1917), lack of communication between the generations is an insuperable barrier. In this novel, the father represents the old-fashioned

Liberal who had dominated Uruguayan life in the past. The novel opens with the defeat of his party; the son, long disillusioned with Liberalism, goes to Cuba where, momentarily, he finds the energy and purpose lacking in his own country.

In the modern Chilean novel, the generation conflict has been related to the decline of a social class. In *Coronación* (Coronation, 1959), by José Donoso (b. 1925), two of the central characters – a very old woman, now mad, and her ineffectual, lazy, middle-aged son – are members of the upper-class. A young peasant girl is employed to look after the old woman. Her presence soon disrupts the household; mother and son become obsessed by her, while the girl herself falls in love with a young criminal who, with her connivance, breaks into the house. This assault on the house symbolizes the eruption of new forces into Chilean life. The culminating scene of the novel, in which the dying old woman is mockingly crowned by her servants, is an ironic comment on the degeneration of a class that had once held real power. Throughout the novel, age and impotence are associated with the old ruling class, vigour and virility with the young and the working or servant classes. Another Chilean novel, *El peso de la noche* (The Weight of the Night, 1964), by Jorge Edwards (b. 1931), again deals with a generations-conflict. This time, however, the conflict is entirely within a social class, the characters representing three generations of a single upper-class family. Señora Cristina, whose illness and death overshadow the novel, represents the older generation that has lived according to traditional codes. Catholic and conservative, they have imposed their order without questioning it. The second generation, represented by a son, Joaquín, is more tormented. Joaquín has rebelled, but his rebellion is a futile one and he has become a dipsomaniac, attempting fruitlessly to find satisfaction in personal relationships. The third generation, represented by Joaquín's adolescent nephew, Francisco, is once again living the conflict between the imposed religious and moral code and its own experience. Whereas Joaquín's rebellion is seen as a temporary one (for, with the death of Cristina, he returns to 'order'), that of Francisco is seen as being more authentic and more definitive.

THE GEOGRAPHICAL DIMENSION

If history is used to question the values of the past, geography is used to raise questions of national identity. By taking his characters into a foreign setting, the modern novelist illuminates the relations of Latin America with other cultures. Much of Julio Cortázar's *Rayuela*, for instance, is set in Paris; the Latin-American characters reveal a typically mocking attitude to the culture which they belong to and yet treat with irreverence. One of Carlos Martínez Moreno's short stories, *Los aborígenes* (1964), is set in Rome and contrasts a Latin-American ambassador, who has been brought up in the backlands of his country and who is now writing a study of 'the aborigines', with his wily Italian chauffeur, whose pattern of life is as ancient as the city itself. The old and the new are presented in startling juxtaposition.

The European setting had been used extensively by writers of previous generations, and the novel dealing with Latin-American 'exiles' in Paris has had a long history, ever since the time of the Chilean nineteenth-century novelist, Alberto Blest Gana (1830–1920). What is new is the appearance in recent years of North America in the Latin-American novel. It is against the background of the United States that some novelists now set their clash of cultures; the story of a Chilean race-horse in California, for instance, is the theme of *Caballo de copas* (Horse of Clubs, 1957) by Fernando Alegría (Chile, b. 1918), and Mario Benedetti's *Gracias por el fuego* has opening chapters set among Uruguayans who are living in New York and whose sense of national identity is weakened by their contact with a nation that is so much more powerful and so different from their own.

Even when novels are not set in the United States, Americans often appear as characters. They are often used in social-protest novels as the hated exploiter figure – the sinister whisky-drinking Yankee has, indeed, a long history in Latin-American fiction. What is surprising is the appearance of the 'good American' in some recent novels. Thus, in Miguel Angel Asturias's *Viento fuerte* (Strong Wind, 1950), the evil American who controls the banana plantations of Guatemala is offset by a good American who tries to help the Indians and fight exploitation. And *La muerte de Artemio Cruz* is dedicated to C. Wright Mills, 'true voice of North America, friend and comrade of the Latin-American struggle'.

The impact of Cuba is perhaps too recent to have been recorded in much modern literature. Carlos Martínez Moreno, in *El paredón* (The Wall, 1962), effectively contrasts the aimless disillusionment of middle-class Uruguayans with the enthusiasm of the Cubans in the early days of their revolution. Both the strengths and the weaknesses of the Castroite revolution are faithfully recorded. The impression is ambiguous, but almost certainly an accurate record of the mixture of enthusiasm and bewilderment with which the Cuban revolution was greeted by the rest of Latin-America's middle-class intellectuals.

A QUESTION OF GOOD AND EVIL

The day when Latin Americans viewed the situation of their countries in terms of social or political solutions has long passed. The ambiguity of Carlos Martínez Moreno's account of the Cuban revolution is characteristic of a generation whose preoccupation is as much ethical as political. This does not mean that the concern for social justice has vanished; it is still there, but more and more the evil is seen as being in men's hearts. A symptom of this shift of emphasis is the extensive use of Christian or general religious symbolism in the modern novel. As has already been pointed out, this symbolism may be a device for giving a local incident universal significance, but the implications are wider than this. The Christ-figure appears again and again in the modern novel, not as a symbol of organized religion – which in Latin America has always been tainted by its alliance with the established order – but as a symbol of true humanity and justice.

The most striking use of Christian symbolism in this way is in the Paraguayan novel, *Hijo de hombre* (1959) by Augusto Roa Bastos. Here, the crude struggle between the governing elite and the oppressed is transformed into a poetic vision of Paraguay between the peasant risings of 1912 and the Chaco war of the 1930s. The village of Itapé is overshadowed by the figure of a crucified Christ which, once a year, is taken down from its cross and paraded through the village. The Christ, carved by a leper, had been put into its position in defiance of the governing elite; it is not a symbol of passive suffering but 'a victim who had to be avenged'. The story tells of the heroism of simple people who, generation after generation, fight against the stifling and all-powerful representatives of the state and who invent their own myths and their own forms of rebellion. One of the culminating incidents of the novel – the tying of an assassinated police chief in the place of the crucified Christ – is a ferocious comment on the Christian ideal. Rebellion and oppression are the two extremes between which Paraguay oscillates: 'There must be some way out of this monstrous absurdity of man crucified by man. If not, we shall have to believe that man is forever cursed and that *this* is hell and that we cannot expect salvation.'[39] A Colombian novel, *En Chimá nace un santo* (In Chimá a Saint is Born, 1963) by Manuel Zapata Olivella (b. 1920) tells the story of a saint cult which begins when a cripple miraculously escapes being burnt to death in a fire. The cripple, during his lifetime and after his death, becomes the object of a fanatical devotion in which the poorest and most oppressed find hope. The authorities of both church and state violently oppress the cult, only to find themselves up against the fury of the peasants, who for the first time have understood their own power.

In several other novels, organized Christianity conflicts with true Christian or human feeling. Eduardo Caballero Calderón's *El Cristo de espaldas* (Christ Turns His Back, 1953), concerns the single-handed efforts of a priest in a conservative Colombian village to prevent the summary execution of an innocent man who happens to belong to the wrong political faction. The priest saves the man but has to leave the village in which the attempt to live according to Christ's law is interpreted as political rebellion. In the Peruvian novel, *Los ríos profundos* by José María Arguedas (b. 1911), the narrator is a boy whose father puts him in a Catholic boarding-school. The school is a microcosm of society outside; the church hierarchy supports the landowners and attempts to stifle the narrator's natural sympathy for the Indians among whom he has grown up and to whom he feels a deep attachment. The boy's love of Indian music, song and myth represents the authentic in his experience, in contrast with the imposed pattern of Christianity which breeds suspicion between people and unhealthy sexual attitudes. The same author's *Todas las sangres* (All the Bloods, 1964) contrasts the perfect dignity of the Indians with the violence and cruelty and materialism of the Whites.

Other authors prefer to go back further than Christianity and pose the problems in terms of the eternal fight between good and evil. Miguel Angel Asturias's *El Señor Presidente* makes the dictator into a demiurge against whom Lucifer (in the person of his secretary, 'Angel Face') rebels. The fight is the eternal fight between the forces of light and the forces of darkness. The monumental Brazilian novel, *Grande Sertão: Veredas* (1956) by João Guimarães Rosa, is a Ulysses-like soliloquy of a north-east bandit who believes that he has sold his soul to the devil. The devil, however, turns out to be a metaphor: 'Men sell their lives of their own accord and without any buyer.' The story of the bandit thus becomes a story of any human existence, with its temptations, its wrong paths and its search for authenticity.

The conclusion to be drawn from this survey of the quest novel is that the overwhelming concern of the novelist, like the essayist, is for 'authenticity', for ethical rather than political solutions.[40]

However, the problem is not invariably put in the form of a quest or transmitted in terms of myth. Many recent novels have adopted a technique which presents a problem of national significance within the bounds of a tight, and limited, situation. Very frequently, the novelist has chosen to set his novel in a closed community, and this very technique of insulation appears to reflect the concern of many writers that the national and social problems they are writing about may, in fact, have no obvious solution. The claustrophobic atmosphere of these novels of insulation – set in an isolated village community or a boarding-school – contrasts with the sweeping canvases of the historical novel. Eduardo Caballero Calderón's *El Cristo de espaldas*, for example, is set in a Colombian village with almost no contact with the outside world. This has enabled the authorities – the mayor and the judge – to wipe out all opposition from the village; they mercilessly hunt down the one man who is in opposition to them. Many Colombian novelists and short-story writers emphasize the isolation of villages in which – because of their remoteness – fanaticism, violence and odd forms of mysticism breed unchecked by contact with the outside world.

The most striking examples of novels of insulation are those written by the Colombian novelist, Gabriel García Márquez, who nearly always sets his stories and novels in remote villages. In *La hojarasca* (1965), in the stories of *Los funerales de la Mamá Grande*, in *La mala hora*, (The Evil Hour), *Cien años de soledad* (A Hundred Years of Solitude, 1967) and *El coronel no tiene quien le escriba* (Nobody Writes to the Colonel, 1961), the isolation of a village or town is presented in such a way that it appears analogous to the isolation of Latin America as a whole. Although not allegorical, the novels do represent mythic versions of Latin-American reality. In *El coronel no tiene quien le escriba*, the protagonist is a retired army colonel, who lives in a remote village, waiting for news of a pension which has been due to him for decades. The village is controlled by political enemies who have killed his son; he has virtually no friends or allies, no one who can overtly support him. Old, starving to death, and with no possibility of change, he presents, nevertheless, a defiant face to the world. The symbol of his pride and rebellion is a fighting cock which had belonged to his son and which he refuses to sell, even though he lacks the food to feed it. At the end of the book, he is still alone, still starving. When his wife asks what they are going to live on until the next cock-fight he can only answer: 'On shit'. García Márquez's novel is a very brief one, little more than a long short story. In it he says more about the Colombian situation than many more overt political or social protest novels. He does it by presenting us with a heroic character who symbolizes the doggedness of the best in Latin America and at the same time the iron-bound nature of its small community life. In *Cien años de soledad*, the town of Macondo is insulated from the rest of the world because surrounded by marshes and impassable jungle. Macondo has been founded by the family of Buendía as far as possible from the sea from which they come, and its inaccessibility means that everything there follows a different rhythm from that of the rest of the world. European inventions – false teeth, ice, the magnet – are capriciously introduced by wandering gypsies, but the place is so cut off from knowledge of the outside world that Aureliano Buendía can discover that the world is round without realizing that this is a commonplace. In the beginning there is an innocence about Macondo. Things have not been named, there is no death and the innocence extends to moral questions, for the Buendías marry their aunts, or girls of twelve; Remedios Buendía walks about naked, unaware of the effect her beauty has on men. Yet this mythic, fantasy world is not unlike Latin America, or at least the remoter parts of the continent. For there, too, during many centuries, people's contacts with the rest of the world were sporadic and whimsical. In Macondo, evil comes from outside. A hundred-year civil war brings death and destruction, a banana company introduces exploitation and oppression. To these are added natural hazards – a four-year rainstorm, a plague of insomnia, a scourge of dead birds, which afflict the town like biblical disasters. Again analogies can be seen with Latin America. In *Cien años de soledad*, García Márquez has created the mythic representation of a third-world culture.

The classic setting for a novel of insulation would, of course, be the prison cell. José María Arguedas's novel *El Sexto* (The Sexto Prison, 1961) is based on his own prison experiences. However, novels such as this differ little from the 'novel of exposure' – the account of unjust social conditions – of previous decades. The effect of prison can be conveyed equally effectively by other means. In the same author's *Los ríos profundos*, the boarding-school effectively conveys the sense of restriction, claustrophobia and the consequent breeding of evil passions as contrasted with the town outside, its saloons and the surrounding countryside of 'deep rivers' and mountains. A similar contrast is conveyed in *La ciudad y los perros* (The City and the Dogs, 1963) by the Peruvian novelist, Mario Vargas Llosa (b. 1936). This is set in a Lima military academy: the 'dogs' of the title are the cadets, a group of whom form themselves into a circle to resist the bullying of older pupils. The leader of the circle, the Jaguar, is a born bully who leads his gang in tormenting the Slave, a cadet who hates fighting. When one of the Jaguar's associates steals the questions to an examination paper, the Slave denounces him and is shortly afterwards shot when they are out on manoeuvres. The world of the 'dogs' is a sordid world of homosexuality and perversion, betrayal and torture. The 'city' represents a freer, more civilized and feminine world. Yet, ultimately, it is for this world that the cadets are trained, and they take from the school the habits and attitudes which had been instilled into them by the combination of discipline and brutality. There is a symbiotic relationship between the city and the academy, for the middle-class parents, who are without discipline and principles, put their sons into the school as an easy way out of their own parental problems. At the same time, they ensure that another generation like themselves will be bred to repeat the same miserable cycle over again. The striking thing about Vargas Llosa's novel is that for him, as for García Márquez, the situation seems to be insoluble. The bully and the victim, the city and the academy, boys and officers, exist because of each other; only the isolated individual questions the rules, but he is impotent to change anything.

Mario Vargas Llosa is concerned with the complexity of human relationships, with the subtly-changing human relationships that make the same man act sometimes like the hero, sometimes like the coward and the web of factors which ultimately restrict his existential choices. This complexity is represented with great skill in a second novel, *La casa verde* (The Green House), which is set in the jungles of the Marañón region and the town of Piura with its dry, sandy surroundings. The 'casa verde' of the title is a brothel in Piura but is also the green house of the jungle. By breaking with chronological sequence and by a technique of constantly shifting to different points of time even within the same sentence or paragraph, Vargas Llosa suggests the intricate woof and warp of existence with criss-crossing threads of relationships, with the conditioning of past actions on the present and the effect of time itself. The main characters are an army sergeant from Piura and a girl from the Marañón selva whom he meets and marries and takes back to Piura. During a spell when he is in prison, she goes to live in a brothel. The girl, Bonifacia, had come from an Indian tribe and has been educated by nuns until, after a misdemeanour, she was expelled from the convent. Another character is a Brazilian-Japanese adventurer, an escaped convict who had engaged in illegal rubber-collecting and who throughout the course of the book is being taken by boat on his last journey to a leper colony. The extraordinarily complex mesh of events, of interweaving lives, faces the reader with such a wealth of evidence that it blurs sharp moral distinctions between good and bad. The analogy of human life and a journey, one of the commonplaces of literature, takes on a new depth in *La casa verde* where the structure becomes an existential analogy. Constantly determining our choices are webs of factors which can be laid out like a time map with networks of rivers and interconnecting roads. And on this existential map, there are also goals – a house, a town, an island, a leper colony, which are ephemeral stages in life's journey.

The richness and variety of the Latin-American novel and short story in the last two decades make it difficult to generalize. Nevertheless, one overwhelming impression remains when one compares the modern novel with the novel of the twenties and thirties. In the latter, it is often assumed that, once the oppressed classes have lost patience and have learnt the value of their united strength, an era of revolution and ultimately of social justice will be at hand. Hence, many novels of this period end with an uprising of the oppressed: an uprising that may fail but which is generally indicated as the first step towards victory. Such an ending is occasionally found in more modern novels – José María Arguedas's *Todas las sangres* is an example – but they are much rarer. In the modern novel, revolution is no longer seen as a panacea; at best, it is only an essential first step. The real battle, it is suggested, is now within the human mind and particularly within the minds of the upper and middle classes, whose failure to construct a reasonable society is one of the tragedies of Latin America.

THE THEATRE

Many writers tend to have romantic ideas about the theatre as a genre because of the more immediate contact between the author and the public. In recent years in Latin America, there has been great enthusiasm for the drama, despite the absence of a commercial theatre of any importance in the sub-continent except in Argentina and Mexico. The universities often play an important role in encouraging theatrical groups. Chile, for instance, has a professional theatre company which is run by Santiago University. Even so, for all the importance attached to the theatre during the colonial period and the popularity of the theatre throughout the nineteenth century in cities like Buenos Aires, Rio de Janeiro and Mexico City, the emergence of drama of any national significance has been very recent and sporadic, and it has not yet replaced the novel or the short story for the writer with a serious social message. Up to the 1940s, plays written by Latin Americans tended to be of one or two types: either plays depending very heavily on regional or local dialect, or plays on 'universal' themes.

In the thirties, in Mexico, the first serious attempt to create a drama relevant to the contemporary national scene was made by Rodolfo Usigli and Xavier Villaurrutia. Villaurrutia, founder of the company, Orientación, wrote a series of psychological plays dealing with the inner tensions of family life. *La Hiedra* (The Ivy, 1941), *La mujer legítima* (The Legal Wife, 1943), *El yerro candente* (The White Hot Iron, 1945), *El pobre Barba Azul* (Poor Bluebeard, 1948), *Juego peligroso* (Dangerous Game, 1950) are concerned with the psychological conflicts that arise out of family and marital relationships. Usigli, who has been very much influenced by Bernard Shaw, declares that a country without a theatre is a country without truth. His plays are greatly concerned with the exposure of hypocrisy but they also make direct comment on political situations. His three 'unpolitical' comedies, for instance, are satires on the regime of President Calles, in which a democratic revolutionary façade covers up corruption and fraud. One of his most important plays, *El gesticulador* – discussed earlier on page 228 – probes deeply into the Mexican love of the collective myth. The hero, César Rubio, a failed university teacher who has just returned to his native province after years in Mexico City, seems doomed to live a life of humiliation and frustration until he begins to impersonate a dead revolutionary leader of the same name. The myth he creates proves more powerful than the truth, and persists even when he is shot by a political enemy. The play thus probes the lack of authenticity in Mexican life, which is also one of the main themes of the modern novel. Usigli has also written two ambitious historical dramas that are concerned with national identity. *Corona de sombra* (Crown of Shadow, 1943) is set in the days of the Emperor Maximilian. *Corona de luz* (Crown of Light, 1965), with its setting in the period soon after the Conquest, relates the origins of the cult of the Virgin of Guadelupe, which marks the moment, as Usigli puts it, when Mexico really began to separate from Spain. All major preoccupations of the modern novelists are present in Usigli's work: the concern for authenticity, the questioning of the historical past, the concern for Mexico's identity and its relations with other civilizations (North-American and Spanish).

A concern for national identity is also the feature of the plays of the Puerto Rican playwright, René Marqués, who, in *La carreta* (The Cart, 1953), examines the fate of a Puerto Rican immigrant to New York and his subsequent loss of identity. Like Usigli, Marqués is concerned with the man who lives a lie or betrays his revolutionary principles. In *La muerte no entrará en palacio* (Death Will Not Enter the Palace, 1957), there is a clash of generations similar to that in many modern novels, with the older generation representing corruption (in the person of a despot who is ready to sell his country to a foreign power), and the young generation (the despot's daughters) representing the 'new spirit' which, however, cannot survive. Many of Marqués's plays reflect a despair which is the theatrical equivalent of the novel of insulation. Indeed, in one of them, *Los soles truncos* (The Truncated Suns, 1958) two old women live in a house that is cut off from the outside world. Here, in isolation, they attempt to stave off the invasion of the modern which, however, is destined to triumph.

The theatre is also concerned with examining the bases of morality both in a Latin-American and also in a universal context. The plays of the talented Salvadorian playwright, Walter Beneke (b. 1928), particularly *Funeral Home* (1959), are concerned with the alienation of modern man and with his inhumanity to his fellows. The play, which takes place at Christmas in a funeral parlour, is an ironic comment on the Christian idea of salvation and its inapplicability to the real human situation.

Carlos Solórzano (Guatemala, b. 1922), who has written on the modern Latin-American theatre and who is himself a playwright, has commented on the absence of any general trend in the drama in the last two decades, and also on the fact that plays contain little overt comment.[41] Instead, there is simply a presentation of a problem which is allowed to develop naturally to a dénouement in which no definite solution is given. The theatre, like the novel, has thus forgone any attempt to provide answers.

The Latin-American theatre has not yet attained the importance of the novel, and the attempt of the dramatist to act as the conscience of society is still very largely made in the borrowed mould of European drama. But in young Latin-American talent there is a vigour and a spontaneity and a natural love of spectacle which has just begun to be explored. One of the most interesting new trends has been the emergence of a non-realistic drama. Vigorous experimental theatre has transformed the theatrical scene in Chile, Argentina, Mexico and Brazil. Dramatists are too numerous to mention but the work of Juan José Arreola (b. 1918) in Mexico, and of Luis A. Heiremans (b. 1928) in Chile, is of special interest. In all these countries the work of theatrical groups connected with universities has been of great importance.[42]

The theatre of the absurd and the theatre of cruelty have found their counterparts in the Latin-American theatre. Interestingly, it has been Cuba which has seen some of the most successful avant-garde drama, despite the populist tendencies of some early post-revolutionary plays. In Virgilio Piñera (1912), a dramatist and short story writer who has been writing for some years, we find black humour, fantasy and Beckett-like situations. His plays are primarily expressionist but he insists that in a country so poor in tradition as Cuba, there can be no absolute guide lines. The first Cuban dramatist to become well known outside his country has been Jose Triana (b. 1931) whose *La noche de los asesinos* (Night of the Assassins, 1931) represents a game played by three children in which they mimic murder. Many European critics found the play derivative but the absence of tradition helps to explain why this should be so. Obviously Cuban theatre is still in its infancy, but readiness to experiment is one of its most encouraging features and the combination of puppets and live actors now being used in the marionette theatre is its most original contribution to the technique of drama.

8

The Writer and the National Situation

For a century and a half, the republics of Latin America have been following different paths. Mexico has undergone a social revolution, Paraguay has lived under a series of dictators, Argentina's population has been transformed by immigration from Europe. Obviously such factors have their repercussions on the sub-continent's arts and in particular on its literature which, besides common Latin-American features, has also specifically Argentinian, Mexican or Paraguayan characteristics. These local variants are not necessarily political. The incidence of illiteracy, the presence of a large rural population, the existence of a publishing trade are a few of the many social factors which can also affect the quality and quantity of writing. This does not necessarily mean that socially backward countries do not produce good literature, but simply that in such places the artist's task is lonelier and more difficult. For instance, a collection of poems like César Vallejo's *Trilce* (1922), many of which were written in prison, is likely to be different in form and intention from poems written for a mass audience, like Neruda's *Canto general* (1950). In *Trilce*, Vallejo is not immediately concerned with the question of communication, and therefore experiments in an extreme fashion; in the *Canto general*, Neruda has to meet the demands of rhetoric; the poem is therefore less dense, more immediately communicable than those of Vallejo.

It is therefore the purpose of this chapter to outline some local conditions, with reference to the regions where they prevail and the effect of such conditions on the arts – particularly on literature.

POLITICAL OPPRESSION

Most countries in Latin America have experienced political oppression during the present century and, in many, the condition has been endemic. Long dictatorships – like those of Estrada Cabrera (1898–1920) and Jorge Ubico (1931–44) in Guatemala, of Rafael Trujillo (1930–60) in the Dominican Republic, of Juan Vicente Gómez (1908–35) in Venezuela, and the long reign of the Somoza family in Nicaragua – reduced to cultural deserts the countries subjected to them. In other Latin-American countries there have been shorter but equally devastating periods of oppression. The ten-year dictatorship of Perón in Argentina, for instance, sent many scholars into exile. Getúlio Vargas's rise to power in Brazil was accompanied by mass arrests of writers and other intellectuals along with workers, peasants and labour leaders, especially during the critical years of 1936 and 1937.

Contemporary literature abounds with the personal testimonies of men who have been imprisoned and persecuted by dictators. Neruda's *Canto general*, for instance, includes a bitter attack on González Videla, from whom the poet had to flee in 1949. Graciliano Ramos and Jorge Amado were both arrested during the Getúlio Vargas regime in 1936 and Ramos wrote a fine account of his experiences in one of the dictator's penal colonies. No less than three contemporary Peruvian novelists, José María Arguedas, Gustavo Valcárcel (b. 1921) and Juan Seoane (b. 1898) have based novels on their personal experiences as political prisoners. Arguedas's *El Sexto* (1961) was the fruit of a period of imprisonment during the dictatorship of General Benavides. Valcárcel's *La prisión* (1951) documents the ruthless crushing of the personality that took place in Peruvian prisons during the regime of Manuel Odría. Juan Seoane's *Hombres y rejas* (Men and Bars, 1936) is the crude and pathetic outcry of a man who was unjustly imprisoned for ten years. In Venezuela, imprisonment during the Gómez dictatorship was described in *Puros hombres* (Real Men, 1938) by Antonio Arráiz (b. 1903). Prison literature is thus common all over Latin America and there are masterpieces of the genre.

In many countries, however, the problem of dictatorship and

oppression is much wider than the immediate physical consequences. The writer suffers from the much slower torments of frustration, lack of freedom to write as he wishes, and a crushing intellectual environment. To be born and grow up in a Latin-American dictatorship is, to use the words of Miguel Angel Asturias, to be born into a tomb.[1] To protest means to risk death or, at best, exile; even to record a protest in literary form often meets with frustration. Books are banned or simply left unpublished. Yet, despite these discouraging conditions, writers continue to write. They are often provincials whose early careers follow closely the description given by Mario Monteforte Toledo (b. 1911) of the Guatemalan writers:

They begin to make themselves known at a very early age in student publications and in small reviews which appear sporadically. The acceptance of some of their work in the pages of the newspapers in the capital starts their recognition on a bigger scale and a chain of events which usually transforms them into professional journalists. More than half of the young writers register at university, especially in the faculties of Law and Humanities where they form 'generations' or literary groups and edit reviews which almost never go beyond ten numbers.

Almost all are self-educated and fall in love with their profession after avid reading in private libraries or under the tutelage of some intellectual who encourages their questionings. Many of those who come from the provinces thus read the classics. Only exceptionally, in the case of true professionals of letters, does one come across writers who speak a foreign tongue adequately. Equally rare are those who know the literature, the social and economic problems and the history of their countries.[2]

This poor intellectual background and training is, nevertheless, the first stage in a career which either ends in conflict with a dictator for whom any intellectual activity is dangerous, or, in many anonymous cases, in an ignominious defeat by the environment. Such a defeat has been recorded by the Paraguayan novelist, Gabriel Casaccia (b. 1907), in his novel *La babosa* (The Slimy One, 1952), in which he traces the slow degeneration of a writer in a backward Paraguayan village. The hero, a man of poor background who had published a volume of poems while at university, marries the daughter of a well-to-do lawyer and thus has the leisure to write. But he is unable to stand up to the intellectual isolation and the pettiness of village life, and he ends as a sordid drunkard.

This intellectual isolation is a feature of life in small towns and all over Latin America but, under a dictatorship, the situation is aggravated by the insulation from the outside world which almost inevitably occurs during periods of political oppression. It follows that intellectuals in such areas are slow to hear of artistic trends in the outside world and even slower to adopt them, and, since frequently they are also discouraged from travelling, they remain enclosed in attitudes long since superseded elsewhere. In Paraguay, for instance, Romanticism was still the prevailing literary school at the turn of the century, and Modernism did not become dominant until 1923 with the appearance of the journal *Juventud*.[3]

The writer can overcome this isolation in various ways. The Modernists, for example, made a virtue of isolation and were proud of being misunderstood. Yet the careers of the less successful Modernists of Central America show the sad fate that awaited those for whom outside recognition failed to come. The Nicaraguan poet, Solón Arguello (1880–1920), joined Zapata's forces and died, assassinated; his compatriot Angel Salgado (1894–1920) died early of tuberculosis; Luis Angel Villa (Nicaragua, 1886–1907) committed suicide; and one of the most interesting of Central American poets, Alfonso Cortés (b. 1889), has been in a lunatic asylum since 1927. In Honduras, Juan Ramón Molina (1875–1909) committed suicide. Only those Modernists – like the Guatemalan Enrique Gómez Carrillo (1873–1927), the Peruvian José Santos Chocano (1875–1934) and the Nicaraguan Rubén Darío (1867–1916) – who managed to win an international reputation were able to survive successfully.[4] And it is interesting that all three of these were sufficiently self-centred to collaborate with and even adulate dictators.*

* José Santos Chocano's friendship for the Guatemalan dictator Estrada Cabrera nearly led to his execution on the dictator's downfall. Gómez Carrillo was responsible for an adulatory defence of Cabrera in *La verdad sobre Guatemala*, Hamburg and Paris 1907.

More recent generations have tended to spurn the ivory tower in favour of a more militant attitude. Many joined left-wing parties, and some met their death in the political struggle. Others went into exile either because of political difficulties or simply because there was no other way of pursuing their art. Buenos Aires and Mexico are full of distinguished Paraguayan and Central American exiles: for example, Augusto Roa Bastos (Paraguay, b. 1917), the Guatemalans Luis Cardoza y Aragón (b. 1904), and Carlos Solórzano (b. 1922), and the Nicaraguan Ernesto Mejía Sánchez (b. 1923). A Honduran critic has described the alternatives that face the Central American writer as 'the escape across the frontiers' or 'losing oneself in the mountains'.[5] This escape to the mountains may be not merely a physical escape. Nature poetry and religious and mystical poetry occur quite commonly in dictatorships; indeed, they represent permitted 'literary territory'. The same is true of folk-lore and legend: a genre that abounds, for instance, in Honduras.[6] However, it is significant that there are limits even in those fields and certainly to the writer's interpretation of the 'folk'. The Dominican Republic, for example, has been alone among the Spanish-speaking Caribbean islands in standing aloof from the Afro-Antillean movement in literature, despite the fact that there are Negroes and Mulattos in the population. In part, this is attributable to historical factors and particularly to the Dominican Republic's long-standing feud with predominantly Negro Haiti; but the aloof attitude to the Negro in literature also reflects Trujillo's racial policy. Whereas, in Cuba, Afro-Cubanism has developed into a genuinely felt need to integrate all the races into the national culture, the Dominicans have ignored this aspect of their culture. The exception is the avant-garde poet Manuel del Cabral (b. 1907) who, for all that his prologue to a collection of his poems denies the existence of an American art and a Negro poetry, nevertheless has published *Doce poemas negros* (Twelve Negro Poems, 1935). But even these poems, according to one critic, emphasize 'the primitive aspects of the Negro in a negative sense'.[7] A more recent trend apparent in some oppressed countries (e.g., Nicaragua) has been the association of the avant-garde with revolt. Nicaragua's major poet, Ernesto Cardenal, has been imprisoned for political reasons. A deeply religious man, who writes in a Whitmanesque style, his poetry unites political, religious and moral themes. Thus his *Apocalipsis* deals with the H-bomb and the modern world and also with the nature of evil.

It would seem, then, that the experience of people in countries with long-standing dictatorships must go unrecorded except in the memoirs of exile. But this is not quite true. Two outstanding writers, Augusto Roa Bastos and Miguel Angel Asturias – the first from Paraguay and the second from Guatemala – have succeeded in gaining a continental and even international reputation, despite the inhibitions of their background. The careers of these two writers have been very similar. Both lived through comparatively liberal periods of government in their countries which enabled them to pursue their writing and studies. Both spent several years working as radio commentators and journalists before eventually going into exile.* Their work shows a similar approach to the problem of writing a novel about an oppressed country, for both have abandoned the documentary technique, using instead fantasy, legend and myth to present the subconscious forces at work in the minds of their fellow-countrymen. Both have realized that the only way the international public (generally ignorant about their countries of origin) can be engaged by the narrative is to present a complete picture of the nation in all its complexity and richness.

Asturias's *El Señor Presidente* (1946) covers every strata of the population from beggar to president, and shows how all are in the grip of fear and the menace of death. His *Hombres de maíz* (1949) is set over a long historical period and traces the dispossession of the Indians and the commercialization of agriculture. Similarly, Roa Bastos's *Hijo de hombre* (1959) covers the history of Paraguay from the mid-nineteenth century to just after the Chaco war. In *Hombres de maíz* and *Hijo de hombre*, this historical perspective helps the authors to overcome one of the difficulties of presenting a picture of national life that is not completely black. By showing a process of struggle over a long period, a sense is given of the continuity of human sacrifices and struggle.

*Miguel Angel Asturias has been Ambassador in Paris since 1966.

Nevertheless, both writers also show the other side: the utter waste of human material which, even more than physical suffering, is the tragedy of life under a dictator. Asturias's novel *El Señor Presidente* and Roa Bastos's short story 'La excavación' present a nightmare of frustration in which those who rebel against the *status quo* are ignominiously murdered.[8]

The works of writers such as Roa Bastos and Asturias, and the sudden flowering of the arts in short periods of liberalization, serve only to emphasize the tragic waste of human potential inherent in a dictatorship. And yet dictators might not be the artists' worst enemies. Estrada Cabrera and Trujillo, for instance, even made clumsy and misguided efforts to help the arts. In fact, the national culture of a country like El Salvador – which is not really a dictatorship, but has been ruled by a selfish and insensitive oligarchy – might well suffer more in the long run than neighbouring Guatemala, where periods of light have followed periods of darkness.

THE PROBLEM OF THE SMALL COUNTRY: THE CASE OF URUGUAY

Even if there were no dictatorships in the countries mentioned above, there would still be a serious problem facing their writers: the problem of a public. The Central-American republics, the Caribbean islands and many of the countries on the mainland of the sub-continent have populations which are too small to provide a mass public, particularly in view of the incidence of illiteracy. Costa Rica, Nicaragua, Panama and Paraguay have less than two million inhabitants each; Bolivia, the Dominican Republic, El Salvador, Guatemala, Honduras and Uruguay have less than four million each. Obviously, none of these countries can expect to have a large commercial theatre or large-scale editions of books produced by commercial publishers. In itself, this already represents a restriction on the artist, as one critic has pointed out: 'To sell a novel in Costa Rica is a labour of Hercules. Editions are rarely bigger than a thousand copies and although we have good publishing houses, these rarely pay ... because of the small size of the national market.'[9] Writers resort in such cases either to having their works published by a government publishing house or to writing short stories which appear in newspapers or periodicals. Indeed, in Uruguay and Costa Rica and many other small countries, it is the short story rather than the novel which is the most favoured literary genre. And it is significant that Roque Dalton, one of El Salvador's leading poets, now lives and works in Cuba.

Another serious problem faced by the small country is the brain-drain of writers who emigrate in order to seek the stimulus lacking at home. Uruguay has suffered very badly in this respect, many of the leading Uruguayan writers – such as Florencio Sánchez (1875–1910) and Horacio Quiroga (1878–1937) – having left their native land to live in the Argentine. El Salvador illustrates yet another of the cultural problems of the small country: the difficulties in the way of those who want to become professional writers. Since in a small country talent is limited, the literary man often acts as politician, journalist or diplomat. The three great names of Salvadorian literature – Francisco Gavidia (1875–1955), Alberto Masferrer (1858–1932), Arturo Ambrogi (1875–1936) – have all been men of letters with multifarious activities in public life.[10] The writer in such small countries also has a special burden of responsibility, since he perforce acts as mediator between his own provincial environment and the broad movements in world culture. Cosmopolitanism, therefore, is a vital aspect of the writer's role in society. Where the cosmopolitan note is lacking, writing in small countries is imperilled by a narrow provincialism. In Costa Rica, for instance, there are many writers of charming stories – Claudio González Rucavado (1865–1925), Carmen Lyra (1888–1949), Ricardo Fernández Guardia (1867–1950), Manuel González Zeledón (1864–1936) – whose scope seems to have been limited in this way.[11]

Of the small countries, Uruguay has been most successful in creating a distinctive culture. This is partly due to the stimulus of neighbouring Buenos Aires, and also to the fact that Montevideo is a big international port. But there are other significant factors. Alone of all Latin-American countries, Uruguay has a really high rate of literacy (97 per cent of the population). The middle class is of substantial proportions, and includes some 250,000 civil servants: an enormous figure in so small a country. These two factors – a high level of literacy and a large middle class – enable Montevideo to boast of an intellectual climate that is far more stimulating than that of the capitals of some much larger states. It has a good commercial publishing house (Alfa) and a first-class literary magazine (*Número*); there have developed original Uruguayan trends in literature and painting (e.g., Constructivism),[12] and the standard of literary criticism is high. Yet, as we have noted, the smallness of the country has had a decisive effect on the attitudes of writers for, feeling cramped by the local scene, they have naturally tended to look beyond national boundaries. José Enrique Rodó, the leading Latin-American intellectual of the first decade of this century, was almost certainly led by the thinness of the Uruguayan cultural tradition to consider himself a Latin American first and foremost. It is a Uruguayan writer, the poetess Juana de Ibarbourou (b. 1895), who has been given the name of 'Juana de América'. And we find Horacio Quiroga, the Uruguayan short story writer who spent most of his adult life in Argentina, speaking scathingly, in one of the stories in his *La patria* (The Fatherland),* of man's foolish regard for national boundaries: a cosmopolitan sentiment that undoubtedly reflects his own experience.

This being so, one would expect Uruguayan writing to be cosmopolitan in the way that much of Argentinian writing is; but this is by no means the case. Poetry, it is true, tends to deal with general themes, and this holds true particularly for 'Juana de América', whose best poems are about 'nature' in general and not Uruguayan nature. The other major poets – Julio Casal (1889–1954), Emilio Oribe (b. 1893), Carlos Sabat Ercasty (b. 1887), Sara de Ibañez (b. 1910), Idea Villariño (b. 1920) – have also explored areas of feeling and experience that have little to do with national sentiment. But the expression of a specifically 'Uruguayan' experience is very marked in the novel and the short story.[13] Up to the 1940s, close interest in specifically Uruguayan aspects of experience meant writing about rural areas. The gaucho tradition survives in the stories of Fernán Silva Valdés (b. 1887) and Pedro Leandro Ipuche (b. 1899).

* Included in the collection, *El desierto*.

However, two writers who came to the fore in the 1930s – Francisco Espínola (b. 1901) and Enrique Amorim (1900–1960) – have broken away from the gaucho cliché to show the poverty and conflicts of the rural population in all their sombre intensity. While Espínola tends to deal with the emotional relationships of very simple people, Amorim, a prolific novelist, covers all the major social conflicts of rural life: the clash between Creole and immigrant in *El caballo y su sombra* (The Horse and its Shadow, 1941), the alienation of the city-dweller from the land in *El paisano Aguilar* (Farmer Aguilar, 1934). And in *La desembocadura* (The Meeting of the Waters, 1958), he epitomizes the history of the country in the figure of a lusty pioneer, begetter of a legitimate and an illegitimate family, who witnesses the transformation and destruction of the wild and lonely life he had loved.*

In recent years, however, it has become apparent that the heart of the Uruguayan problem is no longer the country areas. Modern Uruguay is a country of clerks and civil servants, and the hazards that face them are not those of violence and oppression but of smugness and the excessive concern for security. Hence it is that two contemporary writers, Mario Benedetti and Carlos Martínez Moreno, write stories and novels set among office workers and members of the middle class, whose problems are much more typical of the country as a whole than are those of country folk. The protagonist of Martínez Moreno's *El paredón* (1962), for instance, is a journalist whose visit to Cuba throws into contrast the flat indifference and quiet desperation of his own countrymen. The characters of 'El presupuesto' (The Budget), a short story by Mario Benedetti, are employees in the civil service whose only purpose in life is waiting for a pay rise.[14] Both in Benedetti's novel *La tregua* (The Truce, 1960) and in Martínez Moreno's short story 'Paloma' (The Pigeon), the characters' low-key lives take on a tragic tinge simply because they are caught in the trap of routine. In the latter, a retired civil servant lives for the day when his pigeon will again win the first race of the season.[15]

*Totally apart from other writers of this generation is Felisberto Hernández, whose stories bear some resemblance to the Argentine 'literatura fantástica'.

With such modern writers, it will be observed, the very concern with the Uruguayan situation does in fact create a literature of more than national relevance, for such characters and problems as are depicted by Benedetti and Moreno have close similarities with characters and problems in European fiction. Thus, by an interesting circular development, a good deal of modern Uruguayan writing, ostensibly concerned solely with the local experience, appears to be much more in the international mainstream than the literature of other small countries in Latin America. However, one of the most outstanding contemporary Uruguayan writers, Juan Carlos Onetti (b. 1909), hardly comes into a Uruguayan context at all, for he has lived many years in Buenos Aires and this city is the setting of some of his novels. His works deal with tortured and isolated people who inhabit a misty, featureless no-man's-land.* The hero of *El astillero* (1961), for example, is the manager of a yard into which no ship ever puts for repairs, and the emptiness of his work-place parallels the emptiness of his life. Onetti's themes and settings are therefore anything but regional or local, yet there is, perhaps, some significance in the fact that his major interest is degeneration and the loneliness that comes from inability to communicate. For him maturity is equated with decay and the very process of living corrodes. Such a view is not that of a man living in a young country that is full of promise. It is rather the vision of a man who feels himself the victim of events over which he has no control. Ultimately this is also the dilemma of the small country in a world where size is increasingly important, for in such a situation, understanding can bring only disappointment and acknowledgement of limitations.

THE PROBLEM OF IDENTITY: PANAMA
AND PUERTO RICO

Panama and Puerto Rico are two small countries where the problem of national identity is particularly acute. Panama, as a

---

*The influence of the North-American novelist, William Faulkner, is interesting in the case of Onetti, for Faulkner showed how the regional tragedy of the South could take on universal significance.

nation state, is not much older than its canal. It is not surprising, therefore, that its writers and intellectuals should be moved by the need to emphasize that their country has a separate identity. For the Puerto Rican intellectual there is the problem of reconciling his country's past as part of the Spanish-speaking world with its present status as dependant of a predominantly Anglo-Saxon state.

Panama's major writers – such as Guillermo Andreve (1879–1940) and the poet Ricardo Miró (1883–1940) – have been mainly concerned with creating a sense of national consciousness. Miró, for example, wrote poems for schoolchildren celebrating the native land: poems that he deliberately intended to be read and learned in childhood. Despite such conscious efforts to create a national literature, it needed the encouragement of a literary prize – the Ricardo Miró Prize – before Panamanian novelists and short-story writers had sufficient stimulus to make a significant contribution to developing a strong sense of Panamanian nationality. Many contemporary Panamanian novelists first had their works published thanks to this literary award.[16]

Not surprisingly, the Panamanian novel has concentrated on themes of protest. For example, Joaquín Beleño Cedeño (b. 1922), a winner of the Miró prize, has described in *Luna verde* (Green Moon, 1951) the injustices committed in the Canal Zone. And the best poetry – that of Demetrio Korsi (1899–1957) – captures the cosmopolitan turbulence of the area of which he claimed: 'I know the White men, the Negroes, the Half-Castes/I know all their lives and miracles.'[17] This is also true of Panama's outstanding contemporary writer, Rogelio Sinán (b. 1904), who, despite his use of fantasy and avant-garde techniques and despite his cosmopolitan outlook, brilliantly conveys the strange nature of his native land. His novel *Plenilunio* (Full Moon, 1947) takes us deep into a world of sexual violence, turbulence, material wealth and the mixture of races and nationalities that constitutes the canal zone. The lives of the characters in this novel reflect the tension between the Panamanian and North American worlds as well as the repercussion of international events as felt in the Isthmus.

In Puerto Rico the main problem facing modern writers has

been the threat to traditional culture offered by the United States. A critic has described the situation in these terms:

> The American way of life, through its many contacts with the island – through schools, books, magazines, through journeys made by many Puerto Ricans to the States, through the education there of our professional classes, through trade relations, through the cinema and, on a lesser scale, the radio and television – exercises a dominating influence over our environment. Despite the fact that, under the new regime, schools in the country have increased and that we have had a university since 1903, the general education system had lost ground by attempting . . . to carry on the teaching of young people in English, relegating Spanish to a secondary role.[18]

United States money has poured into the University of Puerto Rico, making it one of the best equipped in the Americas. Most leading intellectuals, none the less, are deeply concerned about the preservation of the island's Hispanic tradition. It is no accident that Puerto Rico produces some of the best and most devoted Hispanists, and that in *La Torre*, the university quarterly, articles on Spanish literature predominate.

In common with most Latin-American countries, Puerto Rico numbers among its writers many who have dealt with nature or rural life. The most important of these have been the poet Virgilio Dávila (1869–1943) and the novelist Enrique A. Laguerra (b. 1906). And, despite Puerto Rico's being predominantly a White island, with only a small Negro element in the population, it can boast an outstanding poet of the Afro-Antillean school: Luis Palés Matos (1890–1959), whose frequently humorous evocations of Africa are to be seen as an indirect comment on the 'overcerebralized' White civilization, and hence on Anglo-Saxon culture as a whole.[19] The poetry of Palés Matos, however, has remained an isolated phenomenon in Puerto Rican literature, because there is less justification there than in other Caribbean countries for considering African tradition as an important part of the national cultural character.

Contemporary writers in Puerto Rico have concerned themselves directly with the problem of identity. The most important of them is René Marqués, both a short-story writer and a dramatist. His play *La carreta* (1953) deals with the significant subject of emigration to the United States. The main character is a peasant who returns to Puerto Rico after living in New York, only to find that he no longer fits into his former way of life. One of the most moving of Marqués's short stories, 'En la popa hay un cuerpo reclinado' (There is a Body Lying in the Stern), is, on the immediate level, the tragic story of a marriage in which a dominated male kills his wife and then castrates himself; but, at a deeper level, it also reflects an awareness of Puerto Rico's domination and emasculation by an alien and materialistic culture.[20]

THE PROBLEM OF VIOLENCE: VENEZUELA AND COLOMBIA

Venezuela and Colombia, with populations of 8 million and 15 million respectively, have both had to face the problem of integrating disparate and widely separated regions, and of establishing the rule of law over vast territories, including high mountain regions and parts of the Amazonian basin. In both countries, backward rural populations and high levels of illiteracy (58 per cent in Venezuela and 37 per cent in Colombia) have laid the rural areas open to the evils of *caciquismo* and of outbursts of lawless violence. The cultured intellectual in the main cities of Venezuela and Colombia has little in common with his compatriot in the interior, where chaos and barbarism reign. Indeed, it is perfectly possible for the artist or writer to live entirely in the enclave of urban civilization, identifying himself completely with Europe and with European culture. This was certainly the case with the poets of the Modernist generation who cultivated an elegance and refinement which was in itself a form of defiance. The Colombians José Asunción Silva (1865–96), Porfirio Barba Jacob (1883–1942) and Guillermo Valencia (1873–1943), and the Venezuelans Manuel Díaz Rodríguez (1871–1927) and Pedro Dominici (1872–1954), all had in common this attitude of disdain or defiance towards their environment.

Many of the Modernists, and many of the other leading writers of the first decades of this century, were drawn from the upper ranks of society and not unnaturally reflected elite attitudes. Two outstanding Venezuelan writers, Rufino Blanco Fombona (1874–1944) and Teresa de la Parra (1891–1936), came from the upper classes. The latter, one of Latin America's outstanding woman novelists, expressed in her *Ifigenia* (1924, the translated subtitle of which reads *Diary of a Bored Young Lady*) the frustration of a European-educated young lady living in provincial and backward Caracas. Teresa de la Parra's affection for her native country was associated with nostalgia for the sugar plantation on which she had been brought up as a child, and which she recalled in *Las memorias de Mama Blanca* (Mama Blanca's Souvenirs, 1929). Half the charm of this novel is its nostalgia for a patriarchal way of life that was already in decline when she wrote. By deliberately circumscribing his art to the experience of the urban or provincial middle classes, a writer was able to work with traditional artistic moulds and had no need to invent new forms. There are many Venezuelan and Colombian writers of this traditional type, the best known being the Colombian Tomás Carrasquilla (1858–1940), whose novels and short stories are immediately familiar in theme and style to anyone acquainted with the Hispanic literary tradition. He seldom strayed from the life and manners of the provincial town of Antioquia, the customs and human relations of which are revealed as being very similar to those of a Spanish provincial town. His frequent use of folk tales also gives his work a familiar ring. Indeed, readers both of his works and of those of Teresa de la Parra may well be excused for believing that life in Venezuela and Colombia differed very little from life in Spain. Such writers as these at times allow us a glimpse of the turmoil beneath the urbanized surface, but they do not explore a situation for which the European literature of their generation offers no parallel.

It is true that there are writers of this generation who saw things differently. The true situation in Colombia and Venezuela was aptly illustrated, for example, in 'Que pase el aserrador' (Let the Sawyer Pass),[21] a short story by Jesús del Corral of Colombia (1871–1931) in which the action takes place in a foreign-owned mine. Inside the mine, work and social life go on as they do in similar places elsewhere, but the mine is a private world of its own, connected with the real world around it only by a basket slung on a rope over a ravine. At the other side of the ravine there is civil war. The situation in the mine paralleled almost exactly that of the Colombian or Venezuelan upper and middle classes who lived in a civilized enclave while the country was in turmoil.

Even so, it was not until the 1920s that writers in these two countries generally began to describe the reality of their local world: a world, hitherto largely unknown to their national literatures, of violence and chaos.[22] The pioneer novel here (discussed already on pp. 100 and 142) is *La vorágine* (1924) by José Eustasio Rivera of Colombia (1888–1928). The novelist still used a familiar convention – that of a hero's romantic flight from civilization – but with the difference that, whereas the hero in the tradition of nineteenth-century romanticism frequently escapes into a dream world, Arturo Cova meets with the implacable reality of the jungle, which slowly breaks down his personality and his sense of humanity. Rivera's novel shows with devastating force the terror of the artist in the face of the hitherto unimagined nature of experience in the jungles and plains of his native land. In subsequent writers, the fear and horror that are the predominant emotions in *La vorágine* are replaced by a feeling of fascination. Eduardo Zalamea Borda (1907–63), in particular, expresses the wonder of primitive life in Colombia in his *Cuatro años a bordo de mí mismo* (Four Years Aboard Myself, 1934), a novel set in the almost deserted salt flats of La Guajira.

In the Venezuelan novel, a mixture of attraction and repulsion towards the primitive marks some of the best writing. The tension between the two attitudes is central to three major novels (discussed on p. 101) by Rómulo Gallegos (b. 1884): *Doña Bárbara* (1929), *Canaima* (1935) and *Cantaclaro* (1934). In each of these, the hero is a civilizer who sets out to combat the dangerous lawlessness of his country; and in each case there is a point in the story where the law-respecter commits or projects an act of violence. The barbarism of the environment proves overwhelming for Gallegos's characters. Similarly, in *Las lanzas coloradas* (The Coloured Lances, 1931) by Arturo Uslar Pietri, which is set in the Independence period, the two main characters – a Creole landowner and a Mulatto foreman – represent civilization and barbarism respectively. For all that, the barbarous foreman who fights against Bolívar's forces is not presented as an entirely despicable figure. In a novel set in more recent times, *El mar es como un potro* (The Sea is Like a Stallion, 1943)* by Antonio Arráiz, sea and stallion symbolize the barbaric, virile strength of the smuggler-hero, Dámaso Velázquez, who is sharply contrasted with the cowardly accountant who falls in love with Velázquez's wife and who is finally killed by him. The themes of chaos, violence and barbarism do not lend themselves easily to literary form and cannot be shut within the tidy bounds of the neatly structured novel, as Gallegos's rambling and disordered novels illustrate.

The younger generation of novelists has tried to solve the problem in other ways. In a satirical novel, *La misa de Arlequín* (Harlequin's Mass, 1962), Guillermo Meneses (b. 1911) makes use of fantasy and the absurd to expose the evils of military rule and the connivance of the middle classes with the oppressors. The novel ends with a 'dance of the colonels', a fantasy which exposes the corrupt political situation in the country. Another contemporary novelist, Miguel Otero Silva (b. 1908), attempts to put violence and disorder into perspective by showing it as part of a historical development. Two novels of his – *Casas muertas* (Dead Houses, 1955) and *Oficina Número 1* (Office Number 1, 1961) – epitomize the country's history by depicting two contrasting communities. In the first novel, the setting is a decayed town, symbol of the old Venezuela, whose economy was predominantly rural, its social structure feudal and its tradition Hispanic. But the town is now dead; its inhabitants, no longer able to make a living, either inertly await death or emigrate. *Oficina Número 1* on the other hand, shows an entirely different community, one set in an oil field. Lawless and brash as this is, it nevertheless represents for the author the foundation for a new future. Although the wealth from the oil fields has not yet brought a very high standard of life and culture to most Venezuelans, Otero Silva sees in it the necessary basis for a modern state. The

---

* The original title was *Dámaso Velázquez*.

change in the social environment in Venezuela since Rómulo Gallegos began to write is reflected in a new type of novel written by Salvador Garmendia (b. 1928). In *Los pequeños seres* (The Little People, 1959), *La mala vida* (Low Life, 1968), *Día de ceniza* (Day of ash, 1954) and *Los habitantes* (The Inhabitants, 1968), he deals with the lives of marginal types, unemployed men or lower-middle-class office workers. An ironic, pitiless realism lifts these themes out of the banal and gives the novels great intensity.

The problem of violence has also been the main theme of the modern Colombian novel, particularly since 1947 when, following the election of a conservative president on a minority vote, civil war broke out. During this period of brutal slaughter and violence, 150,000 to 200,000 Colombians died and, not surprisingly, many of the novels relating to the fighting have a polemic quality. *Viento seco* (Dry Wind, 1954), by Daniel Caicedo* is probably the best-known example. However, a great many Colombian novels could be listed which have excellent but less direct or obviously polemical treatments of the theme of violence: novels such as *El Cristo de espaldas* (1953) and *Siervo sin tierra* (Landless Serf, 1954) by Eduardo Caballero Calderón, *El coronel no tiene quien le escriba* (1961) and *La mala hora* (The Evil Hour, 1962) by Gabriel García Márquez, *El día señalado* (The Appointed Day, 1964) by Manuel Mejía Vallejo (b. 1924), and *En Chimá nace un santo* (1963) by Manuel Zapata Olivella. All these novels are situated in isolated towns and communities where men and women are still a prey to drought, flood, fanaticism and senseless waves of violence, a situation which gives a distinctive medieval atmosphere. In García Márquez's novels and short stories, for instance, men are visited by mysterious plagues and curses, like the rain of dead birds that falls on one village in his *El día después del sábado* (The Day after Saturday, 1962). And this medieval atmosphere is reinforced by the many novels in which serfs seek a lord or protector when menaced with attack by hostile raiders. This feudal relationship between protector and serf also occurs in Caicedo's *Viento seco* and in Caballero Calderón's *Siervo sin tierra*; and in the latter's

*I have been unable to trace the date of his birth.

Manuel Pacho (1964), the character of the eponymous hero is as strange as that of the protagonist of a medieval ballad. The story concerns an adolescent boy who, from the boughs of a mango tree in which he is sheltering, witnesses the massacre of his mother, his putative grandfather and the whole of their huge household. When the raiders gallop off, the boy comes down from the tree, stuffs the body of his grandfather into a sack and sets off to the nearest town to claim his inheritance. When he reaches his destination several days later, the body of the old man is a putrefying mass. The fact that the latter stage of the journey is completed by aeroplane drives home the point that, in countries such as Colombia, a medieval mind can coexist with the most modern forms of communication.

Venezuela and Colombia illustrate the phenomenon of the survival of social structures and ways of life which have much in common with medieval Europe. The remarkable feature, particularly of contemporary Colombian writing, is the way that novelists have made an imaginative effort to explore creatively a situation where the archaic survives alongside the most modern instruments and inventions. Both countries have also seen in recent years an upsurge of 'beat' poetry movements, which combine in their aims social and poetic revolution: in Colombia, the 'Nadaista' movement; in Venezuela, the avant-garde gathered round the magazine *El Techo de la Ballena*.

RACIAL AND NATIONAL INTEGRATION IN THE ANDEAN REPUBLICS

Writers in the Andean republics share a common problem: that of living in countries with two cultures, one stemming from Hispanic tradition, the other from the Indian past. Bolivia, Ecuador and Peru are also divided into very disparate geographical regions, ranging from high Andean plateaux to tropical jungles or lowlands. At the same time, since the Indian way of life tends to be preserved in the most remote regions, regional and racial differences are often coincidental. Despite these similarities, each of the Andean countries has quite a distinct culture. Peru is the country with the sharpest division between the Hispanic and the indigenous; Bolivia's population is almost wholly Indian or Mestizo; while in Ecuador there has traditionally existed a strong regional rivalry between Quito and Guayaquil, between mountain and coastal plain. In addition to these problems, Bolivia and Ecuador are both small countries which have, in the past, offered a poor cultural environment. Hence we find among the Modernists – as in Central America – a pattern of suicides and early deaths or of semi-permanent exile, as typified by two such distinguished figures as the Bolivian poet Ricardo Jaimes Freyre (1868–1933) and the Ecuadorian novelist and essayist Gonzalo Zaldumbide (b. 1885).

The greatest single problem that has faced, and still faces, the Andean republics is that of the Indian. A Peruvian thinker, Manuel González Prada (1848–1918), was one of the first to realize that the culture and politics of a country with an Indian majority could not be confined to a tiny White or Mestizo minority living in the capital; and in Bolivia and Ecuador writers such as Alcides Arguedas (1879–1946) and Pío Jaramillo Alvarado (b. 1889) came to the same conclusion.[23] Up to the 1920s, as has been noted in chapter 2, most of such thinkers believed that the problem could be solved by education, and by exposing the injustices committed against the Indian. Novels of this period – like *Aves sin nido* (1889) or *Raza de bronce* (1919) – are primarily works of protest designed to arouse the conscience of the ruling elite. But this initial humanitarian approach was followed by more radical attitudes. These ranged from the idealistic racial theories of the Bolivian Franz Tamayo (1879–1956) – who suggested that the Indian was the true source of Bolivian nationality and national energy, and that to destroy him and his way of life meant 'destroying the only sources of life and energy that nature offers us' – to the Socialism of the Peruvian José Carlos Mariátegui (1895–1930), who believed that the Indian *ayllu* or commune could form a sound basis for a distinctively Peruvian type of modern Communism.[24]

The influence of essayists and thinkers in regard to social justice is soon reflected in the novel. Whereas Clorinda Matto de Turner's *Aves sin nido* and Alcides Arguedas's *Raza de bronce* are primarily protests against unjust treatment of the Indian, later

279

novels tend to stress economic exploitation. In many of them, the main incident is no longer the rape of the Indian girl by the White or Mestizo boss but the expulsion of the Indians from their lands to make room for a more commercial form of exploitation. *Plata y bronce* (Silver and Bronze, 1927) by the Ecuadorian Fernando Chaves (b. 1902); *Altiplano* (High Plateau, 1945) by the Bolivian Raúl Botelho Gosálvez (b. 1917); *Todas las sangres* (1964) and *Yawar Fiesta* (1941) by the Peruvian José María Arguedas (b. 1911); *Tungsteno* (1931) by the Peruvian César Vallejo (1892–1938) – all these deal with the proletarianization of the Indian, as we saw in chapter 4. There it was also noted that two of the best Indianist novels – *Huasipungo* (1934) by the Ecuadorian Jorge Icaza (b. 1906) and *El mundo es ancho y ajeno* (Broad and Alien is the World, 1941) by the Peruvian Ciro Alegría (b. 1909) – both centre on the landowner's deliberate attempt to deprive the Indians of their land in order to turn them into an easily exploitable labour force. Both novelists depict the Indians' rebellion in the face of this prospect.

The cultural implications of the suggestion made by Franz Tamayo and other Bolivian essayists – that the Indian is the true source of national energy – is also found in the novel, particularly in the works of José María Arguedas of Peru. Arguedas believes that fear and denial of the Indian as a human being has led to the alienation of the White and Mestizo Peruvians, who prefer to adopt an alien culture rather than recognize that an authentic Peruvian culture is indigenous. This conflict of 'true' and 'alien' cultures forms the theme of his masterpiece, *Los ríos profundos* (1958), discussed on pp. 250–51. The boy-protagonist in the 'unauthentic' atmosphere of a Catholic boarding-school feels only distaste for this European-imported culture; his real emotions arise from experience of life among Indians or *cholos* (Mestizos). The instinctive love he feels for the Indian and for Indian music and lore conflicts with the patterns that civilized society seeks to impose on him.

Another major problem facing writers in the Andean republics is the narrowness of life in and around the capital, out of which they must break if they are to discover and understand the country as a whole. As has been noted (pp. 76–7), one of the first writers to do this was the Ecuadorian Luis Martínez (1869–1909) in his pioneer novel *A la costa* (To the Coast, 1904), in which the hero leaves the capital, Quito, to become manager of a coastal plantation. This novel made little immediate impact, and it is not until 1930 that there appears literary work in the Martínez tradition. In that year, a group of writers from Guayaquil – Demetrio Aguilera Malta (b. 1909), Joaquín Gallegos Lara (b. 1911) and Enrique Gil Gilbert (b. 1912) – published a collection of stories, *Los que se van* (Those Who Go Away), which explored life among the lower strata of Ecuadorian society, and especially among the *montuvios* (the inhabitants of the Guayaquil coastal area). These writers are the initiators of the Ecuadorian realist novel.[25] The two major novelists of this region are Alfredo Pareja Diez-Canseco (b. 1908) and José de la Cuadra (1903–41), whose masterpiece, *Los Sangurimas* (The Sangurima Family, 1934), is a savage story of a feud in a Mestizo family.

In Bolivia, this journey of exploration has carried writers to remote regions.[26] Some of them have exposed conditions in the mines: for example, *Metal del diablo* (The Devil's Metal, 1946) by Augusto Céspedes (b. 1904). Others have turned to the little-known tropical region of the Chaco, scene of the terrible war against Paraguay. The finest of such works, Augusto Céspedes's *Sangre de mestizos* (1936), consists of a series of harrowing scenes from this war, in which the natural environment was as menacing as the human enemy. This work overcomes exoticism, one of the dangers incidental to regional writing, by continually relating events in the Chaco to events in Quito. In this way, Céspedes emphasizes that the region is not simply another remote and strange phenomenon but an area of national significance. By using something akin to a picaresque technique, the Ecuadorian Adalberto Ortiz (b. 1914) conveys the sense of regional unity in his *Juyungo* (1943), and the Peruvian writers, Ciro Alegría and José María Arguedas, both move their characters from countryside to city and from city to country so that the regional incidents are always related to the national scene in general.[27]

A third problem in the Andean republics – and one which has scarcely been touched on by writers until quite recently although it was certainly perceived by César Vallejo, the great Peruvian poet – is that of the psychological attitudes inculcated by social pressures. *La ciudad y los perros* (1963) by Mario Vargas Llosa of Peru is one of the few novels to explore the education of a caste. Its setting in a military academy in Lima is extremely significant, for it is here that boys from all regions of Peru are sent to be educated and, above all, 'disciplined'. The relationship between bully and bullied in the school is a micro-model of the state of society at large. In exposing the weaknesses of the school, Vargas Llosa also exposes the weaknesses of Peruvian society. (There is a fuller discussion of this novel on pp. 253–4.) As has already been pointed out, Vargas Llosa's second major novel, *La casa verde*, was concerned with the ambiguous and shifting nature of human relationships. But as with *La ciudad y los perros*, these relationships are essentially rooted in Peruvian attitudes. Hence *machismo* with its offshoots of violence and exploitation underlies the actions of the male characters. The convent and the brothel are the two contradictory projections of *machismo* into social life. However, the novel really deals with an immense complex of moral attitudes that can scarcely be summarized thus briefly. More obviously symbolic is the short novel, *Los cachorros* (The Puppies, 1967), in which the accidental castration of the protagonist at the beginning of the novel leads to over-compensation in his early adolescent and adult life. It is clear that while Vargas Llosa does not write documentary novels, his exploration of existential attitudes cannot be separated from the Peruvian background of his characters.*

As can be seen from this short survey, the novel of the Andean republics is largely about injustice. Suffering and injustice are also themes of the greatest poet of the Andean region, César Vallejo, although in general poetry has been less socially concerned. Many fine poets, such as the Peruvians José María Eguren (1874–1942) and Carlos Germán Belli (b. 1927), the Bolivian Ricardo Jaimes Freyre and the Ecuadorian Jorge Carrera Andrade (b. 1903), have created a poetic world which

---

*His most recent novel, *Conversación en la Catedral* (1970), is a sophisticated political novel which reveals the ambiguities and tensions of a group of characters in relation to the dictatorship of Odría.

has little to do with national boundaries. Jaimes Freyre drew his myths and symbols from Norse mythology, Eguren from a fairy-tale world, while Carrera Andrade, whose diplomatic career took him to the far corners of the world, became interested in the Japanese *haiku* and wrote *Microgramas* (1940) in imitation of these. In his other poetry, he uses a virtuoso imagery to convey the wonders of ordinary material reality. His poetry and that of many other poets from the Andean countries illustrates that the writer is no less 'national' in his function if he keeps open the lines of communication between his own country's culture and Western culture as a whole. Belli, the outstanding poet of contemporary Peru, follows in the tradition of Vallejo. His poems are statements of personal anguish or explorations of the self in which he extends the usual meanings and associations of words to create his own symbolic pattern.

As in many other Latin American countries where the social structure has not kept pace with the modern world, poets increasingly make their poetry the expression of social criticism. In Ecuador, the 'Tzántzicos' group combine avante-garde techniques and social commitment. In Peru much important recent poetry is social poetry. Among contemporary Peruvian poets of this type, the following deserve mention: Alejandro Romualdo (b. 1926), whose books include *Poesía, 1945–54* and *Edición extraordinaria* (1958); Washington Delgado (b. 1927), author of *Días del corazón* (Days of the Heart, 1957), *Para vivir mañana* (To Live Tomorrow, 1959) and *Parque* (Park, 1965); Javier Heraud (1942–62), who was killed when fighting with the guerrillas and whose poetry has been published posthumously; and Antonio Cisneros, author of *Comentarios reales* (Royal Commentaries, 1964) and winner of the *Casa de las Américas* prize with his collection, *Canto ceremonial contra un oso hormiguero* (Ceremonial Chant Against an Anteater, 1968).

THE PROBLEM OF ROOTS: ARGENTINA AND CHILE

Though there are great differences between Argentina and Chile, both countries face the problem of national identity; and much of what has been said under this head in regard to Uruguay (pp. 266–70) is applicable to these bigger nations. The indigenous American element is virtually non-existent, and the original Spanish stock has been greatly modified by immigration on a colossal scale. The immigrants in Argentina and Chile have presented a serious cultural problem, for many of them, coming from uneducated European families, have not been equipped to play any part in the culture of their adopted country. Far from being a cultural asset, they have threatened existing standards. At the same time, the immigrant tends to have well-defined material ambitions; these make him a dynamic member of the community and eager for social advancement. His children are likely to be better educated than himself, and many of the second and subsequent generations of immigrants enter the professions.

The larger of the two countries, Argentina, is something of a paradox. Although it has a vast rural area, it also contains one of the most highly urbanized regions of Latin America. The capital city, Buenos Aires, has a population of 4·5 million, and 62·5 per cent of the country's entire population live in towns. Even in the rural areas, there is a high degree of social organization, with good communications, and this means that Argentinians are very rarely as remote from civilization as the rural inhabitants of Colombia or Venezuela. Yet, despite the essentially urban character of the majority of the population, the pampa remains a reality, and these two poles of pampa and city are so diverse that one commentator has declared that it is impossible to consider them together.[28]

The middle class in Argentina is large by European standards. There is a high level of literacy, and the proportion of university students in the population is among the highest in the world. Unfortunately, the country has not been able to use these intellectuals with full effectiveness, and there has been a good deal of emigration of technicians, professionals and scholars, particularly to the United States. Despite this brain-drain, there is an excellent publishing trade, a good theatre (although the most advanced productions are done by small non-commercial companies), a large number of art galleries and many literary reviews. Buenos Aires is a city with great cultural potential and with something of a tradition in the arts. It is also a city which exercises an important role in Latin America as a whole, attracting artists and writers from smaller and poorer countries. The Losada and Sudamericana publishing houses have done important work by publishing novels and short stories by promising writers from all over the sub-continent.

The salient factor in Argentinian culture is its elite nature. In no other Latin-American country has literature remained so exclusively the province of the fortunate few, whose values it reflects. This is surprising for, early in this century, many prominent intellectuals belonging to Socialist or Anarchist groups and, in the 1920s, the *Boedo* group who admired Gorky, were vocal in their insistence that art should not be the province of an elite. *Boedo* counted in its ranks many intelligent and dedicated novelists, including Alvaro Yunque (b. 1890), Roberto Mariani (1893–1945), Elías Castelnuovo (b. 1893), Max Dickman (b. 1902), Lorenzo Stanchina (b. 1900) and Roberto Arlt (1900–1942). And there are still a number of writers – for instance, Bernardo Verbitsky (b. 1907), David Viñas and the poet García Robles – who follow in this stream of committed literature. Yet the fact remains that the best-known names among modern Argentinian writers are of men who represent an elite outlook. Leopoldo Lugones, Ricardo Güiraldes, Jorge Luis Borges, Eduardo Mallea, Ernesto Sábato – these all stand far apart from any social and realist school of writing, and some of them belong to a distinctly conservative tradition. This tradition undoubtedly owes much of its strength to the confusion of values which followed the arrival of vast numbers of immigrants at the turn of the century. The peak year, 1910, when it was recorded that over forty per cent of the population had been born abroad, was also the centenary of Argentinian independence. It is significant that this is also a period when writers begin to turn to the past and to idealize the gaucho way of life or the pioneer values. Two of the most important centenary tributes – Leopoldo Lugones's *Odas seculares* (1910) and Alberto Gerchunoff's *Los gauchos judíos* (The Jewish Gauchos, 1910) – praised the virtues of honest toil upon the land. With the increasing industrialization of Argentina and the growth of the urban population, writers increasingly tend to idealize a way of life that has either disappeared or is on its way out – the life of the gaucho.

In the novels of Benito Lynch (1885–1952), for instance, the simple and honest gaucho or the country girl come to grief when confronted with the man or woman from the city or from Europe. Behind the simple plot, there is the confrontation of two totally different and conflicting attitudes to life. The idealization of the gaucho received its finest expression in Ricardo Güiraldes's *Don Segundo Sombra* (1926). As we have seen (pp. 104 and 144), this is the story of the way a boy comes to manhood through his life as a cattle-herder and with the guidance of Don Segundo Sombra, who epitomizes the spirit and lore of the pampa. But noble as the picture is, there is no escaping the fact that the world of Don Segundo Sombra is one which is already disappearing, even as Güiraldes is praising its virtues. By the mid-1920s, the majority of Argentinians no longer lived on the land, and many of those who owned estates were no longer close to the land. The aristocratic and sophisticated landowners of Enrique Larreta's *Zogoibi* (1926) or of Eduardo Mallea's *Las Aguilas* (The Eagles, 1943) were probably far commoner than the Don Segundo Sombras. Certainly, by the twenties, it was already difficult for the writer to identify Argentinian culture with that of the gaucho.

In fact, from the 1920s onwards, many writers show themselves aware that a big city like Buenos Aires, open to influences from all parts of the civilized world, a polyglot and cosmopolitan city, cannot limit its conception of a national cultural tradition to that of nineteenth-century popular culture. A number of periodicals founded in this period acted as media for the introduction of European culture. The most notable of these, *Sur*, was founded in 1931 by Victoria Ocampo who admired English and North American as well as French writers. Over the years, *Sur* has brought together the best of contemporary writing throughout the world, and has set the tone for the Argentinian avant-garde.

The conscious cosmopolitanism of *Sur* and of much Argentinian writing from the twenties onwards is attributable to a number of factors, the two most significant of which are the elite's sense of alienation and the intellectuals' anxiety over cultural standards. First and most important has been the elite's inability, isolated and without roots in a native or in any one European culture, to identify itself either with the gaucho tradition or with the urban immigrant[29] – hence the recourse to aesthetic values in the belief that these transcend national and racial boundaries. Secondly, some Argentinian writers have seen in immigration a threat to cultural standards. Many of the first generation of immigrants spoke little Spanish, their vocabulary was poor and their grammar imperfect. Many Argentinian artists have been alarmed by the risk of Argentinian Spanish degenerating into a crude dialect; the only possible recourse for them in this situation has been to set a standard, in the literary language, writing, not in dialect, but in a 'general Spanish'. Intellectuals taking this approach include the Spanish-born scholar Amado Alonso (b. 1896), the poet Arturo Capdevila (b. 1889) and, most notably, Jorge Luis Borges. The spirit informing their work reveals very clearly the anxiety of the elite to keep open the lines of communication with Europe and to identify itself with a culture that transcends national boundaries.

This attitude towards language has its parallel in a certain conservatism of style. Argentina's leading poets – Baldomero Fernández Moreno (1886–1950), Enrique Banchs (b. 1888) and Ricardo Molinari (b. 1898) – have made very little attempt to break with or modify existing Hispanic forms. Fernández Moreno draws heavily on the traditional Spanish forms of popular poetry; Banchs prefers the sonnet; Molinari, after an initial revolutionary period, now combines vers libre and traditional forms. This latter is particularly interesting since Molinari is a contemporary of Vallejo and Neruda, both of whom made violent attacks on the literary language and the literary forms they had inherited. Molinari is far more ambivalent in his attitude. He feels the need to conserve the links with Hispanic tradition as well as to rebel.* Since 1950, the rather tardy influence of Surrealism has been felt. Although Aldo Pellegrini was responsible for the introduction of Surrealism into Argentina in the late 1920s, it has only begun to have a widespread influence in comparatively recent years, with the foundation in 1952 of the review *A partir de O* (From O Onwards). At much the same period a second influential review was founded, *Poesía Buenos Aires* (edited by Raúl Gustavo Aguirre).

Perhaps the best summary of the position of the Argentinian artist has been made by Jorge Luis Borges, who believes that the relation of the Argentinian to Western culture is similar to that of the Jew, who inherits this culture but remains an ironic outsider. Borges's own writing epitomizes this attitude, for it reveals him as a man of immense and eclectic culture for whom philosophical systems are 'games with infinity'.

The fascination that philosophical idealism has for Borges and his generation is also significant. He himself has no positive philosophy. He is a sceptic whose work is a continual questioning of fact, of systems and of all the structures of reality that are normally taken for granted. A good example of this is the short story 'Tlön, Uqbar, Orbis Tertius' (discussed previously on pp. 198-9) in which some scholars create an imaginary planet, objects from which begin to invade the 'real' world. The story is a strange and compelling allegory of the relation between 'creation' and 'reality', and it shows the fascination that the former holds for Borges. In many of the elite writers, the everyday world is presented as a world of appearances. This persistent idealism is reflected in the popularity in Argentina of such genres as mystery and detective stories with metaphysical overtones, or fables, like those of Marco Denevi (b. 1922). The highly complex fictional games of Julio Cortázar represent attempts to shake the reader out of a complacent acceptance of routine of any kind. In the essay, too, there has been a persistent probing beneath surface reality to the 'essential Argentina', as in *Historia de una pasión argentina* (1937) by Eduardo Mallea, or in *Radiografía de la pampa* (1933) by Ezequiel Martínez Estrada.

When the turbulent city of Buenos Aires or the social problems of the immigrant come into Argentinian writing, it is often as the background to a type of fiction that probes metaphysical questions, as in many of the stories of Borges or the novels of Bioy Casares. The city has also been the protagonist of a

Joycian novel, *Adán Buenosayres* (Adam Buenos Aires, 1948) by Leopoldo Marechal (b. 1900). Where social questions come into elite writing, they are nearly always associated with the theme of the decline of the old social structure. The decay of the old land-owning families, the disappearance of their way of life, the degeneration of the traditional elite – these form the themes of several novels by Eduardo Mallea (notably *Las Aguilas*), of Ernesto Sábato's *Sobre héroes y tumbas* (1961), and of *La caída* (The Fall, 1956) by Beatriz Guido (b. 1924). These writers show us that the old Argentina is dead, but Sábato's confused characters and Mallea's pessimistic characters also reveal that the nature of the new Argentina is not yet very clear.[30]

Among the younger writers, however, the claims of the avant-garde have reasserted themselves. Revolutions are now formal ones, and there is an emphasis on technical skill and originality. Néstor Sánchez (b. 1935) is a young novelist who in *Nosotros dos* (1967) creates a literary language closely based on the spoken language of Buenos Aires. In *La traición de Rita Hayworth* (1967), Manuel Puig (b. 1932) uses stream of consciousness and dialogue, again re-created from the spoken language, to present the alienated world of a compulsive movie-going mother and child.

Argentina has a continuous avant-garde tradition associated with an elite attitude to culture. However, it is also one of the few countries in the continent which has a recognizable middle-brow culture. There is also the pop culture of the *tango* and *lunfardo* (the dialect spoken in the city of Buenos Aires). The literary elite tend to waver between total rejection of the middle-brow and the popular (Mallea), parody of the middlebrow with humorous acceptance of the popular (Cortázar) and the populism represented by the *Boedo* group and their descendants.

In Chile, the elite attitude, so marked in Argentinian culture, is greatly attenuated, possibly because many of the leading poets and novelists have come from the lower sectors of the population. Indeed, the background of many is working-class. Pablo Neruda's father was a train driver; Manuel Rojas has worked as a linotype operator and a house painter; and Nicomedes

Guzmán (b.1914) is the son of a street hawker. Moreover, even writers from wealthy families – such as Joaquín Edwards Bello (b. 1887) – are often deeply humanitarian.

In consequence, Chilean literature is frequently documentary and didactic. Many novels exposed bad conditions or the difficulties of life in remote regions. Mariano Latorre (1886–1955), Federico Gana (1868–1926), Marta Brunet (b. 1901), Luis Durand (1895–1954) and Rafael Maluenda (b. 1885) all treat of peasant life. Baldomero Lillo (1867–1923) documents the life of the miners, Edwards Bello that of the city *lumpenproletariat*, while in *Paralelo 53 Sur* (Fifty-Third Parallel South, 1936), Juan Marín (b. 1900) describes life in the extreme south of Chile. This sympathy for the poor and oppressed has even characterized Chilean poetry, thus distinguishing it markedly from that of other Latin-American countries. Nicanor Parra (b. 1914), Gabriela Mistral (1889–1957) and, above all, Pablo Neruda (b. 1904), have devoted poems to 'simple people'. Neruda has stated that his Communism grew out of 'the suffering of the people and their hope of change'.[31] This is not to say that all Chilean writers see the world through the eyes of the humble. It is true, however, that Chilean writers, even when dealing with personal or psychological themes, still tend to anchor their characters very firmly in a social context. Eduardo Barrios (b. 1884), María Bombal (b. 1910) and Augusto González Vera (b. 1897) are primarily concerned with individuals and with their motives and sensations, and yet they invariably show these individuals in their social role. Even a writer like Pedro Prado (1886–1952), whose interests were primarily aesthetic, wrote one novel – *Un juez rural* (The Country Magistrate, 1924) – based closely on his own experiences as a member of the legal profession. But perhaps the point can best be made by contrasting Eduardo Barrios's *Gran Señor y Rajadiablos* (Gentleman and Hell-Raiser, 1948) with the Argentine novel *Don Segundo Sombra*. Both deal with a similar environment but, whereas in the latter the hero's main development takes place in the solitude of the pampa, in *Gran Señor y Rajadiablos* Barrios presents a character-study of a lusty, old-fashioned patriarch who is the backbone of the social and political life of the rural community in which he lives. The Chilean novel never strays far from society.

There is also a significant difference between Argentinian novels chronicling the downfall of an aristocratic family and Chilean novels on the same theme, for the latter tend to show the relationship between classes as well as presenting the story through the eyes of the declining class. Thus, *Coronación* (1957) by José Donoso describes a vigorous and immoral servant class erupting into the lives of ageing and declining members of the upper class. *El peso de la noche* (1964 – discussed on p. 247) by Jorge Edwards shows up the base values of members of the upper class in their love relations with humbler members of society. This master-servant, upper-lower class relationship has also been brought to the theatre in *Mama Rosa* (1958) by Fernando Debesa (b. 1921). The awareness of class relationships perhaps helps to account for the fact that Chile is the one country in South America that has produced an authentic study of crowd psychology. This is Manuel Rojas's *Hijo de ladrón* (1951, published in English as *Born Guilty* – previously discussed on p. 220). One of its central scenes is a city riot in which a few small incidents develop into a wave of destructive violence and looting. Rojas's observation of the way a riot starts and the course it takes is both accurate and acute. Strikes and labour violence come into many Chilean novels, notably those of Juan Marín.

Yet paradoxically, although Chilean writers seem particularly conscious of the overcrowded city poor, they are also among those most absorbed with the virgin nature of America. Many poems of Gabriela Mistral transmit the sense of loneliness that even trees and rocks seem to feel in their remoteness from human eyes. Pablo Neruda tells us in his autobiography what it is like to live in houses newly made from the timber of virgin forests whose insect and wild life are still unnamed. One of the high points of Chilean literature is the passage in the *Canto general* where Neruda describes the flora and fauna of virgin America, revealing a religious awe at the beauty of the as yet unviolated natural life.

> Mas, húmedo como un nenúfar
> el flamenco abría sus puertas
> de sonrosada catedral,
> y volaba como la aurora.[32]

> Humid as a water-lily,
> the flamingo opened the doors
> of its rosy cathedral
> and flew like the dawn.

A similar sense of wonder at the beauty and enigma of primitive life is transmitted in the novel *Jeremy Button* (1950) by Benjamín Subercaseaux (b. 1902). It tells the story of three savages taken by a British ship from Tierra del Fuego to Victorian London, and of the conflict between the primitive and the civilized mind.

Chile's geographical contrasts are thus reflected in a literature in which awareness of the primitive and untamed is conjoined with the anguished self-questioning of poets, such as Enrique Lihn (b. 1923) and Nicanor Parra, and of novelists who deal with class relationships and the behaviour of men in the mass.[33]

BRAZIL, MEXICO AND CUBA

Brazil, Mexico and Cuba are three countries which, for different reasons, have their eyes consciously fixed on the future. In Mexico and Cuba, which have undergone radical political and social revolutions, concern with reform and reconstruction is part of the atmosphere of life at all levels. In Brazil, where there has been as yet no such major social revolution, 'futurism' is very much a concept of intellectuals who are aware of their country's enormous potential.

The most striking feature of Brazil is that it has all the problems of other Latin-American countries on a far larger scale. Its size is enormous and its population very large (there are 75 million Brazilians); its natural regions range from Amazon jungle to pampa; São Paulo is one of the most advanced cities in Latin America, yet Brazil has also some of the most primitive tribes in the world. The racial mixture is the most variegated in the sub-continent for, with large populations both of Negroes and of Indians, Brazil has also been washed over by a wave of immigration from Europe and the Far East that has appreciably modified the original Portuguese stock. The economic and social problems are equally great; the drought-ridden north-east; the evils of regional monoculture; the concentration of wealth in the hands of the few; inadequate capital investment; and the tendency to revert to political oppression whenever the demand for reform gathers enough head of steam to seem to be capable of pushing the country into a radical social transformation.[34]

Yet, if Brazil's problems are those of the rest of Latin America its comparatively calm political development during the nineteenth century and its size and wealth have created a good environment for culture. Thanks to the patronage of the monarchy in the last century, educational and cultural institutions were founded. Before the turn of the century, there was an excellent school of philosophy in Recife; Rio de Janeiro could boast a flourishing book trade; and there was a certain amount of public and private patronage of the arts. In fact, Rio in the 1870s was far more sophisticated and cultured in atmosphere than any other Latin-American city. In more recent times, São Paulo has rivalled Rio and (as we saw in chapter 3) has become the avant-garde centre in both literature and in the arts. It is, in particular, one of the big patron cities for the plastic arts in Latin America, and its wealthy citizens have begun to buy canvases and murals by avant-garde Brazilian artists. But Rio de Janeiro still has the major publishing concerns, notable among which is that of José Olympio, who has made a praiseworthy contribution to Brazilian letters in his encouragement of native writers.

A prominent feature of Brazilian cultural life in the last forty years is the tension between the need for roots and the urge for modernity, between those who want to stress local or regional characteristics and those who want Brazil to be in the forefront of world culture. This tension has given rise to polemics and discussion but it is also not unusual to find the two tendencies at work in the same writer. It is significant that Modernismo began in São Paulo in 1922 with an exhibition of Brazilian painting that included canvases showing the influence of Fauvism; hence, at the outset of this specifically Brazilian cultural movement, the 'modern' and the 'native' came together. This conjunction of the two tendencies has also occurred in literature. Many reviews of the Modernismo period had 'nationalist' titles such as *Pau Brazil* (Brazilian Wood) and *Verde-Amarelo* (Green-Yellow – the colours of the Brazilian flag). And, within Modernismo, there was also a cult of the primitive. Oswald de Andrade launched his *Manifesto Antropofágio* (Cannibal Manifesto) in 1928; the novel, *Mucanaíma* (1928), by Mário de Andrade (1893–1945) is the story of an emperor born in the Amazon jungle, a noble savage who visits São Paulo and who was intended to incorporate a 'composite Brazilian character'. (See pp. 111–12 above.) The poem *Cobra Norato* (1931) by Raul Bopp (b. 1898) concerns a poet's return to his roots in the jungles of Brazil. Again, Jorge de Lima (1895–1953) wrote poetry on Negro themes, identifying himself with this section of the community, before turning to the writing of religious and metaphysical poetry. Thus in Modernismo there was a combination of the avant-garde and the search for roots among the most primitive elements of the population and in primitive nature. Yet at the same time Oswald and Mário de Andrade and others were singing the praises of São Paulo and declaring it the 'city of the future'.[35]

A similar polarity is observable in the novelists of north-east Brazil. They treat of the simple *sertanejos*, sugarworkers, cocoa-planters and fishermen, but many of them show their simple and even primitive characters drawn away from their environment by the magnetic pull of the city – like the cattleman in *Vidas Sêcas* (1938) by Graciliano Ramos (1892–1953) or the starving *sertanejos* in *O Quinze* (The Year Fifteen, 1931) by Raquel de Queirós (b. 1910). However, in the north-east novel, the contrast between the country and the city, between traditional forms of life and modernity, has a significance that differs from that of the roots-modernity polarity of the Modernista writers. To Graciliano Ramos, for instance, the city is the one force that can stimulate the peasant to break out of the eternal cycle of backbreaking labour and starvation. In the 'Sugar Cane Cycle' novels of José Lins do Rêgo (1901–57) – previously discussed on pp. 114 – plantation and city are mutually dependent, like the two scales of a balance. The money from the plantation feeds the shops and brothels of the city; yet it is in the city, where he experiences political and economic struggles, that Ricardo, the plantation boy, learns enough to return to the plantation as an accountant. On the other hand, Carlos Melo, the landowner's nephew who is educated in the city, is also depicted as being made unfit by it for life on the plantation. The city may offer wider horizons but it also corrupts; indeed, in the final volume of this series of novels, the ruin of the plantation comes about partly through the corrupting influence of the city.* In many of the novels of Jorge Amado, the city is the place where the poor sharpen their wits in the class struggle and also where the political rivalries of the feudal hierarchy are fought out.

Roots and modernity come together in two very fine contemporary works: the novel *Grande Sertão: Veredas* (1956) by João Guimarães Rosa, and the poem *Vida e Morte Severina* (Life and Death of a Severino, 1954–5) by João Cabral de Melo Neto (b. 1920). *Grande Sertão* (previously discussed on pp. 251), set among the bandits of the north-east, is written in a Joycean style that manages to capture the psychology of the people of the region. *Vida e Morte Severina*, based on the form of a traditional Pernambucan Christmas play, deals with the universal problem of death and suffering, and the life of those who strive

> to try to bring to life
> a dead and deader land,
> to try to wrest a farm
> out of burnt-over land.[36]

A similar confluence of nativism and modernity marks the contemporary plastic arts, especially the paintings of Cándido Portinari (b. 1903), and also music: for example, the *Cancões Brasileiros* of Heitor Vila-Lôbos (1887–1959).†

---

*This is an oversimplification. In the novels, the situation is presented in all its complexity and in relation to a changing economic situation. All the same, whereas the old patriarch Ze Paulino has little to do with the city, both the son and the grandson are partly city men, and it is they who, in their different ways, help to ruin the estate.

†Although there is at present much more emphasis on the 'international style', as for instance in the sculptures of Sergio Camargo.

Perhaps partly because the city with its promise of change and modernity is so close to the primitive backland in Brazil, writers have been intensely aware of the frustrations and anguish of city life, an awareness which reached its highest artistic expression in the novel *Angústia* (Anguish, 1936) by Graciliano Ramos. This novel relates the story of a man's obsession for the girl next door. He talks to her over the fence, glimpses her through a crack in the bedroom wall, hears her conversations and weeping through the thin walls. Finally, taunted by her nearness and her emotional distance, he kills her – an apt allegory of the torment of living close to other people while yet remaining estranged from them in the unnatural circumstances of modern urban life. Two of the great Brazilian poets – Manuel Bandeira (b. 1886) and Carlos Drummond de Andrade (b. 1902) – have both been concerned with this lack of communication in modern life. For Drummond de Andrade indeed, not only is human communication difficult but even the most humble objects met in daily life are unknowable and enigmatic. His poems are ironic comments on human inadequacy.

Brazil is too big and varied, and too much of a paradox, to be epitomized in a single work. The despair of many Brazilian writers at the very size and variety of their country is given ironical expression by Drummond de Andrade, who urges those obsessed by the Brazilian problem to 'forget Brazil' because:

> Tão majestoso, tão sem limites, tão despropositado
> êle quer repousar de nossos terríveis carinhos.[37]

> So majestic, so endless, so absurd,
> She wants to reject our terrible affection.

Brazil has had a strong tradition of pure poetry, the outstanding exponent being Cecília Meireles (b. 1901), and of religious poetry, such as that published by Jorge de Lima in his *Tempo e Eternidade* (Time and Eternity, 1935). Undoubtedly the most influential poet is Cabral de Melo Neto (b. 1920), whose technical skill and verbal dexterity have transformed Brazilian poetry. As in other parts of Latin America, the most recent poetry movements (associated with the magazines *Praxis* and *Noigandres*) tend to combine avant-garde and social commitment. The most significant new development in the arts is, however, in the Cinema Novo where the analysis of Brazilian myths has become a major theme.

Mexico, unlike Brazil, has undergone a social revolution that has destroyed old structures. It is notable in having a major body of writers who are fundamentally in sympathy with the post-revolutionary establishment, despite some criticisms and reservations; and it is the one country in Latin America which has something of a mass public and in which all the arts – music, painting, ballet, cinema, sculpture, poetry, the novel – are practised and even flourishing. The Spanish Civil War, moreover, had a distinct effect on Mexican culture, since many republican intellectuals settled in the country and helped to found publishing houses and theatre groups, and strengthened the staffs of colleges and universities.

There are plenty of problems however. Even today, 43 per cent of the adult population is illiterate, and connected with this problem of illiteracy is the problem of the Indian and the peasant. Though Mexican post-revolutionary governments have tried to integrate the peasant into national life by redistributing lands and conducting literacy campaigns, this process is not yet complete. Of an estimated four million Indians in the population, two million are still very poor.[38] The criteria by which modern Mexicans judge Indians are cultural and linguistic. Because the Indians speak a language other than Spanish, their integration is difficult, and is aggravated by the fact that most of them, living far from the centres of civilization, have only superficial contacts with any way of life other than their own. However, barriers to integration come not only from the Indian side; many non-Indians are indifferent to or uninterested in the problem. For all the devoted work of anthropologists, teachers and sociologists, Indianism has often remained more of an intellectual pose and not pursued in any practical way. Nevertheless despite barriers on the side of the Indian and indifference on the part of many of the rest, Mexican society and the Indians' outlook are changing, as is shown in the fine study of a Chamula village, *Juan Pérez Jolote* (1952) by Ricardo Pozas (b. 1910).

The main problem which post-revolutionary intellectuals have had to face is the disparity between the promises of the revolution and their fulfilment. Land distribution has been sporadic and imperfect, the majority of businesses still depend heavily on foreign capital and personnel, and the Mexicans themselves seem less interested in industrial development than in the professions. There is also a disparity between Mexico's claim to be 'revolutionary' and the fact that it is still a free enterprise capitalist country. Before the revolution, Mexican society resembled that of most Latin-American countries. There was a small intellectual elite, the members of which wrote for one another and found publication difficult, a theatre that housed foreign companies, and a mass of the population that was illiterate and remote from civilization. But even in the nineteenth century, intellectuals such as Guillermo Prieto (1818–97), Ignacio Ramírez (1818–79) and Ignacio Altamirano (1834–93) showed a deep social concern which has been inherited by subsequent generations. Indeed, one of the remarkable features of Mexican intellectual life is the fact that the generation which included José Vasconcelos (1882–1959), Antonio Caso (1883–1946) and Alfonso Reyes (1889–1959) – intellectuals who had formed part of the *Ateneo* group – gave their support to the revolution. This adhesion was important and had a profound effect on younger generations. These thinkers not only contributed to post-revolutionary Mexican ideology but also set an example of cooperation with the work of the revolution which most intellectuals have since followed. Vasconcelos, in particular, was responsible for starting many projects in the arts which have since come to fruition. His work was indeed, as Octavio Paz declared, 'not that of a technician but that of a founder'.[39] And it is probably true that institutions such as the Institute of Indigenous Studies, the Museum of Anthropology and History (in which history is considered as part of the living present and not as a collection of relics), the Folk Ballet and the National Orchestra would probably not have taken the remarkable form they did without his pioneer work. Certainly, in no other part of Latin America are members of all classes so conscious and proud both of their historical and popular traditions.

Of all the arts, it is mural painting to which we look for the first expression of the spirit of the Mexican revolution. The work of Diego Rivera (1887–1957), Alfaro Siqueiros (b. 1898) and Clemente Orozco (1882–1949), discussed in chapter 3, needs little further comment here except to make the point that, despite their weaknesses, Mexican painters are alone in Latin America in having 'created a truly original style of painting which has influenced the art of many countries in the Western hemisphere'.[40] Mexico has also been one of the pioneers in the modern integration of art and architecture, to which public buildings like the National Autonomous University and the many low-cost housing projects bear witness. The murals of the three great painters, Rivera, Orozco and Siqueiros, pioneered this integration.

Early Mexican muralism tended to be didactic; yet, even when at its height and at its most influential, there have been those standing aside from the view that the artist must teach or preach. Carlos Mérida (b. 1891) and Rufino Tamayo (b. 1899), for example, are painters whose works show us the artist following his own individual path. Although Mérida has executed many murals for public buildings, his work, unlike that of the early muralists, is abstract. Since the 1940s one of the dominating influences of the Mexican artistic scene has been the German-born Mathias Goeritz who is the architect of the impressively sober towers of the Satellite Town near Mexico City and who, in collaboration with Rufino Tamayo and Carlos Mérida (and also Henry Moore), has designed and helped to decorate the experimental museum El Eco, which includes murals, architectural sculpture, and even a 'plastic poem'.[41] It is significant that the plastic arts in Mexico, though the first of the arts to be identified with the spirit of the revolution, have shown in recent years a tendency to break with the earlier nationalist didacticism and to move towards a more international style.

Unlike the muralists, Mexico's poets and novelists were, on the whole, slower to cooperate with the revolution, for writers in the immediate post-revolutionary period had little direct contact with the new public. Mexican poetry of this century for long remains locked in the themes of death and solitude,[42] while the post-revolutionary novel – even where it deals with the revolution – tends to show horror at the grimmer aspects of it. This is natural enough. Mexico's novelists tend to come from middle-class backgrounds, and those of the revolutionary generation, direct witnesses of the fighting – for instance, Mariano Azuela (1873–1952) and Martín Luis Guzmán (b. 1887) – show in their works their horror at the violence and the barbarism unleashed by the revolution. The semi-autobiographical novels of José Rubén Romero (1890–1952) – one thinks particularly of *Apuntes de un lugareño* (Notes of a Provincial, 1932) – depict the disruption of peaceful village life with the coming of the revolution. Nevertheless, there is more to such novels than implicit criticism of aspects of the great upheaval of Mexican society; the novels of the revolution also introduced something new into Latin-American literature: the mass hero. Novels like *Los de abajo* (The Underdogs, 1916) by Mariano Azuela and *Campamento* (Bivouac, 1931) by Gregorio López y Fuentes (b. 1893) show the part played by the anonymous mass in the great events of the country's history.

The first wave of eye-witness accounts of the revolution is followed by many novels exhibiting the frustration or failure of post-revolutionary promises. López y Fuentes's *El Indio* (1935) shows the failure of the revolutionaries to integrate the Indian into national life; and *El Resplandor* (Sunburst, 1937) by Mauricio Magdaleno (b. 1906) demonstrates that the new political bosses can be as unscrupulous as the old. This feeling of disenchantment becomes particularly acute during and just after the presidency of Plutarcho Calles (1924–8), with its apparent attendant danger of Mexico's reverting to dictatorship and rule by the military. Writers of this period are not slow to warn of the danger. *La sombra del caudillo* (Shadow of the Caudillo, 1929) by Martín Luis Guzmán and *¡Mi General!* (General!, 1934) by Gregorio López y Fuentes express a critical attitude towards military leaders who try to interfere in political affairs, and both writers expose the perils that ensue when men who have experienced power and glory on the battlefield cannot reconcile themselves to a minor role in time of peace. An even more open attack on the hypocrisy and demagogy of the Calles regime is made by Rodolfo Usigli in *Tres comedias impolíticas* * (1933–5) and in the play *El gesticulador* (The Gesticulator, 1937).

The threat of a return to authoritarian rule under Calles was fortunately averted. With the coming to power of Lázaro Cárdenas in 1934, many of the promises of the revolution finally became implemented. Subsequent governments have been moderately reformist, offering both a high degree of social security and welfare to the mass of the people, and at the same time allowing private enterprise and foreign capital investment. Writers and intellectuals have therefore tended to direct their criticisms less at the system and more at the character of the Mexicans as a people, seeing in them collective faults and blaming these for the difficulty in properly implementing the revolution. The first analytical essays on the Mexican character appeared during the Calles regime. This analysis has continued to the present day, and includes: *El perfil del hombre y la cultura en México* (Profile of Mexican Man and Culture, 1934) by Samuel Ramos; *Epílogo sobre la hipocresía del mexicano* (Epilogue on Mexican Hypocrisy, 1938) by Rodolfo Usigli; *La propensión mexicana al resentimiento* (The Mexican Propensity to Resentment, 1949) by Agustín Yañez (b. 1904); *El laberinto de la soledad* (1950) by Octavio Paz; *Conciencia y posibilidad del Mexicano* (The Mexican's Self-awareness and Potential, 1952) by Leopoldo Zea; and many others. These studies follow Alfonso Reyes's counsel that men should seek America in their hearts 'with severe integrity instead of lying down as if in paradise and waiting for the fruit to drop off the tree'.[43] Though the writers mentioned here differ among one another in the angles taken for studying the problems of modern Mexico, all agree in pointing out weaknesses in social and political attitudes which act as obstacles to progress, and which stem very often from the circumstances of the country's history and the clash of races.

This critical analysis of the Mexican character and environment is not confined to scholarly studies but is also reflected in literature, both in the theatre (particularly in the plays of Rodolfo Usigli) and in the novel. Here, the early eye-witness

* *Impolíticas* is a play on the numerous meanings of the word, which can mean impolite, tactless and non-politic.

account of the revolution, which treats the events rather in the manner of an adventure story, eventually gives way to more subtle and evocative studies. In contemporary Mexican literature, the revolution is no longer seen as the upsurge of a blind force, as in Azuela, or as the triumph of barbarism, as in Guzmán, nor yet as the movement of an anonymous mass, as in López y Fuentes's *Campamento*. This change in attitude corresponds to the emergence of a new generation for whom the dictatorial regime of Porfirio Díaz and the revolution are events in the historical past and not something directly experienced.

The change in attitude has involved a change in technique. The first revolutionary writers – Azuela and Guzmán – see the revolution through their own eyes or through the eyes of a central character who narrates the events in all their brutal immediacy. In the writings of the new generation, the violence is remembered or recalled, as in *La muerte de Artemio Cruz* (1962) by Carlos Fuentes, where a dying man remembers this now remote past; or – even more distantly – as in *Pedro Páramo* (1955) by Juan Rulfo, where all the main characters are dead and exist only as voices in the air of a deserted village. In *Los recuerdos del porvenir* (1963) by Elena Garro, the persecution of the Catholics by Calles and his followers is presented as if this period already belongs to the mists of legend. Other writers frankly present the revolution in terms of distant personal memories, like the charming reminiscences of Andrés Iduarte (b. 1907): *Un niño en la revolución mexicana* (A Child in the Mexican Revolution, 1951). The bitterness has gone also from literary evocations of the pre-revolutionary period, under the Díaz regime. In Agustín Yañez's *Al filo del agua* (On the Verge of the Rain, 1947), the tragic narrowness of life in a dusty provincial town suddenly appears less tragic by the end of the novel when the revolution blows through the town like a refreshing wind. Juan Rulfo can present the landowner Pedro Páramo with a certain sympathy and understanding since he and his kind are forever dead.

It is for the present rather than for the past that bitterest criticism is reserved. Carlos Fuentes, in particular, agrees with the essayists in attributing the difficulties of modern Mexico to weaknesses in the Mexican character, and especially to the Mexican's need to impose himself violently on other people in order to assert his *machismo*, or masculinity. Fuentes's *Artemio Cruz* is the embodiment of such characteristics. By virtue of the situation in post-revolutionary Mexico, Cruz becomes one of the top men in the country's politics, controlling newspapers and industry. In *La región más transparente* (Where the Air is Clearer, 1958), Fuentes introduces the reader to a whole galaxy of characters who have made their fortunes in the unsettled post-revolutionary era: bankers, poets, spongers, actresses. Here and in *Las buenas conciencias* (1959), he exposes a society in the grip of men who have no scruples about betraying their fellows and rising to the top through playing on ideals which they betray. Fuentes thus warns his readers against accepting the fact that the winning side is necessarily impeccable. He and his generation can no longer think in terms of black and white. Similarly, Rosario Castellanos (b. 1925), whose novel *Balún Canán* (1957) deals with the relationship between Indians and White or Mestizo landowners, shows not a 'good' and a 'bad' side but two mutually uncomprehending races, neither of which is deliberately wicked.[44] The difficulty of attributing guilt and innocence in regard to violent events has also been dealt with in a striking way by Vicente Leñero (b. 1933). His novel *Los albañiles* (The Bricklayers, 1964 – previously discussed on p. 206) is a detective story in which a nightwatchman is murdered. Various characters, including the police, 'confess' in their minds to his murder, Leñero's purpose being to show that the clear-cut division between 'guilt' and 'innocence' is invalid.[45] A younger generation of Mexican novelists have tended to become increasingly sophisticated in the technical devices they use. Fuentes's most recent novel, *Cambio de piel* (A Change of Skin, 1968) is a tribute to the *nouvelle vague* novel and represents a more abstract approach than he had hitherto adopted to the theme of the novel as it consists of the sexual and verbal interplay of four characters. His younger contemporaries, José Agustín, Salvador Elizondo and Juan García Ponce, write for an increasingly sophisticated urban public and make no concessions to regionalism or local colour. Theirs is a middle-class world with its in-jokes and slang and their theme of alienation is common to most countries.

This reluctance of many modern Mexican novelists to associate the established order with the morally good is connected, with the conviction, powerfully expressed by Octavio Paz, Alfonso Reyes and others, that the artist must remain free and uncommitted. This, needless to say, is a view of art quite different from that of the post-revolutionary muralists; but for writers, in the ambivalent atmosphere of modern Mexico, the assertion of this freedom has become increasingly necessary. In the novel, this freedom is demonstrated by the author's insistence on maintaining a critical detachment from events. And in poetry it has meant the assertion of the right to deal with any subject matter. For Octavio Paz, indeed, the poet must remain an outsider in bourgeois society since he is totally opposed to its values. Poetry brings man into contact with that other world, the world of the imagination, and with the underlying unity which society shatters. For a torn and alienated humanity, more and more enslaved by the machine, poetry represents a path of salvation.[46] Much of Paz's own poetry fulfils this function, notably his magnificent 'Piedra de sol' (Sun Stone, 1957) which fuses Aztec and Greek myth to reveal the unity of all things in the eternal cycle of procreation and death.[47] Paz's recent anthology, *Poesía en movimiento* (1966), strikingly illustrates the continuity of the Mexican poetic tradition from López Velarde onwards. There is a notable paucity of anything that can be termed social poetry. José Emilio Pacheco (b. 1939), Jaime Sabines (b. 1925), Marco Antonio Montes de Oca (b. 1932), Jaime García Terres (b. 1924), Rubén Bonifaz Nuño (b. 1923), whilst writing very individual poetry, yet share a common preoccupation for poetic language.

Mexican culture is far too dynamic and varied to be fully considered in such a brief space. Its most remarkable feature is the continuing existence down the years of groups of writers and intellectuals who are passionately involved in their country and its future while maintaining their right to criticism. This attitude of critical involvement goes back to the early nineteenth-century novelist and journalist Fernández de Lizardi (1776–

1827), and has remained a coherent tradition down to the present.

The Cuban revolution has also had a great effect on national cultural life, although the changes in the political and social life of Cuba are still too recent for a solid judgement to be formed.

Until 1959, Cuban culture was very similar to that of the other Spanish-speaking islands in the Caribbean. Pre-revolutionary poets tended to identify themselves with contemporary European trends or to pursue 'pure' poetry. Mariano Brull (1891–1956), Eugenio Florit (b. 1903), José Lezama Lima (b. 1912), Cintio Vitier (b. 1921) and Eliseo Diego (b. 1920) are all excellent poets but they were not primarily concerned with national themes. On the other hand, the novel has been much more socially involved. The novels of Carlos Loveira (1882–1928), Carlos Montenegro (b. 1900) and Enrique Serpa (b. 1899), and the short stories of Lino Novás Calvo (b. 1905), are often set among the underdogs or the ordinary people of Cuba and imply social criticism of the state of the island.[48]

The one truly original movement in the pre-revolutionary culture of Cuba is the Afro-Cuban movement. Certainly, the initial inspiration came from the Negro vogue in Paris in the 1920s (see above, pp. 183–7), but the joy of the Cuban poets of this school in the primitive, uninhibited Negro song and dance rhythms was also an assertion of something specifically Cuban and non-European. In the poetry of Nicolás Guillén (b. 1902), Afro-Cubanism developed into a response to the dehumanized industrial and capitalist civilization of the neighbouring United States. It is no accident that Guillén calls a group of his poems 'Sones para turistas' (Dance for Tourists, 1937) or that, in his verse, he frequently mocks the American tourist whose presence is taken as symbolic of Cuba's economic dependence on the United States.[49]

The Castro revolution of 1959 has changed the social structure of Cuba. Most of the upper class and many of the middle and professional classes left the island. A vigorous campaign against illiteracy has brought into being a new mass readership. New writers have emerged to provide for this readership, encouraged to write and helped to publish by the official Union of Artists and Writers and by the prizes offered by the Casa de la Américas, which acts as a cultural clearing-house. Book production has enormously increased, and there are now available cheap editions of many Cuban and Latin-American classics.

These changes have not yet been reflected in any new or outstanding writing.[50] A group of writers of the older generation – the avant-garde poet José Lezama Lima, Nicolás Guillén and the novelist Alejo Carpentier (b. 1904) – dominate the literary scene. Of these, Carpentier began his career in the Afro-Cuban movement, and the basis of his reputation rests on the novel *Los pasos perdidos* (1953). He has also written a number of novels which delve into the historical past of the Caribbean; the most outstanding of these works are *El reino de este mundo* (The Kingdom of This World, 1949), which deals with the slave risings in Haiti at the end of the eighteenth century, and his remarkable *El siglo de las luces* (1962) the first novel to give a picture of the Caribbean as a whole. Lezama Lima has recently published his major work – a novel, *Paradiso* (1966). This novel, conceived on a grand scale, is undoubtedly one of the major contemporary works of Spanish-American literature. Its principal theme is the adolescent's perception of reality in the widest sense, through sexual, sensual and intellectual experience and the formation of an artistic vocation and consciousness. Among the new names to emerge since the revolution are poets such as Roberto Fernández Retamar (b. 1930), Antonio Arrufat (b. 1935), Fayad Jamís (b. 1930), Pablo Armando Fernández (b. 1930) and Heberto Padilla (b. 1932); among prose writers, Guillermo Cabrera Infante (b. 1929), Virgilio Piñera (b. 1912), Onelio Jorge Cardoso (b. 1914), Rogelio Llopis (b. 1928), Edmundo Desnoes (b. 1930), and Severo Sarduy (b. 1937).

Of these, Guillermo Cabrera Infante and Severo Sarduy are now in exile. The writers who remain in Cuba face totally novel conditions for the writer. On the one hand the successful completion of the literacy campaign gave them a new public. On the other hand conditions imposed by the blockade of the island and the ensuing paper shortage have made publication slow and sometimes difficult. But editions of works which are published are enormous and they normally sell out very rapidly. In 1961 in a speech to intellectuals, Castro guaranteed freedom of literary expression, declaring, 'within the Revolution everything, outside the Revolution nothing', a guarantee that was repeated by other leading intellectuals and which has allowed a remarkable a variety of styles. Unlike Soviet writing, realism has not been the only permitted style. Science fiction, fantasy as in *Tute de reyes*, a collection of stories by Antonio Benitez, black humour as in the short stories of Virgilio Piñera – all these are common. The nearest thing to socialist realism has been the recent interest of some young writers in the documentary approach. The poet, Miguel Barnet (b. 1940) published *Cimarrón* (Memoirs of a Runaway Slave) in which he tape-recorded the memories of an aged former slave who remembered the Wars of Independence.

In poetry, there has been a tendency to turn towards the colloquial poem after the first years of heroic revolutionary poetry. The outstanding example of the latter is a collection by Pablo Armando Fernández, already referred to (p. 178), *Libro de los héroes* (Book of Heroes) in which the poet makes his own roll call of the heroes of the Revolution. Of a different type was Fernández Retamar's *Carta a los pioneros* (Letters to the pioneers, 1962) in which the poet uses 'simple, everyday words'. Here there is an attempt to bridge the gap between the intellectual and common man by using simple language and colloquial expressions. More recent poetry is often ironic, detached and even personal in tone, like the poems of Heberto Padilla's *Fuera del juego* (Outside the Game, 1968) in which the poet reserves the right to criticize the revolution. The Uneac prize awarded to this volume by an international jury proved to be controversial, for some Cuban critics felt that the criticism was counter-revolutionary. But Padilla is something of an eternal outsider. Less bitter but also writing of personal reactions and often using an ironic or throwaway style, two women poets, Belkis Cuza Malé and Nancy Morejón, are characteristic of a younger generation of Cuban poets whose memories scarcely go back to pre-revolutionary times and whose reactions often have a freshness lacking in poets of other countries.

Painting has, perhaps, been more successful than literature in separating political commitment from artistic integrity. The leading Cuban painters can contribute on a practical level with posters and art objects whilst at the same time they continue to paint in abstract or semi-abstract style for a growing public. Although public projects such as murals are not uncommon in contemporary Cuba, easel painting is widely practised and canvases are still sold.

Cuba's promise has always been that its revolution would not follow patterns set elsewhere. Certainly within the first ten years, the struggle for survival has not meant the sacrifice of spontaneity and variety. It will be interesting to see whether, in time, totally new art forms will emerge.*

*For a more recent view of Cuban literature see an article 'Before and After: Contexts of Cuban Literature', written after the author's return from Cuba, and published in the Cambridge Review, March 1970.

In Conclusion

To declare oneself an artist in Latin America has frequently involved conflict with society. In the nineteenth century, the artist was divided from the bulk of his fellow-countrymen because of his culture and upbringing. He represented standards of refinement and civilization which were still alien to the *caudillos*, peasants and shopkeepers of his native land. As we have seen, the majority of nineteenth-century writers were also political fighters dedicated to reforming their societies. It was only towards the end of the century, with Spanish-American Modernism, that a group of poets emerged who regarded art as more important than the political struggle. This did not mean that they had abandoned hopes of social improvement. On the contrary, the Modernists' ideal of society was the exact contrary to the vulgar materialism which they regarded as the symptom of the age, and their way of life was an implicit protest against those who ignored the life of the spirit, and ignored beauty. However, though the Modernists succeeded in winning prestige for the artist in Latin America, they were often frustrated and unhappy because of the gulf between their ideals and the reality of the society in which they lived, and this frustration was also reflected in many of the novels of the period. Without abandoning these ideals of culture and refinement, the Arielist generation turned its attention to the task of bringing the rest of society up to its own standards of civilization. The artist now saw himself as a pedagogue or as a moral leader. He put his faith in education and in the written word as a means of changing society. As González Prada pointed out, this often led the intellectual to feel superior to other members of society, seeing himself as a *lazarillo* guiding the blind. And ultimately neither the written word nor education proved effective. The Arielist generation was overtaken by a rising tide of unrest, by the shattering impact of world events such as the Russian and Mexican revolutions and the First World War. The post-war generation was no longer in a position to feel superior; the masses had come to be a power to be reckoned with, while, on the other hand, Europe – for so long the refuge and backbone of Latin-American intellectuals – proclaimed its own bankruptcy. The intellectual was therefore obliged either to regard himself as an ally of the masses, a helper in their cause, or, if he could not do this, he tended to stand aside, proclaiming that politics and social reform belonged to a world of appearances. Art itself was only a game, but it was, they contended, a game worth playing for its own sake.

In the twenties and thirties, the view predominant among Latin-American writers and painters was that the artist must help further the political struggle, although an important and distinguished minority dissented from this view. Since the thirties, this position has changed. The view that the artist can in any way change or modify society through his art has gradually been abandoned by the majority. This is in itself a reflection of the state of Latin-American political life. Gloomy as the situation was in the thirties, the possibility of revolution did not seem remote. In the sixties, despite the presence of Cuba, there is a growing feeling of impotence, of being caught between the Scylla of North America and the Charybdis of Russia. It is no accident that many contemporary novels are set in microcosmic communities and their characters are caught in situations as inflexible as those of Greek tragedy.

Although to the despairing observer Latin America seems to have made little progress in the direction of the social justice for which its intellectuals have always fought, the artistic scene has not remained static. No one can pretend that the artist is in the same position as he was eighty years ago. The revolution in communications has meant that the artist is no longer totally dependent on a national public; works of art now travel from country to country. Novels are speedily translated and may even bring in enough money for the novelist to live by his writing. Under these circumstances, it is understandable that the artist should tend to rid his work of local or regional characteristics which may make it inaccessible to an international public. Both in painting and in the novel the predominance of the 'international style' is evident and is characterized by abstractionism in painting and, in the novel, by the use of universally understandable symbols and myths, through which a local or regional setting merely becomes the backcloth for the enactment of an archetypal drama. It thus seems rather odd and paradoxical that there should be this stress on similarity with the rest of the world in a sub-continent which, immediately following independence, did so much to emphasize its differences and its originality.

Yet when we look back over Latin-American culture, we find that there are considerable differences from that of the rest of the world. The major difference is not only the obvious one – of different landscapes and races – but also a more significant difference and one which affects basic notions of what art is about. While so much of Western art is concerned with individual experience or relations between the sexes, most of the major works of Latin-American literature and even some of its painting are much more concerned with social phenomena and social ideals (for instance, *Facundo*, *Os Sertões*, the novels of Rómulo Gallegos, Rivera's paintings) or – and it is here that Latin-American art achieves its profoundest vision – with that form of love which the Greeks called *agape* or love for one's fellow men. The strongest emotion in *Martín Fierro* is the sorrow of its protagonist when his friend, Cruz, dies; in *Don Segundo Sombra*, the loyalty of a man to his fellow men is far stronger than love between the sexes. In the poetry of César Vallejo, the most moving poems are those which evoke his sense of separation not from a beloved woman but from humanity in general. Here lies the true originality of Latin-American art: it has kept alive the vision of a more just and humane form of society and it continues to emphasize those emotions and relationships which are wider than the purely personal.

REFERENCES

For publication details of the works cited here, see the Bibliography.

Introduction: The Artist and Social Conscience

1. Esteban Echeverría, *Dogma socialista y otras páginas políticas*, p. 91.
2. Quoted by R. Bazin, *Histoire de la littérature américaine de langue espagnole*, p. 22.
3. Leopoldo Zea discusses the rejection of Spanish culture in Hispanic America in *The Latin American Mind*, pp. 7–26.
4. João Cruz Costa, *A History of Ideas in Brazil*, p. 49.
5. Domingo Sarmiento, *Facundo*, 4th edition, p. 18.
6. Esteban Echeverría, *La cautiva y el matadero*, Prologue by Juan María Gutiérrez, 7th edition, pp. 75–9.
7. Sarmiento, op. cit., p. 254.
8. For his opinion of *Martín Fierro*, see Jorge Luis Borges, *El Gaucho Martín Fierro*.
9. Unfortunately, there is no extensive study of these nineteenth-century literary groups, although some are mentioned *passim* by Marguerite C. Suárez-Murias, *La novela romántica en Hispano-américa*.
10. Zea, op. cit., p. 33.

1. A Symbolic Revolt: The Modernist Movement

1. The best general discussion of Modernism is by Ricardo Gullón in *Direcciones del modernismo*. There is also a very complete account in Max Henríquez Ureña's *Breve historia del modernismo*; references here are from the 2nd edition.
2. For a discussion of the term 'Modernism', see Henríquez Ureña, op. cit., ch. 9, pp. 158–72.
3. These works are included in Rubén Darío, *Poesías completas*. For his prose writings, see his *Obras completas*. The best works on his poetry are Pedro Salinas, *La poesía de Rubén Darío* and Arturo Torres-Rioseco, *Vida y poesía de Rubén Darío*.
4. The issue was particularly lively in Mexico at this period. See, for example, the many articles on the topic by Amado Nervo in *Obras completas*, Vol. II, especially 'El casticismo melindroso', pp. 307–11.

5. Quoted by Henríquez Ureña, op. cit., p. 288.
6. ibid., p. 289.
7. Manuel González Prada, *Páginas libres*, p. 43.
8. Darío, 'María Guerrero', *Obras completas*, Vol. IV, p. 887.
9. A. Bórquez Solar, quoted by John M. Fein, *Modernismo in Chilean Literature*, p. 18.
10. Darío, 'Los colores del estandarte', *Obras completas*, Vol. IV, p. 874.
11. Julián del Casal, 'La última ilusión', *Prosas*, Vol. I, pp. 228–9.
12. Manuel Gutiérrez Nájera, 'La Duquesa Job', *Poesía*, pp. 200–202.
13. Darío, 'Prosas profanas', *Poesías completas*, pp. 611–99; Leopoldo Lugones, 'Las montañas del oro', *Obras poéticas completas*, pp. 51–103; Ricardo Jaimes Freyre, 'Castalia bárbara' in *Poesías completas*.
14. Nervo, 'Nuestra literatura', *Obras completas*, Vol. I, p. 610.
15. Quoted by Fein, op. cit., pp. 20–21.
16. Darío, 'La vida literaria', *Obras completas*, Vol. IV, pp. 750–54.
17. Quoted by Henríquez Ureña, op. cit., p. 289.
18. Casal, *Prosas*, Vol. III, p. 86.
19. José Asunción Silva, 'La realidad', *Prosas y versos*, p. 35.
20. Asunción Silva, 'El paraguas de Padre León', *Prosas . . .*, pp. 45–9.
21. Manuel Díaz Rodríguez, 'Cuento áureo', *Cuentos de color*, pp. 87–93.
22. These stories by Darío are all included in the collection *Azul*, first published in Santiago de Chile in 1888; see *Obras completas*, Vol. V, pp. 624–757.
23. José Martí, 'Versos sencillos', *Obras completas*, Vol. XVI, p. 67.
24. Martí, *Obras completas*, Vol. XV, p. 18.
25. Martí, 'Vivir en sí', *Obras completas*, Vol. XVI, pp. 276–7.
26. Martí, 'Los héroes', from 'Versos sencillos', *Obras completas*, Vol. XVI, pp. 123–4.
27. Raúl Silva Castro, ed., *Obras desconocidas de Rubén Darío*, pp. 266–8.
28. Darío, *Poesías completas*, pp. 1019–26.
29. Quoted by Fein, op. cit., p. 29.
30. ibid.
31. Salvador Díaz Mirón, *Poesías completas*, pp. 101–3.
32. Quoted by Fein, op. cit., p. 30.
33. Díaz Mirón, 'Victor Hugo', *Poesías completas*, pp. 39–44.
34. Darío, 'A Victor Hugo', *Poesías completas*, pp. 208–12.

35. Darío, 'A un poeta', *Poesías completas*, pp. 275–9. Even more exaggerated is his early poem, 'Victor Hugo y la tumba', *Poesías completas*, pp. 435–44.
36. Lugones, *Obras poéticas . . .*, p. 58.
37. José Santos Chocano, 'En la mazmorra' (from 'Iras santas', 1893–5), *Obras completas*, pp. 89–93.
38. Martí, *Obras . . .*, Vol. XV, pp. 361–8.
39. Gutiérrez Nájera, 'Non omnis moriar', *Poesía*, pp. 346–7.
40. Casal, 'Autobiografía', *Hojas al viento*, included in José Monner Sans, *Julián del Casal y el modernismo hispanoamericano*, pp. 123–5.
41. Asunción Silva, 'Ars', *Prosas . . .*, p. 129.
42. Darío, 'La vida literaria', *Obras completas*, Vol. IV, p. 755.
43. Darío, Introduction to 'El canto errante', *Poesías completas*, p. 792.
44. Asunción Silva, 'Paisajes', *Prosas . . .*, pp. 40–42.
45. Asunción Silva, 'Nocturno', *Prosas . . .*, pp. 68–70.
46. Darío, 'Yo persigo una forma', from 'Prosas profanas', *Poesías completas*, p. 699.
47. Darío's use of classical mythology is exhaustively dealt with by Dolores Ackel Fiore, *Rubén Darío in Search of Inspiration*.
48. Darío, 'El reino interior', from *Prosas profanas*, *Poesías completas*, pp. 677–80.
49. Julián del Casal's 'Prometeo' and 'Salome', from 'Museo ideal', are included in Monner Sans, op. cit., p. 166 and 165 respectively.
50. The most striking of such poems by Darío are from 'Cantos de vida y esperanza', *Poesías completas* – especially 'Melancolía', p. 764, 'Nocturno', p. 770.
51. Darío, 'El coloquio de los centauros', *Poesías completas*, pp. 641–9.
52. Yeats's poem is dated 1923: see *Collected Works of W. B. Yeats*, London 1959, p. 241. Darío's poem is from 'Cantos de vida y esperanza', *Poesías completas*, pp. 734–5.
53. Darío, 'La dulzura del Angelus', *Poesías completas*, pp. 740–41.
54. Ricardo Jaimes Freyre, 'El canto del mal', *Poesías completas*, p. 79.
55. Quoted by Mário da Silva Brito, *História do Modernismo Brasileiro*, Vol. I, p. 19. There is an account of the Parnassian poetry movement in Manuel Bandeira, *Antología dos Poetas Brasileiros da Fase Parnasiana*. The poems of João Cruz e Sousa are included in his *Obras Poéticas*.

2. The Select Minority: Arielism and Criollismo 1900–1918

1. Hubert Herring, *A History of Latin America from the Beginnings to the Present*, ch. 55, pp. 798–803.

2. On New Worldism, see Francisco Contreras, *Les Ecrivains Con-temporains de l'Amérique Espagnole*, p. 15; also Fein, op. cit., pp. 90–126. On Literary Americanism, see Francisco García Godoy, *Americanismo literario*, which contains essays on writers such as Rodó and Rufino Blanco Fombona.

3. Rufino Blanco Fombona, *Camino de imperfección: Diario de mi vida, 1906–1913*, pp. 41–2.

4. Joseph Arthur de Gobineau, *Essai sur l'inégalité des races humaines*; Edmond Demolins, *A quoi tient la supériorité des Anglo-Saxons?*

5. *Pueblo enfermo*, by Alcides Arguedas, first appeared in 1909; a revised version is included in his *Obras completas*, Vol. I, pp. 395–617.

6. Francisco García Calderón, *Le Pérou contemporain*: see especially ch. VII, 'L'Avenir'.

7. José Veríssimo, *A Educação Nacional*: especially ch. II, 'As Características Brasileiras', pp. 17–43 of 2nd edition.

8. Euclydes da Cunha, *Os Sertões*; for his views on racial mixture, see 12th edition (revised), p. 108.

9. José Pereira da Graça Aranha, *Canãa*, 8th edition (revised), p. 99.

10. Manuel González Prada, 'Nuestros indios', *Horas de lucha*, 2nd edition, pp. 327–81, especially p. 311.

11. García Calderón, op. cit., p. 328.

12. Arguedas, *Pueblo . . .*, especially ch. XI, 'La terapeútica social'.

13. This reference, and the other conclusions on Mexican attitudes to race at this time, are from an article by Martin S. Stabb, 'Indigen-ism and Racism in Mexican Thought, 1877–1911', *Journal of Inter-American Studies*, Vol. I, No. 4, pp. 405–23.

14. ibid., pp. 419–20.

15. Rufino Blanco Fombona, 'La Barbarocracia triunfante', *Obras selectas*, p. 1192; here he suggests that Venezuela should make up its mind to be a predominantly White nation.

16. Cf. Zea, op. cit., p. 219.

17. Darío, 'Palabras liminares', *Poesías completas*, pp. 612–13.

18. Darío, 'Folklore de la América Central', *Obras completas*, Vol. IV, pp. 858–66.

19. Chocano, 'Quién sabe', *Obras completas*, p. 827–8.

20. For a sympathetic account of José Santos Chocano's poetic career, see Manuel Suárez-Miravel, 'Las letras peruanas en el siglo XX', in *Panorama das Literaturas das Américas, de 1900 a actualidade*, Vol. IV, pp. 1561–1609. Note that his poems on the modern Indian date from the 1920s and do not belong to the earlier period.

21. Sousândrade, 'O Inferno de Wall Street' in Augusto and Haroldo de Campos, eds., *Revisão de Sousândrade*, p. 199.

22. Veríssimo, op. cit., pp. 177–8.

23. References to José Enrique Rodó's work are from the *Obras completas*; 'Ariel' is included, pp. 191–244.

24. Ernest Renan, *Caliban: Drame philosophique*.

25. Rodó, 'Ariel', *Obras completas*, p. 231.

26. Quoted by E. Rodríguez Monegal, Introduction to Rodó's *Obras completas*.

27. Rodó, 'El Mirador de Próspero', *Obras completas*, p. 497.

28. Blanco Fombona, 'La evolución de Hispanoamérica', *Obras selectas*, p. 357.

29. Manuel Ugarte, *El porvenir de la América Latina*, pp. 84–5.

30. Chocano, 'Ofrenda a España' and 'Ciudad Colonial', included in 'Alma América', *Obras completas*.

31. Ugarte, op. cit., pp. 84–5.

32. Francisco García Calderón, 'Las corrientes filosóficas en la América Latina', *Ideas e impresiones*, pp. 41–57.

33. For the role of the *Ateneo* on the formation of this generation, see José Vasconcelos, 'Ulises criollo', *Obras completas*, Vol. I, pp. 507–10; and Alfonso Reyes, 'Pasado inmediato', *Obras completas*, Vol. XII, pp. 182–216.

34. Rodó, *Obras completas*, p. 239.

35. Rómulo Gallegos, 'Necesidad de valores culturales', *Una posición en la vida*, pp. 82–109. This is a collection of essays originally published at various periods; 'Necesidad . . .' is dated 1912.

36. Carlos Reyles, 'Vida Nueva', *Academias y otros ensayos*, pp. 195–206.

37. García Calderón, *Le Pérou . . .*, pp. 319–20.

38. Rodó, 'Ariel', *Obras completas*, p. 224.

39. C. Vaz Ferreira, 'Moral para intelectuales', *Obras*, Vol. III, p. 41

40. Zea, op. cit., pp. 192–3.

41. See Enrique Anderson Imbert, *Tres novelas de Payró*.

42. The story 'El padre Casafús' is included in Tomás Carrasquilla, *Obras completas*, pp. 1251–89.

43. Machado de Assis, *Memórias Póstumas de Brás Cubas*, p. 38.

44. The short stories by Machado de Assis mentioned here have been published in English in *The Psychiatrist and Other Stories*.

45. *La Revista de América*, Paris, No. I.

46. Leopoldo Lugones, *El payador*, p. 19.

47. García Calderón, 'La originalidad intelectual de América', *Ideas e impresiones*, pp. 72–3.

48. Ugarte, op. cit., pp. 297–306, especially p. 300.

49. Mariano Latorre, *Autobiografía de una vocación*, p. 50.

50. There is a discussion of the Chilean Tolstoyans in Fernando Alegría, *Las fronteras del realismo: literatura chilena del siglo xx*, pp. 47–67.

51. Quoted by Enrique Molina, *La filosofía en Chile en la primera mitad del siglo xx*, pp. 31–2.

52. See, for example, Carlos Pezoa Véliz, *Alma chilena*.

53. Baldomero Lillo, *Sub terra*, pp. 19–36.

54. E.g., Mariano Latorre, 'Risquera vana' in the collection *Cuna de cóndores*.

55. Rufino Blanco Fombona, *Dramas mínimos*, p. 111.

56. 'Pago de deuda' from the collection of that name. The best collections of Javier de Viana's stories are *Campo* (1896) and *Gurí y otras novelas* (1916). For a discussion of his work, see Alberto Zum Felde, *Proceso intelectual del Uruguay*, pp. 302–15.

57. Alberto Gerchunoff, *Los gauchos judíos*; the quotation is taken from the English translation, *The Jewish Gauchos of the Pampa*, p. 1.

58. Manuel Ugarte, *La dramática intimidad de una generación*, pp. 14–15.

59. Rodó, *Obras completas*, p. 1318.

60. Manuel Gálvez, *El mal metafísico*, p. 226. This novel is a document of Argentine life of the period, many of the characters being thinly disguised members of the Argentine literary scene; one of them, for instance, was based on Gerchunoff.

61. In, for example, Lillo's 'La barrena', *Sub sole*, pp. 91–100.

62. In Venegas's 'Cartas al Excelentísimo Señor Don Pedro Montt sobre la crisis moral de Chile en sus relaciones con el problema económico de la conversión metálica', quoted by Enrique Molina, op. cit., pp. 33–5.

63. Quoted by Mário da Silva Brito, *História do Modernismo Brasileiro*, p. 84.

3. *Back to the Roots: 1. Cultural Nationalism*

1. Alberto de Oliveira, quoted in Silva Brito, *História do Modernismo Brasileiro*, p. 33.

2. José Ingenieros, 'El suicidio de los bárbaros', *Los tiempos nuevos*, pp. 11–14.

3. Pedro Henríquez Ureña, 'La Utopía de América', *Plenitud de América: ensayos escogidos*, p. 11.

4. ibid., p. 13.

5. See Vasconcelos' autobiography, 'La Tormenta', *Obras completas*, Vol. I, pp. 790 and 900–905.

6. ibid., p. 892.

7. Vasconcelos, 'El monismo estético', *Obras completas*, Vol. IV, pp. 91–2. The whole essay is written round this theme.

8. Vasconcelos, 'La raza cósmica', *Obras completas*, Vol. II, p. 912.

9. Vasconcelos, 'Conferencia leída en el "Continental Memorial Hall" de Washington', *Obras completas*, Vol. II, p. 874.

10. Vasconcelos, 'Discurso de Cuauhtémoc', *Obras completas*, Vol. II, pp. 848–53.

11. Fernando Peñalosa, *The Mexican Book Industry*.

12. Vasconcelos, 'De Robinson a Odiseo', *Obras completas*, Vol. II, pp. 1674–8; here he gives his own account of the beginnings of the Mexican mural movement.

13. Jean Charlot, *The Mexican Mural Renaissance, 1920–25*, p. 99.

14. ibid., p. 103.

15. ibid., p. 202.

16. ibid., p. 230.

17. ibid., pp. 259–60.

18. Pedro Henríquez Ureña, op. cit., p. 14.

19. Quoted by Rivera's biographer, Bertram D. Wolfe, *Diego Rivera: His Life and Times*, p. 183.

20. Quoted in Charlot, op. cit., pp. 226–7.

21. José Luis Cuevas, 'The Cactus Curtain: An Open Letter on Conformity in Mexican Art', *Evergreen Review*, Winter 1959, pp. 111–20.

22. Enrique Sánchez Pedrote, 'Consideraciones sobre la música en Hispanoamérica', *Estudios Americanos*, No. 32, pp. 417–26.

23. Vasconcelos, 'Simón Bolívar', *Obras completas*, Vol. II, pp. 1721–66.

24. Ramón López Velarde, 'El retorno maléfico', *Poesías completas y el minutero*, pp. 174–6.

25. Octavio Paz, in *El laberinto de la soledad*, has some interesting remarks on the position of the intelligentsia after the revolution; see especially pp. 122–3. Francisco Monterde was one of the first critics to call for a novel which would reflect the experience of the revolution: see his introduction to the *Obras completas* of Mariano Azuela, in which he recalls the literary history of the period.

26. The novels of the revolution mentioned here are all included in the anthology, Antonio Castro Leal, ed., *La novela de la Revolución Mexicana*, 2 vols.

27. On José Rubén Romero, see *Obras completas*, with a preface by Antonio Castro Leal.

28. Alberto Zum Felde, *Indice crítico de la literatura hispanoamericana*; Vol. I, *Los ensayistas*, pp. 487–94.

29. See Eugenio Chang Rodríguez, *La literatura política de González Prada, Mariátegui y Haya de la Torre*.

30. José Carlos Mariátegui, 'El proceso de la literatura', *Siete ensayos de interpretación de la realidad peruana*, 9th edition, pp. 198–305.

31. César Vallejo, 'El espíritu universitario', *Variedades*, Lima, 8 October 1927.

32. Vallejo, 'Los escollos de siempre', *Variedades*, Lima, 22 October 1927.

33. Manuel Suárez Miravel states in 'Las letras peruanas ...' – included in *Panorama das Literaturas ...*, Vol. IV – that *La venganza del condor* dates from 1919, but the earliest edition the author of this work has traced was published by Mundo Latino, Paris, 1924.

34. For this quotation and for López Albújar's views on race, the author is indebted to the account by Suárez Miravel, op. cit., pp. 1723–40. See also Earl M. Aldrich, Jr, *The Modern Short Story in Peru*, pp. 39–51.

35. See the biography of José Eustasio Rivera by Eduardo Neale Silva, *Horizonte humano: vida de José Eustasio Rivera*.

36. Quoted by Lowell Dunham, *Rómulo Gallegos: vida y obra*, p. 39.

37. Dunham, op. cit., p. 61. All these novels by Gallegos are included in his *Obras completas*.

38. Earl T. Glauert, 'Ricardo Rojas and the Emergence of Argentine Cultural Nationalism', *Hispanic American Historical Review*, Vol. XLII, No. 1, p. 19 ff.

39. On Ricardo Güiraldes, see Giovanni Previtali, *Ricardo Güiraldes and Don Segundo Sombra*.

40. Leopoldo Lugones, 'Himno a la luna', in 'Lunario sentimental', *Obras poéticas ...*, p. 206.

41. Adolfo Prieto discusses the role of *Martín Fierro in* 'El Martin-fierrismo', *Revista de Literatura Argentina e Iberoamericana* Vol. I, No. 1, pp. 9–31.

42. Jorge Luis Borges, 'Arrabal', in 'Fervor de Buenos Aires', *Poemas* (1923–58), pp. 34–5.

43. Jorge Luis Borges, 'El escritor argentino y la tradición', *Discusión*, 2nd edition, pp. 151–62.

44. ibid., p. 161.

45. Wilson Martins, '50 anos de literatura brasileira', in *Panorama das Literaturas* . . ., Vol. I, pp. 103–241, especially p. 112.
46. See, for instance, Ronald de Carvalho and Elysio de Carvalho, *Affirmacões: Um ágape de Intellectuaes*.
47. Quoted by Mário da Silva Brito, *História do Modernismo Brasileiro*, p. 125.
48. ibid., p. 179.
49. Ronald de Carvalho, *Pequena História da Literatura Brasileira*, p. 372.
50. Manuel Bandeira, 'Poética', in 'Libertinagem', *Poesia e prosa*, Vol. I, p. 188–9.
51. Quoted by Haroldo de Campos in his preface to Oswald de Andrade, *Memórias Sentimentais de João Miramar*, pp. 13–14.
52. Quoted by Silva Brito, op. cit., p. 177.
53. Gilberto Freyre, *Manifesto Regionalista de 1926*, p. 16.
54. José Aderaldo Castello, *José Lins do Rego: Modernismo e Regionalismo*, p. 103.
55. José Lins do Rego is here commenting on Gilberto Freyre's ideas: see José Aderaldo Castello, op. cit., p. 105.
56. On the Brazilian regional novel, see Fred P. Ellison, *Brazil's New Novel*.

4. Back to the Roots: 2. The Indian, the Negro, the Land

1. César Vallejo, 'La conquista de París por los negros', *Mundial*, Lima, 11 December 1925.
2. According to G. R. Coulthard, *Race and Colour in Caribbean Literature*, pp. 30–31.
3. D. H. Lawrence, *The Plumed Serpent*, p. 431.
4. Count Hermann Keyserling, *South American Meditations*, p. 157.
5. Mariátegui, op. cit., p. 292.
6. The author consulted Antonio Mediz Bolio's Spanish translation, *Libro de Chilam Balam de Chumayel*.
7. Giuseppe Bellini, *La narrativa di Miguel Angel Asturias* is a good study of Asturias's work.
8. Aída Cometta Manzoni, *El indio en la novela de América*, deals with most novels of Indian life.
9. Ciro Alegría, *La serpiente de oro*, 1963 edition, pp. 186–7.
10. José María Arguedas, prologue to *Canto Kechwa*.
11. ibid.
12. See José Antonio Portuondo, *Bosquejo histórico de las letras cubanas*, p. 47; and José Luis Varela, *Ensayos de poesía indígena en Cuba*, pp. 91–2.

13. Nicolás Guillén, 'Pequeña oda a un negro boxeador cubano', *Sóngoro cosongo*, 2nd edition, pp. 15–17.
14. Quoted by Coulthard, op. cit., pp. 30–31.
15. Luis Palés Matos, 'Pueblo negro', included in the anthology, José Sanz y Díaz, ed., *Lira negra*, pp. 275–7.
16. Palés Matos, 'Ñam-ñam', in *Lira negra*, pp. 282–3.
17. Quoted in Varela, op. cit., p. 96.
18. Quoted in Coulthard, op. cit., p. 29.
19. ibid.
20. Guillén, 'Balada del Güije', in 'West Indies Ltd', *Sóngoro cosongo*, pp. 62–4.
21. Guillén, 'Sensemayá', in 'West Indies Ltd', *Sóngoro cosongo*, pp. 68–70.
22. Guillén, 'Tú no sabe inglés', in 'Motivos de son', *Sóngoro cosongo*, p. 47.
23. Adalberto Ortiz, *El animal herido*, p. 7.
24. ibid., p. 57.
25. Raymond S. Sayers, *O Negro na Literatura Brasileira*.
26. Jorge de Lima, 'Poemas negros', *Obras completas*, Vol. I, pp. 373–4.
27. Glauert, op. cit.

5. Art and the Political Struggle

1. Cf. David Caute, *Communism and the French Intellectuals, 1914–60*, p. 70.
2. Chang Rodríguez, op. cit., p. 137.
3. Raúl Silva Castro, *Pablo Neruda*, pp. 29–35.
4. Silva Brito, op. cit., pp. 131–2.
5. From the biographical note by Raúl Roa in the Introduction to Rubén Martínez Villena, *La pupila insomne*, p. 32.
6. José Ingenieros, op. cit., pp. 11–14.
7. Henri Barbusse, *Manifeste aux intellectuels*, pp. 9–10.
8. José Carlos Mariátegui, 'La revolución y la inteligencia', *La escena contemporánea*, pp. 193–245, especially p. 196.
9. Percy Alvin Martin in an appendix to João Pandiá Calogeras, *A History of Brazil*, p. 346.
10. Graciliano Ramos, *Memórias do Cárcere*, p. 69.
11. Victor Alba, *Historia del movimiento obrero en América latina*, pp. 20 and 463.
12. Martínez Villena, op. cit., p. 40.
13. ibid., p. 41.

14. César Vallejo, 'Las lecciones del marxismo', *Variedades*, Lima, 19 January 1929.

15. Vallejo, 'El apostolado como oficio', *Mundial*, Lima, 9 September 1927.

16. Vallejo, 'Obreros manuales y obreros intelectuales', *Variedades*, Lima 2 June 1928.

17. Vallejo, 'Autopsia del superrealismo', *Variedades*, Lima, 25 March 1930.

18. Vallejo, *Tungsteno*, p. 148.

19. Vicente Huidobro, 'Ecuatorial', *Poesía y prosa*, pp. 241–51.

20. Manuel Maples Arce, 'Urbe', quoted by Raúl Leiva in *Imagen de la poesía mexicana contemporánea*, p. 69.

21. Quoted in Wolfe, op. cit., p. 169.

22. ibid., p. 167.

23. José Clemente Orozco, 'New World, New Races and New Art', *Textos de Orozco*, pp. 42–3.

24. According to Charlot, op. cit.

25. For discussion of Socialist realism, see Caute, op. cit., pp. 318–24, especially p. 323. For recent Cuban criticism, see Juan Marinello, *Conversación con nuestros pintores abstractos*.

26. Orozco, *Textos* . . ., p. 81. The quotations are from the catalogue of an exhibition held in 1947.

27. Manuel Maples Arce, *Modern Mexican Art*; see also Justino Fernández, *Arte moderno y contemporáneo de México*.

28. Reproduced by Margarita Nelkin, *El expresionismo en la plástica mexicana de hoy*, p. 15.

29. Maples Arce, op. cit., p. 20.

30. Nelkin, op. cit., pp. 33–6.

31. Orozco, *Textos* . . ., pp. 42–3.

32. Quoted in José Antonio Portuondo, *Bosquejo histórico de las letras cubanas*, pp. 62–3.

33. Martínez Villena, op. cit., pp. 95–6.

34. Vallejo, *Trilce*, poem LVIII.

35. Vallejo, 'Masa', *España, aparta de mí este cáliz*, p. 81.

36. Vallejo, 'Los nueve monstruos', *Poemas humanos*, pp. 57–9.

37. Vallejo, 'Parado en una piedra', *Poemas humanos*, pp. 117–18.

38. Vallejo, 'Voy a hablar de la esperanza', *Poemas humanos*, pp. 153–4.

39. Vallejo, 'La rueda del hambriento', *Poemas humanos*, pp. 40–41.

40. The best study to date of Vallejo's poetry is Luis Monguió, *César Vallejo, 1892–1938: Vida y obra – bibliografía, antología*.

41. Guillén, 'La canción del Bongó', *Sóngoro cosongo*, pp. 12–13.

42. Guillén, 'Soldado muerto', from 'Cantos para soldados y sones para turistas', *El son entero*, p. 12.
43. Guillén, 'Llegada', *Sóngoro cosongo*, pp. 9–11.
44. Guillén, 'Visita a un solar', from 'Cantos para soldados . . .', *El son entero*, pp. 40–42.
45. Silva Castro, *Pablo Neruda*, p. 83.
46. ibid., p. 96.
47. Pablo Neruda, 'Canto General', *Obras completas*, p. 668.
48. ibid., p. 674.
49. Neruda, 'Oda a la madera', 'Odas elementales', *Obras completas*, pp. 1035–8.
50. Nicanor Parra, *Poemas y antipoemas*, pp. 55–6.
51. ibid., pp. 137–41.
52. Jorge Amado, *Cacau*, included in the edition, *O País do Carnaval, Cacau, Suor: Obras de Jorge Amado*, Vols. I–III, p. 139.
53. Roberto Arlt, Preface to *Los lanzallamas*. Arlt also boasts of the speed with which the novel was written and says that the last pages were still being written while the first were with the printer.
54. ibid., p. 6.
55. Joaquín Edwards Bello, *El roto*, p. 57.
56. A list of such novels can be found in Luis Alberto Sánchez, *Proceso y contenido de la novela hispanoamericana*, chs. 18–20.
57. Jorge Icaza, *Huasipungo*, p. 15.
58. ibid., p. 27.
59. ibid., p. 175.
60. Graciliano Ramos, *Vidas Sêcas*, pp. 170–71.
61. Rafael Arévalo Martínez, 'Por cuatro cientos dólares', *El hombre que parecía un caballo*, pp. 53–81.

6. Cosmopolitan or Universal?

1. Alfonso Reyes, 'En el Día Americano', *Obras completas*, Vol. XI, p. 68.
2. ibid., p. 69.
3. Reyes, 'Ciencia social y deber social', *Obras completas*, Vol. XI, p. 123.
4. Vallejo, 'Contra el secreto profesional: a propósito de Pablo Abril de Vivero', *Variedades*, Lima, 7 May 1927.
5. Jorge Mañach, quoted by Carlos Ripoll, 'La Revista de Avance, 1927–30', *Revista Iberoamericana*, Vol. XXX, No. 58, 1964.
6. Hans Richter, *Dada Art and Anti-Art*, p. 34.
7. ibid., p. 57.
8. ibid., p. 64.

9. ibid., p. 65.
10. Patrick Waldberg, *Surrealism*, p. 84.
11. ibid., p. 76.
12. André Breton, 'Second Manifeste du Surréalisme', *Manifestes du Surréalisme*, p. 194.
13. Breton, 'Discours au congrès des écrivains', *Manifestes . . .*, p. 285.
14. Jorge Luis Borges, *Otras inquisiciones*, p. 259.
15. Jorge Luis Borges, *Historia universal de la infamia*, p. 10.
16. Jorge Luis Borges, *Ficciones*, pp. 13–14.
17. Borges, 'Nueva refutación del tiempo', *Otras inquisiciones*, p. 256.
18. Borges 'La muralla y los libros', *Otras inquisiciones*, p. 12.
19. Borges, 'Anotaciones al 23 de agosto de 1944', *Otras inquisiciones*, p. 185.
20. Ana María Barrenechea, *Borges, the Labyrinth Maker*, p. 17.
21. J. L. Borges, *The Spanish Language in South America: A Literary Problem*, p. 13.
22. ibid., p. 6.
23. Adolfo Bioy Casares, *El sueño de los héroes*, p. 46.
24. Julio Cortázar, *Rayuela*, p. 438.
25. ibid., p. 442.
26. ibid., p. 442.
27. ibid., pp. 31–2.
28. From 'Del sentimiento de no estar del todo', in *La vuelta al día en ochenta mundos*, p. 26.
29. J. Mario, 'Poeta con revolver', *El corno emplumado*, 7 July 1963, pp. 96–8.
30. Editorial in *El corno emplumado*, 7 July 1963, p. 92.
31. ibid., 9 January 1964, p. 5.
32. ibid., 1 January 1962, p. 5.
33. Augusto de Campos, Décio Pignatari, Haroldo de Campos, *Teoria da Poesia Concreta: Textos Críticos e Manifestos, 1950–60*, p. 23.
34. ibid., p. 55.
35. ibid., p. 133.
36. ibid., p. 93.
37. ibid., p. 90.
38. ibid., p. 5.
39. ibid., pp. 151–2.
40. For an evaluation of Concrete poetry, see J. Reichardt, 'The Whereabouts of Concrete Poetry', *Studio International*, London, February 1966, pp. 56–9.
41. From 'Los signos en rotacion', *Sur* B. A., 1965.
42. Frank Dauster, *Ensayos sobre poesía mexicana*, pp. 8–9.

43. ibid., p. 32.
44. José Gorostiza, *Muerte sin fin*, p. 49.
45. Salvador Novo, 'Diluvio', *Poesía*, pp. 57–8.
46. Novo, 'Poemas proletarios', *Poesía*, pp. 109–15.
47. Octavio Paz, 'La poesía', *Libertad bajo palabra*, pp. 246–8.
48. Octavio Paz, *El arco y la lira*, p. 149.
49. ibid., p. 40.
50. ibid., pp. 40–1.
51. Octavio Paz, *Piedra de sol*; quotation from Muriel Rukeyser's translation, pp. 44 and 45.
52. Paz, *El arco . . .*, p. 259.
53. Marta Traba, *Seis pintores colombianos*, Introduction.
54. ibid.
55. Lawrence Alloway, 'The International Style', *Encounter*, September 1965, pp. 71–4, especially p. 74.
56. There are illustrations of these projects in Paul F. Damaz, *Art in Latin American Architecture*.
57. E.g. the towers at the entrance to the satellite city. See Damaz, op. cit.

7. The Writer as Conscience of his Country

1. Samuel Ramos, *Historia de la filosofía en México*, p. 149.
2. Leopoldo Zea, *Esquema para una historia de las ideas en Iberoamérica*, p. 112.
3. Paz, *El laberinto . . .*, p. 61.
4. Sebastián Salazar Bondy, *Lima la horrible*, p. 77.
5. Mario Benedetti, *Literatura uruguaya, siglo xx*, pp. 9–10.
6. Rudolfo Usigli, 'Epílogo sobre la hipocresía del Mexicano', *El gesticulador*, p. 172.
7. Fernando de Azevedo, *A Cultura Brasileira*; from English translation, *Brazilian Culture*, pp. 489–92.
8. Sérgio Buarque de Holanda, *Raízes do Brasil*, p. 133.
9. Usigli, 'Epílogo . . .', *El gesticulador*, p. 163.
10. Paz, *El laberinto . . .*, p. 34.
11. Ezequiel Martínez Estrada, *Radiografía de la pampa*, Vol. II, p. 149.
12. Eduardo Mallea, 'Historia de una pasión argentina', *Obras completas*, Vol. I, p. 348.
13. Salazar Bondy, op. cit., p. 75.
14. Benedetti, op. cit., p. 35.
15. Luis Cardoza y Aragón, *Guatemala, las líneas de tu mano*, p. 289.

16. Fernando de Azevedo, op. cit., see especially Part III.
17. Martínez Estrada, op. cit., Vol. II, p. 153.
18. Salazar Bondy, op. cit., p. 15.
19. Cardoza y Aragón, op. cit., especially sections II and III.
20. Otto Morales Benítez, *Muchedumbres y banderas*.
21. Leopoldo Zea, *Conciencia y posibilidad del mexicano*, pp. 10–11.
22. ibid., pp. 54–5.
23. Benedetti, op. cit., p. 36.
24. ibid., p. 37.
25. Paz, *El laberinto . . .*, p. 151.
26. Mallea, 'Historia . . .', *Obras completas*, Vol. I, p. 432.
27. Leopoldo Zea, 'Dialéctica de la conciencia en México', *La filosofía como compromiso*, p. 197.
28. Hector Murena, *El pecado original de América*, p. 26.
29. Luis Alberto Sánchez, op. cit., p. 62; Murena, op. cit., especially pp. 13–42.
30. Alfonso Reyes, 'En el Día Americano', *Obras completas*, Vol. XI, p. 69.
31. Paz, *El laberinto . . .*, p. 148.
32. Mallea, 'Historia . . .', *Obras completas*, Vol. I, p. 436.
33. Hernando Téllez, *Literatura y sociedad*, p. 74.
34. Benedetti, op. cit., p. 34.
35. Mallea, 'Historia . . .', *Obras completas*, Vol. I, pp. 432–5.
36. Eduardo Mallea, 'La bahía del silencio', *Obras completas*, Vol. I, p. 854.
37. ibid., p. 986.
38. Carlos Fuentes, *Las buenas conciencias*, p. 190.
39. Augusto Roa Bastos, *Hijo de hombre*, p. 229.
40. Interviews with many contemporary writers such as Mario Vargas Llosa, Miguel Angel Asturias and Gabriel García Márquez are included in Luis Harss, *Los nuestros*. Translations of some contemporary writers are included in J. M. Cohen, ed., *Latin American Writing Today*.
41. Carlos Solórzano, *Teatro latinoamericano del siglo xx*, pp. 73–5.
42. A special number of the Madrid magazine, *Primer Acto*, No. 75, 1966, was devoted to Brazilian theatre and included Spanish translations of Cabral de Melo Neto's *Vida e Morte Severina* and the successful *O Pagador de Promesas* by Alfredo Días Gomes.

8. *The Writer and the National Situation*

1. Miguel Angel Asturias puts these words into the mouth of the imprisoned student in *El Señor Presidente*.

2. Mario Monteforte Toledo, *Guatemala, Monografía sociológica*, pp. 390–91.
3. Rubén Bareiro Saguier, 'Panorama de la literatura paraguaya, 1900–1959', in *Panorama das Literaturas . . .*, Vol. III, pp. 1265–95.
4. For surveys of Honduran and Nicaraguan writers, see: Juan Felipe Toruño, 'Sucinta reseña de las letras nicaraguenses en 50 años, 1900–1950', *Panorama das Literaturas . . .*, Vol. III, pp. 1093–1202; Humberto Rivera Morillo, 'La literatura hondureña en el siglo XX', and Jorge Fidel Durón, 'La prosa en Honduras', in *Panorama das Literaturas . . .*, Vol. II, pp. 673–778.
5. Rivera Morillo, op. cit., p. 694.
6. ibid.
7. G. R. Coulthard, op. cit., pp. 37–8.
8. 'La excavación' is included in Augusto Roa Bastos's collection, *El trueno entre las hojas*. For a survey of Paraguayan literature, see Rubén Bareiro Saguier, op. cit. For surveys of Guatemalan literature, see: Otto-Raúl González, 'Panorama de la literatura guatemalteca', *Panorama das Literaturas . . .*, Vol. III, pp. 1017–71; and Seymour Menton, *Historia crítica de la novela guatemalteca*.
9. Alfonso Ulloa Zamora, 'Panorama literario costarricense, 1900–1958', *Panorama das Literaturas . . .*, Vol. III, pp. 923–1016.
10. Luis Gallegos Valdés, 'Panorama de la literatura salvadoreña', *Panorama das Literaturas . . .*, Vol. II, pp. 495–588.
11. Cf. Zamora, op. cit.
12. Cf. Damaz, op. cit., pp. 57–8.
13. Cf. Zum Felde, *Proceso intelectual . . .*, and Benedetti, op. cit.
14. Mario Benedetti, 'El presupuesto', *Montevideanos*.
15. Carlos Martínez Moreno, 'Paloma', *Los aborígenes*.
16. Rodrigo Miró, 'La literatura panameña de la República', *Panorama das Literaturas . . .*, Vol. III, pp. 1203–64.
17. Demetrio Korsi, quoted by Miró, op. cit., p. 1237.
18. Josefina Rivera de Alvarez, 'Panorama literario de Puerto Rico durante el siglo xx' *Panorama das Literaturas . . .*, Vol. II, p. 745.
19. Coulthard, op. cit., pp. 30–31.
20. René Marqués, 'En la popa hay un cuerpo reclinado', *En una ciudad llamada San Juan*.
21. Included in Gertrude M. Walsh's collection *Cuentos criollos*.
22. On Venezuelan writing, see Dillwyn F. Ratcliff, *Venezuelan Prose Fiction*. On Colombian writing, see Javier Arango Ferrer, 'Medio siglo de literatura colombiana', *Panorama das Literaturas . . .*, Vol.

I, pp. 329–428; and *Diccionario de la literatura latinoamericana: Colombia.*

23. The racial question is discussed by Arguedas in *Pueblo enfermo,* and by Pío Jaramillo Alvarado in *El indio ecuatoriano.*

24. Mariátegui, 'El problema de la tierra', *Siete ensayos . . .,* pp. 41–89.

25. On the Ecuadorian novel, see Angel F. Rojas, *La novela ecuatoriana.*

26. On Bolivian literature, see *Diccionario de la literatura latinoamericana: Bolivia*; and Aída Cometta Manzoni, op. cit., pp. 32–49.

27. On Peruvian literature, see Manuel Suárez-Miravel, 'Las letras peruanas en el siglo XX', *Panorama das Literaturas . . .,* Vol. IV, pp. 1529–1895.

28. R. M. Albérès, *Argentine: Un Monde, Une Ville.*

29. On Argentinian rootlessness, see Julio Mafud, *El desarraigo argentino.*

30. On Argentinian literature, see *Diccionario de la literatura latinoamericana: Argentina,* 2 vols. On the non-elite tradition, see Alvaro Yunque, *La literatura social en la Argentina.* On the non-realistic tendency, see Ana María Barrenechea and Emma Susana Speratti Piñero, *La literatura fantástica argentina.* On poetry, see C. Fernández Moreno, *La realidad y los papeles,* Aguilar, Madrid, 1967.

31. Cf. report on the 1966 PEN international conference, *The Times,* 18 June 1966.

32. Pablo Neruda, 'La lámpara en la tierra', 'Canto general', *Obras completas,* p. 302.

33. On the Chilean novel, see Raúl Silva Castro, 'Historia crítica de la novela chilena, 1943–1956', *Panorama literario de Chile.*

34. For an introduction to Brazil, see Roger Bastide, *Brésil: Terre des contrastes.* A useful survey of the political and social forces is given by Emanuel de Kadt, 'The Brazilian Impasse', *Encounter,* London, September 1965, pp. 55–8. On contemporary writing, see Emir Rodríguez Monegal, 'La novela brasileña', *Mundo Nuevo,* December 1966.

35. Cf. Mário da Silva Brito, op. cit.

36. João Cabral de Melo Neto, from a translation of *Vida e Morte Severina* by Elizabeth Bishop, part of which was published in *Encounter,* London, September 1965, pp. 49–50.

37. Carlos Drummond de Andrade, 'Hino Nacional', *Poemas,* pp. 49–50.

38. Howard Cline, *Mexico: Revolution to Evolution, 1940–1960*, especially ch. 9, 'The Elusive Indian'.

39. Paz, *El laberinto* . . ., p. 118.

40. Damaz, op. cit., p. 52.

41. ibid., pp. 222–5.

42. Cf. Dauster, op. cit.

43. Reyes, *Obras completas*, Vol. XI, p. 142.

44. See also Castellanos's *Oficio de tinieblas* on the same theme.

45. Luis Leal gives a brief survey of recent Mexican novelists in 'La literatura Mexicana en el siglo XX', *Panorama das Literaturas* . . ., Vol. IV, pp. 1998–2050; see also José Luis Martínez, *Literatura Mexicana siglo xx*, 2 vols, Mexico, 1950. See also the recently published J. Sommers, *After the Storm*, 1968, and J. Brushwood, *Mexico in its Novel*, 1966.

46. Paz, *El arco* . . ., pp. 260–64.

47. Some poems by younger poets are included in Pellegrini, *Antología de la poesía viva latinoamericana*.

48. Salvador Bueno, 'La literatura cubana en el siglo XX', *Panorama das Literaturas* . . ., Vol. II, includes a brief discussion of these social novels, pp. 448–53.

49. For details of the Afro-Cuban movement, see Varela, op. cit.; Coulthard, op. cit.; Portuondo, op. cit.

50. The author is indebted to J. M. Cohen for much information on the post-revolutionary literary scene in Cuba and also for the opportunity of seeing his extensive collection of recent Cuban writing. There are also references to post-Castro writers in Portuondo, op. cit. For Cuban poetry to 1953, see Roberto Fernández Retamar, *La poesía contemporánea en Cuba (1927–53)*. For post-Castro poetry, see the literary review, *Revista de la Casa de las Américas*, which includes contemporary writing. The Penguin collection, *Writers in the New Cuba*, ed. J. M. Cohen, 1967, gives a selection of post-revolutionary writing, and there is an anthology of Cuban poetry in original and translation, *Concuba*, ed. Nathaniel Tarn, London 1969.

BIBLIOGRAPHY

Note: Full details of publisher and place of publication are given wherever they are known. Where the edition consulted is of later publication, the date of first publication is given in brackets immediately after the title.

WORKS AND GENERAL REFERENCE

Bailey, Helen Miller, and Nasatir, Abraham P., *Latin America: The Development of its Civilization*, Prentice-Hall, Englewood Cliffs N.J., 1960.

Encounter, September 1965, special issue, 'Rediscovering Latin America'.

Herring, Hubert C., *A History of Latin America*, 2nd revised edition, Knopf, New York 1963.

Pendle, G., *A History of Latin America*, Penguin, Harmondsworth 1963.

Penguin Companion to World Literature, Vol. 3 (American and Latin-American section, due to be published in 1970).

Stabb, Martin S., *In Quest of Identity. Patterns in the Spanish American Essay of Ideas (1890–1960)*, North Carolina University Press, London 1968.

Worcester, Donald E., and Schaeffer, Wendell G., *The Growth and Culture of Latin America*, Oxford University Press, New York and London 1956.

Literary History

Alegría, Fernando, *Breve historia de la novela hispanoamericana*, 3rd edition, revised, Studium Andrea, Mexico 1966.

Anderson Imbert, Enrique, *Historia de la literatura hispanomericana*, 2 vols., 3rd edition, Fondo de cultura económica, Mexico 1961; *Spanish American Literature: A History*, trans. John V. Falconieri, Wayne State University, Detroit 1963.

Brushwood, J. S., *Mexico in its Novel*, Texas University Press, Austin 1966.

Diccionario de la literatura latinoamericana, Union Panamericana, Washington D.C. This began publication in 1957 and has completed the following volumes: *Argentina*, 2 vols., 1960–66; *Bolivia*, 1957; *Chile*, 1958; *Colombia*, 1959; *Ecuador*, 1962; *Central America* – Vol. 1, *Costa Rica, El Salvador and Guatemala*, 1963; Vol. 2, *Honduras, Nicaragua and Panama*, 1963. No more volumes are to be published.

Englekirk, John E., ed., *Outline History of Spanish American Literature*, 3rd edition, Appleton-Century-Crofts, New York 1965.

Franco, J., *An Introduction to Spanish American Literature*, Cambridge University Press, 1969.

Harss, L., *Los nuestros*, Sudamericana, Buenos Aires, 1966; published in English as *Into the Mainstream*, trans. L. Harss and Barbara Dohmann, Harper Row, New York 1967.

Henríquez Ureña, Pedro, *Las corrientes literarias en la América hispánica*, 2nd edition, Fondo de cultura económica, Mexico 1954; *Literary Currents in Hispanic America*, Harvard University Press, Cambridge Mass., 1945.

Ortega, Julio, *La contemplación y la fiesta*, Ed. Universitaria, Lima 1968.

Putnam, Samuel, *Marvellous Journey. A Survey of Four Centuries of Brazilian Writing*, Alfred A. Knopf, New York 1948.

Roggiano, A. *En este aire de America*, Mexico, 1966.

Sommers, Joseph, *After the Storm, Landmarks of the Modern Mexican Novel*, University of New Mexico Press, 1968.

Torres-Rioseco, Arturo, *The Epic of Latin American Literature* (paperback), University of California Press, Berkeley and Los Angeles 1959.

Anthologies

Alegría, Fernando, *Novelistas contemporáneos hispanoamericanos*, Heath, Boston 1964.

Arciniegas, Germán, *The Green Continent*, Editions Poetry, London 1947.

Bandeira, M., *Apresentação da poesia brasileira*, Edições de Ouro, n.d.

Candido, Antonio, and Castello, José Aderaldo, *Presença da literatura brasileira*, Difusão Européia do Livro, São Paulo, 1964.

Cohen, J. M., ed., *Latin American Writing Today*, Penguin, Harmondsworth 1967.

Cohen, J. M., ed., *Writers in the New Cuba*, Penguin, Harmondsworth 1967.

Florit, Eugenio, and Jiménez, José Olivio, *La poesía hispanoamericana desde el modernismo*, Appleton-Century-Crofts, New York 1968.

Bibliography

Franco, J., *Short Stories in Spanish*, Penguin Parallel Texts, Penguin, Harmondsworth 1966.

Onís, Federico de, *Antología de la poesía española e hispanoamericana (1883–1932)*, 2nd edition, Las Américas, New York 1961.

Paz, Octavio, et al., ed., *Poesía en movimiento, Siglo XXI*, Mexico 1966.

Pellegrini, Aldo, *Antología de la poesía viva latinoamericana*, Seix Barral, Barcelona 1966.

Tarn, Nathaniel, ed., *Concuba*, Jonathan Cape, London 1969.

WORKS CITED OR CONSULTED

Abreu Gómez, Ermilio (Mexico, b. 1894), *Quetzalcóatl, sueño y vigilia*, Antigua Librería Robredo de José Porrúa e hijos, Mexico 1947.

Ackel Fiore, Dolores, *Rubén Darío in Search of Inspiration*, Las Américas, New York 1963.

Aguilera Malta, Demetrio (Ecuador, b. 1909), in collaboration with D.A.M., Joaquín Gallegos Lara and Enrique Gil Gilbert, *Los que se van* (Guayaquil 1930), 2nd edition, Casa de la Cultura Ecuatoriana, Quito 1955; *Don Goyo*, Cenit, Madrid 1933; *La isla virgen* (1942), Casa de la Cultura Ecuatoriana, Quito 1954.

Agustini, Delmira (Uruguay, 1886–1914), *Poesías completas*, 3rd edition, Losada, Buenos Aires 1962.

Alba, Víctor, *Historia del movimiento obrero en América latina*, Editorial Mexicanos Unidos, Mexico 1954; *Las ideas sociales contemporáneas en México*, Tierra Firme, Fondo de cultura económica, Mexico 1960.

Albérès, R. M., *Argentine, Un Monde, Une Ville*, Hachette, Paris 1957.

Aldrich, Earl M., Jr, *The Modern Short Story in Peru*, University of Wisconsin Press, Madison, Milwaukee and London 1966.

Alegría, Ciro (Peru, 1909–67), *La serpiente de oro* (1935), Ediciones Nuevo Mundo, Lima 1963, published in English as *The Golden Serpent*, trans. Harriet de Onís, Signet Classics, New York 1963; *Los perros hambrientos* (1939) included in *Novelas completas*, Aguilar, Madrid 1959; *El mundo es ancho y ajeno* (1941), 20th edition, Losada, Buenos Aires 1961, published in English as *Broad and Alien is the World*, trans. Harriet de Onís, Farrar and Rinehart, New York 1941; Nicholson and Watson, London 1942.

Alegría, Fernando (Chile, b. 1918), *Breve historia de la novela hispanoamericana*, Ediciones de Andrea (Colección Studium), 3rd edition, Mexico 1966; *Las fronteras del realismo: literatura chilena del siglo xx*, Zig-Zag, Santiago 1962; ed., *Novelistas contemporáneos hispano-americanos* (anthology), Heath, Boston 1964; *Caballo de copas*, Nascimento, Santiago de Chile 1957.

Alloway, Lawrence, 'The International Style', *Encounter*, London September 1965.

Almeida, José Américo de (Brazil, b. 1887), *A Bagaceira* (1928), 7th edition, José Olympio, Rio de Janeiro 1937.

Alone, *see* Díaz Arrieta.

Altamira, Rafael, *Mi viaje a América*, Victoriano Suárez, Madrid 1911.

Altamirano, Ignacio (Mexico, 1834–93), *El Zarco* (1901), 5th popular edition, Espasa Calpe, Buenos Aires 1958.

Amado, Jorge (Brazil, b. 1912), *País do Carnaval* (1932); *Cacau* (1933); *Suor* (1934); these three novels have been published together in *Obras de Jorge Amado*, 4th edition, Vol. I, Martins, São Paulo 1955; *Jubiabá* (1935), *Obras . . .*, 6th edition, Vol. IV, Martins, São Paulo 1951; *Mar Morto* (1936), *Obras . . .*, 5th edition, Vol. V, Martins, São Paulo 1955; *Capitães de Areia* (1937), *Obras . . .*, 4th edition, Vol. VI, Martins, São Paulo 1947; *Terras do Sem Fim* (1942), 3rd edition, Livros do Brasil, Lisbon n.d., published in English as *The Violent Land*, trans. Samuel Putnam, Knopf, New York 1945; *São Jorge dos Ilhéus*, Martins, São Paulo 1944; *Gabriela, cravo e canela* (1958), Martins, São Paulo 1961, published in English as *Gabriela, Clove and Cinnamon*, trans. William L. Grossman, Knopf, New York 1962; *Os Velhos Marinheiros: Duas Histórias dos Cais da Bahia*, Martins, São Paulo 1961, published in English as *Home is th Sailor*, trans. Harriet de Onís, Knopf, New York 1964; Chatto and Windus, London 1964.

Amorim, Enrique (Uruguay, 1900–1960), *El paisano Aguilar* (1934), Editor Siglo Veinte, Buenos Aires 1946; *El caballo y su sombra* (1941) Losada, Buenos Aires 1945; published in English as *The Horse and its Shadow*, trans. R. O'Connell and J. Graham, Scribner, New York 1943; *La desembocadura*, Losada, Buenos Aires 1958.

Anderson Imbert, Enrique, *Tres novelas de Payró* Facultad de Filosofía y Letras, Tucumán 1942.

Andrade, Mário de (Brazil, 1893–1945), *Há uma Gôta de Sangue em cada Poema* (1917), included in *Obra Imatura*, Martins, São Paulo 1960. All other poems are included in *Poesias completas*, Martins, São Paulo 1955; *Macunaíma, o Herói sem Nenhum Caráter* (1928), Cem bibliófilos do Brasil, Rio de Janeiro 1957; 'O Movimento Modernista', *Aspectos da Literatura Brasileira*, *Obras completas de Mário Andrade*, Vol. X, Martins, São Paulo 1959.

Andrade, Oswald de (Brazil, 1890–1954), *Memórias Sentimentais de*

Bibliography

João Miramar (1924), 2nd edition, Difusão Européia do Livro, São Paulo 1964; *Poesias Reunidas de Oswald de Andrade*, Difusão Européia do Livro, São Paulo 1966.

Aranha, José Pereira de Graça (Brazil, 1868–1931), *Canãa* (1902), published in English as *Canaan*, trans. Marián Joaquín Lorente, London 1921.

Arévalo Martínez, Rafael (Guatemala, b. 1884), *El hombre que parecía un caballo* (1915), Editorial Universitaria, Guatemala 1951.

Arguedas, Alcides (Bolivia, 1879–1946), *Pueblo enfermo* (1909); *Raza de bronce* (1919); included in *Obras completas*, 2 vols., Aguilar, Mexico 1959.

Arguedas, José María (Peru, b. 1911), *Canto Kechwa*, Ediciones Club del libro Peruano, 1938; *Yawar Fiesta* (1941), Populibros Peruanos, n.d.; *Los ríos profundos*, Losada, Buenos Aires 1958; *El sexto* (1961), Ediciones Merlin, Lima n.d.; *Todas las sangres*, Losada, Buenos Aires 1964; *Agua* (1935), Ediciones Nuevo Mundo, Lima, 1961; *Diamantes y pedernales*, Juan Mejía Baca, Lima 1954.

Arlt, Roberto (Argentina, 1900–1942), *Los siete locos*, Claridad, Buenos Aires 1929; *Los lanzallamas*, Claridad, Buenos Aires 1931; *Novelas completas y cuentos*, 3 vols., Fabril, Buenos Aires 1963.

Arráiz, Antonio (Venezuela, b. 1903), *Puros hombres* (1938), Editorial Latinoamericana, Lima, included in the series 'Segundo Festival del libro Venezolano', n.d.; *El mar es como un potro*, first published as *Dámaso Velázquez* (1943).

Asturias, Miguel Angel (Guatemala, b. 1899), *Leyendas de Guatemala*, Editorial Oriente, Madrid 1930; *El Señor Presidente* (1946), published in English as *The President*, trans. Frances Partridge, Gollancz, London 1963; *Hombres de maíz* (1949); (*El Señor Presidente* and *Hombres de maíz* are included in *Obras escogidas*, Vol. I, Aguilar, Madrid 1955); *Viento fuerte*, Losada, Buenos Aires 1950; *El Papa verde*, Losada, Buenos Aires 1954; *Los ojos de los enterrados*, Losada, Buenos Aires 1960; *Mulata de tal*, Losada, Buenos Aires 1963, published in English as *The Mulatta and Mr Fly*, trans. Gregory Rabassa, Peter Owen, London 1967; *see also* Bellini.

Ataíde, Tristão de (pseudonym of Alceu Amoroso Lima) (Brazil, b. 1893), *Contribuição à História do Modernismo*, Vol. I, José Olympio, Rio de Janeiro 1939.

Azevedo, Fernando de (Brazil, b. 1894), *A Cultura Brasileira* (1943), 2nd edition, Companhia Editôra Nacional, São Paulo, Rio de Janeiro, Bahia, Pará, Pôrto Alegre, 1944, published in English as *Brazilian Culture*, trans William Rex Crawford, Macmillan, New York 1950.

Azuela, Mariano (Mexico, 1873–1952), *Los de abajo* (1916), published in English as *The Underdogs*, trans. Enrique Munguía, Signet Classics, New York 1963; *Los caciques* (1917) and *Las moscas* (1918) published in one volume in English as *Two Novels of Mexico: The Flies – The Bosses*, trans. Lesley B. Simpson, University of California Press, Berkeley and Los Angeles 1964; *Obras Completas*, 3 vols., Fondo de cultura económica, Mexico 1958–60, with an introduction by Francisco Monterde.

Baciu, Stefan, 'Beatitude South of the Border, Latin America's Beat Generation', *Hispania*, Vol. XLIX, No. 4, December 1966.

Ballagas, Emilio (Cuba, 1908–54), *Antología de la poesía negra hispano-americana*, Aguilar, Madrid 1944; *Mapa de la poesía negra*, Pleamar, Buenos Aires 1946.

Banchs, Enrique (Argentina, b. 1888), *Poemas selectos*, ed. Francisco Monterde, Cultura, Mexico 1921.

Bandeira, Manuel (Brazil, b. 1886), *Poesia e Prosa*, 2 vols., Aguilar, Rio de Janeiro 1958, with an introduction by Sérgio Buarque de Holanda and Francisco de Assis Barbosa; *Antología dos Poetas Brasileiros da Fase Parnasiana*, 3rd edition, Departamento da Imprensa Nacional, Ministério da Educação e Saúde, Rio de Janeiro 1951.

Barbusse, Henri, *Manifeste aux intellectuels*, Les écrivains réunis, Paris 1927.

Barnet, Miguel (Cuba, b. 1940), *Cimarrón*, Gente Nueva, La Habana 1967, published in English as *Memoirs of a Runaway Slave*, Bodley Head, London 1968.

Barrenechea, Ana María, *Borges, the Labyrinth Maker*, New York University Press, New York 1965; in collaboration with Emma Susana Speratti Piñero, *La literatura fantástica argentina*, Imprenta Universitaria, Buenos Aires 1957.

Barrios, Eduardo (Chile, 1884–1963), *Un perdido* (1917); *Gran Señor y Rajadiablos* (1948); *Obras completas*, 2 vols., Zig-Zag, Santiago 1962.

Bastide, Roger, *Brésil: Terre des contrastes*, Hachette, Paris 1957.

Bazin, R., *Histoire de la littérature américaine de langue espagnole*, Paris 1953.

Beleño Cedeño, Joaquín (Panama, b. 1922), *Luna verde*, Panama 1951; *Gamboa Road Gang (Los forzados de Gamboa)*, Ministerio de Educación, Departamento de Bellas Artes y Publicaciones, Panama 1960.

Bellini, Giuseppe, *La narrativa di Miguel Angel Asturias*, Vol. I: *Dalle 'Leyendas' a 'Hombres de Maíz'*, La Goliardica, Milan 1965.

Bibliography

Bello, Andrés (Venezuela, 1781–1865), *Obras completas*, Ministerio de Educación, Caracas 1952.

Benedetti, Mario (Uruguay, b. 1920), *Montevideanos* (1959), 3rd edition, Alfa, Montevideo 1964; *La tregua* (1960), 2nd edition, Alfa, Montevideo 1963; *Literatura uruguaya, siglo xx*, Alfa, Montevideo 1963; *Gracias por el fuego*, Alfa, Montevideo 1964.

Beneke, Walter (El Salvador, b. 1928), *Funeral Home* (1959), included in *El teatro hispanoamericano contemporáneo* (anthology): *see* Solórzano.

Benítez, Antonio (Cuba, b. 1931), *Tute de reyes*, Ediciones Premio, Casa de las Américas, La Habana 1967.

Benítez, Fernando (Mexico, b. 1910), *Los indios de Mexico*, Era, Mexico 1967.

Berisso, Luis (Argentina, 1866–1944), *El pensamiento de América*, 1898.

Bioy Casares, Adolfo (Argentina, b. 1914), *El sueño de los héroes*, Losada, Buenos Aires 1954; *La invención de Morel* (1940), 2nd edition, Sur, Buenos Aires 1948; in collaboration with Ocampo, Silvina, *Los que aman, odian*, Emecé, Buenos Aires 1946.

Blanco Fombona, Rufino (Venezuela, 1874–1944), *El hombre de hierro*, Tipografía Americana, Caracas 1907; *Dramas mínimos*, Biblioteca nueva, Madrid 1920; *La evolución política y social de Hispanoamérica*, Madrid 1911; *Camino de imperfección: Diario de mi vida, 1906–13*, Editorial América, Madrid 1933; *Obras selectas*, ed. Gabaldón Márquez, Ediciones Edime, Madrid and Caracas 1958.

Bopp, Raul (Brazil, b. 1898), *Cobra Norato e outros poemas* (1931), Livraria São José, Rio de Janeiro 1956.

Borges, Jorge Luis (Argentina, born 1899), *Poemas* (1923–58), Emecé, Buenos Aires 1958; *Otras inquisiciones* (1937–52), Sur, Buenos Aires 1952; 2nd edition, Emecé, Buenos Aires 1960; *Discusión* (1932), Emecé, Buenos Aires 1957; *Historia Universal de la Infamia* (1935), Emecé, Buenos Aires 1954; *Ficciones* (1935–44), 3rd edition, Emecé, Buenos Aires 1961; *El Aleph* (1949), 3rd edition, Emecé, Buenos Aires 1957; *El hacedor*, Emecé, Buenos Aires 1960; *El idioma de los Argentinos* (1928), included in a collection of essays by Borges and others and published under the same title, Emecé, Buenos Aires 1963; *The Spanish Language in South America: A Literary Problem* and *El Gaucho Martín Fierro* (texts of lectures given at the Hispanic Council, London, and Bristol University), Diamante, London 1964; English translations of Borges's stories have been published as *Labyrinths: Selected Stories and other Writings*, New Directions, Norfolk Conn., 1962, ed. by Donald A.

Yates and James E. Irby with preface by André Maurois; *Ficciones*, London 1962, edited and with an introduction by Anthony Kerrigan; *A Personal Anthology*, trans. Anthony Kerrigan, Jonathan Cape, London 1968.

Botelho Gosálvez, Raúl (Bolivia, b. 1917), *Borrachera verde*, Zig-Zag, Santiago 1938; *Altiplano*, Ayacucho, Buenos Aires 1945.

Brandão entre o mar e o amor, a composite Brazilian novel by Jorge Amado, José Lins do Rego, Aníbal Machado, Raquel de Queirós and Graciliano Ramos, 1942.

Breton, André, *Manifestes du Surréalisme*, Éditions Jean Jacques Pauvert, Paris 1962.

Brunet, Marta (Chile, b. 1901), *Montaña adentro*, Nascimento, Santiago 1923; 2nd edition, 1933; *María Nadie*, Zig-Zag, Santiago 1957.

Buarque de Holanda, Sérgio (Brazil, b. 1902), *Raízes do Brasil*, José Olympio, Rio de Janeiro 1936.

Bulnes, Francisco (Mexico, 1847–1924), *El porvenir de las naciones latinoamericanas*, 1899.

Bunge, Carlos Octavio (Argentina, 1875–1918), *Nuestra América*, Barcelona 1903.

Caballero Calderón, Eduardo (Colombia, b. 1910), *El Cristo de espaldas*, Losada, Buenos Aires 1953, 4th edition, Espiral, Bogotá 1961; *Siervo sin tierra* (1954), 2nd edition, Guadarrama, Madrid 1955; *Manuel Pacho*, Bolsilibros, Bedout, Medellín 1964; *Americanos y europeos*, Guadarrama, Madrid 1957.

Cabral de Melo Neto, João (Brazil, b. 1920), *Duas águas, poemas reunidos*, José Olympio, Rio de Janeiro 1956; *Terceira feira*, Editôra do Autor, Rio de Janeiro 1961; *Poemas Escolhidas*, Portugália, Lisbon 1963; *Antologia Poetica*, Rio de Janeiro 1965.

Cabral, Manuel del (Dominican Republic, b. 1907), *Doce poemas negros*, Ciudad Trujillo 1935.

Cabrera, Lidia (Cuba), *Cuentos negros de Cuba*, La Verónica, La Habana 1940.

Cabrera Infante, Guillermo (Cuba, b. 1929), *Así en la paz como en la guerra*, 4th edition, Ediciones Revolución, Havana 1964; *Tres tristes tigres*, Seix Barral, Barcelona 1967

Caicedo, Daniel (Colombia), *Viento seco*, 3rd edition, Losada, Buenos Aires 1954.

Cambaceres, Eugenio (Argentina, 1843–88), *Obras completas*, ed. E.M.S. Danero, Santa Fé, Argentina, 1956.

Campos, Augusto de (Brazil), in collaboration with Décio Pignatari and Haroldo de Campos, *Teoria da Poesia Concreta: Textos Críticos e Manifestos, 1950–60*, Edições Invenção, São Paulo 1965; in collaboration with Haroldo de Campos, *Revisão de Sousândrade*, Edições Invenção, São Paulo 1964.

Campos, Haroldo de (Brazil), *see* Campos, Augusto de.

Candido, Antônio, *Literatura e Sociedade*, Companhia Editôra Nacional, São Paulo 1965.

Capdevila, Arturo (Argentina, b. 1889), *Babel y el Castellano*, Losada, Buenos Aires 1940.

Cardenal, Ernesto, *Poemas*, Casa de las Américas, La Habana 1967.

Cardoza y Aragón, Luis (Guatemala, b. 1904), *Guatemala, las líneas de tu mano*, Fondo de cultura económica, Mexico 1955.

Carpentier, Alejo (Cuba, b. 1904), *Ecué-Yamba-O*, Editorial España, Madrid 1933; *El reino de este mundo* (1949), Organización Continental de los Festivales del Libro, Lima 1958; *Los pasos perdidos* (1953), Compañía General de Ediciones, Mexico 1959, published in English as *The Lost Steps*, trans. Harriet de Onís, London 1956; Knopf, New York 1956; *El acoso*, Losada, Buenos Aires 1956; *Guerra del tiempo*, EDIAPSA, Mexico 1958; *El siglo de las luces*, EDIAPSA, Mexico 1962, published in English as *Explosion in a Cathedral*, London 1963.

Carrasquilla, Tomás (1858–1940), *Frutos de mi tierra*, (1896); *Obras completas*, EPESA, Madrid 1952, prologue by F. de Onís.

Carrera Andrade, Jorge (Ecuador, b. 1903), *Boletines de mar y tierra*, Barcelona 1930; *Rol de la manzana: poesías* (1926–29); *Biografía para uso de los pájaros*, Paris 1937; *Registro del mundo: antología poética* (1922–39), Imprenta de la Universidad, Quito 1940; *Edades poéticas* (1922–56), Casa de la Cultura Ecuatoriana, Quito 1958 (includes *Microgramas*, 1940).

Carvalho, Ronald de (Brazil, 1893–1935), *Pequena História de Literatura Brasileira*, 7th edition, Briguiet e Companhia, Rio de Janeiro 1944; in conjunction with Elysio de Carvalho, *Affirmações: Um ágape de Intellectuaes*, Monitor Mercantil, Rio de Janeiro 1921.

Casaccia, Gabriel (Paraguay, b. 1907), *La babosa*, Losada, Buenos Aires 1952.

Casal, Julián del (Cuba, 1863–93), *Poesías completas*, Ministerio de Educación, Havana 1945; *Prosas*, 3 vols., Consejo Nacional de Cultura, Havana 1961; *see also* Monner Sans.

Castellanos, Rosario (Mexico, b. 1925), *Balún Canán*, Fondo de cultura económica, Mexico 1957, published in English as *The Nine Guardians*, London 1959; *Oficio de tinieblas*, Joaquín Mortíz, Mexico 1962.

Castello, José Aderaldo, *José Lins do Rego: Modernismo e Regionalismo*, Edart, São Paulo 1961.

Castro Leal, Antonio, ed., *La novela de la Revolución Mexicana*, 2 vols., Aguilar, Mexico 1958–60.

Caute, David, *Communism and the French Intellectuals, 1914–60*, Deutsch, London 1964; Macmillan, New York 1964.

Céspedes, Augusto (Bolivia, b. 1904), *Metal del diablo* (1946), Palestra, Buenos Aires 1960; *Sangre de mestizos: Relatos de la Guerra del Chaco* (1936), Ministerio de Educación y Bellas Artes, La Paz 1962.

Chang Rodríguez, Eugenio, *La literatura política de González Prada, Mariátegui y Haya de la Torre*, Ediciones de Andrea, Studium, Mexico 1957.

Charlot, Jean, *The Mexican Mural Renaissance, 1920–25*, Yale University Press, New Haven 1963.

Chaves, Fernando (Ecuador, b. 1902), *Plata y bronce* (1927), Casa de la Cultura Ecuatoriana, Quito 1954.

Chocano, José Santos (Peru, 1875–1934), *Obras completas*, Aguilar, Mexico 1954, with a prologue by Luis Alberto Sánchez.

Cisneros, Antonio (Peru, b. 1942), *Comentarios reales*, La Rama Florida, Lima 1964; *Canto ceremonial contra un oso hormiguero*, Casa de las Américas, La Habana, 1968; Selection of poems published in English as *The Spider Hangs Too Far from the Ground*, trans, Various, Jonathan Cape, 1970.

Cline, Howard, *Mexico: Revolution to Evolution, 1940–1960*, Oxford University Press, London and New Yo rk 1962.

Cohen, J. M., ed., *Latin American Writing Today*, Penguin, Harmondsworth 1967.

Cometta Manzoni, Aída, *El indio en la novela de América*, Editorial Futuro, SRL, Buenos Aires 1960.

Contreras, Francisco (Chile, 1877–1933): *Les Ecrivains contemporains de l'Amérique Espagnole*, La Renaissance du Livre, Paris 1920.

Corno Emplumado, El, Mexico City, No. 1, January 1962, to present day.

Corral, Jesús del (Colombia, 1871–1931), 'Que pase el aserrador' included in Walsh, Gertrude M., *Cuentos criollos*, Heath, Boston 1941.

Cortázar, Julio (Argentina, b. 1914), *Final del juego* (1964), 2nd edition, Editorial Sudamericana, Buenos Aires 1964; *Los premios* (1960), 3rd edition, Editorial Sudamericana, Buenos Aires 1965, published in English as *The Winners*, trans. Elaine Kerrigan, Souvenir Press, London 1965; Pantheon, New York 1965; *Rayuela*, Editorial Sudamericana, Buenos Aires 1963, published in English as *Hopscotch*, trans. Gregory Rabassa, Pantheon, New York 1966; Collins,

London 1967; *Historias de cronopios y de famas* (1962), Minotauro, Buenos Aires 1964; *La vuelta al día en ochenta mundos*, siglo xxi, Mexico 1967; *62. Novela para armar*, Sudamericana, Buenos Aires, 1968.

Costa du Rels, Adolpho (Bolivia, b. 1891): *see* Francovitch, Guillermo.

Coulthard, G. R., *Race and Colour in Caribbean Literature*, Oxford University Press, London and New York 1962.

Cruz Costa, João, *Contribição a história da idéias do Brasil*, Coleção Documentos Brasileiros, Rio de Janeiro 1956; published in English as *A History of Ideas in Brazil*, trans. Suzette Macedo, University of California Press, Berkeley and Los Angeles 1964.

Cruz e Sousa, João (Brazil, 1861–98), *Obras Poéticas*, Valverde, Rio de Janeiro 1945.

Cuadra, José de la (Ecuador, 1903–41), *Repisas* (1931); *Horno* (1932); *Guasintón* (1935); *Los Sangurimas* (1934); *Obras completas*, Casa de la Cultura Ecuatoriana, Quito 1958, with a prologue by Alfredo Pareja Díez-Canseco.

Cuevas, Jose Luis, 'The Cactus Curtain: an open letter on conformity in Mexican Art', *Evergreen Review*, Vol. 2, No. 7, Winter 1959, pp. 11–120.

Cunha, Euclydes da (Brazil, 1866–1909), *Os Sertões* (1902), 12th revised edition, Rio de Janeiro 1933, published in English as *Rebellion in the Backlands*, trans. Samuel Putnam, University of Chicago Press, Chicago 1944; condensed edition, *Revolt in the Backlands*, Gollancz, London 1947.

Damaz, Paul F., *Art in Latin American Architecture*, Reinhold, New York 1963, with a preface by Oscar Niemeyer.

Darío, Rubén (1867–1916), *Azul* (1888); *Los raros* (1896); *Prosas profanas* (1896); *Cantos de vida y esperanza* (1905); *El canto errante* (1907); *Obras poéticas completas*, 9th edition, Aguilar, Madrid 1961; *Obras desconocidas de Rubén Darío escritas en Chile y no recopiladas en ninguno de sus libros*, ed. Raúl Silva Castro, Universidad de Chile, Santiago 1934; *Obras completas*, 5 vols., Aguado, Madrid 1950–55.

Dauster, Frank, *Ensayos sobre poesía mexicana*, Ediciones de Andrea, Studium, Mexico 1963.

Debesa, Fernando (Chile, b. 1921), *Mama Rosa*, Editorial del Nuevo Extremo, Santiago 1958.

Delgado, Wáshington (Peru, b. 1927), *Días del corazón*, Cuadernos de composición, Lima 1957; *Para vivir mañana*, Lima 1959; *Parque*, La Rama Florida, Lima 1965.

Demolins, Edmond, *A quoi tient la supériorité des Anglo-Saxons?*, Paris 1897.

Denevi, Marco (Argentina, b. 1922), *Ceremonia secreta*, Doubleday, Garden City N.Y., 1961.

Díaz Arrieta, H. (Alone), *Historia personal de la literatura chilena*, 2nd edition, Zig-Zag, Santiago 1962.

Díaz Mirón, Salvador (Mexico, 1853–1928), *Lascas* (1901), included in *Poesías completas*, 3rd edition, Porrúa, Mexico 1952.

Díaz Rodríguez, Manuel (Venezuela, 1871–1927), *Idolos rotos* (1901); *Cuentos de color* (1899), Ediciones Nueva Cádiz, Caracas 1952.

Donoso, José (Chile, b. 1925), *Coronación*, Nascimento, Santiago 1957, published in English as *Coronation*, Bodley Head, London 1965; Knopf, New York 1965.

Droguett, Carlos (Chile, b. 1915), *100 gotas de sangre y 200 de sudor*, Zig-Zag, Santiago 1961; *El hombre que había olvidado*, Buenos Aires 1968; *Eloy*, Seix Barral, Barcelona 1960.

Drummond de Andrade, Carlos (Brazil, b. 1902), *Poemas*, José Olympio, Rio de Janeiro 1959.

Dunham, Lowell, *Rómulo Gallegos, vida y obra*, Ediciones de Andrea, Studium, Mexico 1957.

Echeverría, Esteban (Argentina, 1805–51), *Dogma socialista* (1837–46), published as *Dogma socialista y otras páginas políticas*, Editorial Estrada, Buenos Aires 1958; *El matadero* (published posthumously in *Obras completas*, 5 vols, 1870-74); *La cautiva y el matadero*, 7th edition, Sopena, Buenos Aires 1962, with a reprint of the prologue by Juan María Gutiérrez.

Edwards, Jorge (Chile, b. 1931), *El peso de la noche*, Seix Barral, Barcelona 1964.

Edwards Bello, Joaquín (Chile, b. 1887), *El roto*, Editorial Chilena, Santiago 1920.

Eguren, José María (Peru, 1874–1942), *Vida y obra, Antología Bibliografía*, Hispanic Institute, New York 1961.

Ellison, Fred P., *Brazil's New Novel*, University of California Press, Berkeley and Los Angeles 1954.

Erro, Carlos Alberto (Argentina, b. 1899), *Tiempo lacerado*, Ediciones Sur, Buenos Aires 1936.

Espejo Asturrizaga, Juan, *César Vallejo: itinerario del hombre*, Mejía Baca, Lima 1965.

Espínola, Francisco (Uruguay, b. 1901), *Raza ciega* (1927), Ediciones de la sociedad Amigos del Libro Rioplatense, Montevideo and Buenos Aires 1936.

341

Bibliography

Fallas, Carlos Luis (Costa Rica, b. 1909), *Mamita Yunäi* (1941), 2nd edition, Nascimento, Chile 1949.

Fein, John M., *Modernismo in Chilean Literature*, Duke University Press, Durham N.C., 1965.

Fernández, Justino, *Arte moderno y contemporáneo de México*, Imprenta Universitaria, Mexico 1952; ed., *Textos de Orozco*, Instituto de Investigaciones Estéticas, Universidad Nacional Autónoma de México, Mexico 1955.

Fernández, Macedonio (Argentina, 1874–1952), *Papeles de un recienvenido*, Ediciones Revolución, La Habana 1961.

Fernández, Pablo Armando (Cuba, b. 1930), *Libro de los héroes*, Casa de las Américas, Cuba 1963; *Toda la poesía*, Ediciones Revolución, La Habana 1961.

Fernández de Lizardi, José Joaquín (Mexico, 1776–1827), *El Periquillo Sarniento* (1816), 4th edition, Porrúa, Mexico 1962.

Fernández Guardia, Ricardo (Costa Rica, 1867–1950) *Cuentos ticos*, San José de Costa Rica 1901.

Fernández Moreno, Baldomero (Argentina, 1886–1950), *Las iniciales del misal* (1915); *Aldea española* (1925); *Poesía* (1928); *Décimas* (1928); *Dos poemas* (1935); *Seguidillas* (1936); *Romances* (1936); *Antología, 1915–50*, 6th edition, Espasa-Calpe, Buenos Aires 1954.

Fernández Retamar, Roberto (Cuba, b. 1930), *La poesía contemporánea en Cuba: 1927–53*, Orígenes, Havana 1954; *Vuelta a la antigua esperanza*, Havana 1959; 'Carta a los pioneros' included in the collection *Con las mismas manos*, Ediciones Unión, Poesía, Havana 1962.

Francovitch, Guillermo, *El pensamiento boliviano en el siglo xx*, Fondo de cultura económica, Mexico 1956.

Freyre, Gilberto (Brazil, b. 1900), *Casa Grande e Senzala* (1933), published in English as *The Masters and the Slaves*, trans. Samuel Putnam, 2nd edition, Knopf, New York 1956; *Manifesto Regionalista de 1926*, Ministério da Educação e Cultura, Rio de Janeiro 1955; *Interpretação do Brasil* (1947), Livros do Brasil, Lisbon, n.d., originally published in English as *Brazil: an Interpretation*, Knopf, New York 1945.

Frías, Heriberto (Mexico, 1870–1928), *Tomóchic*, Biblioteca Mexicana, Barcelona 1899.

Fuentes, Carlos (Mexico, b. 1929), *Las buenas conciencias* (1959), 3rd edition, Fondo de cultura económica, Mexico 1961; *La región más transparente* (1958), 4th edition, Fondo de cultura económica, Mexico 1965; *La muerte de Artemio Cruz*, Fondo de cultura económica, Mexico 1962, published in English as *The Death of*

Artemio Cruz, trans. Sam Hileman. Collins, London 1964; Farrar, Straus, New York 1964; *Cambio de piel*, Joaquín Mortíz, Mexico 1968; *La nueva novela hispanoamericana*, Joaquín Mortíz, Mexico 1969.

Gallegos, Rómulo (Venezuela, 1884–1969), *Reinaldo Solar* (1920); *La trepadora* (1925); *Doña Bárbara* (1929); *Cantaclaro* (1934); *Canaima* (1935); *Pobre negro* (1937); *Una posición en la vida* (essays), Ediciones Humanismo Mexico 1954; all the novels are included in *Obras completas*, 2 vols., Aguilar, Madrid 1958.

Gallegos Lara, Joaquín: *see* Aguilera Malta.

Galván, Manuel de Jesús (Dominican Republic, 1834–1911), *Enriquillo, leyenda histórica dominicana* (1882), published in English as *The Cross and the Sword*, trans. Robert Graves, Gollancz London 1956

Gálvez, Manuel (Argentina, 1882–1962), *El mal metafísico* (1916); *Nacha Regules* (1919); *Obras escogidas*, Aguilar, Madrid 1949.

Gamboa, Federico (1864–1939), *Obras completas*, Fondo de cultura económica, Mexico 1965, with a prologue by Francisco Monterde.

García Calderón, Francisco (Peru, 1883–1953), *Le Pérou contemporain*, Paris 1907; *Ideas e impresiones*, Madrid 1919; *Les Démocraties Latines de l'Amérique*, Paris 1912.

García Calderón, Ventura (Peru, 1886–1959), *La venganza del cóndor*, Mundo Latino, Madrid 1924.

García Godoy, Federico (1857–1924), *Americanismo literario*, Editorial América, Madrid 1917.

García Márquez, Gabriel (Colombia, b. 1928), *La mala hora*, Esso Colombiana, 1962; *El coronel no tiene quien le escriba* (1961), 2nd edition, Era, Mexico 1963; 'Un día después del sábado' included in *Los funerales de la Mamá Grande*, Jalapa, Mexico 1962; *La hojarasca*, Arca, Montevideo 1965; *Cien años de soledad*, Sudamericana, Buenos Aires 1967.

García Robles, Victor (Argentina, b. 1933), *Oíd mortales*, Las Americas, Havana 1965.

Garmendia, Salvador (Venezuela, b. 1928), *Los pequeños seres* (1959); *La mala vida*, Arca, Montevideo 1968; *Día de ceniza* (1964), Monteavila, Caracas 1968; *Los habitantes*, Monteavila, Caracas 1968.

Garro, Elena (Mexico, b. 1917), *Los recuerdos del porvenir*, Joaquín Mortíz, Mexico 1963.

Gerchunoff, Alberto (b. Russia 1884, died Argentina 1950), *Los gauchos judíos* (1910), new edition, Biblioteca de escritores argentinos, Buenos Aires 1936, published in English as *The Jewish Gauchos of the Pampa*, trans. Prudencio de Pereda, Abelard Schuman, London and New York 1959.

Gil Gilbert, Enrique (Ecuador, b. 1912), *Nuestro pan*, Librería Vera, Guayaquil 1942, published in English as *Our Daily Bread*, trans. Dudley Poore, New York and Toronto 1943; in collaboration with Joaquín Gallegos Lara, Demetrio Aguilera Malta, *Los que se van; cuentos del cholo y del montuvio*, Guayaquil 1930.

Glauert, Earl T., 'Ricardo Rojas and the Emergence of Argentine Cultural Nationalism', *Hispanic American Historical Review*, Vol. XLII, No. I, p. 19.

Gobineau, Joseph Arthur de, *Essai sur l'inégalité des races humaines*, Paris 1884.

Gómez Carrillo, Enrique (Guatemala, 1873–1927), *Literatura extranjera*, Garnier, Paris 1895.

González Martínez, Enrique (Mexico, 1871–1952), *Antología poética*, 3rd edition, Espasa-Calpe, Buenos Aires and Mexico 1944.

González Prada, Manuel (Peru, 1848–1918), *Páginas libres*, Paris 1894; *Horas de lucha* (1908), 2nd edition, Lux, Lima 1924.

González Vera, Augusto (Chile, b. 1897), *Cuando era muchacho*, Nascimento, Santiago 1956.

Gorostiza, José (Mexico, b. 1901), *Muerte sin fin* (1939), Imprenta Universitaria, Mexico 1952; *Poesía*, Fondo de cultura económica, Mexico 1964.

Guido, Beatriz (Argentina, b. 1924), *La caída*, Losada, Buenos Aires 1956.

Guillén, Nicolás (Cuba, b. 1902), *Motivos de son* (1930); *Sóngoro cosongo* (1931), 2nd edition., Losada, Buenos Aires 1957; *Cantos para soldados y sones para turistas* (1937); *El son entero*, Pleamar, Buenos Aires 1947; *Cantos para soldados y sones para turistas* is included in the 2nd edition of *El son entero*, Losada, Buenos Aires 1957.

Guimarães Rosa, João (Brazil, b. 1908), *Grande Sertão, Veredas* (1956), 3rd edition, José Olympio, Rio de Janeiro 1963, published in English as *The Devil to Pay in the Backlands*, trans. James Taylor and Harriet de Onís, Knopf, New York 1963; *Corpo de Baile* (Sete novelas), 2 vols., José Olympio, Rio de Janeiro 1956.

Güiraldes, Ricardo (Argentina, 1886–1927), *Don Segundo Sombra* (1926), included in *Obras completas*, Emecé, Buenos Aires 1962, with a prologue by Francisco Luis Bernárdez; published in English as *Don Segundo Sombra*, trans. Harriet de Onís, Penguin Books, Harmondsworth 1948.

Bibliography

Gullón, Ricardo, *Direcciones del modernismo*, Gredos, Madrid 1963.

Gutiérrez Nájera, Manuel (Mexico, 1859–95), *Obras de Manuel Gutiérrez Nájera*, ed. Justo Sierra, Mexico 1896; *Poesías completas*, 2 vols., Porrúa, Mexico 1953.

Guzmán, Martín Luis (Mexico, b. 1887), *El águila y la serpiente* (1928), published in English as *The Eagle and the Serpent*, trans. Harriet de Onís, Knopf, New York 1930; *La sombra del caudillo* (1929); *Obras completas de Martín Luis Guzmán*, 2 vols., Compañía General de Ediciones, Mexico 1961, with an introduction by Andrés Iduarte.

Guzmán, Nicomedes (Chile, b. 1914), *Los hombres oscuros* (1939), 6th edition, Zig-Zag, Santiago 1964; *La luz viene del mar* (1950), 2nd edition, Zig-Zag, Santiago 1963.

Heiremans, Luis A. (Chile, 1928–66), *La jaula en el árbol y dos cuentos para teatro*, Editorial del Nuevo Extremo, Santiago 1959.

Henríquez Ureña, Max, *Breve historia del modernismo* (1954), 2nd edition, Fondo de cultura económica, Mexico 1962.

Henríquez Ureña, Pedro (Dominican Republic, 1884–1946), *Plenitud de América, ensayos escogidos*, Peña, del Giudice, Buenos Aires 1952.

Heraud, Javier (Peru, b. 1942), *Poesías completas y homenaje*, La Rama Florida, Lima 1964.

Hernández, José (Argentina, 1834–86), *Martín Fierro* (1872); *La vuelta de Martín Fierro* (1879), 8th edition, Losada, Buenos Aires 1953, ed. Eleuterio F. Tiscornia.

Herrera y Reissig, Julio (Uruguay, 1875–1910), *Los éxtasis de la montaña* (1904); *Sonetos vascos* (1906); *Poesías completas*, 3rd edition, Losada, Buenos Aires 1958.

Herring, Hubert, *A History of Latin America from the Beginnings to the Present*, 2nd edition, Knopf, New York 1963.

Huidobro, Vicente (Chile, 1893–1948), *Poesia y prosa*, Aguilar, Madrid 1957, with a preface by Antonio de Undurraga.

Ibarbourou, Juana de (Uruguay, b. 1895), *Obras completas*, Aguilar, Madrid 1960.

Icaza, Jorge (Ecuador, b. 1906), *Huasipungo* (1934), 2nd edition, Losada, Buenos Aires 1953, published in English as *Huasipungo*, trans. Mervyn Savil, London 1962; *Cholos* (1938), 2nd edition, Atahualpa, Quito 1939.

Iduarte, Andrés (Mexico, 1907), *Un niño en la revolución mexicana*, Editorial Ruta, Mexico 1951.

Ingenieros, José (Argentina, 1877–1925), *Los tiempos nuevos, reflexiones optimistas sobre la guerra y la revolución*, Buenos Aires 1921.

345

Bibliography

Isaacs, Jorge (Colombia, 1837–95), *María* (1867), Espasa-Calpe, Buenos Aires and Mexico 1949.

Jaimes Freyre, Ricardo (Bolivia, 1868–1933), *Castalia bárbara* (1897), included in *Poesías completas*, Claridad, Buenos Aires 1944, with an introduction by Eduardo Joubín Colombres.

Jaramillo Alvarado, Pío (Ecuador, b. 1889), *El indio ecuatoriano, contribución al estudio de la sociología nacional* (Quito 1922), 4th edition, Casa de la Cultura Ecuatoriana, 1954.

Keyserling, Count Hermann, *Sudamerikanische Meditationen*, published in English as *South American Meditations*, Jonathan Cape, London 1932.

Korsi, Demetrio (Panama, 1899–1957), *Pequeña antología*, Panama 1947.

Lafourcade, Enrique (Chile, b. 1927), *La fiesta del Rey Acab*, Editorial del Pacífico, Santiago 1959.

Laguerra, Enrique A. (Puerto Rico, b. 1906), *Solar Montoya*, 1947.

Larreta, Enrique (Argentina, 1875–1961), *La gloria de Don Ramiro* (1908); *Zogoibi* (1962); *Obras completas*, Plentitud, Madrid 1958.

Latorre, Mariano (Chile, 1886–1955), *Cuentos de Maule* (1912); *Cuna de Cóndores* (1918); *Autobiografía de una vocación*, Universidad de Chile, Santiago 1956; *Sus mejores cuentos*, 3rd edition, Nascimento, Santiago 1962.

Lawrence, D. H., *The Plumed Serpent*, 3rd reprint, Penguin Books, Harmondsworth 1961.

Leiva, Raúl, *Imagen de la poesía mexicana contemporánea*, Imprenta Universitaria, Mexico 1959.

Leñero, Vicente, (Mexico, b. 1933), *Los albañiles* (1964), 2nd edition, Seix Barral, Mexico 1964.

Lezama Lima, José, *Paradiso*, Contemporáneos, Havana 1966.

Lihn, Enrique (Chile, b. 1929), *La pieza oscura* (1955–62), Editorial Universitaria, Santiago 1963; *Agua de arroz*, Ediciones del Litoral, Santiago 1964.

Lillo, Baldomero (Chile, 1867–1923), *Sub terra*, Imprenta Moderna, Santiago 1904; *Sub sole*, Imprenta Universitaría, Santiago 1907. References in the text are to the first editions but there have been recent editions: *Sub terra*, 5th edition, Nascimento, Santiago 1956; *Sub sole*, 3rd edition, Nascimento, Santiago 1943.

Lima, Jorge de (Brazil, 1893–1953), *Bangüê e Negra Fulô* (1928); *Obra completa*, Aguilar, Rio de Janeiro 1958, ed. Afrânio Coutinho.

Lima Barreto, Afonso Henrique de (Brazil, 1881–1922), *Recordações do Escrivão Isaías Caminha* (1909); *Triste fim de Policarpo Quaresma* (1915); *Obras de Lima Barreto*, Editora Brasiliense, São Paulo 1956. The two novels are included in Vols. I and II of the *Obras* respectively.

Lins do Rêgo, José (Brazil, 1901–57), *Menino de Engenho* (1932), 4th edition José Olympio, Rio de Janeiro 1943; *Doidinho* (1933), 4th edition, José Olympio, Rio de Janeiro 1943; *Banguê* (1934), 2nd edition, José Olympio, Rio de Janeiro 1943; *O Moleque Ricardo* (1935), 3rd edition revised, José Olympio, Rio de Janeiro 1940; *Usina* (1936), 2nd edition, José Olympio, Rio de Janeiro 1940; *Fogo Morto* (1943), 2nd edition, José Olympio, Rio de Janeiro 1944.

Lira Negra (Anthology of Afro-American and Afro-Spanish poetry), *Crisol*, No. 21, Aguilar, Madrid 1945, ed. José Sanz y Díaz.

López Albújar, Enrique (Peru, b. 1872), *Cuentos andinos* (1920); *Matalaché* (1928); *De mi casona* (1924); *Nuevos cuentos andinos*, Ercilla, Santiago 1937; *Los mejores cuentos*, Patronato del Libro Peruano, Lima 1957.

López Portillo y Rojas, José (Mexico, 1850–1923), *La parcela* (1898).

López Velarde, Ramón, (Mexico, 1888–1921), *Poesías completas y el minutero*, Porrúa, Mexico 1957, with a prologue by Antonio Castro Leal.

López y Fuentes, Gregorio (Mexico, b. 1897), *Campamento* (1921); *Tierra* (1932); *Mi general* (1934); these novels are included in *La novela de la revolución mexicana*, 2 vols., Aguilar, Mexico 1964, ed. by Castro Leal; *El indio* (1935), 3rd edition, Botas, Mexico 1945, published in English, with illustrations by Diego Rivera, as *They That Reap*, trans. Anita Brenner, Harrap, London 1937; Bobbs Merrill, Indianapolis and New York 1938.

Loveira, Carlos (Cuba, 1882–1928), *Generales y doctores* (1920), Oxford University Press, London and New York 1965, ed. by Shasta M. Bryant and J. Riis Owre; *Juan Críollo* (1927), Consejo Nacional de Cultura, Havana 1962.

Lugones, Leopoldo (Argentina 1874–1938), *Las montañas del oro* (1897); *El libro de los paisajes* (1917); *Romances del Río Seco* (1938); *Obras poéticas completas*, 3rd edition, Aguilar, Madrid 1959, with a prologue by Pedro Miguel Obligado; *La guerra gaucha* (1905), Ediciones Peuser, Buenos Aires 1946; *El payador* (1916), Ediciones Centurión, Buenos Aires 1961.

Machado de Assis, Joaquim Maria (Brazil, 1839–1908), *Memórias Póstumas de Brás Cubas* (1881), published in English as *Epitaph for a Small Winner*, trans. William L. Grossman, Noonday Press, New York 1952; W. H. Allen, London 1953; *Quincas Borba* (1891), published in English as *The Heritage of Quincas Borba*, trans. Clotilde Wilson W. H. Allen, London 1954; *Dom Casmurro* (1899), published in English with same title, trans. Helen Caldwell, Noonday Press, New York 1953; W. H. Allen, London 1953; *Esaú e Jacó* (1904), published in English as *Esau and Jacob*, trans. Helen Caldwell, Peter Owen, London 1965; University of California, Berkeley 1965; *Papéis Avulsos* (short stories), Lombaerts, Rio de Janeiro 1882; *Relíquias de Casa Velha* (short stories), Garnier, Paris 1906; a selection of short stories has been published in English under the title *The Psychiatrist and Other Stories*, trans. William L. Grossman and Helen Caldwell, Peter Owen, London 1963; University of California, Berkeley, 1963.

Mafud, Julio, *El desarraigo argentino*, Americalee, Buenos Aires 1959.

Magaña Esquivel, Antonio, *La novela de la revolución*, Vol. I, Instituto Nacional de Estudios Históricos de la Revolución Mexicana, Mexico 1964.

Magdaleno, Mauricio (Mexico, b. 1906), *El resplandor* (1937), included in Vol. 2 of *La novela de la revolución mexicana*, Aguilar, Mexico 1964, ed. by Castro Leal, published in English as *Sunburst*, trans. Anita Brenner, Lindsay Drummond, London 1945.

Mallea, Eduardo (Argentina, b. 1903), *La ciudad junto al río inmóvil* (1936); *Historia de una pasión argentina* (1937); *La bahía del silencio* (1940); *Las Aguilas* (1943); *Los enemigos del alma* (1950); *Obras completas*, 2 vols., Emecé, Buenos Aires 1961, with a prologue by Mariano Picón Salas.

Maples Arce, Manuel (Mexico, b. 1898), *Modern Mexican Art, El arte mexicano moderno*, Zwemmer, London 1946.

Marechal, Leopoldo (Argentina, b. 1900), *Adán Buenosayres* (1948).

Mariátegui, José Carlos (Peru, 1895–1930), *Siete ensayos de interpretación de la realidad peruana* (1928), 9th edition, Biblioteca Amauta, Lima 1964; *La escena contemporánea*, Editorial Minerva, Lima 1925.

Marín, Juan (Chile, b. 1900), *Paralelo 53 sur*, Nascimento, Santiago, 1936; *Viento negro* (1944), 2nd edition, Zig-Zag, Santiago 1960.

Marinello, Juan (Cuba, b. 1898), *Conversación con nuestros pintores abstractos*, Universidad de Oriente, Santiago de Cuba 1960.

Marqués, René (Puerto Rico, b. 1919), *La carreta* (1953), Editorial Cultural, Rio Piedras, Puerto Rico, 1961; *La muerte no entrará en palacio* (1957) included in *Antología del teatro latinoamericana*, Vol. I (*see* Solórzano); *Los soles truncos* (1958); *En una ciudad llamada San Juan*, Universidad Nacional Autónoma, Mexico 1960.

Martel, Julián (pseudonym of José María Miró) (Argentina, 1868–96), *La bolsa* (1891), Estrada y Cía, Biblioteca de Clásicos Argentinos, Buenos Aires 1946, with a prologue by Adolfo Mitre.

Martí, José (Cuba, 1853–95), *Ismaelillo* (1882); *Versos libres* (1919); *Versos sencillos* (1891); *Obras completas de Martí*, 23 vols., Editorial Nacional de Cuba, Havana 1963–5.

Martínez, José Luis, *Literatura mexicana, siglo xx: 1910–49*, 2 vols., Antigua Librería Robredo, Mexico 1950.

Martínez, Luis (Ecuador 1869–1909), *A la costa* (1904), 2nd edition, Casa de la Cultura Ecuatoriana, Quito 1959.

Martínez Estrada, Ezequiel (Argentina, b. 1895), *Radiografía de la pampa* (1933), 2 vols., Losada, Buenos Aires 1942.

Martínez Moreno, Carlos (Uruguay, b. 1917), *Los aborígenes*, Alfa, Montevideo 1964; *El paredón*, Seix Barral, Barcelona 1962.

Martínez Villena, Rubén (Cuba, 1899–1934), *La pupila insomne* (a biography and an edition of his poems), Publicaciones del Gobierno Provincial Revolucionario de la Habana, Havana 1960, with an introduction by Raúl Roa.

Matto de Turner, Clorinda (Peru, 1854–1909), *Aves sin nido*, Buenos Aires 1889, published in English as *Birds without a Nest: a story of Indian Life and Priestly Oppression in Peru*, trans. C. J. Thynne, 1904.

Mazzei, Angel, *La poesía de Buenos Aires*, Editorial Ciordi, Buenos Aires 1962.

Mediz Bolio, Antonio, ed. and trans., *Libro de Chilam Balam de Chumayel*, Universidad Nacional Autónoma de México, Mexico 1941.

Meireles, Cecília (Brazil, b. 1901) *Obra poética*, Aguilar, Rio de Janeiro 1958.

Mejía Vallejo, Manuel (Colombia, b. 1924), *El día señalado*, Seix Barral, Barcelona 1964.

Mendoza, Jaime (Bolivia, 1874–1939), *El macizo boliviano*, Arnos hijos, La Paz 1935; *En las tierras de Potosí*, Barcelona 1911; *La tesis andina* (1920), *see* Francovitch, Guillermo.

Meneses, Guillermo (Venezuela, b. 1911), *La misa de Arlequín*, Ateneo de Caracas, Caracas 1962.

Menotti del Picchia, Paulo (Brazil, b. 1892), *Juca Mulato* (1917), 16th edition, Companhia Editora Nacional, São Paulo 1937.

Menton, Seymour, *Historia crítica de la novela guatemalteca*, Ed.

Universitaria, Guatemala 1960; *El cuento costarricense*, Ediciones de Andrea, Studium, Mexico 1964.

Mera, Juan León (Ecuador, 1832–94), *Cumandá* (1879), Heath, Boston and New York 1932, with notes and a vocabulary by Pastoriza Flores.

Miró, Ricardo (Panama 1883–1940), *Versos patrióticos y recitaciones escolares* (1925); *Antología poética, 1907–37*, Edición Homenaje, Panama 1937; *Cien años de poesía en Panamá, 1852–1952*, Departamento de Bellas Artes del Ministerio de Educación, Panama 1953.

Mistral, Gabriela (pseudonym of Lucila Godoy Alcayaga) (Chile, 1889–1957), *Desolación*, (1922); *Ternura* (1924); *Tala* (1938); *Poesías completas*, Aguilar, Biblioteca Premios Nobel, Madrid 1958.

Molina, Enrique, *La filosofía en Chile en la primera mitad del siglo xx*, second edition enlarged, Nascimento, Santiago 1953.

Molinari, Ricardo (Argentina, b. 1898), *Umida noche*, Emecé, Buenos Aires 1957.

Monguió, Luis, *César Vallejo (1892–1938): Vida y obra – bibliografía – antología*, Hispanic Institute, New York 1952.

Monner Sans, José Maria, *Julián del Casal y el modernismo hispanoamericano*, El Colegio de México, Mexico 1952.

Monteforte Toledo, Mario (Guatemala, b. 1911), *Guatemala, Monografía sociológica*, Instituto de Investigaciones Sociales, Universidad Nacional Autónoma de México, Mexico 1959.

Monteiro Lobato, José Benito (Brazil, 1882–1948), *Urupês* (1918); *Obras completas de Monteiro Lobato*, Editôra Brasiliense, São Paulo 1956.

Montes, Hugo, *Antología de Medio Siglo* (anthology of Chilean poetry) Editorial del Pacífico, Santiago 1956.

Montes de Oca, Marco Antonio, *Fundación del entusiasmo*, U.N.A.M., Mexico 1963; *Vendimia del juglar*, Joaquín Mortiz, Mexico 1965; *Las fuentes legendarias*, Joaquín Mortiz, Mexico 1966; *Pedir el fuego*, Joaquín Mortiz, Mexico 1968.

Morales Benítez, Otto, *Muchedumbres y banderas*, Tercer Mundo, Bogotá 1962.

Murena, Hector (Argentina, 1920), *El pecado original de América*, Sur, Buenos Aires 1954.

Neale Silva, Eduardo, *Horizonte humano, Vida de José Eustasio Rivera*, Fondo de cultura económica, Mexico 1960.

Nelkin, Margarita, *El expresionismo en la plástica mexicana de hoy*, Instituto Nacional de Bellas Artes, Mexico 1964.

Neruda, Pablo (pseudonym of Neftalí Reyes) (Chile, b. 1904), *Veinte poemas de amor* (1924); *Residencia en la tierra* (1933–7); *España en el corazón* (1937); *Canto general* (1950); *Odas elementales* (1954–7); *Obras completas*, Losada, Buenos Aires 1957; *Plenos poderes*, Losada, Buenos Aires 1962; *Memorial de isla negra*, 5 vols., Losada, Buenos Aires 1964; there is an English translation of part of the *Canto general*, trans. Nathaniel Tarn and published as *The Heights of Macchu Picchu*, Jonathan Cape, London 1966; *20 poems by Pablo Neruda*, trans. Robert Bly and James Wright, Rapp and Whiting, London 1967.

Nervo, Amado (Mexico, 1870–1919), *Obras completas*, 2 vols., Aguilar, Madrid 1955–6.

Nicholson, Irene, *Firefly in the Night*, *A Study of Ancient Mexican Poetry and Symbolism*, Faber and Faber, London 1959.

Novo, Salvador (Mexico, b. 1904), *Poesía* (includes *xx poemas, Espejo, Nuevo amor y poesías no coleccionadas*), Fondo de cultura económica, Mexico 1961.

Nueva poesía nicaraguense, Madrid 1949, with an introduction by Ernesto Cardenal.

Onetti, Juan Carlos (Uruguay, b. 1909), *El astillero*, Compañia General Fabril Editora, Buenos Aires 1961; *El pozo* (1939), Ara, Montevideo 1965; *Tierra de nadie* (1941), Ediciones de la Banda Oriental, Montevideo 1965; *La vida breve*, Buenos Aires 1950; *Juntacadáveres*, Montevideo 1965; *Novelas cortas*, Monteavila, Caracas 1968.

Orozco, José Clemente (Mexico, 1883–1949), *Textos de Orozco*, ed. Justino Fernández, Instituto de Investigaciones Estéticas, Universidad Nacional Autónoma de México, Mexico 1955.

Ortiz, Adalberto (Ecuador, b. 1914), *Juyungo* (1943), Casa de la Cultura Ecuatoriana, Quito 1957; *El animal herido*, Casa de la Cultura Ecuatoriana, Quito 1959.

Ortiz, Fernando (Cuba, b. 1881), *Hampa afrocubana: los negros brujos*, Madrid 1906; *Hampa afrocubana: los negros esclavos*, Madrid 1916.

Ortiz de Montellano, Bernardo (Mexico, 1899–1949), *Sueños*, Contemporáneos, Mexico 1933; *Muerte de cielo azul*, Cultura, Mexico 1937.

Otero Silva, Miguel (Venezuela, b. 1908), *Casas muertas*, Losada, Buenos Aires 1955; *Oficina número 1*, Losada, Buenos Aires 1961.

Pacheco, José Emilio (Mexico, b. 1939), *Los elementos de la noche* (1963), *El reposo del fuego* (1966), *Morirás Lejos*, Joaquín Mortiz, Mexico 1967.

Bibliography

Padilla, Heberto, *Fuera del juego*, Uneac, La Habana 1968.

Palés Matos, Luis (Puerto Rico, 1898–1959), *Tuntún de pasa y grifería* (1937), Jaime Benítez, San Juan de Puerto Rico 1950.

Palma, Ricardo (Peru, 1833–1919), *Tradiciones peruanas completas*, 3rd edition, Aguilar, Madrid 1957, edited by Edith Palma.

Pandiá Calogeres, João, *A History of Brazil*, University of North Carolina Press, Chapel Hill N.C., 1939, trans. and additions by Percy Alvin Martin.

Panorama das Literaturas das Américas, de 1900 à actualidade, 4 vols., Edição do Municipio de Nova Lisboa, Angola 1958–63, ed. Joaquim de Montezuma de Carvalho.

Pardo y Aliaga, Felipe (Peru, 1806–68), *Poesías y escritos en prosa de don Felipe Pardo*, Paris 1865.

Pareja Diez-Canseco, Alfredo (Ecuador, b. 1908), *La Beldaca, novela del trópico* (1935), 2nd edition, Casa de la Cultura Ecuatoriana, Quito 1954; *Los nueve años*, 2 vols., Quito 1956, and Buenos Aires 1959.

Parra, Nicanor (Chile, b. 1914), *La cueca larga*, Editorial Universitaria, Santiago 1955; *Poemas y Antipoemas*, 2nd edition, Nascimento, Santiago 1956.

Parra, Teresa de la (Venezuela, 1891–1936), *Ifigenia, diario de una señorita que escribió porque se fastidiaba*, Paris 1924; *Las memorias de Mama Blanca*, Editorial Le Livre Libre, 1929; published in English as *Mama Blanca's Souvenirs*, trans. Harriet de Onís, Pan American Union, Washington D.C. and Mexico 1959.

Payró, Roberto (Argentina, 1867–1928), *Divertidas aventuras del nieto de Juan Moreira* (1910), Losada, Buenos Aires 1957.

Paz, Octavio (Mexico, b. 1914), *Libertad bajo palabra* (*Obra poética, 1935–58*), Fondo de cultura económica, Mexico 1960 (an edition of *Libertad bajo palabra* first appeared in 1949); *Piedra de sol* (1957), original with trans. by Muriel Rukeyser, The World Poets Series, New Directions, New York 1963; Villiers, London 1963; *El laberinto de la soledad* (1950), 3rd edition, Fondo de cultura económica, Mexico 1963, published in English as *The Labyrinth of Solitude: Life and Thought in Mexico*, Grove Press, New York 1961; *El arco y la lira*, Fondo de cultura económica, Mexico 1956; *Corriente alterna*, Siglo XXI, Mexico 1967; *Los signos en rotacion*, Siglo XXI, 1966; *Salamandra*, Joaquín Mortiz, 1962.

Blanco, folding scroll, Joaquín Mortiz, Mexico 1968; *Ladera Este*, Joaquín Mortiz, Mexico 1969.

Pedroso, Regino (Cuba, b. 1896), *Antología poética, 1918–38*, Municipio de la Habana, Havana 1939.

Peñalosa, Fernando, *The Mexican Book Industry*, Scarecrow Press, New York 1957.

Pezoa Véliz, Carlos (Chile, 1879–1908), *Alma chilena* (1911); *Antología*, ed. Nicomedes Guzmán, Zig-Zag, Santiago 1957.

Piñera, Virgilio, *Teatro completo*, Ediciones Revolución, La Habana 1960; *Cuentos*, Uneac, La Habana 1964.

Portuondo, José Antonio, *Bosquejo histórico de las letras cubanas*, Ministerio de Relaciones Exteriores, Havana 1960.

Pozas, Ricardo (Mexico, b. 1910), *Juan Pérez Jolote* (1952), 5th edition, Fondo de cultura económica, Mexico 1965.

Prado, Paulo (Brazil, 1869–1943), *Retrato do Brasil* (1928), 4th edition, Briguiet, Rio de Janeiro 1931.

Prado, Pedro (Chile, 1886–1952), *Alsino* (1920), 2nd edition, Nascimento, Santiago 1928; *Un juez rural*, Nascimento, Santiago 1924.

Praz, Mario, *The Romantic Agony*, 2nd edition, Oxford University Press, London and New York 1951.

Previtali, Giovanni, *Ricardo Güiraldes and Don Segundo Sombra*, Hispanic Institute, New York 1963.

Prieto, Adolfo, 'El Martinfierrismo', *Revista de Literatura Argentina e Iberoamericana*, Vol. I, No. I, Mendoza 1959; *Literatura autobiográfica argentina*, Facultad de Filosofía y Letras, Rosario 1962.

Primer Acto, Madrid, No. 75, 1966.

Queirós, Rachel de (Brazil, b. 1910), *O Quinze* (1931), included in *Três romances*, José Olympio, Rio de Janeiro 1948.

Quiroga, Horacio (Uruguay, 1878–1937), *Cuentos de amor, de locura y de muerte* (1917), 3rd edition, Losada, Buenos Aires 1964; *Cuentos de la selva para niños* (1918), 7th edition (published as *Cuentos de la selva*), Losada, Buenos Aires 1963; *Anaconda* (1921), Losada, Buenos Aires 1963; *Los desterrados* (1926), 2nd edition, Losada, Buenos Aires 1964; *Cuentos escogidos*, Pergamon, Oxford 1968.

Ramos, Graciliano (Brazil, 1892–1953), *Vidas Sêcas* (1938), quotations are from the undated Portuguese edition, Portugália, Lisbon; *São Bernardo* (1934), quotations are from the Portuguese edition, Ulisseia, Lisbon 1957; *Angústia* (1936); *Obras*, 10 vols., José Olympio, Rio de Janeiro 1947; *Memórias do Cárcere*, 4 vols., José Olympio 1954.

Ramos, Samuel (Mexico, 1897–1959), *El perfil del hombre y de la cultura en México*, Mexico 1934.

Ratcliff, Dillwyn F., *Venezuelan Prose Fiction*, Instituto de las Españas, New York 1933.

Bibliography

Reichardt, J. 'The Whereabouts of Concrete Poetry', *Studio International*, February 1966.

Renan, Ernest, *Caliban, Drame philosophique*, Paris 1878.

Revueltas, José (Mexico, b. 1914), *El luto humano*, Editora México, Mexico 1943.

Reyes, Alfonso (Mexico, 1889–1959), *Obras completas de Alfonso Reyes*, 15 vols., Fondo de cultura económica, Mexico 1955–63.

Reyles, Carlos (Uruguay, 1868–1938), *Beba* (1894); *El terruño* (1916), Losada, Buenos Aires 1945; *El embrujo de Sevilla* (1922), Espasa-Calpe, Buenos Aires 1944; *Academias y otros ensayos* (1884), Biblioteca Rodó, Montevideo n.d.

Richter, Hans, *Dada Art and Anti-Art*, Thames and Hudson, London 1965.

Ripoll, Carlos, 'La Revista de Avance (1927–1930); Vocero de Vanguardismo y Pórtico de Revolución', *Revista Iberoamericana*, 1964, Vol. XXX, No. 58, pp. 261–82.

Rivera, José Eustasio (Colombia, 1888–1928), *La vorágine* (1924), 6th edition, Losada, Buenos Aires 1957; *see also* Neale Silva.

Roa Bastos, Augusto (Paraguay, b. 1917), *El trueno entre las hojas* (1953); *Hijo de hombre* (1959), 2nd edition, Losada, Buenos Aires 1961; published in English as *Son of Man*, trans. Rachel Caffyn, Gollancz, London 1965.

Rodó, José Enrique (Uruguay, 1871–1917), *Ariel* (1900); *Los motivos de Proteo* (1909); *El mirador de Próspero* (1913); *Obras completas*, Aguilar, Madrid 1957, with a prologue and notes by Emir Rodríguez Monegal; English edition of *Ariel*, ed. J. G. Brotherston, Cambridge University Press, Cambridge 1967.

Rodríguez Monegal, Emir, *El juicio de los parricidas*, Deucalion, Buenos Aires 1956; 'La novela brasileña,' *Mundo Nuevo*, December 1966.

Rojas, Angel F., *La novela ecuatoriana*, Fondo de cultura económica, Mexico and Buenos Aires 1948.

Rojas González, Francisco (Mexico, 1903–51), *El diosero* (1952), 5th edition, Fondo de cultura económica, Mexico 1964.

Rojas, Manuel (Chile, b. 1896), *Hijo de ladrón* (1951), published in English as *Born Guilty*, trans. Frank Gaynor, Library Publishers, New York 1955; Gollancz, London 1955; *Obras completas*, Zig Zag, Santiago 1961.

Rojas, Ricardo (Argentina, 1882–1957), *La Argentinidad*, Librería La Facultad de Juan Roldán, Buenos Aires 1916; *Blasón de plata* (1909); *Historia de la literatura argentina*, 9 vols., Kraft, Buenos Aires 1960.

Romeo, José Rubén (Mexico, 1890–1952), *Apuntes de un lugareño* (1932); *Desbandada* (1934); both these novels are included in the Aguilar anthology *La novela de la Revolución Mexicana*, ed. Castro Leal; *La vida inútil de Pito Pérez* (1938), Porrúa, Mexico 1946; *Obras completas*, Oasis, Mexico 1957, with a preface by Antonio Castro Leal.

Romualdo, Alejandro (Peru, b. 1926), *Poesía 1945–54*, Mejía Baca, Lima 1954; *Edición extraordinaria*, Cuadernos Trimestrales de Poesía, Lima 1958.

Rubín, Ramón (Mexico, b. 1912), *El callado dolor de los tzotziles*, 1949.

Rulfo, Juan (Mexico, b. 1918), *El llano en llamas*, Fondo de cultura económica, Mexico 1953; *Pedro Páramo* (1955), 4th edition, Fondo de cultura económica, Mexico 1963; published in English as *Pedro Páramo*, trans. Lysander Kemp, Grove Press, New York 1959.

Sábato, Ernesto (Argentina, b. 1911), *Sobre héroes y tumbas* (1961), 3rd edition, Mirasol, Compañía General Fabril, Buenos Aires 1964.

Salazar Bondy, Sebastián (Peru, 1924–65), *Lima la horrible*, Era, Mexico 1964.

Salinas, Pedro, *La poesía de Rubén Darío*, 2nd edition, Losada, Buenos Aires 1958.

Sánchez, Florencio (Uruguay, 1875–1910), *La gringa* (1904); *M'hijo el dotor* (1903); *Barranca abajo* (1905); *Teatro completo*, 2nd edition, Claridad, Buenos Aires, ed. Dardo Cúneo; some of the plays are translated into English and published as *Representative Plays of Florencio Sánchez*, Pan American Union, Washington D.C. 1961.

Sánchez, Luis Alberto (Peru, b. 1900), *La literature peruana*, 6 vols., Guaranía, Asunción, Paraguay, 1950–51; *Proceso y contenido de la novela hispanoamericana*, Gredos, Madrid 1953.

Sánchez Pedrote, Enrique, 'Consideraciones sobre la música en Hispanoamérica', *Estudios Americanos*, No. 32 (1954), pp. 417–26.

Sarduy, Severo, *De donde son los cantantes*, Mexico 1967.

Sarmiento, Domingo (Argentina, 1811–88), *Facundo; Civilización y barbarie* (1845), Espasa-Calpe, Buenos Aires 1958.

Sayers, Raymond S., *O Negro na Literatura Brasileira*, Edições o Cruzeiro, Rio de Janeiro 1956.

Seoane, Juan (Peru, b. 1898), *Hombres y rejas* (1936).

Silva, José Asunción (Colombia, 1865–96), *Prosas y versos*, Biblioteca de Autores Hispanoamericanos, Ediciones Iberoamericanas, Madrid 1960, ed. Carlos García Prada.

Silva Brito, Mário da, *História do Modernismo Brasileiro*, Vol. I, Edição Saraiva, São Paulo 1958.

Bibliography

Silva Castro, Raúl, ed., *Obras desconocidas de Rubén Darío, escritas en Chile y no recopiladas en ninguno de los libros*, Universidad de Chile, Santiago 1934; *Panorama literario de Chile*, Editorial Universitaria, Santiago 1961; *Pablo Neruda*, Editorial Universitaria, Santiago 1964.

Silveira, Valdomiro (Brazil, 1873–1941), *Os Caboclos* (1920), 2nd edition, Companhia Editôra Nacional, São Paulo 1928.

Sinán, Rogelio (pseudonym of Bernardo Domínguez Alba, Panama, b. 1904), *Plenilunio* (1947), Editorial Constancia, Mexico 1953.

Solórzano, Carlos (Guatemala b. 1922), *Teatro latinoamericano del siglo xx* Editorial Nueva Visión, Buenos Aires 1961; ed., *El teatro hispanoamericano contemporáneo* (anthology), 2 vols., Fondo de cultura económica, Mexico and Buenos Aires 1964.

Sousa Andrade (Sousândrade), Joaquim de (Brazil, 1833–1902), *Obras Poéticas*, New York 1874. See the anthology and study of Sousândrade by Augusto and Haroldo de Campos, published under the title, *Revisão de Sousândrade*, Edições Invenção, São Paulo 1964.

Stabb, Martin S., 'Indigenism and Racism in Mexican Thought, 1877–1911', *Journal of Inter-American Studies*, Vol. 1, No. 4, 1959.

Suárez-Murias, Marguerite C., *La novela romántica en Hispanoamérica*, Hispanic Institute of the United States, New York 1963.

Subercaseaux, Benjamín (Chile, b. 1902), *Jeremy Button* (1950), published in English with same title, W. H. Allen, London 1955; *Chile o una loca geografía*, 12th edition, Ercilla, Santiago 1961.

Tamayo, Franz (Bolivia, 1879–1956), *Creación de la pedagogía nacional* (1910), 2nd edition, Ministerio de Educación, La Paz, 1944.

Téllez, Hernando (Colombia, b. 1908), *Literatura y sociedad*, Ediciones Mito, Bogota 1956.

Torres, Carlos Arturo (Colombia, 1867–1911), *Idola fori* (1910), Minerva, Bogota 1935.

Torres Bodet, Jaime (Mexico, b. 1912), *Poesías escogidas*, Espasa-Calpe, Buenos Aires 1957.

Torres-Ríoseco, Arturo, *Vida y poesía de Rubén Darío*, Emecé, Buenos Aires 1944.

Traba, Marta, *Seis pintores colombianos*, Bogota, n.d. (1965?).

Triana, José, *La noche de los asesinos*, Casa de las Américas, La Habana 1964; *La muerte del ñeque*, Ediciones Revolución, La Habana 1964.

Ugarte, Manuel (Argentina, 1878–1951), *El porvenir de la América Latina*, Valencia 1911; *La dramática intimidad de una generación*, Prensa Española, Madrid 1951.

Uribe Piedrahita, César (Colombia, 1897–1953), *Toá, narraciones de caucherías*, Espasa-Calpe, Buenos Aires 1942.

Usigli, Rodolfo (Mexico, b. 1905), *El gesticulador* (1937); *Epílogo sobre la hipocresía del Mexicano*, from 2nd edition of *El Gesticulador*, Ediciones Letras de México, Mexico 1944; *Teatro completo*, Vol. 1, Fondo de cultura económica, Mexico 1963; *Corona de luz*, Fondo de cultura economica, Mexico 1965; *Corona de sombra* (1947), 3rd edition, Cuadernos Americanos, Mexico 1959.

Uslar Pietri, Arturo (Venezuela, b. 1906) *Las lanzas coloradas*, Zeus, Madrid 1931.

Valcárcel, Gustavo (Peru, b. 1921), *La prisión* (1951), 2nd edition, Peru Nuevo, Lima 1960.

Valdelomar, Abraham (Peru, 1888–1919), *Los hijos del sol* (1921); *Cuentos y poesía*, ed. Augusto Tamayo Vargas, Universidad Nacional Mayor de San Marcos, Lima 1959.

Valencia, Guillermo (Colombia, 1873–1943), *Obras poéticas completas*, Aguilar, Madrid 1955, with a prologue by Baldomero Sanín Cano.

Vallejo, César (Peru, 1892–1938), *Los heraldos negros* (1918); *Trilce* (1922); *Poemas humanos* (1939); *España, aparta de mí este cáliz* (1938); quotations in the text are from the four-volume edition of Vallejo's poems published under the above titles by Editora Peru Nuevo, Lima n.d.; *Tungsteno y Paco Yunque*, Mejía Baca and P.L Villanueva, Lima 1957; *Tungsteno* was first published in 1931.

Varela, José Luis, *Ensayos de poesía indígena en Cuba*, Ediciones cultura hispánica, Madrid 1951.

Vargas Llosa, Mario (Peru, b. 1936), *La ciudad y los perros*, Seix Barral, Barcelona 1963; *La casa verde*, Seix Barral, Barcelona 1966; *Los cachorros*, Lumen, Barcelona 1967.

Vasconcelos, José (Mexico, 1882–1959), *El monismo estético* (1918); *Pitágoras, una teoría del ritmo* (1916); *Indología* (1927); *De Robinsón a Odiseo* (1935); *La raza cósmica* (1925); *Ulises criollo* (1936); *Obras completas*, 4 vols., Libreros Mexicanos Unidos, Mexico 1957–61.

Vaz Ferreira, Carlos (Uruguay, 1878–1958), *Moral para intelectuales* (1908), *Obras*, Vol. III, Homenaje de la Cámera de Representantes de la República Oriental del Uruguay, Montevideo 1957–8.

Veríssimo, Erico (Brazil, b. 1905), *O Tempo e O Vento*, trilogy which includes *O Continente* (1929), 2nd edition, Globo, Rio de Janeiro, Pôrto Alegre and São Paulo 1950; *O Retrato*, Globo, Rio de Janeiro, etc. 1951; *O Arquipélago*, 3 vols., Globo, Rio de Janeiro, etc. 1961.

Bibliography

Veríssimo, José (Brazil, 1857–1916), *A Educação Nacional* (1890), 2nd edition, Livraria Francisco Alves, Rio de Janeiro 1906.

Viana, Javier de (Uruguay, 1868–1926), *Campo* (1896), García, Montevideo 1945; *Gaucha* (1899), Ministerio de Educación Pública, Montevideo 1956; *Gurí y otras novelas*, Editoria América, Madrid 1916; *Pago de deuda, Campo amarillo y otros escritos*, García, Montevideo 1936.

Villaurrutia, Xavier (Mexico, 1903–50), *Nostalgia de la muerte* (1938); *Poesía y teatro completo*, Fondo de cultura económica, Mexico 1953.

Villaverde, Cirilo (Cuba 1812–94), *Cecilia Valdés o la loma del Angel* (1882), Consejo Nacional de Cultura, Havana 1964.

Viñas, David (Argentina, b. 1929), *Literatura argentina y realidad política*, Alvarez, Buenos Aires 1964; *Los dueños de la tierra*, Losada, Buenos Aires 1958.

Waldberg, Patrick, *Surrealism*, Thames and Hudson, London 1965.

Walsh, Gertrude M., *Cuentos criollos*, Heath, Boston 1941.

Wolfe, Bertram, D., *Diego Rivera: His Life and Times*, Robert Hale, London 1939; *Fabulous Life of Diego Rivera*, Stein & Day, New York 1963.

Yañez, Agustín (Mexico, b. 1904), *Al filo del agua* (1947), 3rd edition, Porrúa, Mexico 1961; *La creación* (1959), 3rd edition, Fondo de cultura económica, Mexico 1963; *Las tierras flacas*, Joaquín Mortiz, Mexico 1962.

Yunque, Alvaro (Argentina, b. 1889), *La literatura social en la Argentina: historia de los movimientos literarios desde la emancipación nacional hasta nuestros días*, Buenos Aires 1941.

Zalamea Borda, Eduardo (Colombia, 1907–63), *Cuatro años a bordo de mí mismo, diario de los cinco sentidos*, 1934.

Zapata Olivella, Manuel (Colombia, b. 1920), *En Chimá nace un santo*, Seix Barral, Barcelona 1963.

Zea, Leopoldo (Mexico, b. 1912), *Dos etapas del pensamiento hispano-americano*, published in English as *The Latin American Mind*, trans. James H. Abbot and Lowell Dunham, University of Oklahoma Press, Norman, Oklahoma 1963; *La filosofía como compromiso*, Tezontle, Mexico 1952; *Conciencia y posibilidad del Mexicano*, Porrúa y Obregón, Mexico 1952; *El occidente y la conciencia de México, Esquema para una historia de las ideas en Iberoamérica*,

Filosofía y Letras, Universidad Nacional Autónoma de México, Mexico 1956.

Zum Felde, Alberto, *Indice crítico de la literatura hispanoamericana*, 2 vols., Guaranía, Mexico 1954–9; *Proceso intelectual del Uruguay*, Claridad, Montevideo 1941.

Indexes

INDEX OF SUBJECTS AND
TITLES OF WORKS

Index of Subjects and Titles

Index of Subjects and Titles

MORE ABOUT PENGUINS
AND PELICANS

Penguinews, which appears every month, contains details of all the new books issued by Penguins as they are published. From time to time it is supplemented by *Penguins in Print*, which is a complete list of all books published by Penguins which are in print. (There are well over three thousand of these.)

A specimen copy of *Penguinews* will be sent to you free on request, and you can become a subscriber for the price of the postage. For a year's issues (including the complete lists) please send 4s. if you live in the United Kingdom, or 8s. if you live elsewhere. Just write to Dept EP, Penguin Books Ltd, Harmondsworth, Middlesex, enclosing a cheque or postal order, and your name will be added to the mailing list.

Two other Pelican books are described on the following page.

Note: *Penguinews* and *Penguins in Print* are not available in the U.S.A. or Canada.

A HISTORY OF LATIN AMERICA
Revised Edition

George Pendle

This history has been written by a specialist who has been closely connected with Latin America for the last forty years. In tracing the development of civilization from the earliest times down to Fidel Castro, the author helps to place current events in their context. Many races and classes have contributed to the civilization of this great land-mass: Indians, European *conquistadores*, priests, planters, African slaves, *caudillos*, liberal intellectuals, commercial pioneers.

Political Leaders of the Twentieth Century

POLITICAL LEADERS OF LATIN AMERICA

Richard Bourne

Latin American politics are of increasing importance in world affairs. This volume contains portraits of six political leaders of the region: individually they stress the diversity that lies between caudillo and Communist; together they may be taken to typify the face of Latin American government and the special problems confronting it.

Che Guevara	The Argentinian revolutionary who conquered in Cuba and died in Bolivia
Eduardo Frei	The President of Chile and the first Christian-Democratic president in Latin America
Alfredo Stroessner	The Army dictator of Paraguay
Juscelino Kubitschek	The President of Brazil from 1956 to 1960 and founder of Brasilia
Carlos Lacerda	who has helped to overthrow three Brazilian presidents
Evita Peron	The glamorous wife of the Argentinian dictator who combined military and labour supporters in a powerful nationalist movement.